# Believing in Baptism

# Believing in Baptism

*Understanding and Living God's Covenant Sign*

Gordon Kuhrt and Stephen Kuhrt

LONDON • NEW YORK • OXFORD • NEW DELHI • SYDNEY

T&T CLARK
Bloomsbury Publishing Plc
50 Bedford Square, London, WC1B 3DP, UK
1385 Broadway, New York, NY 10018, USA

BLOOMSBURY, T&T CLARK and the T&T Clark logo
are trademarks of Bloomsbury Publishing Plc

First published in Great Britain 2020

Cover design: Terry Woodley
Cover image: Wirestock Images/Shutterstock

A catalogue record for this book is available from the British Library.

Library of Congress Control Number: 2020932385

ISBN:    HB:     978-0-5676-9444-7
         PB:     978-0-5676-9443-0
         ePDF:   978-0-5676-9446-1
         eBook:  978-0-5676-9445-4

Typeset by Integra Software Services Pvt. Ltd.
Printed and bound in Great Britain

To find out more about our authors and books visit www.bloomsbury.com
and sign up for our newsletters

*To Olive Kuhrt*
*with love and gratitude*

# Contents

# Preface

Confusion about baptism is obvious and widespread. This book is the result of pleas by clergy and ordinands for a single volume that treats coherently the major issues. I am grateful for encouraging responses to lectures and seminars throughout England and, in January 1987, in Pakistan and South India.

The numerous booklets by Bishop Colin Buchanan have exercised a great influence, and I gladly acknowledged my indebtedness. He and other friends have read parts of the manuscript and made valuable criticisms: Roger Beckwith, Leslie Houlden, John Balchin, Wilfred Kuhrt. My colleague David Richardson contributed both encouragement and many helpful suggestions. My secretary, Valerie Gower, typed with great accuracy. I am deeply grateful to each of them.

Baptism is a precious gift of God, in the name of Jesus, and in the Spirit. I pray this book will bring glory to the triune God and assist in making disciples, baptizing and teaching them (Matthew 28.19-20).

Gordon Kuhrt
1987

Over thirty years have passed since Gordon Kuhrt wrote the first edition of *Believing in Baptism*. Several of the reasons for this fresh edition lie in the enduring strengths of the original version and the help that many Christians received from it. Over the years I have met a number of ordinands and clergy who have spoken of the book appearing at a vital time to provide them with much greater confidence in their understanding of baptism. Some have even commented on the role that it played in confirming their calling to minister with integrity within the Church of England. The clarity of its approach and careful handling of the biblical material was clearly crucial here. Another helpful aspect of the book was its eirenic nature. Much of what is written about baptism can be rather polemical in its tone but my father's upbringing as a Strict Baptist before joining the Church of England was probably an important factor preventing this. The result was a book where even those in disagreement with its conclusions could recognize the integrity of its convictions: the biblical basis of a covenantal understanding of baptism and its endorsement of infant baptism within the commitment to seeing children brought up within the family of the church living out their baptism with the response of faith. For this reason, it even featured as 'Book of the Month' in *The Baptist Times*. All of this convinced me that a fresh publication of the book was needed to make its contents available to a new generation of readers.

A number of additional factors have influenced the revised elements within this edition of *Believing in Baptism*. The most important of these are the developments in biblical theology that have taken place over the last thirty years, most obviously through the work of Tom Wright. I have written elsewhere of the transforming effect that Wright's theology can have and has had upon church life.[1] In relation to baptism and this particular book, this is evident in the way in which the covenantal theme so strongly present in the original edition of *Believing in Baptism*, has received such reinforcement from Wright's scholarship. Through Wright's influence, the original chapter on 'God's Covenant' has been very considerably expanded into two much larger chapters, one dealing with the Old Testament and the other on the New Testament, and each containing a great deal more detail on the covenant theme. Those whose interest in baptism is primarily liturgical or pastoral may consider the detail within these chapters rather excessive and even pulling the book considerably out of shape. The temptation to prune back this material has been felt but then resisted for the vital reason that proper, sustained and serious engagement with the covenant theme is the crucial factor upon which everything connected with baptism depends. Too often books on baptism, whatever their perspective, fail to approach the covenant theme with any genuine thoroughness. Reference is usually made to the covenant and key covenantal passages may be discussed. However this is almost always in isolation from the overall biblical narrative in which these passages find their place.[2] The result of this is failure to take the covenant context of baptism seriously, usually based upon a failure to recognize the true nature of the covenant within the Old Testament and a consequent dismissal of its relevance. The conviction of this book is that, unless *the pervasive covenant narrative of the entire Bible is recognized and engaged with, its centrality for a full understanding of baptism will always be missed.* This is the reason for the considerable detail contained in Chapters 3 and 4. Rather than becoming impatient and regarding this as an undisciplined digression, readers are encouraged to live within the covenant theme and its fulfilment in Christ within these chapters in order to recognize it as the indispensable foundation for everything about baptism that follows.

Closely related to this, and another aspect of Tom Wright's influence, is the way in which the new creation or 'new heavens and new earth' as the goal of God's covenant plan has made much greater sense of the value and logic of the sacraments. The original edition of this book was written within a context where vagueness over the nature of the Christian hope was still the norm. An essentially 'other worldly' understanding of this hope left the sacraments making less than full sense. Recovering a properly biblical eschatology has been the critical factor in changing this because once the hope of 'new heavens, new earth' replaces 'going to heaven when you die', the sacraments gain a much fuller significance within God's project to redeem the whole of his creation, rather than simply his chosen people. This leads to a much greater appreciation of the practical ways in which a richness of sacramental worship, more associated with the catholic tradition, can be combined with an equally enhanced understanding of evangelical truth.

Finally, the revision of this book is marked by the desire to draw out more fully the practical implications of its theology of baptism for the life of the local church. For the importance of baptism to be fully reflected in our churches, much greater work needs to be done on its ongoing significance and application. Amongst these are its implications for equality, particularly in regard to the development of a fully all-age approach to church. This should be seen as an indispensable part of any claim to practise infant baptism with integrity. Lots of excellent books and resources now exist about how to create child-friendly models of church. However it is within a fully worked-out theology of baptism that such approaches find the vital foundation upon which they need to be built. A completely new chapter entitled 'Baptism and its completion?' has also been added, chiefly to highlight how often the importance of baptism is undermined in church life and the serious implications of this.

There will probably be some who prefer the original version of this book! A number of evangelicals, in particular, will probably be rather nervous about the greater centrality given to sacraments as a result of the 'new heavens, new earth' eschatology. Those who are used to debates about baptism staying safely away from the practical challenge of providing meaningful church for children may also find it slightly uncomfortable. The urgency needed here means this is part of the book where its eirenic nature is less maintained! Some will also consider that when it comes to describing my church's attempts to put this theology into practice, too many concessions are made to an 'open' perspective. But as with the original version of this book, the aim of this revised edition is to demonstrate the fundamental importance of believing in baptism.

There are a number of people to whom I am extremely grateful for their contributions to the writing of this book. My former colleague Helen Hancock has played a crucial role in both encouraging its writing and providing much of the inspiration for its contents through her dynamic and imaginative ministry. I owe as much thanks to my more recent colleagues: Tim Davis, Helen Durant-Stevensen, Elizabeth Hill, Nathan and Anna Larkin, Katy Loffman, Becky Mills, Eils Osgood and Sarah Parker and the way in which both our regular discussions and partnership in Christian ministry have helped to inform and shape my thinking about the theology and practice of baptism. An equally valuable source of encouragement has come from my friend, the historian Tracy Borman. As Tracy has completed her succession of accomplished historical books and novels, she has also found the time to cajole this much less-gifted writer into finishing this one! My final thanks go to my family: my brothers Martin and Jon Kuhrt for the valuable perspectives that they have offered from their own Christian ministries and to my dear wife, Katie, and our children, Rebecca, James and Abigail, for their steadfast and loyal support. To be the father of three very different children responding with ongoing faith to the promises of God declared in their baptism is something that I am constantly grateful for. Rewriting a book by one's own father is a somewhat strange experience but has brought home how amazingly blessed I have been through the integrity, wisdom and godliness that has characterized Gordon's life and ministry. I'm grateful for the freedom that he gave me to amend and expand this book in any way that I wished. There is, however, one omission from the original version of *Believing in Baptism* more obviously corrected now. A central theme of this book is the vital role that churches have alongside parents in bringing up their children in the Christian faith. In both of our parents, my brothers and I have witnessed the most wonderful example of the integration of these roles. It may be over thirty years late, but the second edition of this book is therefore offered in grateful thanks to Olive Kuhrt, a wife, mother and grandmother who has demonstrated so faithfully and fully what it means to believe in, live out and share the reality of what is proclaimed in Christian baptism.

Stephen Kuhrt
Christmas 2019

# Foreword

It is one of the great ironies of the Christian church that baptism, which was meant to be a point of unity between those who shared it, has served to divide us more than most things. I know this only too well. My father was a Baptist minister who had strong views against infant baptism. In fact, I once came across a letter of his, pointing out to a prospective church that had asked him to become their minister, that he was uneasy about performing infant dedications, in case they gave a false security – the implication that because the child was dedicated they were therefore saved without personal faith.

When as a twenty-something I started exploring the possibility of becoming a church minister, I was going to an Anglican church at the time, and so the natural thing was to explore that route. I went to see a tutor in an Anglican theological college, a friend of my parents, who immediately asked me if I would baptize a baby. I hesitated for a moment, and he chipped in quickly saying that if I couldn't do that, I shouldn't go any further with exploring ordination within the Church of England, as that's what Anglicans do. He sent me away to think hard about it, which I did, and you can guess the conclusion I came to. I'm glad that friend made me think hard about baptism and what it meant. I'm also glad to say that although my dad and I differed over infant baptism, we still recognized in each other a true Christian faith, which was always a lesson to me that theological difference doesn't mean we have to fall out and refuse to see the light of Christ in each other.

However it wasn't easy to do that thinking. In those days before the internet, there was no handy website or podcast to help sift throughout the different arguments, and it was hard to find books for the non-specialist (as I was at the time) that went into the questions of what baptism is, what different Christians think about it, who you should baptize and when. I wish I'd had this book to read carefully then.

Since then, I have spent most of my ministry in theological education and over the years have come across many people who faced the same issues I did. Some have been unsure about infant baptism; some were trying to work out whether you should baptize anyone who asks for it or just the children in churchgoing families; some concerned about how they could safeguard the integrity of baptism if they suspect the parents are just going through the motions to get their kids into a church school; others were wondering how they would relate to other denominations who think differently about it, and many more.

Now as a bishop, I spend quite a few of my Sundays confirming people. Before the service I usually ask each one why they want to be confirmed, and I get a predictably mixed set of answers. Even amongst clergy I find at best a range of views and at worst a haziness on why we confirm adults and exactly what it means when we do this. It has made me go back and think through my own approach to confirmation; yet, again it is hard to find books that explore in good detail the meaning of confirmation and its relation to baptism.

This book therefore has the potential to be something of a landmark. It is on the one hand an absorbing exercise in inter-generational theology. Gordon Kuhrt was a significant figure in Anglican Church life in the 1990s and beyond an Archdeacon who became Director of Ministry in the Church of England, a key role shaping the church's training of its ministers. I got to know his son Stephen as a lively, intelligent ordinand with a passionate faith and a good, energetic mind, whilst I was teaching at Wycliffe Hall in Oxford around the same time. Gordon's original book on baptism came out in the mid-1980s (a little while after I was doing my own amateur explorations on the topic). It was a thorough, well-researched book from the evangelical stable in the church, and it is fascinating to see Stephen's later adaptation of the original book in the light of further insights from his own long experience of parish ministry in more recent, much-changed times and also his engagement with the theology of N. T. Wright, a major new reading of the New Testament which has gradually emerged between the original publication of the book and today.

The result of this collaboration between father and son is a fine treatment of baptism that is theologically informed and sympathetic to different perspectives on baptism in the church. Covenantal theology has been an aspect of Anglican thinking on baptism for centuries yet is given fresh life here by drawing in the new perspectives developed in recent years in Pauline theology. The book is thorough in its arguments and offers an intriguing evangelically shaped sacramental theology that is steeped in rich biblical reflection. At the same time, this is a book that does not just explain theory. It has a welcome emphasis on exploring the implications of a deeply considered theology of infant baptism, in building a church that takes children seriously and puts resources into ensuring they feel every bit as included as adults do.

Martin Luther once wrote, 'There is no greater comfort on earth than baptism.'[1] He found in this sacrament an objectivity and therefore a reassurance that gave him a security and hope that held him through the shifting tides of his own emotions and self-perception. Likewise, St Paul spoke about being 'buried with Christ in baptism', like a bulb planted in the ground, ready to rise to new life. If this book helps its readers find the security that Luther found in times of doubt, and at the same time, to put roots down deep into Christ in a life of discipleship, as St Paul saw in baptism and its hope of resurrection, it will have done us a great service.

Graham Tomlin
Bishop of Kensington

# Acknowledgements

1. Scripture quotations are taken from *The Holy Bible, New International Version* (Anglicized Edition) Copyright © 1979, 1984, 2011 by Biblica (formerly International Bible Society). Used by permission of Hodder & Stoughton Publishers, an Hachette UK company. All rights reserved. 'NIV' is a registered trademark of Biblica (formerly International Bible Society). UK trademark number 1448790.
2. Extracts from *The Book of Common Prayer* of 1662, which is Crown Copyright in the United Kingdom, are reproduced by permission of Eyre and Spottiswood (Publishers) Ltd., Her Majesty's Printers, London.
3. Extracts from *Common Worship* are copyright © The Archbishops' Council, 2000, and is reproduced by permission. All rights reserved. copyright@churchofengland.org
4. Extracts from *Canons of the Church of England* 7th Edition are copyright © The Archbishops' Council, 2011, and are reproduced by permission. All rights reserved. copyright@churchofengland.org
5. The extract from *Letters of C.S. Lewis* is copyright © CS Lewis Pte Ltd 1966 and used by permission.

# Introduction

## Baptism in Melton Sudbury

The title of this book is deliberately ambiguous. This is because 'believing in baptism' can be taken in at least two ways. In the first place, it may refer to *the element of faith in Jesus Christ* that is present when Christian baptism occurs: Who has to have faith? What kind of faith should it be? When must they hold it? Secondly, 'believing in baptism' may refer to *the importance of baptism* itself: Do we believe that baptism is important? If so, then to what extent? Why do we practise baptism, and who is it for? In both of these senses believing in baptism raises important issues for the church today and the conviction behind this book is that, in grappling with these questions, the church can find its way towards a much greater clarity regarding not only its understanding and practice of baptism but also its broader mission and ministry within the twenty-first century. But to set the scene for these questions and the issues attached to them, the reader will firstly be invited within five Christian churches in the (fictional) English town of Melton Sudbury to observe how each of these very different churches approaches baptism.[1]

## 'St Mary's Melton Sudbury' (Church of England)

The oldest church in Melton Sudbury and one of its two Anglican parish churches is St Mary's. Led by its rector, Father Martin Derwent, St Mary's possesses a beautiful medieval building and two congregations attending the weekly Eucharistic services held at 8.00 am and 11.00 am on a Sunday morning. St Mary's, described as moderately Anglo-Catholic, possesses an impressive choir providing its ageing but loyal congregations with a reverence and beauty that many find helpful. Father Martin is viewed as a kindly face around the town and sees his role as making himself available to as many within the parish as want him for help and support. Whilst he wishes that more people within his parish felt the need for God outside of the times when disaster strikes their lives, Father Martin is convinced that a properly Christian approach is one that avoids drawing clear lines between 'insiders' and 'outsiders' and seeks to meet everyone with the inclusive love of the God revealed in Jesus Christ.

All of this has a significant impact upon the way in which St Mary's approaches baptism. A number of parents approach St Mary's each year to ask if Father Martin will christen their child. This is often shortly before their child reaches their first birthday in the hope that the two events can coincide. Often it is the first time that Father Martin has met the family and he responds with enthusiasm visiting the parent/s at home to book a date for the baptism, complete the paperwork and explain something of the significance of Christian baptism. Father Martin's preference is for the christening to take place at St Mary's main service at 11.00 am. If this takes place the congregation is almost doubled by the smartly dressed family and friends present for the occasion with the rector taking the opportunity to make them thoroughly welcome and balance solemnity with kindly enthusiasm about the child becoming a member of God's church. The regulars within the congregation also make a strong effort to be welcoming and generally accept that on 'Baptism Sundays' things need to be a little different with so many visitors present. As well as the certificates for them and the godparents, the child and parents are presented with a Baptism or Paschal Candle. Sometimes the parents request 'something more private' than the 11.00 am service and when this is the case, Father Martin conducts the christening at St Mary's on a Sunday afternoon with just the baptism party present. In more recent times, Father Martin has also agreed to include the baptism of children within the wedding service conducted for their parents, usually on a Saturday.

Whatever the setting, Father Martin always emphasizes his hope that those present at the baptism will return to St Mary's. However, whilst some sort of bond has usually been established between him and the family, they hardly ever become regular worshippers. On the few occasions that a parent and child do return, the lack of provision for children at St Mary's means that the parents usually struggle to cope with their child during the service and rarely continue coming. An important exception is those children who enjoy singing and eventually make their way into St Mary's choir with the choirmaster, Mr Bridges, who sees it as an important part of his role to encourage the growth of their Christian faith alongside the development of their singing. It is from this group that Father Martin often recruits those from fourteen upwards to join his Confirmation class although they are also joined by a number of local teenagers whose parents are keen for them to get confirmed. A small number of these young people continue coming to St Mary's as they reach their later teens and twenties. However Father Martin is rather sad as he reflects upon how, for a greater number of these teenagers, Confirmation has more of the appearance of a 'passing out' ceremony than a strong and personal affirmation of the promises made for them at their baptism.

## 'St Francis Melton Sudbury' (Roman Catholic)

In terms of the style of its services, the church in Melton Sudbury that probably has most in common with the worship at St Mary's is actually the Roman Catholic Church of St Francis led by its priest, Father Lawrence Innes. Several congregations attend the masses at St Francis either on a Sunday morning or on a Saturday evening with Father Lawrence making it clear that weekly attendance is something expected of committed Catholics. When a child is born to those attending St Francis, the child is usually christened/baptized at some point during the year following the child's birth and always at one of the Sunday or Saturday masses. The local Catholic schools also require children to be baptized Catholics, alongside regular attendance by the family at Mass, if they are to secure 'church points' in their application for a place at the school. It is rare for non-Catholics to approach St Francis for baptism and if they do, Father Lawrence points them in the direction of St Mary's or Holy Trinity, the other Anglican Church in Melton Sudbury. Every few years, however, an adult who has not been brought up Catholic decides to 'convert' and on these occasions (provided they have not been baptized already) they are baptized with a sprinkling of water and anointing with oil similar to when a child is christened. It is more common for lapsed Catholics to approach Father Lawrence for the baptism of their child and, in these cases, he is firm in stipulating that they must be regularly attending for a year before a christening takes place and two years before he is willing to sign any school form verifying their membership of St Francis. Both the parents and godparents must provide evidence that they are also baptized Catholics. Children baptized as Catholics can receive their First Communion at St Francis at the age of seven and Confirmation typically takes place for ten to thirteen-year-olds with Father Lawrence conducting preparatory classes for this, assisted by a couple in his congregation. Whilst the various masses at St Francis make few concessions for children in their liturgy, the aim is that their Christian nurture is provided by such rites and their classes.

## 'Melton Sudbury Baptist Church'

Vastly different in its style to both St Francis and St Mary's is Melton Sudbury Baptist Church (MSBC), led by its affable pastor, Johnny Smith. With most of its worship during services led by a band, MSBC lay a very conscious emphasis upon greater freedom of worship and informality through the absence of written forms of liturgy and frequent use of personal testimony. One area of greater formality at MSBC, however, is the role of 'Church Membership'. Here, attendees at the church, in a process separate from their baptism, have to be nominated and then approved by the other church members before they can fully participate in its meetings and governance.

Central to the ethos at MSBC, like other Baptist Churches, is 'Believer's Baptism'[2] – i.e. the conviction that baptism is a witness to the faith of the person being baptized and, in consequence, should only be administered to someone who is able to make a personal profession of faith. When children are born into the families of members of MSBC, they frequently have a 'Dedication' when their child is committed to God's love and care and these are often very moving occasions. Baptism, however, is quite distinct from this. Whilst it has been known for children as young as nine to be baptized at MSBC, there has been a certain amount of disagreement about the appropriateness of this, with the result that the majority of those baptized are now aged from their mid to late teens upwards. The process towards baptism normally starts with the person expressing the wish to be baptized and, after a period of preparation overseen by Johnny Smith, the baptism takes place. Baptism at MSBC is always by full immersion (i.e. the person being submerged below water). Most of these baptisms take place within the specially built pool that exists below the platform at the front of the church, although it has also been known for them to travel down to

Littlehampton where people are baptized in the sea! Before the baptisms take place it is customary for those about to be baptized to speak about the development of their Christian faith and what has led them to the point of wanting to get baptized. MSBC runs the Alpha Course, and times of particular joy at the church are when those who have come on this course 'make a commitment' and go on to express this in their baptism. Only those who have undergone 'Believer's Baptism' are eligible to become church members at MSBC and so it is usually after this point that they are asked about whether they want to apply for this. Those who have previously received 'Believer's Baptism' at another church and wish to become members have to go through the same process of being nominated and then approved by the other church members at MSBC.

## 'Holy Trinity Melton Sudbury' (Church of England)

In many ways most similar to MSBC in its style and 'feel' is the other Anglican Church in Melton Sudbury, Holy Trinity, led by its energetic vicar, Sally Jaggers. Like MSBC, Holy Trinity is strongly evangelical with a major emphasis upon preaching, lively worship, mission and evangelism. Holy Trinity has two Sunday services – one at 10.30 am which seeks to cater for all ages and includes Sunday groups for children and another at 6.30 pm attended, for the most part, by 'twicers'. Both services have Holy Communion just once a month (rather than being Eucharistic every week like St Mary's) and seek to use liturgical forms of worship but in a flexible manner. Through much of its history, Holy Trinity has been more of a 'gathered' than parish church with many within its congregation (including a large number from non-Anglican traditions) commuting some distance to attend its services, chiefly because of its preaching. Particularly since the arrival of Sally Jaggers as vicar, however, Holy Trinity has sought to combine its strongly evangelical style with an equal priority upon trying to draw newcomers from the parish into the church. Alpha, 'Messy Church' (once a month on a Wednesday), a Lunch Club and a Toddler Group form an important part of this strategy. When questioned about this, Sally Jaggers speaks of the importance of sharing God's love with people 'where they are'. An additional factor at Holy Trinity is the popularity of its Church School, Holy Trinity Primary. Unlike the Catholic school, baptism is not a requirement for a school place. The families have to attend church twice a month for two years before 'Church affiliation' and the 'points' that it gains can form part of their child's application for a place at the school.

Against this background, Holy Trinity has had a somewhat ambivalent approach to baptism reflecting the church's traditional evangelical wariness of an over-emphasis upon ritual and 'sacramentalism'. Being an Anglican Church, the baptism of children has always taken place at Holy Trinity but in a fairly low-key manner prompted by the church's desire to keep the emphasis upon personal conversion. In fact, throughout much of its history, baptisms only took place at Holy Trinity on a Sunday afternoon. It was under Sally's predecessor as vicar, and against some resistance from the regular congregation, that baptisms became part of the 10.30 am service, taking place on the second Sunday of the month. The combination of this legacy with more recent developments has resulted in the somewhat strange situation where a number of the most committed members of Holy Trinity choose a Service of Thanksgiving for their children, whilst baptism (for their child) is often sought with the greatest enthusiasm by those parents living within the parish of Holy Trinity but not attending the church.

It is in response to the latter category that Holy Trinity has developed a 'Baptism Policy'. This policy requires those seeking baptism for their child to attend the church on a regular basis for nine months before the baptism is booked. It is explained to the parent/s that since baptism is a sign of entry into the church, it only makes sense in the context of the commitment by them to attend services with their child. Where this is met with unwillingness, Sally Jaggers has to go through the difficult process of telling the parents that a christening is therefore not appropriate and offers them the alternative of a Service of Thanksgiving instead. This is rarely accepted, with some of these families then approaching St Mary's where Father Martin (following an awkward phone call to Sally Jaggers to seek 'permission') is usually prepared to conduct the christening. In a greater number of cases, however, the family are prepared to attend Holy Trinity for the length of time stipulated by the policy, with the attraction of a place at Holy Trinity Primary School often appearing an important additional factor. Rather than the Paschal Candle given at St Mary's, each child baptized at Holy Trinity is presented with a Children's Bible. Once or twice a year adults are also baptized at Holy Trinity and, in these cases, Sally Jaggers offers them the choice of being sprinkled or full immersion. If the latter is chosen, a baptismal pool is borrowed for the occasion from Harvest Community Church.

Whilst inheriting the Baptism Policy at Holy Trinity, Sally Jaggers accepts its aim to preserve the integrity and importance of baptism. She is also, however, increasingly aware of the tension between this policy and the more recent changes within the nature of the church and its approach to mission. Much of the success of the Alpha Course, the Lunch Club and 'Messy Church' appears based upon trying to make people as welcome as possible and reducing the distinction between 'insiders' and 'outsiders'. Sally is also uncomfortably aware that much of the discomfort which 'outsiders' have with the services at Holy Trinity owes rather more to their resistance to an alien subculture than an unwillingness to 'have God in their lives'. One example of this is unease at leaving their young children in a crèche or even their older children within the Sunday school groups. She also worries at the greater ease with which middle-class people appear able to attend Holy Trinity compared to those of poorer backgrounds, particularly when the former soon drop away having secured a place at Holy Trinity School. Whilst remaining resistant to a policy of open/indiscriminate baptism such as that at St Mary's, all of this reinforces Sally's growing sense that something needs to change in the approach of Holy Trinity if it is going to fit with the surrounding culture and be integrated into the increasingly 'incarnational' nature of the church's mission.

## 'Harvest Community Church'

The fifth church within Melton Sudbury is Harvest Community Church led by its minister Bernie Thompson. Bernie came to Melton Sudbury some twenty years ago attending both Holy Trinity and then Melton Sudbury Baptist Church for a time before feeling that God was calling him to establish a new church within the town. Much of Bernie's motivation was based on wanting to establish a church where the gifts of the Holy Spirit could flourish more freely within services – particularly speaking in tongues, 'words of knowledge' and healing. Harvest Community Church originally used the buildings of a local secondary school but in more recent times purchased a local disused factory for its Sunday morning service. At the time of its establishment, there was quite a lot of ill feeling within the other churches in Melton Sudbury, chiefly because of the number of members of MSBC and Holy Trinity who followed Bernie to Harvest. Over the passage of time, however, many of these wounds have healed, partly through Bernie now enjoying a much better relationship with the other church leaders in Melton Sudbury.

When it comes to its understanding and practice of baptism, Harvest Community Church shares most in common with Melton Sudbury Baptist Church. Like the Baptist Church, Harvest understands baptism as a witness to one's personal faith in Jesus Christ and rejects infant baptism (rather more vocally than at MSBC) as both unbiblical and dangerous. 'God has no grandchildren' is Bernie's favourite way of summing this up. In contrast to MSBC, however, a much greater emphasis is placed upon 'baptism in the Holy Spirit' understood as believers receiving a deep sense of God's reality and power quite separate from their baptism with water. Whilst water baptism is important, it is 'baptism in the Holy Spirit', usually signified by the person receiving the gift of tongues, that Bernie proclaims to be the most significant event that can happen in a Christian's life because of the inward rather than outward transformation it effects. Whilst it *may* coincide with water baptism, 'baptism in the Holy Spirit' is commonly separate from it, leading Bernie to preach that this is 'the real baptism' that should be most sought and prayed for, if Christians are to receive the fullness that God intends for their lives.

St Mary's, St Francis, Holy Trinity, Melton Sudbury Baptist Church and Harvest Community Church thus form the five major churches within the town of Melton Sudbury. In a neighbouring town, to which some members of Melton Sudbury travel to worship, is a Methodist Church practising infant baptism and a Society of Friends (also known as Quakers) Meeting House where neither baptism nor Holy Communion forms part of their worship. But it is the five churches detailed above which form 'Churches Together in Melton Sudbury' and whose leaders meet every three months for lunch and discussion at the 'Melton Sudbury Ministers' Meeting'. Normally this is a highly affable affair helped by the unusually good relationships now existing between Martin Derwent, Lawrence Innes, Johnny Smith, Sally Jaggers and Bernie Thompson. There was one notable occasion, however, when relationships between the leaders and their churches came under particular strain. And the presenting issue was baptism!

## 'The Michelle Gough (re-)baptism controversy'

At the centre of the controversy was a girl called Michelle Gough. Michelle's family were long-time members of Holy Trinity with Michelle baptized as a baby at the church and growing up through the various children's and youth groups there. Throughout this time, Michelle was one of the quieter young people at the church but with a growing faith eventually finding expression in her Confirmation at the age of fifteen. What happened soon after this surprised everyone at Holy Trinity, not least her family. Michelle discovered alcohol and boys, abandoned church and its youth group, and went completely off the rails. Various disasters and hardships followed for Michelle and her family who were at their wits' end over what to do with their previously compliant daughter. Eventually, however, Michelle came through this time chiefly through kind and constant support provided by Sally Jaggers and also Lucy Brown, a Christian friend at Michelle's school and a member of Melton Sudbury Baptist Church. Her attendance, alongside Lucy at the 'New Wine' Christian Festival, in the summer of her seventeenth birthday was an especially important time for Michelle as she made a heartfelt recommitment to her Christian faith. To the delight of her family, Michelle returned to regularly worshipping at Holy Trinity, attended the Alpha Course run by Sally Jaggers and, strengthened by her close relationship with Lucy Brown, began to really deepen in her Christian faith.

The complications arose after Michelle attended Lucy's baptism at Melton Sudbury Baptist Church. Lucy spoke during the service about the forgiveness, acceptance and purpose that she had found through a personal relationship with Jesus Christ and her belief that God was calling her to express her commitment to this relationship through her baptism. As Michelle watched this and Lucy's subsequent baptism by Johnny Smith, she felt an overwhelming sense of the Holy Spirit affirming her own relationship with Jesus Christ and calling her to respond in a similar manner. When Lucy spoke afterwards about the powerful experience of God's presence that she had had at her baptism, Michelle decided that this was definitely something she wanted for herself. Having seen Sally Jaggers conduct adult baptisms before at Holy Trinity, Michelle made an appointment to see her fully expecting a response of enthusiasm and endorsement.

The meeting was far from straightforward. Sally was tired and caught off guard by Michelle's request and rather too sharp in informing her that since she had already been baptized, any further baptism was out of the question. Stung by the unexpected nature of Sally's response, Michelle countered by saying that surely her 'christening' was something very different. She argued the unfairness of allowing a decision taken for her as a baby to now bar her from expressing her commitment to Jesus Christ. Realizing that her initial response had been too strong, Sally tried to calm things down by explaining that baptism is primarily a sign of God's grace rather than a witness to our faith and that Michelle had already publically declared her faith at her Confirmation two years earlier. 'But that didn't mean anything to me!', Michelle blurted out, realizing even before she saw the hurt on Sally's face that she had overstated the case. 'What I mean', she said in a quieter voice, 'is that, after messing up so badly, I now feel God's love and forgiveness more strongly than I ever have before. And if baptism is a sign of God's grace, it's one that's more meaningful to me now than ever before as well.' 'I'll need to think this through', Sally responded, anxious to call a halt to the meeting and any further confrontation.

The following week was a difficult one for both women. Sally alternated between hurt at what had occurred, especially after all the time she had spent helping Michelle during the last year and self-recrimination for not handling the meeting better. Michelle felt guilt over the hasty and inaccurate words that she had used towards someone to whom she felt genuinely indebted, but also increased confusion, especially after her parents expressed little of Sally's resistance to the idea of another baptism. 'We're just so grateful that you've come back to God … and us,' her Dad eventually said. 'But if that's the rules of the Church of England, we can't blame Sally Jaggers for keeping them.' It was the last part of what her Dad had said that stayed with Michelle as she met up with Lucy Brown later that day and a solution suddenly appeared to present itself. 'Do you think Johnny Smith would baptize me?' she asked. 'I guess we'd better ask him,' responded her friend.

Johnny Smith was as unprepared as Sally Jaggers had been for the conversation that took place a few days later with Michelle and Lucy. Michelle explained the situation and made her request. 'Well, it's rather tricky,' he began. 'Sally and I are good friends, you're a member of Holy Trinity rather than MSBC and the last thing I want to be doing is causing trouble in another church.' 'But you don't believe in infant baptism Johnny!', Lucy broke in accusingly. 'Well, no', Johnny responded, 'but I do believe in the oneness of the church and respect for another minister, and whatever our disagreements about baptism, it would be quite wrong for me to undermine Sally's ministry in this way.' Frustrated and confused still further, Michelle had finally had enough. 'All I seem to be getting is church rules and politics!' she snapped. 'I simply want to express my faith in God and experience his love in my baptism just as Lucy did, and none of you want to know.' 'I need to talk to Sally' was all Johnny said as another difficult meeting came to an end.

It was a few weeks later that the situation played out its final stages. Johnny phoned Sally and explained what had happened giving assurances that he wouldn't do anything further without Sally's involvement. He asked Lucy to pass a similar message on to Michelle. In the meantime and after lots of prayer, Sally started to ponder whether the answer was to offer Michelle the chance to reaffirm her baptism through full immersion. But this presented problems as well. 'What if everyone at Holy Trinity starts wanting one?' she thought out loud as she talked it through in the kitchen with her husband Peter. 'Sometimes you've got to take the path of least resistance and give people what they want,' he responded, trying to be helpful. 'Yes, but baptism isn't just about the individual', Sally countered, 'and I'm worried that doing this for Michelle will introduce a complete confusion into the meaning of baptism at Holy Trinity. She's grown up in the church, developing her faith in Jesus Christ through the ups and downs of her life and should be one of my best examples of what infant baptism is all about'. The conversation was interrupted by the ringing of Sally's phone in her study and when she answered it, the voice was that of Michelle's Dad. 'I just thought I ought to let you know', he said in a clearly nervous voice, 'that Michelle has done the baptism thing'. Once again taken off guard and puzzled after her conversation with Johnny, Sally remained silent not knowing what to say. 'Harvest Community Church and Bernie Thompson?' Michelle's father continued, seeking to convey his distance from events. 'Michelle heard from a friend that they were having baptisms at their church last Sunday and apparently this Bernie Thompson was happy to do it for her. I think Michelle was rather hoping that you wouldn't find out but Angela and I thought that was wrong and I said I'd ring you. Michelle is actually rather sad about it all. I think she wanted something similar to Lucy's baptism. But with only a few of her family and friends there I don't think it was quite what she was hoping for.' Unsure of what to say but desperate not to respond badly, Sally thanked Graeme for letting her know and asked him to pass on her love and best wishes to Michelle. When Sally emerged from her study, Peter could tell by the look on her face that silence was the best option. 'Bernie Thompson' were the only words that came from Sally as she sunk into a chair, breathed out slowly and gestured to Peter to put the kettle on.

Over the next few months, relationships started to be resolved at Holy Trinity, with Sally and Michelle trying almost too hard to be positive towards one another, culminating in a meet-up where both admitted to mistakes, insecurities and things they wished they had done differently. Without directly addressing 'rebaptism', Sally felt the need to preach more regularly about baptism and its meaning, and many within the congregation at Holy Trinity expressed how helpful and informative they found these talks. Where reconciliation appeared a more difficult matter was between Sally and Bernie Thompson, particularly with the quarterly ministers' meeting approaching. Sally had resisted contacting Bernie after the news of Michelle's baptism but had spoken to Johnny Smith about how upset she was at what Bernie had done. Johnny in turn spoke to Bernie who was genuinely surprised at the angst that had been caused. 'I thought I was doing everyone a favour – Sally included' was his response 'and surely the most important thing is that this young woman got to express her faith in the way she chose to?' 'It's a bit more complex than that,' Johnny replied, and suddenly conscious that he had overstepped the mark, Bernie penned a note to Sally apologizing for not speaking to her before going ahead with the baptism. Sally replied with a grateful note in response, but it was clear to all five of the Melton Sudbury ministers that further and fuller resolution was needed. With Bernie expressing uncertainty to Johnny and Martin Derwent about whether he should come to the next meeting and perhaps any further ones, something was clearly needed to ensure that the fellowship and collegiality that they had previously built up could continue.

Father Martin was due to host the next meeting at the vicarage of St Mary's and it was he who came up with the idea of how to approach the matter. 'We simply can't let this undo what we've worked so hard for,' he declared in a pre-meeting with Father Lawrence and Johnny Smith. 'The truth is that *all* of us see baptism differently and what we need is an open discussion about where we're each coming from so that we can understand one another better and work together, as the Lord surely wants us to.' Even as Father Martin spoke these words he could feel his nervousness rising at the prospect of such a discussion, but despite similar emotions, Father Lawrence and Johnny Smith agreed. So did Sally Jaggers and Bernie Thompson when the idea was put to them a few days later. Sally's curate, Alex Sainsbury, was invited to come along as well.

## 'The discussion of baptism at the Melton Sudbury ministers meeting': Initial statements and questions

The day of the meeting duly arrived. It had been agreed that there would be longer than usual for discussion and that each of the church leaders would be given a short time to explain their understanding of baptism with the others only responding initially to ask questions for clarification. Lunch would then be shared together before a broader discussion and interaction with one another's perspectives.

First to go was Father Lawrence. 'Well the teaching of the Catholic Church is that baptism is a sacrament which God uses to build up his church and impart his grace to those who receive it. It's not the only sacrament', Lawrence continued, 'God uses others as well to convey his presence and blessings – and receiving the sacraments of Communion and Confirmation form further crucial stages in the journey of a person's Christian life. But baptism is the start of the Christian life and the point where God imparts his Holy Spirit to the person being baptized and fills them with his grace which is then renewed and deepened as they continue within the sacramental life to which God has called them.' 'But what about faith?', Johnny asked, with nodding approval from Bernie. 'Doesn't your understanding of baptism include that as well?' 'Well, Catholic teaching is that baptism is a sacrament', Lawrence replied, 'meaning that it is something which God is doing rather than us. Faith is obviously vital to the Christian life but baptism is all about God giving his Church the grace that makes that faith possible'. 'And is that why you're happy to baptize babies?', Bernie asked, 'because you believe the baptism is all about God's action and nothing to do with our response to God?' 'I'm not saying it's got *nothing* to do with our response to God', Lawrence gently replied, strengthened by a smile from Martin, 'I'm saying that baptism imparts God's grace to his church in a way that makes faith and indeed every positive response that we make to God possible. The greatest Christian truth is that God has entered this world in Jesus Christ and is present within the sacraments that he has given to the Church.'

Once Lawrence had finished, it was Martin's turn. 'Well I'm coming from a very similar standpoint to Lawrence', he began. 'Baptism for me and my Anglo-Catholic tradition is also a sacrament, where just as he does through the bread and wine of the Eucharist, the Triune God takes something ordinary and earthly – in this case the water of baptism – and invests it with his heavenly presence. Just as God brought order to creation through the waters of chaos and brought the people of Israel from slavery to freedom through the waters of the Red Sea, so God now uses the water of baptism to bring us from death to new life through his son, Jesus Christ. Through baptism we are joined to the risen Jesus Christ, receive his Holy Spirit and are made sons and daughters of God.'

There was a moment's pause as those in the room took time to think about what Martin had said. Johnny looked as though he was about to speak but was then quiet and the next voice was Bernie's. 'So clearly, like Lawrence, you believe that baptism, whilst done by a priest or whoever, is an act of God himself?' Martin nodded his head in agreement. 'So is that why you're happy to baptize babies?', Bernie asked, 'because once you've baptized them, they'll be safe and go to heaven?' The atmosphere in the room was suddenly slightly tenser since the validity of infant baptism had now been raised twice by Bernie and earlier than most had hoped it would. 'Well, yes,' said Martin, looking sideways to Lawrence and then to Sally for some support, 'I do believe that God imparts his grace to those babies in baptism and starts working in their lives.' Martin paused before making his final statement: 'My task and that of every Christian minister, I would hope, is that of seeking to share God's grace with as many people as possible and to pray that that grace would work in their lives. And since the Church of England is still the official church of this country, I believe that it's my duty to respond positively to anyone and everyone seeking baptism and strongly affirm their search, however vague I might see it, for God in their lives.'

Following Martin, it was Johnny's turn. 'Well, as a Baptist minister, I'm obviously coming from a rather different perspective', he began, 'and see baptism rather differently from Lawrence and Martin. I totally believe that we are saved by God's grace rather than anything that we do by way of response to God but I'm unhappy to see any ritual or ceremony as bringing that grace about. That's why I'm uncomfortable with the word *sacrament* being used of baptism or anything else really. For me it gets too close to making baptism into a lucky charm or piece of magic and puts the emphasis upon outward rituals rather than the genuine response from the heart that God wants from us. The major message of the Old Testament prophets, as I understand them, was to warn people of the danger of the former and need for the latter, and it is the coming of the Holy Spirit in the New Testament era (following the saving death of Jesus Christ) that makes a response of the heart possible. And baptism, as I understand it', Johnny went on, 'is something given by God to form an outward sign of that inward response of faith in Jesus Christ and acceptance of this gift of salvation. It's a command of the Lord that those who have been born again need to obey so that we can publically witness to our faith in him. That's the reason why the apostles, like Peter, told their hearers to "repent and be baptised" – that inward response of repentance or turning from our sins to Christ comes first, with believers then called to express their faith through being symbolically cleansed, and also buried and raised with Jesus Christ through their baptism. That's why we like those being baptized to speak beforehand to the church about their journey to commitment of faith and that's why I couldn't, with any good conscience, baptize a baby. We need to love children, teach and pray for them so that they too will eventually turn to Jesus Christ in repentance and faith and it's when that happens, I believe, that baptism is appropriate and an amazingly powerful demonstration and reminder to all of us of what following Jesus is all about.'

There was a pause as those present sought to take in what Johnny had said and its implications. 'So am I right', Lawrence said, 'that you don't see baptism as actually bringing anything about? Would you regard it as idolatrous to see God as acting through the water of baptism?' Although gently expressed, the directness of Lawrence's question appeared to take Johnny slightly aback, and he was clearly thinking carefully before he replied. 'I think what I'm saying', he eventually replied, 'is that such thinking is dangerous because it can take us in that direction and away from the really important thing which is placing our faith in the free gift of Jesus Christ. In a world full of ritual, priests and ceremony, I believe that Jesus was drawing people away from all that and towards a much simpler faith in him alone as the route to forgiveness and rescue by God.'

'So how do you square that with the language used about baptism in the epistles Johnny?', Sally broke in. 'How do you mean?' Johnny replied. 'Well, in most of the references to baptism in the epistles', Sally continued, 'the language appears to refer to actions which God alone can take. "Baptism that now saves you also" in 1 Peter 3, "We were … buried with him through baptism" in Romans 6 and so on. How do you reconcile those passages with your understanding of baptism being about a believer's act of witness to their faith rather than an act of God himself?' Johnny thought for a moment. 'It's a good question', he said, 'and I admit that this language can be read in a sacramental way. Some Baptists do in fact understand it that way but in a manner that they still wish to express in believer's baptism. But for myself, I see these passages as taking advantage of the powerful symbolism which baptism provides to speak of the action of God which it points to. I take a similar view of Holy Communion or the Lord's Supper. God gives us these signs to point us beyond them to Jesus Christ and that's where he wants our focus to be rather than on the signs themselves.'

There was a pause as the group expected to move on to Bernie. But before this happened a new voice spoke. 'Am I allowed to ask Johnny a question?' asked Alex. No one had expected this since Sally had asked if she could bring her curate Alex along as an observer. A quick glance around the room reassured Sally that the others were happy and she smiled at Alex who then spoke: 'The question I want to ask you Johnny is about the status of the children at MSBC? Including your own two boys. Are they part of God's family or not?' 'Well, yes', Johnny said, 'I do believe that they are part of the family of MSBC and God's wider family as well, but not full members in the way that they will be once they've reached that point of repentance and turning to Christ for themselves. Once they've done that – and my task is to pray and work for that outcome – they can proclaim their faith through being baptized and become full members of the church.' 'Except', cut in Martin a little more sharply than he had intended, 'baptism still doesn't make someone a member at MSBC, does it? Why is that?' 'Well, believer's baptism is a condition of membership at MSBC', said Johnny, 'but it doesn't automatically bring membership and that's because we want to draw a distinction between someone witnessing to their personal faith and being welcomed as a full member into the church. Normally speaking, the two will be closely related but we resist making them identical because there may be pastoral reasons for holding off from granting church membership for a time, even to someone just baptized.'

Martin nodded to the group signalling that he felt that Johnny had faced enough questions. He also suggested that a break was needed, and for fifteen or so minutes the group wandered into the Rectory garden as Martin showed them his roses and served coffee. The conversation was friendly along with periods of silence that indicated that both the format and content of the meeting were taking everyone out of their comfort zones.

Once they were back in Martin's lounge, it was the turn of Bernie to speak. 'Well, to be honest, and not wanting to be offensive', he began, 'I sort of believe that everything said so far has been rather missing the point.' Whilst sounding provocative, Bernie's opening statement was gently expressed, drew smiles from the group and in a strange way diffused some of the tension that had been building up. 'What I mean is this', Bernie went on, 'baptism with water is important, and when it comes to what it is and who it should be for, I'm definitely with Johnny. It's a sign of commitment to Jesus Christ and for those who are able to make a conscious and public affirmation of their faith. But when John the Baptist was administering water baptism he said, "I baptise you with water for repentance. But after me will come one who is more powerful than me … He will baptise you with *the Holy Spirit and with fire*" (Matthew 3.11). That's the baptism that God is really interested in – baptism with the Holy Spirit – and, I suggest that it's the baptism that we've got to be most interested in as well. The wonderful truth of the gospel is that God has come in Jesus so that those who turn to him can be filled with his Holy Spirit transforming every part of their lives. Water baptism is simply a sign pointing to the far greater reality we should be praying and working for – people's lives being drenched in the Holy Spirit as they become spiritually reborn through being buried and raised with Jesus Christ. That, in my opinion, is what those passages mentioned earlier are referring to when they speak about baptism saving us, burying us with Christ and so on, and it is this baptism in the Holy Spirit that we should be focusing upon. Too many people coming to our churches, like those Samaritan believers in Acts 8 have simply been baptized into the name of the Lord Jesus, and the Holy Spirit has not yet come on them. Peter and John placed their hands on these believers so that they might receive the Holy Spirit and we need to foster a similar hunger and expectation for the Spirit today. Baptism in the Holy Spirit may come before water baptism and it may come after it, but that is the real deal, the real McCoy!'

Bernie's ending drew further smiles from the group at both his humour and the earnest nature of his enthusiasm. Martin was the first to respond. 'I hope we'd all agree, Bernie, that baptism with the Holy Spirit is vital. But what convinces you that such an action of the Holy Spirit is absent from the water baptism that we – and you – practise?' Bernie paused for a moment, less to consider what to say than to give his response impact. 'Because, quite frankly, it's obvious. Churches in this country are simply full of people who have been baptized – many of them as babies but some of them as adults – who have no knowledge whatsoever of the depth of relationship that they can have with God through the Holy Spirit. They're like those disciples that Paul met in Ephesus in Acts 19 who had received the baptism of John but had not even heard that there is a Holy Spirit. One of the reasons that infant baptism is so dangerous is because it formalizes this ignorance of the Holy Spirit and lack of expectation regarding his presence. But even within churches that have rightly rejected infant baptism and adopted believer's baptism, like MSBC, that gulf between water baptism and baptism in the Holy Spirit still remains. Some experience it, but God wants *every* believer to receive it.'

Sally was next to ask a question. 'How do you know whether someone has been baptized with the Holy Spirit, Bernie?' The atmosphere suddenly became tense once again with everyone aware that the issue of judgementalism was being raised. 'You know', Bernie said, 'because the Spirit takes hold of them and brings them to a place they couldn't be otherwise. They're empowered to speak in tongues, receive words of knowledge, discern between spirits – basically all the stuff that Paul speaks of when he talks in his letters about the gifts of the Holy Spirit.' 'And Marjorie Pullen?', Sally said. There was silence with Martin, Lawrence and Johnny unaware of whom Sally was referring to. 'You remember Marjorie Pullen from your time at Holy Trinity, Bernie?' Bernie nodded. 'Marjorie has been baptized for about eighty-two years and does none of those things you've just mentioned, certainly not in any obvious way. But she loves God, is full of joy and goodness despite the suffering she has had to endure, helps with our Climbers group (for 5–7's), gives others a lift to both church and our widows' group, and visits those who are in hospital or housebound. Is she baptized with the Holy Spirit?' Bernie paused and gave a look of slight frustration. 'I'm not saying that the Holy Spirit isn't working through Marjorie and others like her. Of course he is, and Marjorie is a wonderful Christian. But this doesn't undermine my point that God wants his supernatural power to flood through our lives and give us an experience of his power that is so much deeper than we often want to allow him. And my concern, if I'm honest, is that even the most earnest Christians in our churches are not always encouraged to let go of control and allow God to take them to that fullness that he intends them to possess.'

The final church leader to give their summary of baptism was Sally. 'OK', she said followed by a deep breath as she paused for energy, 'baptism for me, like Martin and Lawrence, is indeed a sacrament through which God gives us all the blessings of the gospel – forgiveness of our sins, adoption as his children, incorporation into the death and resurrection of Jesus Christ, entry into God's family of the church and possession of the Holy Spirit. It's a sign of God's grace rather than a sign of our response to him, and rather than simply being a picture of these things, it is, I believe, a symbol that actually brings about these blessings. But – and this is crucial – I believe that baptism brings about or effects these blessings as they are responded to with faith. That's why I probably wouldn't use the language of baptism *imparting* these blessings, as I think Martin and Lawrence did. That, for me, makes the blessings of baptism sound a bit unconditional, whereas our response is actually vital, with the grace of God enshrined in baptism needing to be received through *faith* in Jesus Christ. And the reason why I am more than happy to baptize babies and children from believing families is because I firmly believe that God's ideal is for children to grow up never knowing a time when they were outside of his family and responding from their very earliest years with faith in him. My problem with the practice sometimes known as open or indiscriminate infant baptism is that it appears to sit too lightly to the vital role of faith and discipleship in receiving the gift of grace that God gives us in Jesus Christ. That's what we're trying to give expression to through our baptism policy at Holy Trinity. We want infant baptism to take place when it is accompanied by the child being brought up, however falteringly, within the community of faith. If there is no evidence that this will happen because the parents are uncommitted, then it is much better for that child not to be baptized until he or she makes their own response to God later on. Anything else, I believe, brings infant baptism into disrepute and brings understandable accusations that those who practise it don't believe that a personal response to God is important or even necessary. Implementing a baptism policy is hard and frequently causes me no end of grief. But it's our attempt at Holy Trinity to show integrity between what we believe and what we practise in regard to baptism.'

Sally finished there and looked around to see whether the first response would come from Martin and Lawrence on the left of her or Johnny and Bernie to the right.

It was Martin who spoke first. 'I've appreciated what you've said about the sacramental nature of baptism, Sally, and you've also given me a lot to think about in terms of the importance of that grace being received through faith. But how would you respond to the accusation of your baptism policy being a little exclusive and judgemental, especially for an Anglican Church seeking to minister to a parish rather than simply to your regular congregation? Isn't it rather unfair to make it all focused on the commitment or otherwise of the parent or parents? There are, after all, plenty of other means by which children can be influenced to respond to God in their lives. Doesn't a policy of open baptism, such as that we practise at St Mary's, mean that no one is denied access to the grace of God?'

'I can see your point', Sally responded, 'but, in reality, open baptism doesn't expect or even encourage the child to be brought up having faith in Jesus Christ. I don't believe that we should set the bar too high in terms of Christian commitment but I do believe that we are only practising infant baptism with integrity when we expect some evidence that the parents intend to put into practice those very serious promises that they make when their child is baptized. If we don't expect or require any commitment to those promises to bring up their child as a Christian, then we're really only encouraging parents to perjure themselves.' 'And the point about Christian influence being able to come from places other than the family?' said Martin, thinking of the work done at St Mary's with the younger members of the choir by Giles Bridges. 'Well, infant baptism is founded upon the distinctive role that the Bible gives to the family in nurturing Christian faith,' said Sally. 'That's why some prefer to call it "family baptism". Whilst other adults can have a decisive influence upon children, their parent/s are really the only ones with the ability and indeed the right to bring them up within the Faith. And when that commitment isn't present within the parent/s, it's both more helpful and appropriate, I think, for baptism to wait until they have taken that decision towards Christian faith for themselves.'

It was Johnny who spoke up next. 'Sally I'm grateful for what you've said which has helped me to understand the rationale behind infant baptism a lot more. I can see that you're trying to implement it with integrity and with a great deal of importance attached to believing faith. But isn't the difficulty that you experience implementing your baptism policy evidence that it is based upon a rather flawed model? Infant baptism doesn't occur, explicitly at any rate, within the New Testament, and surely this is because faith can only be expressed in a meaningful way once someone is old enough to make a confession of faith based upon really understanding the good news of Jesus Christ?'

'Well, in the first place', Sally responded, 'all the baptisms recorded in the New Testament are those of adult converts to Christianity. There is no example of a child brought up in a Christian family being baptized later on in their life either, so the evidence is actually silent in both directions. But the really important point is that children can and do express very genuine faith in Christ from very early on in their lives. I go into our Tiddlywinks, Scramblers and Climbers groups at Holy Trinity pretty regularly and what I see from these 2–7's is really strong believing faith as they sing, pray and try to understand how God wants them to live. Most of them with really obvious conviction. Those of us who are parents want our children to know from their very earliest moments that they totally belong to us and for the security of knowing this to then play a role in them leading the best lives possible. And I believe that it is precisely the same with God. Implementing our policy on infant baptism is tricky and I am sometimes envious of the greater simplicity and lack of conflict that comes with open baptism and believer's baptism. But I believe that a properly implemented approach to infant baptism gives the best expression to God's wish for children born into the church to grow up in the security of never knowing a time when they didn't belong to him. Confirmation can provide a helpful point for people being able to give their personal affirmation to the promises made for them at their infant baptism but I wouldn't want to put it any stronger than that. What God wants, I believe, is children baptized as infants growing up within the family of the church and constantly responding in faith, hope and love to him in a way appropriate to their age and development.'

'Well, now that all of us have spoken and fielded some questions about our different positions', Martin said cheerily, 'it's time for lunch! Let's chat about anything but baptism as we eat together but then have ten or so minutes after lunch by ourselves to reflect on what we've heard and said this morning, pray about it and consider the further points that we wish to raise as we continue our discussion.'

## 'The discussion of baptism at the Melton Sudbury ministers meeting': Baptism as sacrament or not?

After lunch and the period of quiet, which most of the leaders spent in different parts of Martin's rose garden, they reconvened in his lounge. 'Well, we've had a bit of a rest from the subject of baptism', Martin smiled, 'and hopefully a bit of an opportunity to reflect and pray. So let's now really go for it and, in an atmosphere of Christian love, really push one another on all of those issues surrounding baptism that most concern us.'

First to speak was Lawrence. 'I'd like to pursue things a little more in regard to sacraments', he said. 'Johnny, you said earlier that you weren't happy with the idea of baptism or anything else really being a sacrament because this put the emphasis on outward rituals rather than an inner response of the heart. I'm taking that to mean that you don't believe that God, at least from Pentecost and the time of the Holy Spirit onwards, speaks or acts through physical things like the water of baptism?' Johnny and also Bernie nodded their agreement with this. 'But what about the occult', Lawrence continued, 'because it strikes me that we're all sacramental when it comes to that?' Johnny and Bernie, but also the others, looked slightly confused about where Lawrence was going with this. 'What I mean', continued Lawrence, 'is that if a teenager in your church came to you and said that someone had asked him to have a go with a Ouija board or Tarot cards you'd warn them off pretty strongly, wouldn't you?' This time everyone in the room nodded. 'And I'm guessing', Lawrence said, 'that you'd warn them off, not because those physical things are a nonsense but because they possess the genuine power to put you into contact with some really dark and dangerous forces?' There was silence in the room as the leaders acknowledged the point. 'And so are we really saying that the devil or the powers of evil can speak and act through created things but the one who actually created them cannot? The reason sacraments, including baptism, are so central to my Christian faith is because I firmly believe that the God of the Incarnation, the God who took on flesh in Jesus Christ, is the God whose very "modus operandi" is to take the ordinary things of this world, invest them with his presence and speak through them.'

Johnny was clearly thinking very hard as he responded to what Lawrence had said. 'Lawrence', he said gently, 'that is a really clear and helpful way for me, and I'm sure Bernie as well, to think about what you've said about sacraments, and I clearly need to go away and think a bit more about this. But what about the big emphasis within the Bible upon the danger of idolatry, and confusing or at least blurring the distinction between created things and God? Doesn't an emphasis upon sacraments take us down that dangerous path?' 'Perhaps I could say something about this', cut in Martin. Martin had been quiet for some time and everyone now turned to face him. 'Both sacraments and idolatry make sense when we have a strong doctrine of creation', he said. 'What I mean is this: God is the creator and everything that he has created is good and is intended to bless us.' Everyone in the room now nodded at what Martin had said. 'But', he went on, 'place any created things above their creator or in place of him and because they are transient rather than eternal, these earthly things then cease bringing us God's blessings. In fact', Martin continued, 'they become a curse because, cut off from the life-giving creator, they promise to give us life and demand sacrifices from other good things in our life in return for delivering this, but then completely fail to do so. That's idolatry – when we place created things *above* the Creator God. However place created things in their proper place *below* God – as good but transient things – and everything, without exception, that God has created can then become sacramental, through becoming a potential channel for his blessing. And against that context, I believe that God has chosen particular parts of creation – most notably the water of baptism and the bread and the wine of the Eucharist – to convey his sacramental blessing to us. Idolatry is a big danger and I know that those of us who love ritual and ceremony in our worship can sometimes drift towards that danger. But surely a dualism that separates God from his creation and ends up denying its essential goodness, and God's ability to speak and act through it, is just as much a danger to orthodox Christian faith?'

'I'd also like to add something here, if I may', said Sally, 'and it's because I've gone through quite a shift in regard to sacraments over the last ten or so years. I grew up within thoroughly evangelical circles – the churches I attended, the Christian summer camps I loved so much and my Christian Union at University. But I can see now that, even in an Anglican setting, none of these Christian communities were ever quite sure what to do with sacraments. Partly, I think, because of the fear of idolatry and ritualism that Martin has just spoken about. But also because evangelicals, by and large, simply don't "get" them. When I was a member of my Christian Union Executive at University, for instance, most of us, if asked, could probably have pulled off a fairly good talk about the dangers of sacraments. But we'd have been far more hard-pressed if any of us had been asked to do a talk about sacraments *that was exclusively positive*. In fact most of the talks I remember about baptism and Holy Communion from my upbringing said little more positively about them than their being a divinely authorized visual aid. My own grandfather was a Baptist minister and a wonderfully godly man but whenever I asked him about why we should practise baptism and Holy Communion he would simply reply that it was because they were "a command of the Lord." Much as I loved him, I can now see that his response was a fairly successful way of closing down the conversation, and looking back, I think he was effectively saying that, whilst these things didn't make any obvious, rational sense, Jesus had commanded them and we were to do them anyway. And whilst I've always *wanted* to have something more positive to say about the sacraments – particularly once I firmly committed myself to the Church of England – for many years, if I'm honest, I rather struggled to find out what that was.'

'But two things have made all the difference to my understanding of sacraments', Sally continued, 'and in both cases, it involved grasping a far more biblical understanding of key foundational issues than my evangelical tradition gave me. Firstly, my discovery of what I consider to be a more biblical understanding of *the relationship between heaven and earth* and, secondly, my discovery of a more biblical understanding of *the Christian hope*. I want to affirm everything that Martin said a few moments ago about the need for a strong doctrine of creation, understanding everything that God created as a potential channel of his blessing and seeing baptism and Holy Communion as specially given by God for this purpose. But all of that is hugely reinforced when we adopt a more biblical understanding of *cosmology* (in other words the true relationship between heaven and earth) and *eschatology* (the true nature of the Christian hope).'

'You see when it comes to the first of these', Sally continued 'I grew up with an unquestioned assumption that heaven was another place and that its primary significance lay in being the place where those of us who were Christians would go when we died. But I've now realized that this is not the cosmology reflected in the Scriptures. The Bible doesn't present heaven as a faraway place but as God's dimension of present reality – the spiritual realities that are usually unseen but constantly surrounding us. Rather than being distant and separate from one another, heaven and earth are realities that are distinct from one another and yet also intersecting and interlocking at special points. It's that cosmology, I've come to realize, which is the basis for God's revelation of his presence within the Old Testament, most obviously within the Temple, and supremely, within the New Testament, in the coming of Jesus Christ. The resurrection of Jesus, the ascension of Jesus into heaven and the coming of the Holy Spirit all take on a much deeper significance for me in the light of this overall framework because I now understand all of them as being, in different ways, about God's great project to bring heaven and earth together.'

'And that's the link to how I've also changed in terms of my understanding of the Christian hope', Sally continued. 'You see like most evangelicals – perhaps most Western Christians – I grew up with an understanding of the Christian hope that could basically be summarized as "going to heaven when you die." Throughout my time in Sunday school, Christian summer camps, my Christian Union at university, the various churches to which I belonged and even at my theological college, this wasn't so much taught as simply assumed to be the Christian hope. There was hardly any reflection about how "the sure and certain hope of the resurrection" fitted in with this. But I've now realized, as I say, how inadequate that understanding is. The Christian hope, as presented by the New Testament, is much richer than that of "going to heaven when we die" because it is *the hope of resurrection into a new creation comprising a new heavens and a new earth joined fully and finally together.*

'This has all had major implications for a number of things that I had previously struggled to understand in my Christian life', Sally said to the group, 'and there are loads of things that I've had to rethink in the light of it. But it's got particularly strong implications for understanding the sacraments. Like a lot of evangelical Christians I was pretty nervous earlier in my Christian life about any idea of God being found within physical things. But I can now see how inconsistent this was with both a biblical cosmology and a biblical eschatology. God's presence and the life of heaven are constantly found on earth within the Bible, and it is also made clear that this process will one day be made complete when "the earth will be filled with the knowledge of the glory of the LORD as the waters cover the sea" (Habakkuk 2.14 cf Isaiah 11.9). The risen and bodily ascended Jesus forms the first fruits of this new creation, and if the task of the Holy Spirit is to bring the "deposit" or "first instalment" of that future into the present (Ephesians 1.14), then it is completely appropriate that he brings the presence of God in Jesus Christ within parts of the present creation. That's why I now very firmly believe that the Holy Spirit brings the presence of God in Jesus Christ within the water of baptism.'

'But isn't that putting the significance of baptism in the wrong place?', cut in Bernie. 'I'm not at all sure about the stuff you've said about cosmology and eschatology, Sally, which all sounds a bit unnecessary and overcomplicated. Surely the main significance of water baptism lies in helping believers to look backwards rather than forwards? It's given to help us look back to the way in which the death and resurrection of Jesus brought about an even greater exodus than the original one, from their slavery to sin, so that we can identify ourselves with this act of grace. Baptism in the Holy Spirit, on the other hand, is what brings to people a foretaste of eternity through giving them that depth of personal relationship with God that they will one day enjoy forever. And that's surely all about God being within our hearts rather than within physical things.'

'Well, I think most of us here would probably want to say with Paul in Ephesians 4 that there is just one Christian baptism – of water and of the Spirit', replied Sally. The others nodded. 'And in terms of looking backwards or forwards, I believe that baptism does both. The water of baptism does look back to the death and resurrection of Jesus as the ultimate recapitulation of those great saving events in the Old Testament – the Exodus from Egypt, the Flood and God's act of Creation itself. And the Spirit uses this water of baptism to bring the significance of these events forwards into the present reality of the believer's life. But just as the Passover meal not only looked backwards to the Exodus but forwards to God's future rescue of Israel, so baptism not only looks back to the death and resurrection of Jesus but forwards to the resurrection from death that awaits us in the new creation. And just as the Holy Spirit brings forwards the significance of those past events that baptism recalls to meet us in the present, so he also brings some of those future blessings to us now as well through joining us to the risen Jesus. When we're baptized, the Holy Spirit joins us to Jesus in his death and resurrection and simultaneously provides us with an anticipation of the resurrection that we will receive in the new creation.'

Sally paused, conscious that she had done a lot of talking in the last few minutes. 'I also want to say something in response to Bernie on the whole physical thing, if that's OK?' The others indicated that they would like to hear more and so Sally went on. 'Well, to me, it all comes down to what Martin said earlier about creation being good, and the emphasis I've made upon it being something that God wants to rescue and redeem rather than destroy. It's not just our *souls* that God wants to rescue but *the whole of us*. That's why a physical resurrection – both for Jesus and us – is so important. God's salvation is wonderfully physical as well as spiritual, because its end goal is humans being given resurrection bodies so that we can at last fulfil that calling we were given in creation of caring for a similarly renewed and transformed earth. God's Spirit filling the physical things of creation like the water of baptism and the bread and wine of Communion with Christ's presence points us towards this. The fact that both of these sacraments represent union with Christ's risen body and are also received bodily reinforces this and also the importance of presenting our bodies as living sacrifices to God (Romans 12.1). Paul uses baptism in Romans 6 to insist that what Christians do with their bodies in the present really matters and the physicality of baptism therefore has vital implications for both personal ethics and our commitment to care for the creation that God has entrusted to us. As well as its other associations, it forms a commissioning by God to offer our bodies to him as "instruments of righteousness" (Romans 6.13).'

Once again there was quiet in the room eventually broken by Martin. 'Well, if someone had said all this to me thirty years ago', he said with a broad smile, 'I might have become an evangelical!' 'Well, it's all fairly recent thinking for evangelicals', Sally replied, 'and I am rather embarrassed at how long it has taken me in my Christian life to start understanding sacraments. It's probably taken more unlearning of the implicit teaching that I have received from my evangelical subculture than anything else and that's always a pretty scary thing to do. But I guess I've realized that in regard to sacraments', Sally said glancing at Martin's beloved rose garden and winking at her fellow Anglican, 'my tradition has often been so worried about greenfly on the roses that it has decided to pave over the rose garden with concrete!' The leaders burst into laughter at Sally's provision of a floral metaphor especially for the smiling Martin who then suggested that another short break was taken for people to visit the loo before the last part of the discussion.

## 'The discussion of baptism at the Melton Sudbury ministers meeting': Baptism and the place of faith

It was Martin who spoke first once the group reconvened ten minutes later. 'I've got another issue that I want to raise', he said, 'and I guess it's best expressed in a question for Johnny and Bernie. Both of you place great importance upon baptism (with water, in Bernie's case) being reserved for those who are able to express a clear and conscious decision of faith. I know that believer's baptism sometimes takes place for relatively young children but on the whole it is reserved for those old enough to demonstrate a relatively sophisticated understanding of the Christian message and give a coherent account of their response to this. But how do you reconcile that with Jesus' words about the importance of receiving the kingdom of God like a child (Mark 10.15), and what is your response to those with learning difficulties or other impediments to making a credible confession of faith? That last question isn't an abstract one, by the way. Not long ago I encountered a family who left the Brethren Assembly they attended because the leadership there wouldn't baptise their son because he had Down's syndrome. The irony is that they then joined a church where the same son is the only member of the congregation to attend all three of their Sunday services throwing himself into their worship with as much enthusiasm as I've seen in church. But what's your opinion on that? Was that Brethren Assembly right in their decision and their reason taking for it? Or wrong?'

'Do you want to take this one, Bernie, or should I,' said Johnny with a smile. 'After you,' said Bernie, smiling back. 'Well, I don't know the circumstances, but I think I would have wanted to baptize him,' said Johnny. 'Affirmation of faith can take many forms and if he was expressing that in worship rather than a testimony, that would be good enough for me.' 'OK', said Martin, 'but if I can press you, what if a family possessed a late teenager who was heavily autistic and came to church each week with his family but was unable to show a very coherent response to much. I'm guessing that Lawrence, Sally and I would all baptize him.' Lawrence and Sally both nodded. 'But what would you do, Johnny and Bernie?'

The spikiness in the question had once again produced a rather tense atmosphere in the room with both Johnny and Bernie appearing slightly uncomfortable at the direction the discussion had taken. 'I would probably tell them water baptism wasn't necessary,' responded Bernie eventually. 'We believe in a God of love and it would be enough to commit the boy or girl to God's care without using baptism to do that.' There was a further pause as everyone turned to Johnny for his response. 'I really don't know,' said Johnny. 'It's a good if rather hypothetical question. If I did baptize him or her – and I think I might – I would probably want to see it as a pastoral decision made against a tricky context which warranted a departure from our normal practice. But I would want to make it clear that it was due to exceptional circumstance and very much preserve the norm of baptism being for those able to make a confession of their personal faith.'

By this stage the meeting had been going for some considerable time and most were aware of the need to draw it to a conclusion. 'I'm aware', Martin said, 'that much of the discussion over the last half hour has rather taken your positions to task Johnny and Bernie, and we want this discussion to be even handed. Are there any further issues that you want to raise?'

Johnny and Bernie took a few moments to think. 'Bernie and I have different perspectives on baptism', Johnny eventually said, 'but I guess what unites us is our fear of nominal Christianity and how, if I'm really honest, the practice of your churches in regard to baptism so often appears to endorse that.' Bernie nodded in agreement. 'I don't want to be judgemental of where people are in relation to God', Johnny continued, 'and I can see how the last thing that Sally, in particular, wants to encourage is any idea that a personal response to God doesn't matter. But the truth is that infant baptism and its effects do look for all the world like a vestige of some outdated concept of Christendom. Bernie and I have been challenged pretty strongly this afternoon and so I'd like to issue my own challenge now, particularly to Lawrence and Sally. How many of those children that you baptize each year, do you honestly believe you would be baptizing if you didn't have a school with a churchgoing criterion for admissions? Aren't you (and Martin, even though you haven't got a church school) in major danger of encouraging people to think that Christianity is simply something to pay lip service to as a small part of their life – either for superstitious reasons or because there are some obvious worldly benefits to be got out of it?'

This time it was Lawrence and Sally's moment to look at each other and consider who should make the first response. Eventually it was Lawrence who spoke. 'I think one of the major differences between us', he said slowly, 'lies in the different weight that we seem to place upon the importance of the personal and the corporate in terms of our relationship with God. For Johnny, Bernie and perhaps Sally as well, it does appear from a lot of what you say, that Christianity is overwhelmingly about a *personal* relationship with God and that inevitably shapes a great deal of your approach to baptism. The personal dimension of our relationship with God is clearly important, but one of the things I find most difficult about Protestant Christianity is when this hardens into an individualism that almost forgets that God primarily relates to us as *a people*. For Catholics, like me, the great truth is that of God bringing us through baptism into his community of faith, the church. Of course there is a real mixture of people within the church and I'm as frustrated as anyone when I see nominalism and people just coming to St Francis to seek places at Corpus Christi School. But our Lord warned us in the parable of the wheat and the tares (Matthew 13.24-30) that the church would always contain a mixture of people and the most important thing is that God, through the sacrament of baptism, has called a community into being that brings his presence into the world. That's where I want to place the major emphasis, rather than upon the faith of individuals so evident in the priorities of Johnny and Bernie. Martin may or may not agree with me on this point but I can't get as worked up as them about whether an individual has completely grasped every important aspect of the Christian faith because everyone who is baptised is brought into a community that is so much bigger than the sum of its parts. Not least because it is countercultural communities rather than individuals which really transform the world and bring God's love to it most strongly.'

'I think I want to endorse a great deal of what Lawrence has just said,' added Sally. 'Individualism to the point of almost denying that God can relate to a people is another legacy of my evangelical tradition that I am having to unlearn. But I think I'd want to add, in my response to Johnny, that a really important part of my Anglican ecclesiology (or theology of church) is the desire to be a church that is for everyone within our parish. That doesn't mean that I have any less desire than anyone else here to see people grow into every bit of the fullness that God wants to bring them. But it does shape both the missional approach of trying to "meet people where they are" at Holy Trinity and the level of commitment that we expect before baptism is offered. One of the things that I've noticed throughout my ordained ministry is that when a child is born, a number of changes happen in a family's life to make it more likely that they will come to church. A greater need for local *community* is part of this, as is the sudden parental agenda of needing to locate the source of *values* for their child. But in addition, I would argue that parents frequently have what I call a "God-moment" when their child arrives, as they witness new creation right in front of them, followed by the need for "something spiritual" to speak into this experience. This last factor is, if anything, increasing given the fact that virtually all dads these days are present at the birth. And what we're seeking to do at Holy Trinity is to engage with all of these factors when we encounter new parents including those seeking baptism for their child. We're seeking to affirm both the impulses that have brought them in our direction *and* emphasize the solemn commitment to faith in Jesus Christ and Christian nurture that bringing their child to baptism involves. That's why we warmly welcome them whilst making it clear that we want them to be coming along to services for quite a few months before we set the date for a baptism and it's why we run a baptism preparation evening followed by a visit to their home. It's why we also invite them to our Alpha Course and do everything possible to welcome them into the family of the church. The last thing we're wanting to encourage is nominal Christianity but people can only grow into committed Christians if their search for God, however vague, is affirmed, alongside a real clarity about the commitment involved in baptism.'

'And regarding our church school', Sally continued, 'yes, that is clearly an important factor for many of these parents. But it's important we don't automatically place that agenda within a secular category because it's actually very rare that I don't see a very clear link between this and the factors I mentioned earlier as the Christian community, values and atmosphere of God within the school are a vital part of what is attracting them. That's the reason we invest all the energy we can into building a seamless partnership with our school and particularly the weekly assemblies that our clergy and lay team lead there. The criteria regarding church attendance for school places are applied with meticulous accuracy and fairness and since no one is actually without a whole mixture of motives for attending church, we see it as vital to avoid being judgemental and concentrate on ministering to those who come and praying that God's Spirit would be at work within them.'

'Now I've got to be honest in saying that the results of this approach are mixed. A fair number stay at Holy Trinity and continue growing in their Christian faith and others drift away after gaining school places, which is obviously desperately disappointing. But it doesn't mean that a spiritual agenda was never present or that our response to these people was wrong. The truth is that in all churches, including those practising believer's baptism, people can and do drift away after making a commitment.'

'Well, I think we've had a very profitable time,' said Martin. 'We've heard one another speak about why we practise baptism in the way that we do and we've asked one another some pretty searching and demanding questions. It strikes me that we're all seeking to uphold important principles in how we administer baptism and that we can only profit from further engagement with each other's views and understanding.

This meeting may have been occasioned by conflict over baptism but hopefully its outcome has been for us to develop a deeper understanding of, and respect for, our different ministries. But unless anyone has anything more to say, perhaps it would good if we finish with prayer.'

'I've got something further that I want to ask, if you don't mind.' The voice was that of Alex Sainsbury who in obedience to instruction from Sally had spent most of the meeting listening. The group turned to face the curate. 'It's actually a question for my training incumbent, Sally,' Alex said. After a draining day and all the stress running up to it, this was not something that Sally had expected. Six months of working with Alex, however, had made her accustomed to her curate's ability to spring surprises. 'Yes, Alex?' she smiled. 'Well, having listened to everything that has been said', started Alex, 'my question is this: do you think the Church of England genuinely believes in infant baptism?' There was silence as Sally paused, completely unsure as to what the question meant. 'You see I'm not sure it really does', continued Alex, 'because otherwise I think we'd have a very different church.'

'I'm not sure, I understand', said Sally. 'Are you talking about the issue of whether baptism completes sacramental initiation?' 'Completes what?', exclaimed Bernie, 'I'm sorry, I only speak English!' A burst of laughter triumphed for a moment over the fatigue within the room. 'Sorry', replied Sally, 'I'm talking about the issue of whether baptism completes entry into the church and access to the blessings that it symbolizes. Some in the Church of England, and I think the Roman Catholic Church, would say that Confirmation is a sacrament that is needed to complete this entry as the Holy Spirit is given through this rite to strengthen the adult Christian. I wouldn't say this but I imagine that Martin and Lawrence might?' Lawrence nodded whilst Martin looked more hesitant. 'In some ways, Bernie', Sally continued, 'this understanding of Confirmation is rather similar to your belief that "baptism in the Holy Spirit" is needed to complete what is begun in water baptism. I'm a strong believer that Confirmation isn't a sacrament but instead represents a helpful means for teens or adults baptized as infants to be able to express their personal response to that baptism. Is that what you're referring to, Alex?'

'Well, not really', Alex continued, 'although it's definitely related to that. You see, my understanding, and I think the official position of the Church of England, is that baptism does complete entry into the church and brings all of those baptized into full membership of it.' Sally nodded. 'But I just don't see us as doing that in practice', Alex continued. 'We baptize all of these children and say that they are members of the church but then deny them most of the things that should accompany that membership.' 'Are you talking about Child Communion', Sally responded, 'because, as you know, many Anglican churches are now adopting this?' 'And we Catholics have been doing that for much longer!', added Lawrence.

'Again, not really', said Alex sounding a little frustrated, 'but again it's definitely related. I'm talking about the Church of England baptizing scores of children, and sometimes even admitting them to Holy Communion, without giving any practical expression to what that baptism is meant to represent. When people talk about Baptismal Integrity, for instance, they are usually exclusively referring to whether the parents and godparents can say the promises that they make in an infant baptism with integrity. That's clearly important. But the question I'm more interested in is whether the church can declare with integrity at a child's baptism: "We welcome you into the fellowship of faith; we are children of the same heavenly Father; we welcome you"?[3] The reason I ask this question is because most Anglican churches in this country declare these words whilst simultaneously spending more on their flower budget each year than upon making appropriate provision for these baptized children as full members of their church. I've appreciated Martin's roses today as much as anyone but given our priorities, is it any wonder that we lose most of those children and their parents? Surely the most obvious issue attached to infant baptism and its integrity is the need for us to place the highest priority on delivering church on a weekly basis that is totally relevant, exciting, engaging and age-appropriate to these children whom we have solemnly declared to be full and equal members of God's Church? Surely for infant baptism to have real credibility, it's got to be synonymous with the provision of church that is just as suitable for our children as for any of our other members?'

There was a long pause with everyone too exhausted to respond to a point none of them had expected. 'As I say', said Martin eventually with a warm smile towards everyone in the room, 'let's finish with prayer.'

# 1

# Who believes in baptism?

Although fictional (and perhaps rather unrealistic in the fluency, never mind the collegiality, of its church leaders!), the dialogue at Melton Sudbury demonstrates something of the wide diversity across and within Christian churches regarding baptism. As the discussion at the ministers' meeting indicated, this diversity exists in regard to both the importance and nature of baptism itself, and the importance and nature of the faith that needs to be present within it.

## *Believing* in baptism

The most obvious issue in the theology of baptism today is still that of the necessity and nature of 'believing faith'. All Christian churches who practise baptism at all will baptize an unbaptized adult 'believer' who comes from another religion or from unbelief. This will take place following a personal confession of faith. Beyond these types of baptism, however, there is significant division over the necessity of such a personal confession of faith by the one being baptized. Those from a 'baptist' perspective maintain that such a confession should be required from *all* those being baptized, with the corollary that they must be old enough to understand and express this. Once known as 'adult baptism', this is increasingly known as 'believer's baptism' since older children are sometimes included within it. Even within such 'baptist' approaches, however, there is still a degree of diversity over practice here. Some churches are more cautious than others about encouraging such 'believer's baptism' of children with disagreement about the age they need to have reached for this confession to be credible, personal and responsible. Another issue is whether the baptism even of a 'believing adult' should be as immediate as seems to have been the case in the Acts of the Apostles or whether it should only follow careful preparation over weeks or even months.

Within churches practising the baptism of infants (also known as paedo-baptism) a personal confession of faith is not required from children and is obviously not possible in the case of babies. Strong statements of belief are instead required from the parents and godparents of those bringing these children for baptism. Within the *Common Worship* baptism service, used within the Church of England since 2000, these affirmations are as follows:

> *Do you reject the devil and all rebellion against God?*
> (Answer) *I reject them*

*Do you renounce the deceit and corruption of evil?*
(Answer) *I renounce them*
*Do you repent of the sins that separate us from God and neighbour?*
(Answer) *I repent of them*
*Do you turn to Christ as Saviour?*
(Answer) *I turn to Christ*
*Do you submit to Christ as Lord?*
(Answer) *I submit to Christ*
*Do you come to Christ, the way, the truth and the life?*
(Answer) *I come to Christ*[1]

These liturgical statements are extremely strong in the faith commitment that they require and this is equally true of many of the liturgies of other churches practising infant baptism. Alongside these affirmations, parents and godparents also promise to pray for the child being baptized within the Church of England and 'draw them by your example into the community of faith and walk with them in the way of Christ'.[2] Despite the strength of these promises, however, a major issue surrounds the extent to which such believing faith is, in reality, present or even expected in many infant baptisms. Citing the importance of the baptismal promises being said 'with integrity', some churches discourage such 'christenings' unless the parents are regular members of the church or at least prepared to receive some instruction regarding the promises that they are going to make. At the other extreme are churches where no such demands are made and the desire expressed to avoid making judgements upon the parents' faith or penalizing the child for any lack of it. Such an approach is often described as 'open baptism' by its supporters and 'indiscriminate baptism' by those concerned about whether genuine 'believing' has any part at all in such events. For all Christians then who practise baptism today, there are issues concerning 'believing' in baptism with respect to its timing, its reality, its maturity, its credibility and also the generosity and charitable assumption with which these are viewed.

## Believing *in baptism*

However, and this is the second meaning of the title, there are also Christians today for whom believing in *baptism* itself is (or at least seems to be) of very little importance. The Society of Friends (known as Quakers) do not practise baptism with water or Holy Communion with bread and wine as rites of material signs but seek to practise 'a sacramental life through the living presence of Christ'.[3] Similarly the Salvation Army accept as church members 'all those who are in Christ Jesus' without any rite of initiation by water-baptism.

Surprisingly, moreover, many Baptist Churches too make baptism an entirely voluntary and personal matter sometimes even accepting people into membership and to Holy Communion who are unbaptized. Other Christians will be found worshipping in various congregations and having a living faith in God but who cannot see the point of the sign of water-baptism when they have experienced the reality of spiritual baptism.

There are African Churches which practise 'baptism of the Holy Spirit' without water, through the laying on of hands. But there are also many other Christians who do practise water-baptism but see it as much less significant than 'conversion' or 'baptism with the Spirit'. The one is a *sign* (whether it seems to come before or after what it signifies) whilst the other is the *reality*! Often the sign and the reality are separated by weeks, months or many years, and it is the *reality* (quite understandably) that is prayed and worked for and rejoiced over in the church, whilst the *sign* is but a shadow in comparison.

Such attitudes are often associated with an individualistic and pietistic form of evangelical Christianity. Underlying them is often the fear that too much emphasis upon the sacraments of baptism and Holy Communion will lead to nominal Christianity rather than authentic faith. At a deeper level this is often based upon suspicion of any claim that God can work through physical actions or matter and the fear of this leading to superstition and idolatry. The result is that whilst baptism and communion are usually practised within evangelical churches, they often appear to have far less importance than, for instance, listening to sermons and studying the Bible. In fact there frequently appears to be a greater confidence in describing the dangers associated with the sacraments than understanding their positive importance. A common description of the rationale for baptism and communion amongst such groupings is to call them 'a command of the Lord' betraying a sense that the sacraments ought to be honoured even if their provision seems a little arbitrary and makes little rational sense. The equally frequent description of baptism and communion amongst more 'catholic' Christians as 'holy mysteries' has greater depth but can sometimes appear to be serving the same purpose.

Other churches, by contrast, particularly those which are more Anglo-Catholic, Roman Catholic or Eastern Orthodox, appear to regard baptism in theological terms as highly significant in relation to the gospel and the church of Jesus Christ. Within all of these churches, however, there are also practices rather at odds with this theological status. One example in the Church of England, less prevalent now than thirty years ago but still quite common, is semi-private services of baptism taking place when few (if any) of the church members are present. Or again, when parents and godparents make professions of faith but are never seen in the congregation again (until another baptism – or perhaps a wedding or funeral) and appear to have little intention of truly bringing the children up 'as Christians within the family of the Church'. Another tension evident within many churches is the discrepancy between the declaration that baptized infants are members of the body of Christ and the lack of adequate provision for these children's needs and welfare. The existence of the rite of Confirmation and the frequent restriction of Holy Communion to those who have 'been confirmed' also conveys a degree of ambivalence about the status of those who have 'only' been baptized. Is any of this really believing in baptism?

## A biblical theology

The purpose of this book is to enquire carefully into the biblical theology of baptism. This will involve an understanding of the nature of conversion, repentance and faith. When Paul speaks of Christian unity in Ephesians 4 he declares 'one baptism' alongside 'one body', 'one Spirit', 'one hope', 'one Lord', 'one faith' and 'one God and Father for us all' (Ephesians 4.4-6). One implication of this is that there is *one theology of Christian baptism* which we must endeavour to clarify from the Scriptures. Having done that (and only then) we shall turn to the thorny issue of Christian family baptism (or infant/paedo-baptism) – the view that it is right to baptize the infants of Christian parents and the 'baptist' view that any infant baptism is misguided. One of the strange things about baptism is that many Christians can appear to approach these questions the other way around – firstly, deciding at what stage of life baptism is appropriate and secondly, and on the basis of their answer to the first question, deciding what they consider baptism to actually be. This process is often relatively unconscious but needs to be recognized and reversed if the progress needed within every church and tradition regarding baptism is going to be made.

It would therefore be a theological nonsense for readers to jump to Chapters 9 and 10 without working through the earlier chapters. However, when that point is reached, the authors believe the biblical theology points quite clearly to a particular conclusion. They are concerned though to be gracious and 'eirenical' to those who interpret the evidence differently and to face the pastoral questions of discipline and 're-baptism' in a scrupulous and serious manner.

The book is not intended to be a piece of academic research and so notes and references will be kept to a minimum. It is intended to be a careful and clear enquiry which produces a coherent account, biblically reasoned and pastorally applicable. This point is emphasized because so much of the literature on this subject is on the one hand densely academic, technical and detailed, or on the other hand either very superficial or bitterly polemical and partisan. It is written not for the professional scholar but for clergy, ministers, ordinands, churchwardens, elders, Christian parents and that growing band of lay people who gladly help with baptism preparation, administration and the subsequent nurture of the baptized (both children and adults) but are perplexed as to the real meaning and importance of the whole enterprise.

## A changing scene

Changing contexts have a marked effect on the priorities and practice of theological reflection – whether we are always conscious of it or not. It is helpful to note certain developments during the past generation or so, which have had particular significance for the discussion and practice of Christian initiation.

## The Western world is increasingly seen to be a complex post-modern mission field rather than part of Christendom

In 1981 the number of Christians in Third-World countries surpassed that of the Western world and these respective trends of growth and decline have continued apace since then.[4] The growth of Western secularization has had a crucial impact upon the decline in its churches but the situation has become further complicated over the last thirty years by the certainties of modernism becoming steadily undermined by the range of attitudes and impulses often described as post-modernism. Part of this development has been a marked upsurge during this period of the search for spirituality but with the post-modern assumptions of consumer choice shaping the (largely unconscious) selection and self-assembly of a whole variety of different beliefs and practices. Many forms of post-modernism have reflected a deep suspicion of the traditional institutions seeking to mediate spirituality leading to the rediscovery of Eastern religions and the growth of movements such as the New Age. At other levels, these developments have been more often characterized by a mildly benevolent attitude towards the church accompanied by the assumption that it chiefly exists to mediate the form of spirituality that its individual consumers have decided that they want at that point in their lives.

Particularly from the mid-1990s a decisive shift began amongst perceptive leadership within British churches from the pastoral to the evangelistic, reflected in the announcement by the Church of England of a 'Decade of Evangelism'. The most successful examples of this and subsequent developments have tended to be those churches that have responded most appropriately to the cultural shifts reported above. Where evangelism occurred between the 1950s and 1980s, for instance, it tended to be through large evangelistic rallies, university missions, Sunday schools, youth groups and camps and special 'guest services' where people were invited to hear a specialist speaker and respond to their spoken message. Over the last two decades this has largely given way to approaches more grounded in local engagement with people's search for a spiritual community that will fit their needs. The explosive growth of the Alpha course has formed part of this, as has the development of 'Fresh Expressions of Church' such as 'Messy Church' encouraged by the 'Mission Shaped Church' movement. Changes to the curriculum of theological courses and colleges and criteria for clergy selection have also reflected this major retooling for mission and the need for church leaders to understand something of the changing cultural context in which we are now located.

This changing context has had a significant impact upon baptism. The effects of secularism and the decline of church attendance have resulted in a steady decline, especially since the 1970s, in the number of children being baptized in churches. In many cases the continuing impetus for 'getting the child done' has increasingly come from grandparents (whether churchgoers or not) more familiar with infant baptism/ christening as the norm than the child's parents. One effect of the increasing non-baptism of children has been a marked rise in *adult* baptisms with the number of these within the Church of England frequently exceeding those in Baptist Union churches.[5]

Once again, however, the rise of post-modernism has made the situation more complex, particularly in the greater enthusiasm (however vague and conditioned by a 'pick and mix' mentality) that it has brought for sacramental experiences. Perhaps the most obvious example of this was when one of the most iconic figures of the early new millennium, David Beckham, announced that he and his wife Victoria definitely wanted to get their first child Brooklyn christened but hadn't decided into what religion yet![6] At a more popular level, these developments have resulted in the decline of baptisms in parts of Britain being paralleled in other places by an increased appetite for 'christenings' sometimes resembling a quasi-wedding (particularly given the decline in actual marriages) as the family take the opportunity to put on smart clothes, invoke a sense of God and make a public statement of 'this is who we are'. Some of the recent options introduced into the baptism services of the Church of England, such as the option to reduce what the parents and godparents promise, appear to be prompted by the desire to engage more fully with this context.[7] So has the provision to include the baptism of a couple's children within the marriage service.

The development of 'Fresh Expressions of Church' has encouraged further engagement with all of these factors. Many forms of 'Fresh Expressions', such as 'Messy Church', have particularly engaged with the variety of factors prompting new parents to be open to Christianity. These include parents' increased need for local community and support when a child is born (particularly with many extended families living wider apart than was once the case), the desire to find the source of appropriate 'values' for their child and also the fresh sense of God that frequently accompanies the arrival of a baby.[8] All of this has very obvious implications for initiation with a consequent rise in the prevalence of baptisms (both infant and adult) taking place within 'Fresh Expressions of Church'. One of the key issues within 'Fresh Expressions' is the extent to which they are integrated within traditional forms of church or seen as autonomous churches and this obviously has major implications for the Christian development of those who have been baptized within these churches. All of the changing cultural factors mentioned here thus have a very obvious impact upon the way in which baptism is understood (some would say misunderstood), approached and practised.

## The development of biblical theology

Biblical theology is now more influential in theological discussion and in church life than for several generations past. This is most obviously because of the dramatic decline of theological liberalism in the face of successive developments such as the 'biblical theology' movement, the growth in numbers, confidence and theological integrity of evangelicals, the pervasive spirituality of the charismatic movement and the continuing impact within Roman Catholicism of the Second Vatican Council. Perhaps the greatest factor bringing change within the Church of England over the last forty years has been the astonishing growth of evangelical scholarship with the work of scholars such as Tom Wright, Richard Bauckham, Tony Thiselton, Paula Gooder and Alister McGrath playing a major role in reshaping the church and encouraging a confidence and indeed excitement amongst clergy, ordinands and lay people about the power of biblical theology to address the most pressing issues faced by both the church and society. The development of, for instance, Grove Books and their popularity across all traditions is testimony to the continuing confidence with which biblical theology and church practice are now being regularly integrated.

In regard to baptism, these developments have been highly significant. Back in the 1960s, Colin Buchanan was a lone evangelical voice on the Church of England's

Liturgical Commission. This would be unthinkable now with biblical theology playing a crucial role in shaping the baptism texts contained in *Common Worship* and numerous Grove booklets by Buchanan and others providing commentaries on their biblical basis. Another symptom of this development is the way in which biblical and sacramental theology, once largely separate from one another, are now increasingly being integrated. This confidence in biblical theology has also been demonstrated, with very significant potential fruit for understandings of baptism, in responses to the so-called 'New Perspective on St Paul'. This movement, challenging traditional Protestant readings of St Paul, is usually seen as beginning with the publication of *Paul and Palestinian Judaism* by Ed Sanders in 1977 and has caused considerable controversy through its elevation of ecclesiology (i.e. his theology of church) to a central place in Paul's theology. Some indeed have rejected it out of hand. Others however, most notably Tom Wright, have developed and refined the insights of the New Perspective in a way that has developed, amongst other things, many exciting implications for the understanding and practice of baptism.[9]

At a more popular level, the influence of biblical theology has resulted in a decisive shift from a pragmatic to a principled approach in regard to baptism. One of the most obvious manifestations of this has been the recognition across traditions of the deeply non-theological nature of 'private' baptisms and their widespread relocation to the main Sunday service within each church.

## Increasing pressure for agreed policies of baptismal discipline and discrimination

For a long time, policies regarding baptism remained a matter for individual churches and even more their clergy. Even within the Church of England, with its regulations regarding baptism in Canon Law, the application of these regulations largely remained within the discretion of the local clergyman. One of the results of this and the pragmatic approach mentioned above was the common, if strictly speaking irregular, practice of christenings/baptisms taking place on a Sunday afternoon with just the family and godparents present. In these situations, families would contact the member of clergy and the baptism would be arranged with little involvement by anyone else at the church. If any instruction was provided regarding the meaning and significance of baptism, this would tend to be given by the vicar/priest alone.

This situation has changed quite considerably over the last forty years. Further awareness of the missional context in which the church is placed has brought the much greater involvement of lay people in baptism preparation. The significance of baptism within the missional strategy of churches and greater consciousness of the principles involved has meant that many church councils are discussing baptism policy. The development of 'team ministries' within the Church of England has also prompted the need for wider discussion and agreement between clergy and churches on who should be included within baptism and on what grounds. Every few years there have also been attempts within various dioceses and in General Synod to clarify Church of England policy. Whilst these debates have not resulted in a uniformity of practice, they have brought the issues of baptismal discipline and discrimination to a much greater prominence than existed before.

Another influential factor has been dialogue across the different Christian denominations. This has partly been driven by the greater impetus for cooperation between churches largely fostered by their missional context. The ecumenical movement has had significant influence here particularly through the publication in 1982 of the influential World Council of Churches report *Baptism, Eucharist and Ministry* (also known as the Lima text).[10] This enabled many Christians to study the issues and hear about other approaches to baptism in a dramatically new way.

## The teaching and experience of 'baptism in the Holy Spirit'

One of the most important factors in the development of Christianity within Britain over the last fifty years has been the growth of the charismatic movement. At the heart of this has been a much greater emphasis upon the ministry of the Holy Spirit and, in particular, gifts of the Spirit such as healing, speaking in tongues, receiving 'pictures' and 'words of knowledge' and so on. Rather than being restricted to newer churches, several of the traditional church denominations have been transformed by the charismatic movement with little of the dramatic church growth occurring within this country outside its influence. Within the Church of England, initial wariness has been replaced with a great deal of official endorsement and both Holy Trinity Brompton and the New Wine network now possess a major strategic influence. Just one feature of this is that probably more ordinands are being produced in Britain by charismatic churches than by any others.

The charismatic movement contains a great deal of diversity and it is also fair to say that it has undergone very significant change, particularly in regard to issues such as the expectations surrounding healing. One of its areas of consistent emphasis, however, has been the importance of Christians experiencing a deep and personal experience of God's grace often described as 'baptism in the Holy Spirit'. In many cases, this has been presented by leaders within the Charismatic movement as a second, distinct stage from initial conversion and/or baptism with water leading to a great deal of disagreement and controversy, especially in the 1960s and 1970s. Passages in the Acts of the Apostles where the Holy Spirit appeared to be received at a second stage distinct from conversion were cited to support this. *Baptism and Fullness* was written by the evangelical leader John Stott to oppose any sense of a second and distinct stage of 'baptism in the Holy Spirit' and accusations were made by others that the claims of charismatic leaders were similar to the teaching opposed by St Paul in his letter to the Colossians.[11] It was not uncommon during this period for a number of churches to suffer painful splits with the rightness or otherwise of promoting a 'baptism in the Holy Spirit' often being the most obvious presenting cause.

Nowadays, much of the discussion surrounding these issues is less dogmatic and confrontational, helped by the recognition of the vital role that the charismatic movement has played in renewing some traditional denominations. It is still common to hear charismatic Christians speaking about baptism in the Holy Spirit but with less emphasis upon it as a second, distinct experience bringing its recipient into a fullness of relationship with God that they lacked before. More often, the emphasis is placed upon all Christians receiving the Holy Spirit but needing to be continually refilled with the Spirit and therefore open to and expectant about the new and surprising directions in which this might lead them.

The overall impact of all of these developments has been to raise awareness of the indispensable place of the Holy Spirit within any theology of baptism. The title 'Christ' (the Greek equivalent of the Hebrew word 'Messiah') means 'the anointed with the Spirit one' and the influence of the Charismatic movement over the last fifty years has resulted in a far more serious engagement with what it meant when John the Baptist proclaimed that Jesus would 'baptise with the Holy Spirit and with fire'.

## The issues and expectations surrounding 're-baptism'

One of the symptoms of the modern/post-modern age is its increasing fluidity of movement. Within Christianity, this frequently results in a person growing up within one church or denomination before moving to another, with this process sometimes being repeated several times. Unsurprisingly, given the diversity of practice, this often throws up very significant issues involving baptism. Within the Church of England, Trinitarian baptism (whether as an adult or child) within another denomination is always recognized with no expectation or indeed approval of a 'rebaptism' occurring. In fact adult baptism elsewhere is usually not seen as needing to be supplemented by Confirmation before someone can receive Holy Communion in an Anglican Church. At the basis of this is the conviction that baptism in the name of the Father, the Son and the Holy Spirit brings the baptized person into God's one, worldwide church rather than just into the Anglican branch of it. In practice either Anglican Confirmation (following baptism elsewhere) or formal reception into the Church of England (following baptism and Confirmation elsewhere) is usually only required of those applying for ordination or other positions of authorized authority. The Roman Catholic Church takes the same line on the non-repeatability of Trinitarian baptism with the difference that it does need to be supplemented with Catholic Confirmation if the person is going to receive Holy Communion. Within most other Christian denominations (with significant exceptions amongst the Exclusive Brethren and some Strict or Grace Baptists), adult or believer's baptism (usually when done by immersion) within another denomination is also recognized as valid rather than another baptism being required before the person can apply to become a church member.

Where issues of 'rebaptism' most commonly arise are in relation to a previous infant baptism. Here most Baptist churches stipulate that a person can only become a church member if they have undergone believer's baptism. The validity of a previous infant baptism is usually not recognized. A number of new churches take a similar line. It is then that a rebaptism/proper baptism (depending on your perspective) occurs. There are some Baptist churches that are prepared to recognize infant baptism done in a previous church as 'valid but irregular' but these are normally exceptional.

However, as noted in the introduction to this book, requests for rebaptism can sometimes come from Christians staying within the same denomination. The issue of people being baptized as infants but never brought up in the Christian faith and only coming to faith later on is the most obvious factor prompting this. But also people who have fallen away from a previous Christian faith before returning and wanting to reaffirm their commitment. But the changing cultural context and specifically the greater appetite for the sacramental mean that there are also an increasing number of Christians who simply wish to have the experience of being baptized by full immersion. Ironically given that believer's baptism is generally emphasized by churches that downplay the sacramental power of baptism, such requests can often be accompanied by the hope that the act of rebaptism will bring about a deeper experience of the Holy Spirit's power. Although the issue of rebaptism has always been around, it is sharper now than ever before and is another significant context for our theological enquiry.

## Where shall we start?

We all approach this issue with a particular personal history which may or may not have included experience of particular teaching and practices of baptism. Furthermore such teaching and experience might have been found personally helpful or unhelpful. It might have been in the context of a welcoming Christian community or an apparently harsh and unloving one. It might have been presented by an approachable, kindly member of clergy or an apparently too-busy, uncaring one. It might have been in the context of thoughtful biblical teaching or an apparent appeal to tradition, church rules and Canon Law. Finally, it might have been considered in a careful, leisured, rational way through sermon, preparation class, lecture or book, or in the highly emotional contexts of either adult or peer pressure in adolescence or immediately following the birth of a baby and 'wanting it done' or being under pressure by grandparents to 'have it christened and named proper'. The controversies over infant baptism – whether it is ever right or not and whether it should be administered with careful discrimination or not – especially cast their shadows over any study of baptism.

So every reader will be coming with a different experience and a different agenda of questions, problems and expectations. It is often asserted that 'we must start where people are' and that is usually important in personal conversation and counselling. When preaching to or teaching a group, however, the audience may consist of people who are at many different places in their thinking and experience – so too with a book. For this reason we shall not start with considerations of *psychology* or *sociology*. These issues will play some part later on; the psychology of the child and the teenager is significant in pastoral issues of initiation and nurture, and the sociology of peer pressure on the adolescent, and the greater openness to spirituality of new parents is very relevant too.

Neither shall we start with *church law* or the situation of church *policy* and practice now. As we have seen churches differ widely on these matters, and even within the same denomination there are widely divergent interpretations and practices, it is not an issue that divides neatly along other theological or ecclesiastical lines – for instance it cuts right across the liberal/evangelical, the catholic/protestant, the established/free church and the charismatic/non-charismatic divisions. Canon Law regarding baptism in the Church of England does need to be part of any discussion of baptismal practice and often requires careful examination if it is not to be misunderstood. But it is not the place to begin.

Nor shall we start with a consideration of baptism in *church history*. It is an immensely complex and tangled story, and the interpretation of initiation in the second century and following periods of the early church is a matter of considerable controversy. The impact of *personal* history upon the study of baptism has already been noted but all of us are also influenced by general historical developments in regard to baptism which do repay careful examination and analysis. But to start with these factors is deeply contentious and will usually generate more heat than light.

Neither shall we start with a consideration of *sacramental theology* – the relationship between a sign and the thing that it signifies. To begin in this way is both unhelpfully abstract and makes too many assumptions about the nature of baptism. As with Holy Communion, discussions about the sacramental nature or otherwise of baptism have been hugely controversial and can only proceed once the biblical evidence has been thoroughly examined to see whether or not it points in that direction. Once this has occurred, we will consider the value and significance of using the term 'sacrament' for baptism and the crucial issue of whether it is efficacious, i.e. whether baptism actually brings about the things that it symbolizes or simply represents these things. This will inevitably include examination of the relationship between baptism and other rites and ceremonies often described as sacraments and the broader issues concerning the nature of creation that it also points to. However, loaded as it is with centuries of controversy, such a discussion of sacramental theology is not a good place to begin a study of baptism!

This enquiry will begin unambiguously with the *biblical evidence* – whilst recognizing that quite inevitably we shall all look at that evidence through 'spectacles' misted (more or less) by our own personal experience and the various traditions which have formed us. Different churches have interpreted Scripture differently, and various theological systems have given varying emphasis to the place of tradition, church authority, human reason or conscience and the experienced guidance of the Holy Spirit in a particular situation. However, the overwhelming majority of Christians throughout history, and all major Confessions of Faith, acknowledge unambiguously the unique and normative authority of the Bible for Christian faith. The approach of this study, therefore, will be to start with an examination of the biblical material on baptism paying close attention to its emphases, particularly the contexts within which it claims that baptism should be understood. Thoughtful engagement with the way in which Christian traditions have interpreted this material differently will be attempted with the desire to acknowledge and affirm all of the crucial aspects of baptism that they have recognized and sought to safeguard. Other important factors and considerations will then be approached in the light of this biblical examination. The hope and prayer behind this book is that it will help every Christian who reads it to wrestle afresh with what God has, and is, revealing through the Scriptures about the meaning and significance of baptism, with a particular eye towards its implications for, and challenge to, the church in the twenty-first century.

2

# The Bible and baptism

The problem of where to start when examining baptism is only partially dealt with by turning first to the Bible. The controversy over the legitimacy of infant baptism has tended to polarize those who begin in the Old Testament – because the Bible starts there, and the whole Bible, not just the second part, is Christian Scripture – and those who turn straight to the New Testament – because there Jesus commanded baptism and there the apostles explained it as union with Christ in his death and resurrection.

Later in this chapter a way through this procedural dilemma will become clearer. It will be seen that the New Testament writers themselves, particularly the apostles in their letters, understand baptism in the light of the Old Testament revelation of God's covenant.

First, however, it is helpful to note the variety of approaches by different scholars and their strengths and weaknesses.

## Varieties of starting points for studying baptism

### The alleged antecedents of Christian baptism?

Some begin their study of Christian baptism with its alleged antecedents, i.e. those rituals which could be seen as forerunners of it. Three of these are commonly noted:

*The Jewish ceremony of circumcision* (the removal of the foreskin of a Jewish baby boy on the eighth day of his life)

*The use of water in religious ceremonies* generally and particularly in Jewish rituals of purification

*Jewish proselyte baptism* whereby non-Jews, male and female, underwent a water ceremony to become Jews and 'children of the covenant'.

The first two of these are very definitely biblical and all three clearly of significance to the study of Christian baptism. To begin our enquiry here, however, would be problematic. In regard to circumcision, there are important issues that need to be addressed first, including the relationship of the Old and New Testaments to one another and the nature and distinctiveness of the 'new covenant'. Only after these issues are addressed can the relationship between circumcision and baptism be properly stated. Jewish rituals of purification also possess no unequivocally direct line with Christian baptism and when it comes to Jewish proselyte baptism, there is controversy over the date of its development and no clear reference to it in the New Testament. All of these factors make starting an enquiry into baptism with any of these alleged antecedents highly problematic. In addition starting such an enquiry especially with circumcision is often seen as trying to answer the question about infant baptism before the nature of Christian baptism has itself been examined properly. Both in terms of establishing a proper methodology and safeguarding ecumenical relationships, a better starting point is needed.

## The baptism ministry of John the Baptist?

Other scholars begin where the New Testament begins, with the very obvious antecedent of Christian baptism in the baptism ministry of John 'the Baptist', the forerunner of the Messiah. John's baptism is clearly of great importance with frequent reference made to it in the Acts of Apostles (1.5; 1.22; 10.37; 11.16; 13.24-25; 18.25; 19.3-4), although interestingly not within the epistles. However it is quite clearly pre-Christian with most of these references concerned to stress this difference. In particular, it does not include two of the distinctive features of Christian baptism, namely its being 'into Christ' and associated with 'baptism of the Holy Spirit'. John himself contrasted sharply his own baptism with water and the subsequent Messianic baptism with Spirit (Matthew 3.11-12; Mark 1.7-8; Luke 3.15-17). John's ministry of baptism is highly significant (and will be examined in Chapter 5) but is neither the key to understanding the meaning of Christian baptism nor a good place to start its enquiry.

## The baptism of Jesus?

It seems much more promising to begin at the baptism of Jesus himself. Although this baptism is by John and part of his general programme of baptizing, it has dramatically new features. Jesus (declared as God's Son by the voice from heaven) is at the centre of the episode, and the Holy Spirit descends on him in a clear and dramatic manner. Surely the example of Jesus at the outset of his public ministry is the pattern for a believer at the outset of his or her Christian life and ministry? Attractive and suggestive though this is (and the significance of Jesus's baptism will be expounded in Chapter 6) it must also be noted that distinctive features of Christian baptism are not obviously present. Christian baptism is 'into Christ', involves assurance of forgiveness and marks incorporation into God's people. These features are not present in the baptism of Jesus and suggest that this is primarily a unique event forming a bridge between the baptism of John and the ministry of Jesus which will culminate in Christian baptism. It is only after the death and resurrection of the Messiah and the outpouring of the Spirit at Pentecost that Christian baptism in its fullness can be known. There are brief references in John's Gospel to Jesus and his disciples exercising a ministry of baptism themselves (John 3.22, 26; 4.1-2). However no details are given, and no particular teaching or significance is attached to it. In line with Jesus's first words in Mark 1.14, it is probably best to see these baptisms as an extension of John's ministry and proclaiming the need for Israel to repent in response to the coming of the Kingdom of God.

## The death and resurrection of Jesus Christ?

Others such as Oscar Cullmann have asserted that the very foundation of Christian baptism is to be found only in the death and resurrection of Jesus Christ.[1] One must be born of 'water and Spirit' (John 3.5), and the decisive link between the water (of John's baptism) and the Spirit (of Christian baptism) is to be found in the baptism that Jesus underwent. By this, however, Cullmann does not mean Jesus's baptism in the River Jordan but his baptism of suffering on the cross of Calvary. Jesus seems to refer to this coming experience of distress and desolation as a 'baptism' in Mark 10.38-39 and Luke 12.49-51. The former reference is very allusive, but the latter more explicit – 'I have a baptism to undergo, and how distressed I am until it is completed.' The relationship between baptism and death is clearly of great theological significance in the life of Jesus and in the Christian believer. However, although this relationship is worked out in some detail in Romans 6.1-4 and also mentioned in Colossians 2.12, the death of Jesus is nowhere in the New Testament referred to as a baptism – apart from the two implicit (rather than explicit) references in Mark and Luke referred to above. Its importance will later be examined but again it scarcely seems the place to start to develop a theology of Christian baptism.

## 'The Great Commission'?

Another approach is to commence with the command of Jesus himself in the so-called 'Great Commission' of Matthew 28.19-20: 'Go and make disciples of all nations, baptising them in the name of the Father and of the Son and of the Holy Spirit, and teaching them to obey everything I have commanded you.' Eric Lane asserts that 'these words form the only true basis for the study of Christian baptism'.[2] He goes on to indicate that this clearly implies that baptism is for confessing believers only.

There have been lengthy scholarly debates about the authenticity of this passage where the risen Jesus leaves his marching orders with the disciples. These debates are frequently subjective and inconclusive.[3] We can firmly accept the Great Commission as indicating (if not the actual words of the risen Christ) then at least the very early 'conviction that the practice of Christian baptism had the full authority of Jesus behind it'.[4] Whilst acknowledging the importance of Jesus's authority behind this passage, the significance of the context of evangelism and teaching, and the notable Trinitarian reference, significant features of Christian baptism are still unmentioned. There is no reference to forgiveness of sin, the gift of the Holy Spirit, or incorporation into the church. Important though this passage is, it does not provide the key into the theological significance of Christian baptism.

## The baptismal practice of the early church in the Acts of the Apostles?

Other writers begin with the baptismal practice of the early church as seen in the Acts of the Apostles. There are nine instances of baptism in this story of the growth of early church – the day of Pentecost (2.38-41), in Samaria (8.12-17), the Ethiopian (8.36-38), Saul (9.17-18), Cornelius with his relatives and friends (10.47-48; 11.15-18), Lydia and her household (16.15), the jailer of Philippi and his household (16.31-34), Crispus with his household and others in Corinth (18.8) and the former disciples of John the Baptist at Ephesus (19.1-7).

Across these accounts we find all the distinctive features of Christian baptism:

(a) It is 'in the name of Jesus Christ' implying allegiance to him (e.g. 2.38; 10.48).
(b) It is closely linked to preaching of the gospel and making disciples (in every instance).
(c) It involves repentance and faith and leads to forgiveness of sins (e.g. 2.38; 8.12, etc.).
(d) It usually (though not always) includes the gift of the Holy Spirit (e.g. 2.38; 19.5-6).
(e) It usually implies incorporation into the church (e.g. 2.41).

However, the picture which emerges is not entirely straightforward. Frequently one or several of the five characteristics listed above are omitted, though any argument from silence is of little value. More strange is the baptism by Philip of the believers in Samaria after 'he preached the good news of the kingdom of God, and the name of Jesus Christ' but the Holy Spirit is unmentioned and unreceived. It was some time later that the apostles Peter and John came and prayed for the Holy Spirit who came through the laying on of their hands. The explanation given is 'that the Holy Spirit had not yet come upon any of them; they had simply been baptised into the name of the Lord Jesus' (verse 16). Here, in only the second recorded instance of baptism in the Early Church, baptism seems strangely downgraded and needing 'confirmation' by apostolic hands for reception of the Spirit. Also remarkable is the experience of Cornelius and company who receive the Holy Spirit *prior to* baptism. Then again the disciples at Ephesus had received only John's baptism and not heard of the Holy Spirit, so after Paul had told them of Jesus, they were (re)baptized into his name and received the Holy Spirit through Paul's laying hands on them.

It may well be argued that the Acts narratives indicate a pattern of baptism in the name of Jesus following preaching of Christ which results in repentance and faith. The relationship of the gift of the Spirit and incorporation into the church in this process of initiation is, however, not always clear. Were the believers in Samaria who had been 'baptised into Jesus' really members of the body of Christ before they received the Holy Spirit? What is the significance of 'the laying on of hands' in three (Samaria, Saul, Ephesus) of the four occasions when the receiving of the Holy Spirit is clearly spelled out? And in the fourth (Cornelius), the Holy Spirit precedes baptism.

The whole pattern of initiation does not always follow a logical and ordered progression. Teaching may be inadequate (as in the Ephesus incident) and God's

Spirit is sovereign and free (as in the Cornelius episode). Oddities and inconsistencies therefore occur. It will be seen later that similar issues arise nowadays. Sufficient at the moment to note that it is not as straightforward as some may suggest simply to say that we should follow the pattern of the Early Church. Those narratives that report the spread of the gospel beyond the Jews for the first time (most obviously the Samaritan and Cornelius narratives) appear to contain as much that is special and unique as normative, making them difficult to use in constructing the basis for the theology of Christian baptism. The narratives concerning baptismal practice in Acts clearly do have much to contribute to our theological understanding of Christian baptism, particularly in the cluster of five features associated with baptismal events noted earlier. But it is also clear that we need to look to other parts of Scripture for the clearest insight into the theological basis of baptism.

## The teaching of the New Testament letters on baptism

That place is in the epistles or letters contained in the New Testament. Even here baptism doesn't receive systematic treatment, with no actual instruction about who should be baptized, the manner in which it should be administered and so on. The references in the letters generally use baptism to make or reinforce other points that they want to impress upon their readers. But by examining these references, including carefully noting their contexts, a great deal can nonetheless be grasped about the theological significance of baptism and this is where we will therefore begin our enquiry.

There are ten passages in the New Testament letters where baptism is mentioned explicitly and eight other passages where the reference is probable.

## Explicit references to Christian baptism in the New Testament letters

**Romans 6.3-4** in the context of an appeal for Christian holiness

> All of us who were baptised into Christ Jesus were baptised into his death. We were therefore buried with him through baptism into death in order that, just as Christ was raised from the dead through the glory of the Father, we too may live a new life.

**1 Corinthians 1.13-17** in the context of an appeal for Christian unity

> Is Christ divided? Was Paul crucified for you? Were you baptised into the name of Paul? I am thankful that I did not baptise any of you except Crispus and Gaius, so no one can say that you were baptised into my name. (Yes, I also baptised the household of Stephanas; beyond that I don't remember if I baptised anyone else.) For Christ did not send me to baptise, but to preach the gospel – not with words of human wisdom, lest the cross of Christ be emptied of its power.

**1 Corinthians 10.1-4** in the context of warnings about discipline in the Christian life

> For I do not want you to be ignorant of the fact, brothers, that our forefathers were all under the cloud and that they all passed through the sea. They were all baptised into Moses in the cloud and in the sea. They all ate the same spiritual food and drank the same spiritual drink; for they drank from the spiritual rock that accompanied them, and that rock was Christ.

**1 Corinthians 12.13** in the context of an appeal for unity in Christ

> For we were all baptised by one Spirit into one body – whether Jews or Greeks, slave or free – and we were all given the one Spirit to drink.

**1 Corinthians 15.29** in the context of an argument for resurrection of the dead

> Now if there is no resurrection, what will those do who are baptised for the dead? If the dead are not raised at all, why are people baptised for them?

**Galatians 3.26-29** in the context of an argument for Christian unity through faith in Christ Jesus

> You are all sons of God through faith in Christ Jesus, for all of you who were united with Christ in baptism have been clothed with Christ. There is neither Jew nor Greek, slave nor free, male nor female, for you are all one in Christ Jesus. If you belong to Christ, then you are Abraham's seed, and heirs according to the promise.

**Ephesians 4.3-5** in the context of an appeal for Christian unity

> Make every effort to keep the unity of the Spirit through the bond of peace. There is one body and one Spirit – just as you were called to one hope when you were called – one Lord, one faith, one baptism.

**Colossians 2.11-13** in the context of teaching on true freedom in Christ

> In him you were also circumcised, in the putting off of your sinful nature, not with a circumcision done by the hands of men but with the circumcision done by Christ, having been buried with him in baptism and raised with him through your faith in the power of God, who raised him from the dead. When you were dead in your sins and in the uncircumcision of your sinful nature, God made you alive with Christ.

**Hebrews 6.1-3** in the context of an exhortation to move on from foundational Christian teaching to maturity

> Therefore let us leave the elementary teachings about Christ and go on to maturity, not laying again the foundation of repentance from acts that lead to death, and of

faith in God, instructions about baptisms, the laying on of hands, the resurrection of the dead, and eternal judgement. And God permitting, we will do so.

**1 Peter 3.18-21** in the context of teaching on the place of suffering in Christian life

> For Christ died for your sins once for all, the righteous for the unrighteous, to bring you to God. He was put to death in the body but made alive by the Spirit, through whom also he went and preached to the spirits in prison who disobeyed long ago when God waited patiently in the days of Noah while the ark was being built. In it only a few people, eight in all, were saved through water, and this water symbolizes baptism that now saves you also – not the removal of dirt from the body but the pledge of a good conscience toward God. It saves you by the resurrection of Jesus Christ.

Three features of the apostolic understanding of baptism clearly emerge from these passages.

## The ethical consequences for holiness resulting from baptism

These are apparent from the fact that four of the passages use baptism as an illustration of the radically new behaviour expected of a believer in Christ. A transformed life is expected of those who have been baptized. The Romans and Colossians verses speak particularly of baptism as some kind of identification with the death, burial and resurrection of Jesus whereby the old life is dead, and the believer now lives a new life in Christ. They are now holy or set apart by God and the manner in which they live really matters. A key part of this holiness is being ready to undergo suffering.

## The ecclesiological consequences for unity resulting from baptism

Another four passages use baptism as an indication of and argument for the essential unity of all who share faith in the one Christ and are 'in him'. It is clear that one of the most important features of baptism is the 'oneness' that those who have been baptized share across those divisions separating people in the outside world and which must result in both the rejection of any element of 'tribalism' between Christians, and acts of sacrificial and practical love for one another. The most obvious manifestation of this is the unity that Jews and Gentiles now have through being joined to Christ in baptism.

## The Old Testament covenant context of baptism

This is apparent because in at least four of the passages the writer draws a clear parallel with a key episode from the development of the covenant in the Old Testament. The remarkable nature and significance of these parallels is not generally understood and so needs to be unpacked.

In Galatians 3.26-29 it is asserted that those who belong to Christ through faith and baptism are '*Abraham's seed*, and heirs according to the promise'. Thus not only are the divisions between slaves and free and male and female overcome in Christ but also those between Jews and Gentiles. The declaration here is that, through Christ, the Gentiles (alongside those Jews belonging to the Messiah) have entered into the covenant relationship and promise (and become 'a chosen people, a royal priesthood, a holy nation, a people belonging to God', 1 Peter 2.9). The covenant with Abraham included the promise of a single seed and heirs, not according to human design but by the supernatural and spiritual work of God, i.e. not through Ishmael but through Isaac 'the child of promise'. Paul is saying here that this promise to Abraham is fulfilled in Christ and those who are 'baptised in Christ'. An understanding of baptism into Christ therefore involves knowing about God's covenant promises to Abraham, their history and fulfilment.

In Colossians 2.11-13 it is asserted that in Christ his people receive *circumcision* understood as a moral and spiritual operation and that this happened in association with being buried with Christ in baptism and raised with him through faith. Given that Paul is so adamant in Galatians about Gentile Christians not having to undergo circumcision, it is particularly noteworthy that here he brings so closely together the initiation rites of circumcision and baptism and indicates that they symbolize the same spiritual realities of moral and spiritual transformation in death to a selfish way and new life to a godly way. The implication is that Gentile as well as Jewish Christians now enter through Christ into the spiritual realities of the covenant sign of circumcision by means of the new rite of baptism. Paul is saying without embarrassment that those baptized in Christ are circumcised spiritually. An understanding of baptism therefore involves knowing about God's covenant sign of circumcision, its origin, meaning and use. A further important aspect here is a very precise understanding of the New Testament's perspective upon circumcision and the reason for its cessation as the covenant sign for the people of God.

In 1 Peter 3.18-21 it is asserted that baptism which brings salvation (understood not merely as outward and physical washing but as inward and spiritual renewal) is symbolized in *the water of Noah's flood*, or rather God's flood, through which Noah and his family were kept safe. There are many difficulties in understanding the previous verses, but there can be no doubt that the author draws a clear parallel between the experience of salvation associated with the water of baptism and the salvation through the water of the flood. It may seem a strange comparison to us now, but it obviously had a clear and compelling connection then. An understanding of baptism into Christ will therefore be helped by knowledge of God's salvation of Noah through the flood which is so closely associated with the covenant promise of mercy and the covenant sign in the rainbow.

In 1 Corinthians 10.1-5 Paul speaks about the experiences of *the Israelites journeying with Moses* from Egypt towards the Promised Land. He describes the passing through the sea and being under the cloud as a 'baptism into Moses in the cloud and in the sea'. Furthermore he describes the divinely provided manna and the water that came out of the rock as 'spiritual food' and 'spiritual drink'. In the context of its reference to baptism, this appears to be an allusion to the eating and drinking of Holy Communion. This interpretation is surely made certain by the following words:

'They drank from the spiritual rock that accompanied them, and that rock was Christ.' Just as, in Colossians 2, Paul has no embarrassment about asserting that the same spiritual realities are symbolized in circumcision and baptism, so here he uses baptism to explain the experience of the cloud and the sea, Eucharistic language to explain the provision of food and drink, and caps it all by saying that it was *Christ* who was there sustaining them. Just as Christ, baptism and Holy Communion cast light on the Israelites' experience, so our understanding of Christ, baptism and Communion will surely be enlightened by an appreciation of what God was doing with the Israelites and Moses? The journey they were engaged in was because God remembered his covenant with Abraham, with Isaac and with Jacob (Exodus 2.24), redeeming them from slavery and leading them to a new life. The whole Exodus story refers insistently back to the covenant with Abraham and interprets God's present action as God's faithfulness to and renewal of it. Exodus 6.2-8 should be read carefully, noting the covenant promise of verse 7 'I will take you as my own people, and I will be your God.'

These four references to Abraham's seed, circumcision, Noah and Moses are quite explicit associations of baptism with Old Testament covenant episodes. As a footnote to this section it may be suggested that a fifth passage, 1 Corinthians 12.13, might be relevant too – 'we were all baptised by one Spirit … and were all given the one Spirit to drink'. In the light of Paul's references just two chapters earlier to drinking from the spiritual rock which was Christ, and because it is the Spirit of Christ we drink, the connection seems apparent. But even if not, the case is clearly made in the other four passages. When referring to baptism, the apostles moved naturally to the classic covenant passages of the Old Testament for explanation and illustration.

## Probable references to Christian baptism in the New Testament letters

All the following passages were regarded as baptismal by the (Baptist) theologian G. R. Beasley-Murray in his large and detailed study *Baptism in the New Testament*. The evidence for this conclusion is presented there with meticulous care.[5]

## Passages using the metaphor of washing

Four passages use the metaphor of washing. The idea of cleansing from sin is obvious both in the baptism of John and in Christian baptism. The connection is made explicit in Acts 22.16 where Paul in his testimony quotes Ananias as saying to him, 'Get up, be baptised and wash your sins away, calling on God's name.'

**1 Corinthians 6.11** in the context of teaching that the wicked will not inherit the kingdom of God

> And that is what some of you were. But you were washed, you were sanctified, you were justified in the name of the Lord Jesus Christ and by the Spirit of our God.

**Ephesians 5.25-27** in the context of Christian relationships between husbands and wives

> Husbands, love your wives, just as Christ loved the church and gave himself up for her to make her holy, cleansing her by the washing with water through the word, and to present her to himself as a radiant church, without stain or wrinkle or any other blemish, but holy and blameless.

**Titus 3.5-7** in the context of the decisively new character of life in Christ

> He saved us through the washing of rebirth and renewal by the Holy Spirit, whom he poured out on us generously through Jesus Christ our Saviour, so that, having been justified by his grace, we might become heirs having the hope of eternal life.

**Hebrews 10.22-23** in the context of a call to perseverance in the new life of Christ

> Let us draw near to God with a sincere heart in full assurance of faith, having our hearts sprinkled to cleanse us from a guilty conscience and having our bodies washed with pure water. Let us hold unswervingly to the hope we profess, for he who promised is faithful.

## Passages using the metaphor of a seal

Three passages use the metaphor of the seal. This stamp or mark of God's ownership is the Holy Spirit. Paul uses the same word in Romans 4.11 – Abraham 'received the sign of circumcision, a seal of righteousness'. In the rite of infant circumcision there was a prayer blessing God who 'sealed his offspring with the sign of a holy covenant'.[6] By the second century AD the term 'seal' was used explicitly of Christian baptism. It was, then, commonly used of both rites of initiation – circumcision and baptism. Baptismal ideas are used in each context, so it is widely agreed that these passages refer to baptism. The metaphor of a seal involves an outward sign of an inward reality. If the inward reality is the gift of the Holy Spirit, surely the outward sign is the mark of baptism.[7]

**2 Corinthians 1.20-22** in the context of the faithfulness of God

> For no matter how many promises God has made, they are 'Yes' in Christ. And so through him the 'Amen' is spoken by us to the glory of God. Now it is God who makes both us and you stand firm in Christ. He anointed us, set his seal of ownership on us, and put his Spirit in our hearts as a deposit, guaranteeing what is to come.

**Ephesians 1.13-14** in the context of God's eternal plan and the spiritual blessings in Christ

> And you also were included in Christ when you heard the word of truth, the gospel of your salvation. In him, when you believed, you were marked with a seal, the

promised Holy Spirit, who is a deposit guaranteeing our inheritance until the
redemption of those who are God's possession – to the praise of his glory.

**Ephesians 4.30** in the context of holy living

And do not grieve the Holy Spirit of God, with whom you were sealed for the day
of redemption.

## Passages using the metaphor of anointing

Three passages use the metaphor of anointing. Anointing symbolizes being marked
out and equipped for service by God and is associated with the outpouring of his
Spirit (1 Samuel 16.13; Isaiah 61.1). The apostle Peter says, 'After the baptism that
John preached, God anointed Jesus of Nazareth with the Holy Spirit and power'
(Acts 10.37-38). The association of ideas of separation to God and empowering with
the Spirit point both to the baptism of Jesus, the Anointed One, and to the baptism of
his people who became known as Christians, those separated to Christ and, like him,
baptized in Spirit.

**2 Corinthians 1.20-22** in the context of the faithfulness of God

For no matter how many promises God has made, they are 'Yes' in Christ. And
so through him the 'Amen' is spoken by us to the glory of God. Now it is God
who makes both us and you stand firm in Christ. He anointed us, set his seal of
ownership on us, and put his Spirit in our hearts as a deposit, guaranteeing what
is to come.

**1 John 2.20 and 27** in the context of warnings against false teachings and Antichrists

But you have an anointing from the Holy One, and all of you know the truth. As
for you, the anointing you received from him remains in you, and you do not need
anyone to teach you. But as his anointing teaches you about all things and as that
anointing is real, not counterfeit – just as it has taught you, remain in him.

Features emerge from these passages that are very consistent with those seen in the
passages examined earlier making explicit reference to baptism.

*The ethical consequences of baptism* are clearly seen in every passage. They speak of
the dramatic action of God whereby a new life begins in Christ and by the Spirit. This
life is marked by holiness, purity, perseverance, knowledge of the truth and security
until the eventual 'day of redemption'.

The wider context of a number of the passages also places this calling to a radically
new lifestyle firmly within *the ecclesiological calling of the church to reflect its nature
as a single, united community* brought into being through the death and resurrection
of Jesus Christ (see particularly 1 Corinthians 6.1-8; Ephesians 4.31-32; 5.21;
Hebrews 10.24-25; 1 John 2.19).

*The Old Testament covenant context* is again very apparent because every passage is full of Old Testament covenant imagery. Of the Hebrews passage Beasley-Murray commented, with excusable hyperbole, 'every syllable is reminiscent of the Old Testament cultus' (i.e. the sacrificial system established by Moses).[8] There are at least seven categories to notice.

*Washing and cleansing* was a prominent feature of the ceremonial system. Priests were washed at their consecration (Exodus 29.4) and Levites sprinkled with water (Numbers 8.7). Special washings were required of the chief priest on the Day of Atonement (Leviticus 16.4, 24, 26) and by anyone who was defiled with impurity (Leviticus 11.40; 15.5ff; 17.15; 22.6; Deuteronomy 23.11). The large bronze basin between the tent and the altar was a constant indication of the need for cleansing and purity in the worship and service of God (Exodus 30.17-21). This great emphasis on washing and cleansing was a constant reminder of the holiness of the God who established the covenant and his gracious means for his redeemed people to maintain their response to the covenant in holy separation to God.

*Sealing* was a widely known custom throughout the ancient Near East. Many thousands of individual engraved seals have been discovered. The use of a seal marks ownership and implies security, and the term is used both literally and metaphorically in the Old Testament. Paul's description of circumcision as both a sign and seal to Abraham (Romans 4.11) gives insight into how the covenant sign was understood. It was a mark of God's ownership and a pledge of God's faithfulness – in the context of God's everlasting covenant (see Genesis 15, especially verses 2, 7, 9-11, 13).

*Anointing* was frequently performed in Old Testament times on persons and things to signify holiness, i.e. separation unto God. Kings, priests and prophets were anointed with oil. It was essentially an act of God's authority – as when Samuel poured oil on Saul's head saying 'Has not the Lord anointed you leader over his inheritance?' (1 Samuel 10.1) and is profoundly solemn. As noted earlier, it symbolized equipment for service through the outpouring of God's Spirit (1 Samuel 16.13; Isaiah 61.1). The Hebrew word 'Messiah' and Greek equivalent 'Christ' mean 'the anointed one'. The special task of anointed leaders was to help the people in maintaining the covenant. The Anointed One (Messiah/Christ) would perform this uniquely.

*Promise* is an idea that occurs three times. In 2 Corinthians 1 reference is made to 'God's promises', in Ephesians 1 to 'the Holy Spirit of promise' and Hebrews 10 speaks of God as 'he who promised'. The history of God's salvation (i.e. biblical theology) is a great pattern of promise and fulfilment with lines from Abraham, Moses, David and the prophets converging on Jesus Christ. This is the everlasting covenant through which God makes himself a people as part of his plan for redeeming the world (see Jeremiah 31; Joel 2.28).

*The language of inheritance* occurs twice as does also the closely associated idea of *hope* – in Ephesians 1 'our inheritance', in Titus 3 'heirs having the hope', and in Hebrews 10 'the hope we profess'. The word 'inheritance' is rich with covenant associations. Canaan was God's inheritance (Exodus 15.17; Psalm 79.1) but promised to Abraham (Genesis 12.7; 13.15; 15.18-21; etc.). Spiritually God was to be the inheritance of Israel (Psalm 16.5-6) just as Israel was to be God's (Deuteronomy 7.6; 32.9). The New

Testament picks up this concept and expresses the hope that in Christ his people are heirs of God (Romans 8.17), heirs according to promise (Galatians 3.29) and inheritors of the kingdom of God (Matthew 25.34).

*Redemption* occurs twice in Ephesians 1 and 4. In both cases the Holy Spirit seals or guarantees believers and their inheritance until the final day of redemption. Redemption is used of God's deliverance of the Israelites from Egypt (Exodus 6.6; Psalm 77.15) but this looked forwards to a freedom that was not fully realized until the redemption Christ achieved through his death on the cross, and even that is not fully consummated until his triumphant return. Until then the Holy Spirit is the guarantee that God's covenant is with his redeemed people ahead of that day when the whole of the creation and all 'of those who are God's possession' are redeemed (Ephesians 1.10, 13-14).

*The bridegroom-bride imagery* of God and his people in Ephesians 5.22-33 also comes from the Old Testament covenant promises (Isaiah 54.6; Jeremiah 2.2; 3.20; Ezekiel 16.8; Hosea 2.16).

The Old Testament covenant imagery is overwhelmingly apparent in all of these passages that probably or possibly refer to baptism, just as they were in key passages that spoke explicitly of baptism. This is a matter of cardinal importance because it clearly indicates that baptism is understood by the writers of New Testament letters against this background. Furthermore, this background is not just incidental to understanding baptism – it is *the* theological context and the one in which the ethical and ecclesiological emphases make the sense they do.

The case is clearly made in these pastoral-teaching letters, but when we look back to other references to baptism in the Gospels and Acts we find the same three features of ethical and ecclesiological consequences and covenant language. Later we will examine all of this material in more detail but for the moment we can note that all the same factors are indicated. John's baptism included the call to genuine moral repentance, and through summoning Jews to a ritual previously asked of Gentile proselytes, his baptism was also anticipating something of the ecclesiological emphases we have seen. But most crucially, all of this is found within a firmly covenantal context with the ritual previously used to make Gentiles into 'children of the covenant' now used to summon God's people to the 'fruits worthy of repentance' required of Abraham's children and to prepare the way for covenant renewal in the kingdom-reign of God through the Messiah.

The same emphases are found within the baptism of Jesus particularly in Jesus's comment that it was necessary 'to fulfil all righteousness' (Matthew 3.15). Righteousness is one of the great covenantal words of the Old Testament speaking on the one hand of God's commitment to his covenant purpose and on the other of the ethical conduct required of his covenant people. As the gospels continue, Jesus goes on to fulfil both of these supremely through his commitment to a sacrificial death for sinners, the baptism of Calvary (Mark 10.38-39; Luke 12.49-51), which would establish 'the new covenant in my blood' that he spoke of at the Last Supper (Luke 22.20). The Great Commission of Matthew 28.18-20 also includes the triple emphasis of 'all nations' being taught obedience to everything that Jesus commanded and also the typically covenant promise 'I will be with you always.'

In the Acts of the Apostles, baptism is obviously linked with repentance, forgiveness and new life – the washing away of sins (22.16) and in several cases the welcome for all on equal terms into God's people (8.14-17; 10.44-48; 11.15-18). But it is also explicitly associated with God's covenant promise in 1.4-5 and 2.38-39.

Where shall we start a biblical study of baptism? At the start of this chapter we noted the procedural dilemma over whether to start in the Old Testament or in the New. It has now become clear that any serious consideration of the New Testament references drives us back to the Old Testament to understand the nature of God's covenant. The reason for this is entirely biblical. It is not in order to justify infant baptism (through comparison with circumcision) as argued by Lanc and many other Baptist writers. He says, 'If there had been no argument over the baptising of infants, it is doubtful whether Genesis 17 and the covenant of circumcision would ever have entered into the matter. The appeal to it was made, not to teach *the nature and meaning* of baptism itself, but to justify a certain *way of practising it*' (his italics).[9] This is a tragic misunderstanding. It is the New Testament itself which sends us back to the Old Testament covenant situations to understand the nature and meaning of baptism. If we are to be biblical we can do no other! The argument for or against infant baptism should not be allowed to interfere with following where the evidence requires us to follow. If the covenant context was vital to the apostles, it is of crucial theological import to us too. It is for this reason that we now turn to the vital and central theme of the whole Bible – the story of God's covenant.

# God's covenant (part one)

The Bible is both long and, in places, complex. It represents a vast canvas of history and a whole library of different types of literature: law, prophecy, poetry, proverb, gospel, epistle and apocalyptic. But is there a central theme, a golden thread running throughout its varied contents? Yes – and it is quite simply this: the Bible is the story of God's relationship of love with the earth from its creation through to its new creation, with a particular concentration upon his relationship with the human beings within it.

At the start of the Bible, God creates a good world which he then entrusts to his image-bearing creatures to rule over and care for. The disobedience and sinfulness of these very human beings then result in this creation becoming spoilt and distorted. God, however, remains fully committed to both his creation and the human beings he has charged with ruling over it. To this end, he initiates his plan for the ultimate restoration of human beings and through this, the ultimate restoration and completion, under him, of the entire cosmos.

## The covenant story

This is where the unfolding concept of the covenant is so central to the Bible's story. Rather than being an agreement between equal parties, the covenant is a relationship devised and offered entirely by God in order to undo the problem of sin and put his people and creation back on track. This is what the word 'grace' means in the Bible and it is frequently summarized by God as 'I will be your God, and you will be my people'. The Israelites are initially called to be this people, as God's covenant is continuously revealed to them through and alongside his saving acts, supremely the Exodus (or escape) from slavery in Egypt. The covenant calling of Israel is to live in the light of God's salvation or rescue, shape their lives accordingly and demonstrate to the world what it means to live under his rule. Central to this is the revelation of God as YHWH with covenantal love at the heart of his character. YHWH does not force this covenant upon its recipients, for there can be no compulsion to receive or offer love; it is instead offered as a gift. God's people are called to accept his covenant, believe his promise and actively receive his gift – which is what the Bible means by 'faith'.

The covenant story eventually reaches its climax in the coming of Israel's Messiah, Jesus the Christ, and his proclamation of God's kingdom or sovereign rule. Crucial to this and the bringing of the forgiveness, reconciliation and restoration promised by the covenant is God's defeat of sin and evil. God brought about this victory, not by overlooking this sin, but by bearing it in the body of his Son, Jesus Christ, when he died on the cross. The result of this sacrifice was the defeat of evil, the forgiveness of sins (often known as 'the atonement') and God's kingdom revealed in power through the resurrection of Jesus Christ. Jesus's ascension into heaven to rule the earth and the coming of the Holy Spirit to equip his followers to live as God's renewed people then followed. Central to this fulfilment of the covenant was Gentiles (non-Jews) finally being able to join Jews within the one, united people of God on precisely the same basis of faith in Jesus Christ. Just as central to its fulfilment is the full and final revelation of the one God YHWH as Father, Son and Holy Spirit. The completion of the whole covenant process will be the coming of the new heavens and new earth and God's fully renewed people fully and finally ruling over his perfectly restored new creation.

So from our vantage point in history we can see that the story of God's covenant plan of salvation falls into two phases, BC and AD. Before Christ, the people of the covenant were looking forwards through pictures, types and shadows for the fulfilment of the covenant promises. The coming of Christ ushers in the new era – through his death and resurrection and the gift of the Spirit. The first phase is characterized by 'promise'; the second phase is marked by 'fulfilment'.

The Greek word for 'covenant' (*diatheke*) in the Bible also means testament (i.e. will) and was translated into the Latin 'testamentum' – hence the accepted name for the two sections of the Bible as testaments. The idea of an old and new testament/covenant comes from 2 Corinthians 3 verses 14 and 6. In the Old Testament the covenant was offered in an imperfect, temporary and provisional way (the 'old'), but when Christ came, the covenant was revealed in its perfect, permanent and eternal glory (the 'new' covenant). Thus, as we shall now see from a detailed look at the biblical development of the theme, there is throughout the Bible:

One God – YHWH, the God later revealed as Father, Son and Holy Spirit
One plan of salvation – God's electing love: 'I will be your God and you will be my people'
One basis of atonement – the sacrificial death of Jesus Christ
One way to receive salvation – by faith in God's promises
One goal of salvation – God's renewed people ruling over a renewed creation
One covenant of grace – planned in eternity and worked out in history

We have seen in Chapter 2 that the Old Testament covenant context is the theological context for understanding baptism into Jesus Christ. We shall now find that the covenant is the central theme of the Old Testament. In this summary of the covenant story, we have so far used the advantage of retrospect, of looking at the 'old' through the light of the 'new'. As Augustine said, 'The new is in the old concealed, the old is in the new revealed.' But we shall now examine the development of the covenant concept more sequentially in order to understand it in its own (Old Testament) terms, and not just through Christian (New Testament) spectacles.[1] Tracing its development will allow more of its important features to emerge.

The background to the idea of covenant (Hebrew, *berith*) in the Old Testament is to be found in ancient Near Eastern peace treaties between kings and between nations. These are well known from the third millennium BC. In a friendly relationship between conqueror and vassal the language of 'father and son' was used. In a more stern relationship it was 'lord and servant'. The idea of a covenant relationship between a god and a king or his people was also widespread. It has been suggested that the term *berith* is probably derived from the Middle Assyrian noun *biritu* meaning bond or fetter carrying the sense of a solemn obligation and commitment.

There are 290 references to covenant in the Old Testament. Some of these occur within the context of relationships between human beings with a number referring to treaties made or proposed between nations or tribes. Examples of this include Joshua and the Gibeonites (Joshua 9) and Nahash the Ammonite king and the town of Jabesh-Gilead (1 Samuel 11). At other times covenant is used of a more personal commitment, such as that between David and Jonathan which includes an ongoing commitment to one another's families and descendants (1 Samuel 20, 2 Samuel 9). Sometimes covenants are ratified by elaborate ceremonies and meals (e.g. Genesis 26.30; 31.46, 54) and they generally act to formalize a commitment to an existing relationship.

All of these uses of covenant shed light upon the major way in which it is used within the Bible which is in reference to the relationship between God and his people.

## Covenant introduced – Noah … and Creation?

### The story of Noah

It is in the story of Noah in Genesis 6–9 that the word 'covenant' first occurs in the Bible. God saw how great man's wickedness had become and he 'was grieved that he had made man on the earth, and his heart was filled with pain' (6.6). He therefore announces that he will wipe both humankind and all the other creatures from the face of the earth putting an end to 'all people' and destroying both them and the earth (6.13). Coming just a few chapters after the accounts of creation, it is important to note the way in which this judgement was essentially an act of de-creation. At the flood, God's earlier separation of the waters above and the waters below in Genesis 1 was undone as the waters of chaos flooded back in to fill the space which he had created. The impression given is that God wanted to go back to the start of creation and begin again.

This leads to the role of Noah who, in contrast to the people on earth, 'found favour in the eyes of the LORD' (6.8). Noah is described as 'a righteous man', 'blameless amongst the people of his time' and who 'walked with God' (6.9). God determined to save Noah, instructed him to build the ark and explained 'I will establish my *covenant* with you' (6.18). Certain characteristics of the covenant are clear at this point: (a) It was made at God's initiative; (b) There is a 'family principle' with Noah's 'whole family' included within it; (c) Noah and his family had an obligation of obedience in order to enjoy the covenant – they had to build the ark and enter it; (d) There is continuity with the original mandate to care for the rest of creation with Noah instructed to take pairs of male and female creatures into the ark to preserve their species; (e) Later, after the flood was over, Noah responded to his rescue with worship through building an altar and sacrifice (8.20).

After this, God extended this covenant promising never again to destroy the earth (9.11), in other words a commitment to its preservation and redemption. The characteristics of the covenant are the following: (a) Once again it is a sovereign act of God's grace – '*I* will establish *my* covenant' (9.9); (b) The covenant is not just for Noah and his family but for all humanity (his descendants, 9.9), with every living creature (9.10) and indeed the earth itself (9.13); (c) There is once again continuity with the original creation mandate with a very deliberate repetition of God's instructions in Genesis 1 (albeit in an amended form because of the altered context of a now fallen world) to be fruitful, increase in number, fill the earth and subdue it by ruling over its creatures (9.1-3, 7 cf 1.28); (d) Whilst there are no conditions attached and so the covenant cannot be broken formally, obedience to these instructions represents the response required from those saved by God (9.4-6); (e) The covenant is everlasting (9.16); (f) God gives a 'sign of the covenant between me and the earth' – the rainbow. Remarkably, God says, 'Whenever the rainbow appears in the clouds, I will see and remember the everlasting covenant' (9.16). The sign within the created order (and perhaps symbolizing the relationship between the heavens and the earth) was a pledge of God's faithfulness, of God's memory. It expresses God's commitment to what he had promised and therefore invites the response of trust.

The covenant with Noah is referred to relatively infrequently in the later parts of the Bible. But his 'righteousness' (see later for the covenantal significance of this term) is referred to in Ezekiel 14.14, 20. In Isaiah 54.7-10, God's promise to Noah is also used to assure the exiled Jews in Babylon of God's commitment to rescue them and to his 'covenant of peace'. Rescue from this exile is thus pictured as an act of new creation similar to that within the story of Noah with the redemption of God's people through his 'everlasting covenant' completely interlinked with his redemption of creation (Isaiah 54–55). As we saw in Chapter 2, the story of Noah is explicitly used as an illustration of the significance of baptism in 1 Peter 3.18-22.

### The story of creation

Although the story of Noah contains the first explicit reference in the Bible to God's covenant, several scholars have suggested that the manner in which the term is used there and particularly its lack of introduction and explanation indicates that the creation accounts earlier in Genesis 1 and 2 represent the beginning of the covenant. Dumbrell, in particular, has argued that the 'secular' uses of *berit* in Genesis suggest covenant is a term that is used to formalize and give concrete expression to relationships already established rather than to initiate them.[2] The very fact of creation involved God entering a relationship with the world and the judgement of the flood presupposed an accountability already established by the calling of human beings to rule over creation (1.28, 2.15). It has been further suggested that the language used in

Genesis 1 (particularly the royal sounding fiats of 'Let there be light', etc.) more than anticipate the later connections made between the covenant and God's divine rule. Humans being made in God's image and, through this given the vocation to rule over the other creatures, then assumes the nature of a derived and representative kingship role similar to and anticipating the later covenant with David.

Another feature of the creation story which anticipates the later stories of the covenant is the elements that speak of God's presence being established upon the earth. Walton has suggested that the first creation story (Genesis 1.1-2.3) is deliberately written to evoke the construction of a temple.[3] Human beings, according to this understanding, represent the 'image of God' that was typically placed within a temple after everything else had been completed and the statement that 'on the seventh day he rested from all his work' primarily refers to God taking up residence within the dwelling that he had made for himself. The second creation story also carries the sense of the Garden of Eden being established as a place on earth where the immediacy of God's presence could be encountered (2.4-25 cf 3.8-9). As the location of God's presence, the garden was intended to be the place from which human beings would start building the world that God had given them to take charge of. This calling was set within the command to avoid eating the fruit of 'the tree of the knowledge of good and evil', representing the need for continued trust in the creator's definition of what was good and what was evil within his creation. The alternative to this was human beings asserting their autonomy from God and seeking to define good and evil for themselves. This separation from God as the source of life would result in their death.

The temptation to do this is then provided by the serpent, the craftiest of the wild animals that God had made (3.1ff). The man and the woman duly eat the fruit and immediately experience a sense of vulnerability which was not present before. Their disobedience further results in the couple's expulsion from the Garden of Eden and thus God's special presence, accompanied by curses diminishing their experience of the blessing that they had been given (3.16-19). This is then seen as the template for all the subsequent 'exiles' that follow in the covenant story, as sin and disobedience take hold of the human beings that God has created. Death which now enters the story of the world (3.19; 4.8) forms the ultimate form of this loss of blessing. The vocation given to human beings as God's image-bearers remains but their ability to fulfil this calling is damaged and diminished by their sin.

If this is accurate, it strengthens the understanding that there is one single divine covenant within the Bible of which the various different covenants are subsets. When the prophet Hosea later refers to Israel's unfaithfulness, he declares: 'Like Adam, they have broken the covenant, they were unfaithful to me there' (Hosea 6.7). The covenant is also established very clearly within the context of God's ongoing commitment, despite the sinfulness of human beings, to both creation itself and the role that he established within it for human beings. God's enduring grace means that after every significant advance of sin and judgement, he provides some form of merciful care (e.g. 3.21; 4.15). But the primary way in which God's grace continues to operate is within the constant development of his covenant, beginning most obviously in the story of the flood, as Noah is called to be a new Adam with the vocation given to human beings in creation re-established through him. However the earliest hint at how the covenant story will develop is within Genesis 3 where God tells the serpent that, despite his apparent victory, he is destined for defeat because the woman's seed or offspring will crush his head, as the serpent strikes his heel (3.15). This mysterious promise of a wounded victor refers allusively to two continuing and important aspects of the covenant story. The ultimate defeat of the source of evil and temptation in the world will come from the humanity that God has created, but it will somehow entail the affliction of that humanity as well.[4]

## Covenant clarified – Abram/Abraham

### The story of Babel

It is within the context of a fallen world that the biblical story continues, as the sinfulness of human beings continues to grow even after the flood and the salvation of Noah and his family. This shows itself in the continuing desire of humans to establish their autonomy, climaxing in the story of the Tower of Babel in Genesis 11. The vocation to rule creation on behalf of God has become corrupted by the desire to 'make a name for ourselves' and establish a unity based on this rather than their relationship with God (11.4). In response, God scatters the people and confuses their languages to prevent this happening (11.8–9). The result of all of this is that the calling that God established for human beings in creation is now completely off track.

### The story of Abraham

It is in response to this that the covenant is filled out and clarified within the stories of Abram/Abraham in Genesis 12–24. The Abrahamic covenant, with its remarkable promises, is introduced with a divine call to Abram in chapter 12, developed with divine sacrifice in chapter 15, and confirmed with a divine sign (to the renamed Abraham) in chapter 17.

In chapter 12 the word 'covenant' does not appear, but the promises are clearly made: (a) the promise that God is adopting Abram and his family for blessing (12.1-3); (b) the promise of a great nation and name (12.2); (c) the promise that 'all peoples on earth will be blessed through you' (12.3); (d) the promise of the land is hinted at in verse 1 and clarified in verse 7. All of these promises respond to the problems established in the previous chapters. This is indicated most obviously by the five references to blessings in 12.1-3 countering the five curses announced in Genesis 3–11. The promise to Abram of a 'nation' (rather than simply 'a people') also carries the sense of a system of divine government being established to rescue the world and the promise of a great 'name' suggests that the call of Abram represents the reality to which the Babel story was the parody (12.2b cf 11.4).[5]

Abram's initial response was to believe God's promises and to act on the basis of them. He left his country with his wife Sarai and nephew Lot to travel to Canaan. Frequently he worships YHWH by building altars and calling on YHWH's name. An important feature of these stories is God's presence, with YHWH appearing to Abram in 12.7 and the altars that Abram builds at Shechem (12.6), Bethel (12.8) and Hebron (13.18) to assert God's ownership of the land. Events in chapters 12–14 suggest Abram's hold upon the land is very tenuous and in 13.14-17 the promise regarding it is repeated with the further detail that (a) the gift of the land will be everlasting and (b) that the offspring of Abram that receive it will be as numerous as the dust of the earth.

In chapter 15 God clarifies the covenant (15.18) and develops three of the promises he has already made: (a) the promise of mutual relationship 'I am your shield, your very great reward' (15.1); (b) the promise of a son, and great family (15.4f); (c) the promise of the land (15.7, 18–20). Abram's response is faith in God's promise, 'Abram believed the Lord, and he credited it to him as righteousness' (15.6). God then confirms his promise through a striking act of symbolism. As his presence in the smoking fire pot and blazing torch passes between the pieces of the animals that Abram had provided, God makes a binding oath that Abram's descendants would inherit the land of Canaan (15.9-18). This includes reference to his descendants becoming slaves ahead of receiving this great possession (15.13-16). In the light of similar symbolic oaths using divided animals in Jeremiah 34.18 and 1 Samuel 11.17, God is declaring 'so may it be to me if this oath is broken'.

Earlier we noted the use of the term 'righteous' in reference to Noah and from this point in the Bible 'righteousness' develops into a key covenantal term indicating behaviour consistent with an established relationship. Tom Wright has emphasized the importance of distinguishing between its use in reference to God and to his followers (rather than conflating them through the idea of God 'imputing' his righteousness).[6] Used of *God* (on numerous occasions, particularly in the Psalms), 'righteousness' refers to YHWH's faithfulness to his covenant promises. Used of *YHWH's followers*, 'righteousness' refers to their right response to these promises with both Paul and the writer to the Hebrews later stressing Abram's faith as the fundamental part of this (Romans 4; Galatians 3, Hebrews 11.8-12).

At other points in the stories, however, Abram is far from trusting and obedient. Almost immediately after his calling in chapter 12, he starts to make mistakes as he and his wife Sarai twist and turn in their effort to manage the promises in a *human* way. Their time in Egypt in chapter 12 is an example of this, and an even clearer example is the birth of Ishmael to Abram by Sarai's maidservant Hagar in chapter 16. God meanwhile patiently bides his time to teach Abram and Sarai that there is a better way of covenant promise.

Thus in chapter 17 God confirms the promises to Abram with a covenant sign. Following YHWH's appearance, the promises are again (a) relational – to be 'your God' with the accompanying summons to 'walk before me and be blameless' (17.1, 7); (b) territorial – possession of the land is once again promised (17.8); (c) eternal – the everlasting nature of God's promise in 13.15 is restated as an everlasting covenant between him and Abraham's descendants for the generations to come. An important development is that the covenant promise is now (d) multinational – Abram's name is changed to Abraham because God will make him 'a father of many nations' and 'kings will come from you' (17.4-6). The shift from the promise to make Abram into a 'great nation' (12.2, singular) to the promise to make Abraham 'a father of many nations' (plural) is seemingly connected with the earlier birth of Ishmael and God's promise to both Abraham (and later to his mother Hagar) to make Ishmael, as well as Isaac, into a great nation (17.20; 21.13, 18). But it is Isaac, the child of Sarah (renamed from Sarai), whose impending birth is announced at this point, who is proclaimed as the one with whom YHWH's covenant will be established and inherited by his descendants (17.19, 21).

The confirming covenant sign is circumcision (17.9-14). The cutting off of a small piece of the loose foreskin of the male sex organ was a common practice in the ancient Near East but was usually associated with puberty, coming of age and sexual maturity. God therefore took a common ritual or symbol and invested it with an entirely new significance. It became a mark of God's ownership, God's promises and God's covenant – not a mark any longer of human achievement or maturity, but of God's initiative and grace. Incidentally, it also spoke of the God-given sacredness of sex in a sexually decadent society. Though performed only on the male, the mark and its symbolism would be constantly shared with his wife and would be (as we might say) at the heart of every act of love and procreation.

It cannot be too strongly emphasized that God's covenant of circumcision was never meant to be merely an outward sign of natural birth or racial descent. From the beginning it was a mark of God's ownership, of God's covenant promise and blessing – of God's offer of communion and friendship. It was, therefore, an outward and physical sign of something inwards and spiritual. This is so widely misunderstood that some of the evidence must be set out fully. Because of God's electing love, he expects fearful obedience and loving service and so declares 'circumcise your hearts, and do not be stiff-necked' (Deuteronomy 10.12-16). 'YHWH your God will circumcise your hearts and the hearts of your descendants, so that you may love him with all your heart and with all your soul, and live' (Deuteronomy 30.6). 'If they will confess their sins – their treachery and hostility towards me … then when their uncircumcised hearts are humbled … I will remember my covenant' (Leviticus 26.40-42).

The prophet Jeremiah understood circumcision in the same way as a mark of God's holy covenant which separates people to God and thus calls for the response of a separated, holy life. 'Circumcise yourselves to YHWH, circumcise your hearts' (Jeremiah 4.4). 'Who will listen to me? Their ears are closed (literally, in the Hebrew, "uncircumcised") so that they cannot hear' (Jeremiah 6.10). 'I will punish all who are circumcised only in the flesh … all these nations are really uncircumcised, and even the whole house of Israel is uncircumcised in heart' (Jeremiah 9.25-26). The physical and spiritual aspects of new life are completely interrelated within the covenant.

Once again Abraham's response is trustful worship (17.3) and he is summoned to the obedient keeping of the covenant (17.9-14). Whilst his response to God continues to be flawed and imperfect, his faith in God's promises still plays a vital role (Hebrews 11.8-12). The birth of Isaac to Sarah eventually takes place (21.1-7) and the ultimate test of faith takes place when Abraham is instructed by God to sacrifice Isaac as a burnt offering (22.1-2). At the last moment, an angel instructed Abraham not to slay Isaac and because of his obedience the promises of blessing are confirmed with these expanded to speak of his descendants becoming 'as numerous as the stars in the sky and the sand on the seashore', the promise that these descendants will 'take possession of the cities of their enemies' and that 'through your offspring all the nations on earth will be blessed' (22.15-18). Whilst it is the whole of the land that is promised to Abraham, the first part that he actually owns as a foretaste of what is to come is the field he purchases to bury Sarah and in which he is also buried after his death (23.1-20; 25.7-10).

Generally speaking, the promise that God will bless the nations through Abraham can appear the furthest from being fulfilled within these stories, and indeed within the continuing story of Israel in the Old Testament. In fact Abraham's deceitful actions early on in the story are swiftly seen as bringing just the very opposite, provoking the Pharoah of Egypt's complaint (12.10-20). However in his generosity to his nephew Lot (the father of the future tribes of Ammon and Moab, 19.30-38) in 13.8-13, and in Abraham's pleading for the people of Sodom and Gomorrah in 18.16-33, some indication is given of the way in which these future blessings for the nations will materialize. This continues in the story of Abraham's immediate descendants, most obviously Joseph.

Another noteworthy characteristic of the covenant with Abraham is the *family principle*, similar to that seen with Noah's family entering the Ark. The covenant sign of circumcision includes not only his male infants (from eight days old) but all within Abraham's household (17.12-13). This includes Ishmael (17.23-26). Significantly for the point just made regarding the spreading of the covenant blessing, this household application includes those 'bought with money from a foreigner – those who are not your offspring' (17.12-13, 23–27). The obligation of personal faith and obedience includes these people with the directing of children and household 'to keep the way of the Lord by doing what is right and just' (18.19). This reinforces the consistent emphasis that, whilst the covenant is established by grace and a strong family principle is operating, it is nonetheless *conditional* – the covenant blessings are not automatic, on the basis of either birth or the sign of circumcision.

### The story of Jacob and his sons

As Abraham's family succeed him, the covenant is increasingly known as that which God made 'with Abraham, Isaac and Jacob'. The promises that God has made to Abraham are restated to Isaac (26.1-4) and then to Jacob (28.13-15). Esau and Jacob were twins born to Isaac and his wife Rebecca, with Esau being the older of the two. However through a combination of Esau's complacency and Jacob's deceit, Jacob receives first Esau's birthright (25.29-34) and then the blessing that Isaac intended for Esau (27.1-40). Jacob is forced to flee to escape from Esau's vengeance and experience an 'exile' away from Canaan. This then becomes the consistent pattern of what God's people have to endure as the path to the blessings that he promises them.[7] Another important aspect of Jacob's experience is the major revelation of God's presence that he receives, as he leaves the land to seek descendants (28.10-17) and when he returns with these descendants (32.22-32). Like all the characters with whom God establishes his covenant, Jacob is deeply flawed and yet, as his name is changed to Israel, this reveals God's commitment to a sinful people who have to wrestle or struggle with God in order to receive his covenant promises. Like Abraham's wife Sarah, both Isaac's wife Rebecca (25.21) and Jacob's second and favourite wife Rachel

(30.22-24) are only able to conceive following God's special action, pointing to the way in which the new birth involved in the continuation of the covenant line is completely dependent on God's grace.

Jacob's descendants become the people of Israel and Esau's descendants become people of Edom. This continues an important aspect of Genesis, whereby Israel and the neighbours she later had enmity with are shown as being originally drawn from the same family (e.g. 9.18-27; 19.36-38; 25.1-4). The prophecy of Obadiah shows that this enmity between Israel and Edom was particularly strong, with Edom seizing the opportunity to plunder Judah following the Babylonian destruction of Jerusalem in 587 BC. The reconciliation between Jacob and Esau that occurs after Jacob's return (33.1-20) thus points to the incorporation of Edom within Israel's blessings that would later form an important part of the covenant story (Amos 9.11-12 cf Acts 15.16-18). It further suggests that fulfilment of the promise to Abraham about 'all peoples' being blessed through him would ultimately occur through all of the estranged members of the same family being, somehow, brought back together.

Similar themes recur in the story of Jacob's son, Joseph, who undergoes a similar 'exile' due to the enmity of his brothers (and perhaps his own pride), this time in Egypt. Once again we see familiar covenant themes in God's presence with Joseph during this period of hardship (39.2), the importance of Joseph's righteous response (39.6-10) and God's use of Joseph to bless the Egyptians through the authority he assumes over them (39.4-5; 41.56-57; 47.13-26). A reconciliation between Joseph and his brothers (each representing the later tribes of Israel) eventually occurs with Joseph expressing his consciousness of how God had worked through his hardship to advance his covenant purposes saying 'God sent me ahead of you to preserve for you a remnant on earth and to save your lives by a great deliverance' (45.7 cf 50.20). The deliverance has obvious reference to the salvation from the famine which brought his brothers to Egypt, but also to the greater act of salvation awaiting the people of Israel in the exodus. Genesis draws towards its close with Jacob and his family moving, with God's blessing, to Egypt (46.2-4). Jacob blesses the Pharaoh (47.7, 10) but remains conscious that Canaan is the homeland to which they will return (46.4; 47.28-31; 48.22). God's covenant promises are repeated (48.3-4) and the theme of his purposes being carried forwards through the younger branches of the covenant family continues (48.17-20 cf 27.27-40; 1 Samuel 16.1-13, 1 Kings 1; Romans 9.6-29). By the end of Genesis, Israel are existing in Egypt as a great and populous nation being assured by Joseph that 'God will surely come to your aid and take you up out of this land to the land he promised on oath to Abraham, Isaac and Jacob' (50.24).

A significant interlude in the stories of Joseph concerns his older brother Judah and the role of his daughter-in-law Tamar in preserving the family line (38.1-30). After the death of Tamar's husband Er, both his brother Onan and then his father Judah fail to honour their responsibilities in this regard (38.8-14), causing Tamar to get herself pregnant by Judah (38.15-25). Judah's eventual response to Tamar's action is not only a vindication of her action to safeguard her rights but an affirmation of her role in preserving the covenant line: 'She is more righteous than I, since I wouldn't give her to my son Shelah' (38.26). Judah's chance to show a similar righteousness occurs later in the Joseph story when he offers to take the place of Benjamin to spare

Jacob/Israel further sorrow (44.1-34 cf 37.26-27). This commitment to preserving the covenant family continues in Israel's later history, however questionable the methods (Judges 20-21). More significantly, Judah's offer anticipates the later servant whose death took the punishment of others and 'carries our sorrows' (Isaiah 52.13–53.12). Another familiar element in the Tamar story is her 'second' twin Perez stealing a march on his brother Zerah who had looked like being born first (38.27-30). The advance of the covenant line through Perez continues the emphasis upon God's sovereignty over this process. But the scarlet thread tied around Zerah's wrist both recalls the redness of Esau (25.25) and anticipates the later 'scarlet cord' used to signify Rahab's rescue (Joshua 2), perhaps indicating the later inclusion of those outside of the immediate covenant line and even hinting at the process by which this would come about (cf Matthew 26.27; 27.28; Ephesians 2.13).

Jacob's final blessing upon his twelve sons is particularly significant in relation to Judah, as he predicts that it will be from Judah that the royal leader will come who will command the obedience of the nations (49.8-12). This indicates how the promise made to Abraham about 'all peoples' being blessed through him will occur and its later fulfilment through the Davidic royal line that came from the tribe of Judah (1 Chronicles 2.3–4.23). God's covenant with Abraham is referred to frequently in the later salvation history of the Scriptures (Exodus 2.24; Nehemiah 9.7-8; Psalms 47.9; 105.8-11; Isaiah 29.22; 41.8; 51.2; 63.16; Jeremiah 33.26; Micah 7.20; Luke 1.68-75; Romans 4; Galatians 3; Hebrews 6.13-15) and is clearly of seminal significance. The story of Abraham is particularly used by Paul as he explains how Jesus Christ came to bring the climax of the covenant, and it is also used by the writer to the Hebrews to picture the resurrection and new creation that will form its ultimate fulfilment (Hebrews 11.8-22). For the purpose of the argument here, and in response to some common (and frequently unconscious) misunderstandings, it is to be particularly noted that the Abrahamic covenant is

Holistic – not only material and physical but thoroughly spiritual
Eternal – rather than simply temporal
Universal – not only concerned with ethnic Israel but 'all peoples on earth'
Conditional – established by God's grace but not automatic, requiring the response of faith.

# Covenant developed – Moses

## Exodus

The next major development of the covenant begins in the book of Exodus with the central figure of Moses. By this stage the Israelites had become extremely numerous, leading to their enslavement by a Pharaoh of Egypt 'who did not know Joseph' (Exodus 1.1-14). The Pharaoh eventually attempts to kill the Hebrew boys by having them thrown into the River Nile but the baby Moses is providentially saved after being placed in a basket in the Nile and gains his name through being drawn out of the water (2.10). Moses's own attempt to rescue his people results in his 'exile' but during this period, the Israelites' cry for help was heard by God in the context of the earlier covenant: 'God heard their groaning and he remembered his covenant with Abraham, with Isaac and with Jacob' (Exodus 2.24). God met with Moses at Mount Horeb and explained his plan to rescue his people from Egypt and take them to the land he had promised – 'the land of Canaanites, Hittites, Amorites, Perizzites, Hivities and Jebusites – a land flowing with milk and honey'. During his encounters with Moses, he repeatedly describes himself as the God of Abraham, Isaac and Jacob, i.e. the covenant God (3.6, 16; 4.5; 6.3, 8). God affirms that he had established his covenant with Abraham, Isaac and Jacob and was now remembering his covenant as he promised to bring the Israelites out of Egypt: 'I will free you from being slaves to them, and I will redeem you with an outstretched arm and with mighty acts of judgement. I will take you as my own people and I will be your God' (6.6-7).

Whilst continuity with the earlier covenant episodes is therefore clearly established, a new element surrounds the divine name YHWH. According to 6.3, God had revealed himself to Abraham, Isaac and Jacob as El Shaddai (God Almighty) but 'by my name YHWH I did not make myself known to them'. God's revelation as YHWH is thus presented as having begun with Moses's experience at the Burning Bush in Exodus 3.14-15, establishing a crucial new stage in the covenant story. This is problematic because YHWH is used 116 times between Genesis 12 and Exodus 3, including some forty occasions on the lips of the patriarchs (rather than simply representing statements about God by the narrator). Genesis 4.26 explicitly declares that it was at the time of the birth of Adam's grandson Enosh that 'men began to call on the name of YHWH'. Dumbrell argues that the emphasis must be, therefore, that the *meaning* of the name YHWH was first communicated during the Exodus period.[8] At the Burning Bush, God declared to Moses 'I am who I am' and tells him to say to Israelites that 'I am' had sent him and YHWH is the God of their fathers, Abraham, Isaac and Jacob (3.14-15). There is general agreement that YHWH is derived from the Hebrew verb 'to be'. Rather than being an evasive response to Moses's request for his name, this statement was conveying that God would be known through his future acts, particularly the Israelites imminent liberation from slavery. This fits with God's self-designation at the start of the Ten Commandments: 'I am YHWH who brought you out of Egypt' (20.2). Later we will see how the greatest act of covenant rescue in the New Testament was also accompanied by a fresh revelation of God's name.

The great act of rescue from Egypt occurs in Exodus 14. It follows the plagues YHWH sends upon the Egyptians and the Passover through which the Israelites were protected from the final plague, 'the angel of death'. Annual commemoration of this Passover and the events that followed then becomes a central part of Israel's ongoing covenant relationship with God (Exodus 12). The central event is when YHWH opens the Red Sea to enable the Israelites to escape and then closes it again to consume the Egyptians pursuing them. This is then celebrated in 'The Song of the Sea' in Exodus 15. The first section of this poem pictures YHWH as a mighty warrior defeating Pharaoh (15.1-12) with its language about his control of the waters and seas, recalling both the earlier story of Noah and the creation story, implying that the rescue was an act of new creation. The second part of the poem then speaks of YHWH leading the Israelites through the desert to the land they have been promised (15.13-18). Here the major emphasis is upon Israel being established in the direct presence of God as YHWH reigns in his dwelling place forever. The whole of the Promised Land is thus designated as the divine sanctuary where YHWH will sit enthroned.[9] The chapters that follow then describe how YHWH provided the Israelites with manna and quail to sustain them on the journey and water from the rock that Moses struck with his staff (Exodus 16–17). In the previous chapter we saw how Paul in 1 Corinthians 10 draws a parallel between all of these saving events using baptism, Holy Communion and the Christ/Messiah to explain the spiritual realities that were present within them.

It is when the Israelites reach Mount Sinai that the people are addressed in explicitly covenantal terms. 'You yourselves have seen what I did to Egypt, and how I carried you on eagles' wings and brought you to myself. Now if you obey me fully and keep my covenant, then out of all nations you will be my treasured possession. Although the whole earth is mine, you will be for me a kingdom of priests and a holy nation' (19.4-6). Many scholars have commented on the parallels between the Sinai covenant and the form of ancient near-eastern treaties, and Israel being God's 'possession' carrying the sense of a vassal/suzerain relationship. Israel was thus YHWH's vassal – bound to him yet living in a state of particular privilege. 'Holy' means set apart or withdrawn from general use and here the sense conveyed is of Israel, like Abraham, being called to separate herself from the world. Placed within the overall affirmation that the whole earth is God's, however, the calling of Israel to be a priesthood suggests that, as with Abraham, this separation is in order to serve or bless *the world*. 'Kingdom' and 'nation' are used because Israel was now being formed into a national covenant community with the aim of demonstrating to the world by her distinctiveness what it meant to live under the rule of YHWH.[10] This is emphasized later on in Deuteronomy where Israel is commanded to follow YHWH's decrees carefully 'for this will show your wisdom and understanding to the nations, who will hear about all these decrees and say, "Surely this great nation is a wise and understanding people"' (Deuteronomy 4.6). It is thus through the covenant that the vocation of Israel as God's people is established.

The people said they would accept the covenant, and so they washed their clothes, were consecrated and were led out of the camp to the foot of Mount Sinai 'to meet with God'. YHWH appeared in fire and smoke and then, through Moses, revealed the Ten Commandments and the book of the Covenant (chapters 20–23). Whilst the Decalogue in chapter 20 set out the general principles of how Israel was being called to live, the Covenant Code of chapters 21–23 applied these principles to the needs of an emerging social, economic and agricultural community.[11] The introduction to these laws in 20.1-2 shows that they were given within the context of grace and to outline the nature of life within the relationship that YHWH had established with them. They thus form an equivalent of the faith and obedience that Abraham was called to show in response to God's promises. Whilst YHWH's commitment to his covenant with Israel was eternal, it was made clear that Israel's experience of the divine blessing arising from this depended upon the measure to which the divine will expressed through the law was realized in her life. The covenant was then confirmed with sacrifice, and Moses took some of the blood, sprinkled it on the people and said, 'This is the blood of the covenant that the Lord has made with you' (24.8).

One of the features of the exodus narrative which goes to the heart of the covenant is the *family* terms used of YHWH's relationship with Israel. Alongside the emphasis upon YHWH's holiness and transcendence, these reinforce the sense of his intimacy and presence. Central to this is YHWH's description of Israel as his 'firstborn son' (4.22 cf Deuteronomy 14.1; Hosea 11.1), a term later accorded, in a representative sense, to Israel's king. This motif of adoption then continues and adds further depth to the description of the land as Israel's inheritance. It is within the language of family relationships that we also find the significance of the constant description of the exodus as an act of *redemption*.[12] Redemption happened most often when someone's next of kin acted to buy back the freedom of an enslaved relative, hence the term 'kinsman-redeemer' (*go-el*). When YHWH speaks of the forthcoming rescue from Egypt he declares, 'I will redeem you' (6.6), and the Song of the Sea speaks of him leading the people 'you have redeemed' (15.13). These terms later recur within Isaiah 40–55 when redemption from the Babylonian exile was viewed as a second exodus. All of this conveys the sense that, through the covenant, YHWH had bound himself to Israel as a self-designated relative. In Old Testament law the redeemed and their land came under the power of the relative who had redeemed them, and so the term conveys the sense of Israel moving from slavery to being under the loving rule of their kinsman, YHWH. This is reinforced by the construction of the Tabernacle. Earlier we saw how the close presence of God established in creation was lost after Adam and Eve's disobedience, represented by their expulsion from the Garden of Eden. As God established the covenant in response, his promises were accompanied by fresh revelations of his presence and altars built by the patriarchs to symbolize this and his sovereign rule. These revelations were powerful but also fitful and temporary. In Exodus 25–31, however, Moses was given instructions by YHWH regarding the building of a tabernacle that would now travel with the Israelites as a permanent expression of YHWH's presence and rule. The Tabernacle and the Temple that later superseded it housed the Ark of the Covenant and had the nature of a miniature heaven and earth.[13] It thus represented both Israel's calling to live at the point where heaven and earth had their meeting point and YHWH's commitment to dwell in the midst of his people as a sign of his eventual plan to flood the whole of creation with his presence (Numbers 14.21; Psalm 72.19; Isaiah 11.9; Habakkuk 2.14).

However between the projection of the Tabernacle and its actual building (35–40), the people of Israel committed apostasy by worshipping the Golden Calf (32). In response God resolved to destroy the Israelites but Moses averted this by interceding for them and specifically appealing to covenant promises that YHWH had made to Abraham, Isaac and Jacob (32.13). Following punishments upon the idolaters, Moses makes two new stone tablets to replace those that he destroyed, and a renewal of the covenant and its promises and commitments took place (34.10-27). A key phrase that summarizes YHWH's covenant commitment to Israel is used for the first time at this point with YHWH describing himself as 'the compassionate and gracious God, slow to anger, abounding in love and faithfulness, maintaining love to thousands and forgiving wickedness, rebellion and sin' (34.6-7). This phrase recurs at crucial stages in the covenant story (Numbers 14.18; Nehemiah 9.31, Psalms 86.15; 103.8; Jonah 4.2; Joel 2.13). A particularly important term within it is '*chesed*', variously translated as 'mercy', 'covenant faithfulness' or 'steadfast love'. YHWH is described as 'abounding in *chesed*' (34.6) conveying a sense of undeserved favour similar to the word 'grace' in the New Testament, although this quality is still combined with God's punishment for sin (34.7).

The critical change caused by Israel's apostasy was that YHWH's presence could no longer be encountered by the Israelites with the same immediacy as before (33.3). Instead Moses establishes a 'tent of meeting' where he alone met with and talked with YHWH 'face to face, as a man speaks with his friend' (33.11). In response to Moses's request for God's presence to go with him and the Israelites, he also received a revelation of God's glory (33.12-23). It is the exposure to this glory that led to Moses wearing a veil during the times when he was not speaking with YHWH because the radiance in his face made the Israelites afraid to come near him lest they be destroyed by it (34.29-34). Whilst God's presence with the Israelites thus formed a crucial part of their covenant relationship, Israel's state of sin meant that her experience of this presence and YHWH's glory was limited and partial. Later we will see the use that Paul made of this in explaining the significance of Jesus Christ and the new covenant in 2 Corinthians 3.

After renewing the covenant, YHWH instructs Moses to build the Tabernacle which is then described in great detail (35–40). Once it is completed, the cloud symbolizing YHWH's presence covers the Tent of Meeting and his glory fills the Tabernacle (40.34). At this point, however, Moses cannot enter the Tent of Meeting (40.35), raising the issue of how YHWH's holy presence can exist alongside the ongoing sin and corruption of his covenant people.

## Leviticus

YHWH's answer to this forms the basis of the book of Leviticus which begins with him calling to Moses from the Tent of Meeting (Leviticus 1.1) and establishing the means by which the covenant relationship can be maintained. Central to this were the five main types of sacrifice that were established (1.3–7.38). The grain and fellowship sacrifices expressed thanks to YHWH by symbolically giving back to him what he had given to them and the burnt, purification and restitution sacrifices were understood to bring forgiveness for sin (4.35). The worshipper confessed their sin and laid their hand upon the beast about to be killed. This expressed their personal identification with the sacrifice being made and the death of the animal then brought atonement. The sacrifices thus took place within the context of a relationship already established by God's grace and were given as a continuous demonstration of this. The location of these sacrifices within the Tabernacle showed that God's intention to meet with his people formed the whole basis of the sacrificial system.[14]

This was further established as Aaron and his sons are ordained as priests to enter YHWH's presence and offer these sacrifices on behalf of the people (8.1–9.24). The death of Aaron's sons, Nadab and Abihu, when they entered YHWH's presence in an unauthorized manner (10.1-20), demonstrated the importance of how approach is made to a holy God. This formed the basis of the ritual purity (11.1–15.33) and moral purity (18.1–20.27) required of the people and highest level of moral integrity and ritual holiness required of the priests because of their role in representing the people to YHWH and YHWH to the people (21.1–22.33). Many of the regulations regarding ritual holiness were based upon the stipulation that nothing associated with death or loss of life was allowed into YHWH's presence because of his nature as the source of life. Overall the laws regarding purity served as a symbolic reminder that a response to YHWH's holiness should affect every aspect of Israel's existence.

The basis of all of this in YHWH's grace was shown by the further instruction to observe seven annual feasts, each telling a different part of the story of how YHWH had redeemed Israel from Egypt – Passover, Unleavened Bread, First-Fruits, Weeks/Pentecost, Trumpets, the Day of Atonement and Tabernacles (23.4-44). The instructions about observing the Sabbath and laws of Jubilee were thus given in the context of responding to this grace (23.3; 25.1-55). At the centre of Leviticus is a long description of one of Israel's feasts – the Day of Atonement. This existed because some sins remained uncovered by the individual sacrifices. Once a year, therefore, the high priest would take two goats. One of these became a purification offering and was offered as an atonement for the sins of the people. The other was called the scapegoat, as the priest would confess the sins of Israel, place them on the head of this goat and then drive it out into the desert. This served as a powerful image of YHWH's desire to remove sin and its consequences so that the people can live with him in peace (16–17).

As the Old Testament continues, however, we see an increasingly strong critique of sacrifice and a number of statements about its ineffectiveness (1 Samuel 15.22; Psalm 40.6; Isaiah 1.11; Hosea 6.6; Micah 6.6-8). This was particularly when sacrifices were not accompanied by the obedience and justice that YHWH required. The need for confession before sacrifices were made shows that they were never understood to operate mechanically, and their efficacy always rested in the forgiving love of God. The sheer weight of dissenting Old Testament voices in regard to sacrifice suggests, however, a more fundamental critique of sacrifice than simply its malpractice and fuelled the continuing desire for YHWH to fulfil his covenant promises. This critique of the Levitical sacrifices finds its deepest form in the New Testament letter to the Hebrews and its assertion that it was impossible for the blood of bulls and goats to take away sins and that these sacrifices simply formed an annual reminder of these sins.

Leviticus ends with Moses commanding people to stay loyal to the covenant. He describes the blessings of peace that would result if Israel obeyed and also warned that if Israel was unfaithful and dishonoured God's holiness, the result would be disaster and ultimately exile from the land God had promised to Abraham (26.1-46). The first line of the book of Numbers shows the purpose of Leviticus: 'YHWH spoke to Moses *in* the Tent of Meeting' (Numbers 1.1 cf Leviticus 1.1). Moses was now able to enter God's presence on behalf of Israel indicating that, despite Israel's failure, God has provided a way for Israel to be 'covered' so God can live with sinful people in peace.

**Numbers**

Numbers gains its name from the census by which Israel was numbered (Numbers 1.1-54 cf 26.1-65). Regulations then follow about how the camp was to be arranged. The Tabernacle stood at the centre surrounded by the priests and the Levites and then the twelve tribes carefully arranged with Judah at their head (2.1-4.49). All of this formed an elaborate symbol of how God's holy presence stood at the centre of their existence as a people. This was reinforced by a whole series of laws which then developed the purity laws from the book of Leviticus and indicated that, since God's presence was in their midst, every effort should be made to make the camp pure and a place that reflected God's holiness (5.1-10.10).

The story continues as the cloud of YHWH's presence lifts from the Tabernacle and guides Israel away from Sinai and out into the desert. From here the major theme is the lack of faith that the people show towards YHWH and the ensuing consequences. This begins with the people complaining about their hunger and thirst and expressing the desire to return to Egypt (11.1-35) and continues with Moses's own brother and sister, Aaron and Miriam, opposing him (12.1-16). Once they are in the desert of Paran, YHWH instructs Moses to send twelve spies, one from each tribe to scout the Promised Land (13.1-25). On their return, ten of the spies say that there is no chance that Israel can survive because of the strength of the Canaanites, whilst two spies, Caleb and Joshua, say that YHWH can save them (13.26-33). However, the ten whip up doubts in the people who plan to replace Moses with a new leader and return to Egypt (14.1-4). As happens each time the people rebel, Moses intercedes to YHWH for the Israelites, appealing to his witness to the nations (14.13-16) and asking for forgiveness on the basis of YHWH's covenant love (14.17-19 cf Exodus 34.6-7). This results in YHWH's forgiveness but also his judgement that this generation will stay in the desert until they die, with only their children entering the Promised Land (14.10-35). The rebellion continues as Korah and a whole group of Levites challenge Moses and Aaron before receiving judgement (16.1-50). Whilst the covenant promises are maintained, large numbers of Israelites perish during the desert period because of their disobedience and lack of faith. Even Moses, through dishonouring YHWH, is eventually told he will receive the same fate of not bringing his people into the Promised Land (20.1-13). This is followed by an episode where venomous snakes come upon the people as YHWH's judgement but Moses again intercedes for them and is instructed to make a bronze snake that they can look on and be healed (21.4-9). The contrast is thus made again and again between the people's unfaithfulness to the covenant and YHWH's faithfulness to his promises, even if this still includes his judgement upon Israel.[15]

This is reinforced by the story of Balaam. Just before they reach the plains of Moab, the Israelites are victorious over King Sihon of the Amorites and King Og of Bashan (13.21-35). These victories and the large number of the Israelites cause concern to the King of Moab, Balak, who hires a pagan sorcerer called Balaam to curse them. Three times Balak tries to bring this about, only for Balaam to report that he cannot curse Israel but only speak YHWH's blessings on them (23.1-24.14). His oracles include reference to YHWH bringing his people out of Egypt (23.22; 24.8) and God's promise to Abraham when Balaam declares: 'May those who bless you be blessed and those who curse you be cursed' (24.9 cf Genesis 12.3). In a fourth oracle, Balaam is given a vision of a victorious Israelite king who will bring YHWH's rule over the nations (24.15-19 cf Genesis 49.8-12). The story is intended to reinforce the contrast between Israel down in the camp grumbling and rebelling whilst, in the hills unseen and above, YHWH is still protecting and indeed blessing them.[16]

The importance of faithfulness to the covenant is shown as some of the Israelite men are involved in sexual immorality and idol worship with Moabite and Midianite women. This results in a plague which kills many Israelites. The plague ceases after the action of Phineas, the grandson of Aaron, who kills the couple involved in the most blatant misbehaviour (25.1-17 cf Hosea 9.10). In response, YHWH makes a covenant of peace with Phineas promising that he and his descendants will form an everlasting priesthood 'because he was zealous for the honour of his God and made atonement for the Israelites' (25.10-13). When Psalm 106 refers to this incident, it uses the same language used of Abraham's response of faith to God's promises: 'But Phinehas stood up and intervened and the plague was checked. This was credited to him as righteousness for endless generations to come' (Psalm 106.30-31 cf Genesis 15.6). Elijah later describes his loyalty to the covenant in similar terms to Phineas (1 Kings 19.10, 14). In the last part of Numbers, a fresh census is taken of the new generation who will inherit the land (26.1-65), victory achieved over the Midianites (31.1-54) and details set out of the land they are about to inherit (34.1-29).

The desert period plays an important part in the covenant story and is recalled a number of times in subsequent biblical writings (Psalms 78, 95, 106; Isaiah 63; Jeremiah 7; Ezekiel 20; Hosea 13.5; 1 Corinthians 10; Hebrews 4–5). In most cases, it is used to show that, whilst YHWH will remain faithful to his covenant promises, his people need to walk in faith if they are to avoid facing the consequences that will accompany disobedience. This is particularly evident in 1 Corinthians 10 as Paul draws parallels between baptism and the Lord's Supper and God's acts of covenant salvation during this period. Allusions to several examples of Israel's unfaithfulness and its consequences from Numbers are used to show the importance of responding to God's salvation in Jesus Christ with faithfulness (1 Corinthians 10.1-13).

### Deuteronomy

Deuteronomy records how the covenant was renewed and freshly expounded by Moses on the plains of Moab to Israel's new generation ahead of their entry into the land. The book contains three major addresses by Moses, all focused upon explanation and commendation of the covenant (1.6–4.49; 5–28; 29). A summary of the story so far forms the bulk of the first address highlighting how rebellious the previous generation was in contrast to YHWH's constant grace and provision. YHWH did punish Israel for her unfaithfulness but didn't abandon his covenant promises.

A major emphasis within Deuteronomy is upon the land coming to Israel as a gift because of the promises that YHWH had made to the patriarchs (1.8). Following earlier references, it is idealized as 'a land flowing with milk and honey' (6.3; 11.9; 26.9, 15; 27.3; 31.20) and watered by heaven (11.10-12). At the heart of this land was the one place that YHWH would choose to be a dwelling for his name and where Israel would worship him (12). This was the inheritance of which the people of Israel were now to take possession (26.1).

But the means by which they were to do this were crucial. Previous attempts to possess the land without divine backing had been repulsed (Numbers 14.39ff; Deuteronomy 1.41ff). Central to Israel receiving the land and continuing to enjoy the 'rest' intended for her there was the exhortation that the covenant should not be 'forgotten' (4.23; 6.12). This involved keeping the laws that YHWH had given and, in particular, refraining from the worship of other gods and their idols (4.15-31; 13.1-18). YHWH's ownership of the land provides the rationale for those laws seeking to safeguard this (such as the Sabbath and Jubilee) and its nature as God's dwelling place explains the commands to remove everything that would pollute his sanctuary. The major application of this was Israel avoiding any covenant with the pagan nations currently living in the land and destroying both them and their idols. YHWH's love for Israel's forefathers is presented as the basis of the covenant (4.37; 10.15) and fear of YHWH has a vital role in leading to Israel's obedience in response to this (4.10). But Deuteronomy goes further in requiring a response of *wholehearted love* for YHWH from Israel (6.5; 10.12; 26.16) and, at one point, the circumcision of their hearts (10.16). This includes Israel's leaders with judges, priests and kings (16.18–17.20), all placed under the authority of the covenant laws, and prophets raised up to keep them accountable (18.14-22). Many of the laws that follow include aspects of civil as well as religious life with instructions about the family, business, the legal system and how to protect widows, orphans and immigrants included within Israel's worship (19–26).

Towards the end of Deuteronomy, Moses outlines the blessings that will result from Israel's obedience to the covenant (28.1-14) but also, in a much longer section, the curses that will result from her disobedience (28.15-68). Central to these curses is *exile* which is understood as a loss of those blessings of the covenant already fulfilled, most obviously the land but also including the spoliation of all aspects of the richness of life resulting from Israel's relationship with God.[17] 'It is because this people abandoned the covenant of YHWH, the God of their fathers, the covenant he made with them when he brought them out of Egypt ... In furious anger and in great wrath YHWH uprooted them from their land' (29.25, 28). Assuming that these blessings and curses will occur, Deuteronomy then looks beyond this to a time when YHWH will renew the covenant by ending Israel's exile (30.1-10). Exile is presented as death, enabling restoration to be later presented as resurrection. Central to this will be God's 'circumcision' of the people's hearts mentioned earlier (30.6), which will make their obedience to him possible.

Throughout much of Christian history there has been an understanding that this covenant through Moses was a covenant of *law* (as opposed to *grace*) and rested therefore upon human 'good works' (as opposed to the faith supremely revealed in the Christian gospel). Much of this understanding grew out of the strong dichotomy that Martin Luther believed to exist between law and grace and one of the major benefits of the so-called new perspective on Paul has been the way in which it has challenged the notion that this is how it was understood within Judaism.[18] We have already seen that the covenant with Abraham was a covenant of grace to be met by faith issuing in obedience. So here too, through Moses, is a covenant arising out of an act of gracious rescue to be met by faith and obedience. To have YHWH as God, and to be his people, his precious possession, inevitably involves holiness, separation to him. Enjoyment of fellowship with God involves loving him with all one's heart, soul and strength (Deuteronomy 6.5). 'Be holy, because I am holy,' says the Lord (Leviticus 11.45; 20.26). This should not be understood as earning one's relationship with God but responding to his grace with grateful and loving obedience. But, as Tom Wright has shown, we must go further than this by clarifying *the purpose of the covenant as vocational rather than simply moral*. At its deepest level, the covenant represented a renewal of the vocation given to humankind in creation to rule the earth on God's behalf and reflect creation's praise back to God. Rather than any sort of 'covenant of works', the Mosaic covenant was a covenant of *grace and vocation*.[19]

Part of the reason why the vocational nature of the Mosaic covenant has been missed lies in the failure of Israel to fulfil this calling. It was this failure that Jesus exposed when he performed his action in the Temple and declared, 'It is written "My house shall be called a house of prayer *for all the nations*." But you are making it a den of robbers' (Matthew 21.13; Mark 11.12; Luke 19.46 quoting Isaiah 56.7). Paul is making a similar point when he declares that rather than being 'a guide for the blind, a light for those who are foolish, a teacher of infants because you have in the law the embodiment of knowledge and truth' (Romans 2.19-20), Israel's failure to live by the law had resulted in the very opposite: 'As it is written: "God's name is blasphemed among the Gentiles because of you"' (Romans 2.24 cf Isaiah 52.5; Ezekiel 36.22). Part of Paul's purpose in writing Romans was to show that Israel's very failure to fulfil this calling turned out to be a crucial part of the covenant plan and the way that its aim was paradoxically fulfilled. But, for the moment, it is important to note the central importance of this calling to witness to the nations within the Mosaic covenant, even if Israel's response to this vocation was a conspicuous failure.

We may thus summarize the characteristics of the Mosaic covenant: (a) It is a development of the covenant with Abraham, including the same intention of blessing the peoples of the world; (b) It rests on God's initiative of electing love as the Hebrews are rescued from slavery and sustained by him in the desert, including his provision for the forgiveness of their sins; (c) The covenant promise is holistic comprising a spiritual relationship as well as the land; (d) God's presence amongst his people has become central, enabling them to become a worshipping community, although the people's state of sin means that their experience of this can only be partial; (e) There is an obligation of trust and obedience, i.e. faithfulness to the covenant with very clear consequences attached to this; (f) It looks beyond itself to a future renewal of the covenant with significantly new factors that will ensure its fulfilment.

# Covenant preserved – David

## Joshua

The history of Israel continues in the book of Joshua with their occupation of the land of Canaan, presented as the implementation of the Mosaic programme from

Deuteronomy. In Joshua 1–12 the conquest takes place and in 13–22 the allocation of the land to Israel's tribes. Both before and afterwards, these events are presented as fulfilling YHWH's covenant promises (1.3-6; 23.14; 24.1-12) and Israel is summoned to a steadfast adherence to the covenant laws (1.6-7; 23.6-16; 24.14-24). This is underlined by the River Jordan being parted, in a manner similar to the Red Sea during the exodus, to allow the Israelites led by the Ark of the Covenant to enter the land (3.1–4.24). This was followed by the circumcision of those who had not received the covenant sign during the desert (5.1-9), Israel's celebration of the Passover and their eating of the produce of Canaan (5.10-13).

A notable aspect of the book of Joshua is the role of Canaanite prostitute Rahab who gives shelter to the Israelite spies who enter Jericho and in return is spared from destruction with her family (2.1-24; 6.17-25). The scarlet cord that Rahab is instructed to hang in her window as a sign of this recalls the scarlet thread tied around Zerah's wrist at birth, suggesting some similarity in their inclusion within the people of God (2.18, 21 cf Genesis 38.27-30). The figure of Achan then forms a contrast with that of Rahab. Rahab represents a stereotypically disreputable Canaanite who, by her faith (2.8-11) and solidarity with YHWH's people (2.12-21), gains inclusion for herself and her family within that people (6.25). Achan, by contrast, is an Israelite (from Zerah's line) who, by his disobedience, is cut off along with his family from being part of the people of YHWH (7.1–26).[20]

The book ends with a ceremony of covenant renewal at Shechem which includes Joshua's establishment of a large stone 'near the holy place of YHWH' as a witness to the covenant (24.26-27). Joshua's final two speeches are similar to those of Moses in Deuteronomy reminding Israel of YHWH's generosity and summoning her to be faithful to the covenant through the challenge to serve YHWH.

## Judges

It is in the book of Judges that we see just how far Israel fell short of being faithful to the covenant. Judges opens with Israel's tribes within the Promised Land but also a list of those Canaanite tribes that they failed to drive out (1.1-35). This is interpreted by an angel of YHWH as unfaithfulness to the covenant, and what follows throughout the book is its continued breach by the Israelites and their consequent oppression by the surrounding nations. YHWH then brings about Israel's continued deliverance through twelve successive judges (2.10-23). Raised up by YHWH and endowed with his Spirit (6.34; 11.29; 15.14, etc.), these judges defeat Israel's enemies and are said to exercise authority over all Israel, acting as surrogates for YHWH the Judge (11.27). However, as the book continues, Israel's repentance grows less and less with the judges themselves becoming more and more flawed, and by its conclusion the covenant community is in complete disarray (17–21). The horrific story of the Levite and his concubine bears obvious parallels to that of Sodom and Gomorrah conveying how the covenant people have become indistinguishable from the worst of their pagan neighbours (Judges 19 cf Genesis 19).[21] The moral anarchy is linked by the writer to the absence of a king over Israel indicating where the covenant story will then progress in 1 and 2 Samuel (17.6; 21.25).

## Ruth

Before this, however, we encounter the story of Ruth and the considerable surprise of YHWH's covenant faithfulness being preserved through a Moabite woman. Although Ruth's mother-in-law Naomi is the most obvious recipient of this faithfulness, the last section of the book reveals the wider scope of this for the covenant story of Israel by showing how the arrival of Ruth's son Obed directly led to the coming of Israel's greatest king in David (Ruth 4.17-22). Significantly, before the marriage of Ruth and Boaz takes place, the elders of Bethlehem ask YHWH to make Ruth like Rachel and Leah who 'built up the house of Israel' and through her offspring to make her family 'like that of Perez, whom Tamar bore to Judah' (4.11-12 cf Genesis 38.27-30).

## 1 Samuel

It is in 1 Samuel that we see the path by which Israel's monarchy was established within the covenant. This begins with another act of grace in YHWH's gift of Samuel as a child to the barren Hannah who, in turn, offers him back to YHWH (1.1-28). Hannah's following prayer is centred on the reversal that YHWH brings, reaching its climax in the anointed king that he will raise up (2.1-11). The book then shows how the continuing corruption of Israel and its leaders led to their resounding defeat at the hands of the Philistines and the loss of their key covenant symbol, the Ark of the Covenant, indicating that YHWH's glory had departed from Israel (4.22). From this point, however, YHWH's triumph over the pagan god Dagon and plagues coming upon the Philistines explicitly evoke the earlier exodus from Egypt and signal that a fresh stage in the covenant story is beginning (5–6). This stage with its integration of Israel's monarchy into the covenant is nonetheless surrounded by ambivalence as Israel's elders request a king so that they become 'like other nations' (8.5 cf Exodus 19.3b-6) and Samuel makes it clear that their request is an implicit denial of divine rule (8.7, 10.17-19; 12.12).

This ambivalence continues in the reign of Israel's first king, Saul, culminating in his rejection by YHWH because of his disobedience and his replacement with David (13.1-14; 15.1-35). The establishment of the monarchy within the covenant is nonetheless already demonstrated by features that Saul's kingship shares with the later kingship of David. In both cases their kingship is established by YHWH's choice. This was then confirmed by their anointing, signifying YHWH's appointment of them to the sacred office of leading his people and maintaining the covenant (10.1; 16.13). The Spirit of YHWH came upon them to provide divine empowerment for this role (10.6-7; 16.13) and the king was then further commended to Israel by a public display of prowess – in Saul's case, victory over the Ammonites (11) and in David's case, victory over Goliath (17). Whilst this pattern is not repeated with all the subsequent kings of Israel (particularly YHWH's Spirit coming upon them), the importance of the foundational nature of these royal elements within the covenant is shown by their reappearance within the messianic prophecies in Isaiah 9 and 11 (and much later in the baptism and temptations of Jesus Christ).

Within the figure of Israel's king, we thus see the ideal features of the covenant from Exodus 19.3b-6 being expressed. It is a calling to embody the covenant on behalf of the people and to be an example and enabler to them of preserving it (see Deuteronomy 17.14-20).[22] The failure of Saul indicates the need for something deeper within the king to fulfil this, leading to the major developments within the covenant that we see with David as he is called by YHWH to 'shepherd my people Israel' and 'become their ruler' (2 Samuel 5.2). These begin with his description as 'a man after YHWH's own heart' (13.14) suggesting a similar intimacy with God to that of Abraham and Moses. The humility and trust in YHWH that David shows when he fights Goliath reflects this, as does his refusal to kill Saul when he had the chance (21–26). The Psalms attributed to David during this period also display this same attitude of trust in YHWH (Psalms 18, 53, 57). In his lament for Saul, David's sorrow for the man who sought to kill him acts as a reflection of YHWH's love and compassion for his wayward people (2 Samuel 1).

## 2 Samuel

It was under David that Jerusalem was established as the place of divine presence (6.1-23). The Ark of the Covenant, which had remained in the 'desert' since its 'exodus' from the Philistines, was established in Jerusalem as the visible symbol of the covenant relationship and understood to be the footstall of the divine throne in heaven (Psalm 99.5; 132.7-8; 1 Chronicles 28.2). The death of Uzzah when the Ark's move was first attempted (6.7 cf 1 Samuel 6.19) showed that only YHWH could establish his presence. From this point, Jerusalem became the place from where YHWH himself would exercise his rule. The Ark's contents (the two tablets containing the Ten Commandments) indicated how closely God's rule was connected to conformity with his word.[23]

It is within the following chapter that YHWH announces his everlasting covenant with David (7.1-29). Following the (covenant) blessing of rest from his enemies (7.1 cf Deuteronomy 12.10-11), David had thought to build a house (or Temple) for the Ark of God. YHWH then reveals through the prophet Nathan that he will do something more significant in building a house for David. YHWH affirms his presence with David and then makes him a succession of promises including a great name (7.9), a territory for the people (7.10), freedom from oppression and rest from all his enemies (7.10-11) and a dynasty and kingdom that will be everlasting (7.11-16). Whilst *berit* is not used in 2 Samuel 7, the location of these promises within the covenant is clear from David's subsequent prayer as he refers back to God's gracious redemption from Egypt (7.23) and reiterates that YHWH has established the people of Israel as his own forever and has become their God (7.24).

The most striking part of the covenant with David is the *eternal* nature of the promises regarding his dynasty. David is promised that one of his offspring will succeed him and be the one to build a house for YHWH's name and that the throne of his kingdom would be established forever (7.12-13). The intimate language of father and son is used of YHWH's relationship with David's offspring indicating once again how the covenant promises to Israel have now been drawn into the king as her representative figure (7.14 cf Exodus 4.22). Whilst chastening for wrongdoing will occur, God solemnly promises never to remove his love from David's offspring 'as I took it away from Saul', evoking memories of the similar covenant promise made in Genesis 9.11 after the flood.

The Davidic covenant is explicitly referred to as such in David's last words in 23.5 and is celebrated in Psalms 2; 72; 89, especially verses 1–4 and 26–37 and 132.11-18. 'I have made a covenant with my chosen one, I have sworn to David my servant … I will not violate my covenant or alter what my lips have uttered.' Psalm 110 also asserts the priestly nature of his kingship drawing an implicit contrast with the earlier kingship of Saul (1 Samuel 13.8-14) and suggesting that the covenantal demand for Israel to become a kingdom of priests (Exodus 19.6) had now become embodied in the Davidic king.

Another aspect of the Davidic covenant particularly emphasized in Psalm 72 is the expansion of the king's rule beyond Israel. A major theme of the psalm is the king's justice, but accompanied by emphatic statements about his rule over other peoples: 'All nations will bow down to him and all nations will serve him' with a particular emphasis upon the tribute and gifts they will bring him (Psalm 72.8-15). It is made clear that this rule will represent the fulfilment of the Abrahamic covenant when the psalm declares, 'All nations will be blessed through him, and they will call him blessed' (72.17). The trajectory that this aspect of the covenant with David then takes throughout the rest of the Old Testament is a rather ambiguous one. Rather than being blessed, it often seems that the role of other nations in relation to the fulfilment of the covenant is simply that of being conquered by Israel. This is certainly its most obvious application in terms of the reign of David himself as YHWH gives him successive victories over the Philistines, Moabites, Arameans, Edomites and Ammonites and the king receives their tribute (8, 10). Defeat of Israel's enemies then continues within the Old Testament narrative as a sign of the fulfilment of YHWH's covenant promises. However within the prophets, as we shall see, such passages increasingly sit alongside others which focus more upon the nations being more obviously *blessed* through their coming to Zion and even included within YHWH's covenant people. The way in which this seeming contradiction between the defeat of Israel's enemies and the blessing of the nations through Israel would find its resolution is, for the moment, left mysterious and undisclosed.

YHWH was not therefore changing the subject in 2 Samuel 7 when he responded to David's desire to build a temple with the promise to give David a 'house'. The promise was instead mysteriously affirming that David's son would somehow become the ultimate dwelling place for YHWH and where his covenant blessings would be found.[24]

The characteristics of the covenant with David are thus: (a) It is God's gracious renewal of his former covenant mercy and promises, but made particular to the YHWH's chosen king as the representative and leader of Israel; (b) It involves an intimate spiritual relationship as well as promise of territory, reinforced by the close connection between the Davidic covenant and God's presence within the Temple; (c) It involves the obligation on the king of living by the Spirit of God and preserving the rule and law of God as the pattern for the life of his people; (d) It is an eternal or everlasting covenant which looks ahead to its fulfilment, particularly the rule of Israel's king over all the nations of the world.

However it is from these great heights that the second half of 2 Samuel depicts David's dramatic fall. The catalyst for this is his adultery with Bathsheba and David's consequent murder of her husband, Uriah (11.1-27). Uriah's status as Hittite, i.e. a faithful *Gentile* follower of David, is crucial here. So is his name meaning 'YHWH is my light'. Whilst David admits his sin when he is confronted by Nathan, and is forgiven (12.13 cf Psalm 51), he is also told that his son by Bathsheba will die 'because by doing this, you have made the enemies of YHWH show utter contempt' (12.14). David had not just committed adultery and murder but failed in the covenantal task of displaying YHWH's wisdom to the nations (cf Deuteronomy 4.6; Isaiah 52.5; Ezekiel 36.22; Romans 2.24). A further consequence pronounced by Nathan to David is that 'the sword shall never depart from your house' (12.10). This plays out in the disintegration of David's family, particularly his sons. David's eldest son Amnon rapes David's daughter Tamar (13.1-22), causing Amnon to be murdered by Tamar's brother Absalom (13.23-39). Sometime later, Absalom launches a rebellion causing David to flee from Jerusalem and endure a temporary 'exile', before Absalom too is killed (15.1–18.33). Further rebellion, division and bloodshed then mar the rest of David's reign in stark contrast to its earlier nature (20.1-26).

The book of Samuel ends with a well-crafted epilogue indicating the tension now present within YHWH's covenant promises to David. It begins and ends with stories indicating how Saul and David both took decisions that played out badly for their people (21.1-14; 24.1-25). These are accompanied by stories about David's mighty men which include reference to David's weakness in battle and dependence on others for help (21.15-22; 23.8-39). This even includes the suggestion that the killing of Goliath may have been misappropriated to him (21.19 cf 1 Samuel 17). Significantly, the list of David's warriors contains several Gentiles concluding with Uriah the Hittite (23.24-39). At the centre of the epilogue are two poems which reiterate YHWH's covenant promise to David. The first is set within the context of David reflecting upon the times that YHWH rescued him from danger (22.1-51 cf Psalm 18; Jonah 2) and the second within the context of his death (23.1-7). The message is that, despite David's weakness and failure, YHWH would remain faithful to his eternal covenant commitment that he had made to David and his descendants to bring about the salvation spoken of by Hannah at the start of the book.[25] The sign that YHWH would work through this brokenness and failure is perhaps most strikingly signalled by the Davidic line continuing through the second child that David had with Bathsheba, Solomon, who is given the name Jedidiah, meaning 'loved by YHWH' (12.24-5).

## 1 and 2 Kings

Just as Moses instructed Joshua to keep the covenant, so David before his death instructs his son Solomon to obey the Law of Moses so YHWH would keep his promise about David always having his descendants on the throne of Israel (1 Kings 2.1-4). The ambivalent portrait of David continues, however, in the bloodshed also commanded by David which then accompanies Solomon's accession (2.5-46).

During Solomon's reign the blessing of the covenant appeared to start being fulfilled as he asks for and receives 'a wise and discerning heart' to govern the people (3.5-15). The land of Israel grows to its fullest extent (4.21), its people experience numerous blessings and the language of the Abrahamic covenant is evoked to signify its element of fulfilment (4.20). The covenant concept of 'rest' is also realized (5.4). At the centre of these covenant blessings was God's presence being consolidated amongst his people with the Temple in Jerusalem established as the place of contact between heaven and earth. The detail with which the nature of the Temple is recorded recalls the earlier construction of the Tabernacle (8–9 cf Exodus 35–40). Once the Ark of the Covenant has been moved into the Temple and its dedication has occurred, YHWH appears and once again affirms the paradox of his everlasting covenant with David and the necessity of obedience for its blessings to be received (9.1-9). A further example of the apparent fulfilment of the David covenant during Solomon's reign is the quantity of tribute and wealth that flows into Israel from other nations and also the visit of the Queen of Sheba (10.1-29) who is led by the wisdom and achievement that she witnesses to praise YHWH and his eternal love for Israel in making Solomon king to maintain justice and righteousness (10.9).

Whatever disasters in Israel's history followed, YHWH's promises regarding his presence in Zion (Psalms 46, 48, 76, 84, 87, 122) and the eternal nature of the Davidic dynasty were never forgotten. This was aided by the continuing reign of Davidic kings over the southern kingdom of Judah for four hundred years and the miraculous survival of Jerusalem on more than one occasion when it was threatened with destruction (e.g. 2 Kings 18–19). Both of these were understood as YHWH maintaining his commitment to the Davidic covenant, with this regularly described in the books of 1 and 2 Kings as YHWH fulfilling his promise to maintain 'a lamp in Jerusalem' for David (1 Kings 11.36; 15.4-5; 2 Kings 8.19).

## Covenant broken and renewed – the prophets

Repeatedly, however, both Israel's king and people failed to keep the covenant. We have already seen how, before the end of David's reign, his disobedience led to the start of the breaking down of the 'house' promised to him. Solomon's reign grew from seeds of ambivalence (e.g. 1 Kings 3.1-3; 4.26; 5.13-14; 6.38–7.1; compare Deuteronomy 17.14-20; 1 Samuel 8.10-18) into eventual outright disobedience to the covenant (1 Kings 11). The result was the fracturing of Israel into the two kingdoms of Israel and Judah and further spiritual decline with the rapid growth of idolatry and injustice. There were notable royal attempts at covenant renewal, particularly under the priest Jehoiada and King Joash (2 Kings 11–12) and later King Hezekiah (2 Kings 18–20) and King Josiah (2 Kings 22–23). But these efforts were short-lived and the path towards the exile predicted by Deuteronomy continued.

### 1 and 2 Kings: Elijah and Elisha

Against this background, the essential ministry of the prophets was to recall Israel to the covenant. Elijah was particularly important, emerging in the northern kingdom of Israel to combat the threat posed by King Ahab and his pagan wife, Queen Jezebel of Sidon, as they promoted worship of the Canaanite fertility gods, Baal and Asherah. Elijah, whose name means 'YHWH is God', sought to turn Israel back to the covenant, most notably through the dramatic contest with the pagan prophets on Mount Carmel (1 Kings 18.16-46). After this and Jezebel's attempt to kill him, Elijah travels to Mount Horeb to pronounce his zealousness for YHWH and complain about the Israelites rejection of the covenant (19.10, 14 cf Numbers 26.6-13). Elijah then receives a revelation of YHWH similar but distinct from that received by Moses (19.11-12 cf Exodus 19). The result of this is YHWH's promise to bring judgement upon Israel through those whom Elijah was commanded to anoint, whilst also preserving a faithful remnant in Israel who have not bowed to Baal (19.15-18).

Elijah was succeeded by the prophet Elisha, with this succession signalled by their division of the Jordan in a manner similar to Joshua and Moses (2 Kings 2). Elisha's name means 'God saves' and, like Elijah, his ministry was accompanied by a number of miracles symbolizing the new life that YHWH was bringing to Israel. Most notably, this included the raising of the dead (1 Kings 17.17-24; 2 Kings 8.8-37; 13.20-21). The ministry of Elisha reached its climax in the bloody destruction of Ahab's house and all those who worshipped Baal by the newly anointed King Jehu (2 Kings 9–10). None of this, however, halted the decline of Israel's faithfulness to the covenant and indeed the excesses of Jehu were swiftly seen as an example of her sin (Hosea 1.4-5). Despite this, Elijah and Elisha form crucial figures in the development of the covenant story. Their combination of words of judgement with promises and signs that YHWH would preserve a community faithful to him became central to the proclamation of all the prophets that follow them.

An important aspect of Elijah and Elisha's ministries is the way in which they pointed to YHWH's blessings being carried beyond Israel. Elijah was given refuge in the Baal territory of Zarephath (near Sidon) by a widow whose son is then raised from death (1 Kings 17.17-24). Then it is through Elisha that the Syrian general Naaman was cured of his skin disease by his washing in the River Jordan (2 Kings 5). Given the antagonism and threat that these nations posed to Israel, this is remarkable and points to what would become another important aspect of the development of the covenant by the prophets (cf Luke 4.24-27). Elisha, in particular, anticipated the later prophets by mysteriously combining YHWH's judgement on Israel *by* the nations (2 Kings 8.7-15), deliverance of Israel *from* the nations (2 Kings 6.8-19; 6.24–7.20) and actions which pointed to the *inclusion* of these nations within Israel's blessings (2 Kings 6.20-23).

## Amos, Hosea, Micah and Isaiah

The covenant remains central to the prophets that followed and whose oracles are preserved in the Old Testament books named after them. Whilst some made more use of the language of covenant than others, all of the pre-exilic prophets spoke of how the idolatry and injustice present in the kingdoms of Israel and Judah represented a breach of the relationship that had been established between them and God. Amos proclaimed that Israel had been found wanting in the justice and righteousness that YHWH sought from his people (Amos 5.24 cf Isaiah 5.7). Hosea, making constant reference to earlier traditions (Hosea 2.3; 9.10; 11.1), used the acted metaphor of an adulterous marriage to convey how faithless Israel had been to the covenant (Hosea 6.7; 8.1) and Jeremiah proclaimed a similar message to Judah (Jeremiah 11.6-10). Micah's prophecy begins with an image of YHWH appearing through an earthquake as he did at Sinai but this time to bring judgement upon Judah for her rebellion (Micah 1.3-4) and particularly singles out the way that her leaders and prophets have combined to commit grave injustice (Micah 2.6-11; 3.1-11; 6–7). Isaiah, also in Judah, made it clear how far both Jerusalem and the Davidic kings had fallen from the calling that YHWH had given them and condemned their lack of faith in his promises (Isaiah 1.21; 7.1-9).

The punishment which the prophets announced was severe precisely because Israel were a people who had been chosen, loved and redeemed by YHWH (Amos 3.2), even if their behaviour had reduced them to being like one of the surrounding peoples (Amos 9.7). Amos and Hosea, in particular, used imagery very similar to the covenant curses in Deuteronomy to proclaim the disasters that would happen to Israel as a result. And whilst Isaiah appears to have retained the belief that YHWH's promises regarding David and Jerusalem would ensure their survival (Isaiah 1.7-10, 37.33-35, although see also 39.5-7), his contemporary Micah spoke of Jerusalem becoming a heap of rubble with the temple hill overgrown with thickets (Micah 3.12). Jeremiah a century later had no hesitation in proclaiming that both Jerusalem and its Temple would suffer a similar destruction to that of YHWH's earlier dwelling at Shiloh (Jeremiah 7, 26). The eventual result of Israel and Judah's disobedience was the destruction of the kingdom of Israel by the Assyrians in 721 BC and then the kingdom of Judah, including Jerusalem and the Temple, by the Babylonians in 586 BC. In both cases the writers of their history clearly understand this to have been brought about by disobedience to the covenant (2 Kings 17.7-23; 21.10-15).

Throughout 1 and 2 Kings we see a constant tension between the eternal nature of YHWH's covenant promises and the sin of Israel and Judah. With the destruction of Jerusalem and the Temple, it appeared that the people's faithlessness had finally exhausted the promises of God. However, even within the disaster at the end of 2 Kings, we see a glimmer of light as its final few verses record how the king of Babylon released the king of Judah, Jehoiachin, from prison suggesting that YHWH's grace might yet triumph in the covenant story (2 Kings 25.27-30).[26]

The book of Lamentations provides eloquent witness to the shattering blow which these events, particularly the destruction of the Temple, delivered to the covenant story. The poems that it contains are clear that Israel's sin and the resulting punishment by YHWH were the cause of the exile, and most of these are simply full of grief and lament at this. But even within this anguish, a flicker of hope is found in the assertion to the 'daughter of Zion' that 'your punishment will end, he will not prolong your exile' (4.22).

The message that the judgement of exile would not be YHWH's final word is found with greatest clarity within the prophets. Whether the passages of hope contained within the pre-exilic prophets were actually spoken/written before or after the exile is much debated but they were nonetheless able to see beyond the disaster to a time when YHWH would bring the renewal of the covenant. Whilst Amos's message was overwhelmingly one of doom for Israel, its final section speaks of David's 'fallen tent' being restored and YHWH's people brought back from exile, never to be uprooted again. This restoration includes their possession of 'the remnant of Edom and all the nations that bear my name' (Amos 9.11-15). Within Hosea, the passages of judgement are accompanied by others which use strongly covenantal language to speak of the restoration of YHWH's 'marriage' with Israel. Both the Abrahamic promises (Hosea 1.10) and imagery from the exodus (2.15) are drawn upon by Hosea to picture this restored covenant as an eternal betrothal involving the harmony of the created order and the renewal of creation itself (2.18-23).

Micah too spoke of YHWH like a shepherd regathering the flock (Micah 2.12-13) and raising a Davidic king from Bethlehem to rule over the people (5.1-6) so that Jerusalem and the Temple would be restored as the place of YHWH's presence for the nations to come to (4.1-7). These wonders would be similar to when Israel came out of Egypt (7.15) and, as Israel's sin was dealt with, this would represent YHWH showing compassion and showing mercy to Abraham 'as you pledged on oath to our fathers in days long ago' (7.20).

In Isaiah, it is the Davidic and Zion traditions that were largely used by the prophet to speak of a future time when the present faithlessness of Jerusalem and kings such as Ahaz would give way to YHWH's presence and therefore his righteousness, justice and peace fully realized within both the holy city and rule of its Davidic king which will extend out over the nations (Isaiah 1.24-27; 2.1-5; 4.2-5; 9.1-7; 11.1-16; 19.23-25). The Immanuel prophecy in Isaiah 7.14ff is notoriously complex but within the context of other Isaianic passages appears to be saying that the path towards the fulfilment of YHWH's promises would somehow be through a holy remnant symbolizing 'God with us' through the coming disaster and judgement (Isaiah 6.13; 8.6-10; 8.18; 10.20-23).

## Jeremiah

It was the prophet Jeremiah who spoke explicitly about this future restoration involving YHWH's establishment of a new covenant. Earlier in his prophecy, Jeremiah had drawn contrasts between the earlier covenants and the future that YHWH would bring. In that future, the Ark of the Covenant would become superfluous and neither remembered nor remade as all nations would gather in Jerusalem to honour the name of YHWH (Jeremiah 3.16-18). Having condemned the Davidic kings of his own day as faithless shepherds, Jeremiah spoke of the future days when YHWH would raise up a righteous Davidic branch who (in implicit contrast to Zedekiah, the last king of Judah) would deserve the name 'YHWH is our righteousness' (Jeremiah 23.1-8).

It is in 31.31-34 that Jeremiah's famous prophecy of the new covenant occurs. The Hebrew word *hadash* (and its Greek equivalent *kainos*) can mean 'renewed' (e.g. Lamentations 3.22-23) or 'brand new' (e.g. Exodus 1.8; Deuteronomy 32.17) but the context in Jeremiah points to the newness residing in a qualitatively new dimension being added to the covenant. The discontinuity did not lie, as some have suggested, in the new covenant being an act of grace (as opposed to an earlier earning of forgiveness) since Jeremiah is quite clear that grace was just as central to the Sinai covenant (31.32).

Neither is this found in Jeremiah's emphasis upon the law needing to be placed in people's hearts since this was always YHWH's intention with the Sinai covenant (Deuteronomy 6.4-6; 11.18). The qualitative difference would instead lie *in this actually taking place* – the circumcision of the heart that YHWH required (Deuteronomy 10.16) and which he declared would be wrought after the exile (Deuteronomy 30.1-14) coming to fulfilment. The new covenant was called so, not because new conditions or promises would be established for it, but because a dramatic inward change would occur enabling Israel, and not just YHWH, to keep it.[27] This change would remove the need for the intermediaries associated with the Sinai covenant because the people's wickedness will have been forgiven (Jeremiah 31.34). Like Hosea, Jeremiah then goes on to locate the certainty of the renewed covenant within YHWH's purposes for creation itself (31.35-37). Later on, he confirms that all of this will be in fulfilment of the covenant promises which YHWH has made (33.14-26).

### Zephaniah, Habakkuk, Nahum and Obadiah

Roughly contemporary with Jeremiah, and equally clear about Jerusalem's destruction, was the prophet Zephaniah, who pictured this judgement as a descent into the darkness and chaos that preceded creation (Zephaniah 1.2-3).[28] Shockingly YHWH's judgement upon the nations is extended to Jerusalem because they are no longer recognized as his people (2.4–3.8). However, by the same token, the result of this fire of judgement would be to purify these rebellious peoples and transform all who called on YHWH into one, united people (3.9-10) within a Jerusalem restored with his presence (3.11-20).

Another prophet whose message comes from this period is Habakkuk. Unusually, all of his words are addressed to YHWH as Habakkuk complains, first about the corruption of Judah (Habakkuk 1.2-4) and then about YHWH's use of the even more unjust Babylon as his instrument (1.5–2.1). YHWH's response is to give Habakkuk a vision of the judgement he will bring on such nations, together with the statement that 'the righteous will live by his faith' (2.4). This faith is then presented in Habakkuk's prayer that YHWH will act in the present as he has done in the past. A Sinai-like appearance of YHWH is described (3.3-7 cf Exodus 19; Micah 1.3-4) and the future defeat of evil presented in images that recall the exodus (3.8-15) and allow Habakkuk to face his dark and chaotic world with trust in the covenant promises of YHWH (3.16-19).

As the disaster of exile actually occurred, two other prophets who added their voice to the hope that YHWH would not abandon the covenant were Nahum and Obadiah. Nahum begins his prophecy by describing another Sinai-like appearance of YHWH's glory (cf Exodus 19; Micah 1.3-4; Habakkuk 3.3-7) accompanied by the use of the familiar covenant language about YHWH being 'slow to anger and great in power' (Nahum 1.1-8 cf Exodus 34.6-7). This was in order to assert that YHWH will bring his justice upon the evil of nations that had oppressed Israel such as Assyria and its capital Nineveh (1.8-14; 2.1-13; 3.1-19). Obadiah's short prophecy contains a similar message but in relation to the oppressive Edom which would, like other nations, be brought down from its prideful heights and come to ruin (1.1-16) before it eventually became part of YHWH's kingdom (1.17-21 cf Amos 9.12).

## Ezekiel

The renewal of the covenant is also central to the prophecy of Ezekiel. The first half of the book (1-24) is dominated by judgement upon Jerusalem and the Temple, including the message that YHWH's presence would depart from the Temple prior to its destruction. But even within these chapters we see YHWH's ongoing commitment to the covenant. In chapter 16 Ezekiel recalls the covenant that YHWH made and the faithlessness with which Jerusalem had responded to it as she 'despised my oath by breaking the covenant' (Ezekiel 16.59). In the verses that follow, however, YHWH declares that he 'will remember the covenant I made with you in the days of your youth and I will establish an everlasting covenant with you' (16.60). Mysteriously this restoration will include Jerusalem's sisters (identified earlier as the cities of Sodom and Samaria) 'but not on the basis of my covenant with you' (16.61).

It is in the second half of Ezekiel, and following Jerusalem's destruction by the Babylonians, that more is revealed about how the covenant will be restored. Confidence about continued possession of the land on the basis of its possession by Abraham is shown to be false (Ezekiel 33.24) and the shepherds of Israel (its kings) condemned and then removed because of their lack of care for their flock (34.1-10). In the future, YHWH himself and his servant David would shepherd Israel (34.7-24) and through this 'covenant of peace' creation itself will be renewed for them (34.25-31) and Edom and their other enemies removed (35.1–36.15). YHWH declares that he will do this for the sake of his name and the language of the exodus is evoked as he declares that he will sprinkle clean water upon Israel to make her clean (36.24-25 cf Exodus 24.6). As in Jeremiah 31, this will happen through a change in the people's hearts but greater detail is given about this being effected by YHWH placing his Spirit within the people so that they can keep his laws (36.26-27) as they live once again in the land that has become like the Garden of Eden (36.33-35). Chapter 37 continues to present this as an act of new creation as, recalling Genesis 2.7, YHWH breathes life into the bones of Israel to recreate one united Israel under a single king in David (37.1-24). This covenant will fulfil the promises made to their fathers and at its centre is YHWH's promise to be their God and have his dwelling place within them forever (37.25-28). As assault upon the people of God by Gog of Magog will then follow before Israel's restoration is brought to completion (38–39). The last eight chapters of the book then describe the Ezekiel's detailed vision of the restored Temple in Jerusalem with waters flowing from it recalling Genesis 2 (47.1-12) and the name 'YHWH is there' signifying the permanent establishment of God's presence amongst his people (48.35).

## Isaiah 40–55

The second half of the book of Isaiah is also focused upon the reestablishment of YHWH's 'everlasting covenant', 'my faithful love promised to David' (55.3). Earlier we saw how chapters 1–39 of Isaiah combined condemnation of the Jerusalem and Davidic house of the prophet's day with a vision of YHWH's promises regarding both of them being fulfilled. From chapter 40 the book then addresses Israel's exilic situation with an emphasis upon her return being brought about by the power of

YHWH's word (40.1-11; see also 55.6-13) leading to parallels between this act of rescue and his original act of creation (40.12-31; 41.20; 42.5; 45.12). A strong degree of continuity with the earlier covenant traditions is shown by the depiction of the return from Babylon as a second exodus (40.3-5; 42.16; 43.16, 19; 49.9, 11; 51.10), and numerous references and allusions are made to YHWH's promises to Abraham and Jacob and their fulfilment (41.8; 48.1; 49.5-6, 20ff; 51.1-2; 54.1-3). Particularly noteworthy in this regard is the way in which Isaiah 40–55 (following Isaiah 2.1-4; 19.23-25) looks towards this period of restoration as one that includes the blessing of the nations that was promised through the Abrahamic covenant. Judgement upon the nations that have oppressed Israel in chapters 40–48 gives way in chapters 49–55 to an emphasis upon their incorporation within the good news of YHWH's return to reign in Zion and redeem Jerusalem (52.7-12).

Central to bringing all of this about is the work of a servant of YHWH who would embody the covenant and perpetuate it. Concerning him, God says, 'I will make you to be a *covenant* for the people and a light for the Gentiles' (Isaiah 42.1, 6; see also 49.8; 55.3). The identity of this servant has been much debated as in different passages he seems to represent Israel, a remnant of Israel, possibly the prophet himself and then a later individual figure. Parallels are also found to the royal figures anointed with YHWH's Spirit who occur both earlier and later in the book of Isaiah (9.2-7; 11.1-10; 61.1-4; 63.1-6). Whatever his identity, it is made clear that it will be the arm of YHWH himself that will be working through the servant (52.10; 53.1 cf 40.10; 51.9-10) and that through his work a victory would be won (53.12). Central to the servant's role, however, was the suffering and death that he will endure to bring about the liberation of God's people (Isaiah 52.13–53.12). Isaiah 53.10 presents this suffering in sacrificial terms as 'an offering for sin' with the suffering of the servant seen as somehow redemptive. Suffering is therefore presented, not just as the context for Israel's deliverance by YHWH, but as the *means* of this deliverance as well.

Chapter 54 then elaborates upon this deliverance with allusions to YHWH's promises to Abraham, Moses and Noah (54.1-9) before pointing to the indissoluble covenant of peace that YHWH will establish with the restored Jerusalem inherited by his servants (54.10-17). This is followed in chapter 55 by showing how the renewal of YHWH's covenant promises to David (55.3-4) and the response of the nations will be accompanied by the restoration of the creation itself (55.12-13).

A key covenantal term used within many of the passages in Isaiah which speak about this restoration is 'the *righteousness* of Yahweh' (Hebrew *tsedeq*) (Isaiah 33.5; 45.8, 24; 46.13; 51.6, 8; 54.14; 56.1; 59.16-17; 63.1). Righteousness means right conduct within a relationship. Earlier we saw how the term was used of Abraham to indicate his right response to God's covenant promises. When it is used of YHWH, rather than describing his abstract qualities, it refers quite specifically to his own commitment to fulfil his covenant promises.[29] Later we will see the prevalence of this use of the term within the Psalms. But within the new covenant, just as much as the old, the people are called to respond to YHWH's promises with trust and faithful obedience (Isaiah 55.6-9).

The major development within the prophetic presentation of the covenant is thus the qualitative difference brought to it by the fresh act of YHWH that the prophets envisage.[30] Earlier traditions are used to show how YHWH would bring about a greater exodus through the greater defeat of Israel's enemies by a greater David establishing his greater presence within a greater temple. For much of the time, these enemies were still straightforwardly understood as Israel's oppressors, such as Assyria and Babylon. Increasingly, however, the prophets identify the real enemy as *sin* and the solution needing to be an internal one that would purify people's hearts. This leads to a deeper understanding of the act of YHWH needed to redeem Israel, most obviously through the mysterious role of the Isaianic suffering servant. It also leads to a greater vision of this redemption then including the incorporation of those nations currently outside of YHWH's people. Awareness that a cosmic battle with evil lay behind YHWH's acts of rescue was never absent from Israel's understanding of the covenant (e.g. Exodus 15). But this too becomes steadily clearer within the prophets, leading into the gradual development of the so-called genre of *apocalyptic*. This, as we will see, reaches its fullest form in the post-exilic period. An important consequence of this development, already seen in the pre-exilic and exilic prophets, is growing clarity over YHWH's fulfilment of the covenant leading to the renewal of the whole of creation.

All these factors, however, represent the *fulfilment* of the covenant rather than its replacement. Whilst more permanent and lasting, the new covenant thus stands in striking continuity with the old consisting of (a) a spiritual relationship between God and his people; (b) the restoration of the land to Israel and its renewal; (c) the reestablishment of God's presence amongst his land and people; (d) the provision of forgiveness; (e) the need to respond with the trusting obedience of faith; (f) all peoples on earth, and indeed the whole of creation, being blessed through Israel. These were the very characteristics of the covenant established with Abraham and developed with Moses and David with the 'newness' residing in the new power that God will bring to enable this obedience to finally occur.

## Covenant awaiting fulfilment – the 'post-exilic' period

The exile has usually been seen as coming to an end with the decree of the Persian Emperor Cyrus during the sixth century which allowed the Jews to return from Babylon. Both the end of 2 Chronicles and the start of the book of Ezra record this happening in fulfilment of Jeremiah's prophecy about the exile coming to an end after seventy years. Within the biblical literature produced during this period we see a strong emphasis upon the need to restore the symbols of the covenant, particularly the Temple. This took place under the governor of Judah, Zerubbabel, the High Priest, Joshua, and with the encouragement of the prophets Haggai and Zechariah (Ezra 1-6).

However what we also see throughout this period is a growing realization that, despite the physical return from exile, the covenant still awaited fulfilment. The initial optimism surrounding the return from Babylon swiftly turned to struggle and difficulty which, in turn, led to greater reflection upon the way in which YHWH would fulfil his promises and the inner change needed in his people as part of this.

## Haggai

Within the prophecy of Haggai, we see the use of familiar covenantal terms and concepts to encourage the rebuilding of the Temple. However, it is as the Temple was completed that we see Haggai's witness that the true fulfilment of YHWH's covenant promises still lies in the future. In response to the new temple appearing to lack its former glory, YHWH's message is a strong assurance of his presence, plus the promise of the nations coming to his house and being subject to his chosen ruler. This ruler is identified as Zerubbabel (2.20-23). However the prophecy's preservation, after Zerubbabel's subsequent drift into obscurity, suggests that it was swiftly understood more broadly as a sign that YHWH would keep his covenant promises regarding the Davidic dynasty, of which Zerubbabel was part.

## Zechariah

Zechariah means 'YHWH remembers' and his prophecy is full of the confidence that YHWH will remember the promises that he had made to his people. Endorsement is again made of the authority of Zerubbabel and Joshua but with the major emphasis upon YHWH's Spirit working through them (4.6 cf Haggai 1.13-15). The role of both leaders becomes evident as Zechariah describes Joshua and his associates as 'men symbolic of things to come', followed by more opaque descriptions of YHWH's 'servant', 'the branch' and 'the stone' through which 'the sin of the land will be removed in a single day' (3.8-9). The merging of the royal and priestly roles and the exalted language used indicates that, whilst remaining committed to working through human agents, restoration will occur through YHWH himself becoming king.

This is reinforced in the second half of the book. Zechariah speaks of the rejoicing in Jerusalem as her king comes 'righteous and having salvation, gentle and riding on a donkey, on a colt, the foal of a donkey' bringing peace to the nations and ruling 'to the ends of the earth' (9.9-10). This is followed by the assertion that this freedom and rescue will be brought about 'because of the blood of my covenant with you' (9.11-17). As the prophecy continues, the mysterious connection between YHWH's rescue and his judgement is intensified by pictures such as YHWH using his sword 'against my shepherd, against the man who is close to me' (13.7) but also the people looking to YHWH as 'the one they have pierced' (12.10b-14). New Creation motifs are used (14.6-7) as well as Ezekiel's Edenic symbolism of living waters (14.8) to indicate that YHWH will become king over the whole earth (14.9). Jerusalem's security will be accompanied by exodus-like plagues upon the nations that fought against Jerusalem (14.12-15) but with the intention of the survivors of these nations going up year after year to worship YHWH as king and celebrate the covenantal Feast of Tabernacles (14.16-19). The result of this will be even the most ordinary and everyday items in Jerusalem and Judah such as cooking pots becoming 'Holy to YHWH' and the distinction between Jew and Canaanite in the house of YHWH being no more (14.20-21).

## Joel

One of the features of Haggai and Zechariah is their statements about the covenant promises reaching their fulfilment through a fresh outpouring of YHWH's Spirit. We see the Spirit or breath (Hebrew *ruach*) of YHWH referred to throughout the Old Testament. This is initially within the accounts of creation, as God breathes his Spirit into the man to make him into a living being (Genesis 1.2; 2.7). Then, within the stories of YHWH's covenant relationship with Israel, we see the Spirit of YHWH coming, usually for a temporary period, upon a number of Israel's leaders to empower them to bring about his purposes.

It is within the prophecy of Joel that the vision of YHWH's restoration being accompanied by a fresh and permanent outpouring of his Spirit is most developed. Joel speaks of YHWH's judgement necessitating a genuine response of the heart from his people. This is made possible because, as with Israel's apostasy after the exodus, YHWH 'is gracious and compassionate, slow to anger and abounding in love, and he relents from sending calamity' (2.13 cf Exodus 34). The result of this will be YHWH's rescue and, after this, YHWH will pour out his Spirit 'on all flesh' with the emphasis upon the complete inclusion within this of women as well as men and young as well as old (2.28-29). As with earlier prophets, cosmic imagery is used to indicate the heavenly significance of what will happen as Jerusalem and Mount Zion are delivered and everyone who calls on the name of YHWH is saved (2.30-32). The prophecy concludes with judgement upon the nations who had oppressed YHWH's people as his dwelling on Zion is firmly established, the land once again becomes wonderfully fertile, a fountain flows from YHWH's house and Judah's bloodguilt is removed (3.1-21).

## Isaiah 56–66

Like Joel, the last part of the book of Isaiah is usually seen as representing a 'post-exilic' setting. This is partly because elements within are seen to reflect the difficulties of the impoverished post-exilic community and the disappointment of unfulfilled hopes. This is shown in its criticism of Israel's and its leaders' continued waywardness and its call for a more faithful response to YHWH (56.9-12; 57.1-13; 58.1-14; 59.1-15; 65.1-16; 66.3-4).

However alongside these accusations comes the promise that YHWH will come as a warrior to defeat Israel's enemies and bring about his covenant salvation (59.15-21). The prophecy expands upon this with the full manifestation of YHWH's glory in Zion and the coming of nations to this light with their tribute (60.1-22). Whilst some sections continue to present YHWH's salvation as involving his savage vengeance upon the nations (63.1-6) and their resulting servitude (61.5), other parts emphasize the way that foreigners will be included within its blessings if they 'bind themselves to YHWH to serve him' and 'hold fast to my covenant' (56.6 cf 56.3). The Temple itself would become 'a house of prayer for all nations' as he 'gathers still others to them besides those already gathered' (56.7-8). In another specific reversal of Deuteronomy 23, eunuchs who also 'hold fast to my covenant' will go from being excluded to being welcomed into YHWH's temple (56.3-5). Later it goes even further in envisaging that the non-Israelites who enter YHWH's people will even take their place as priests and Levites (66.18-21 cf Numbers 18.1-7; Ezekiel 44.7-9, 15). This inclusion is because at the heart of YHWH's rescue and restoration will be the full reversal of all current oppression of those who are poor and in captivity (61.1–62.12). Those who follow YHWH are frequently called 'servants', indicating that a calling similar to that of 'the Servant' in Isaiah 40–55 has passed to them (56.6; 63.17; 65.8-9, 13–15; 66.14). In the future, they will also all be priests (61.5) fulfilling Israel's vocation to be a kingdom of priests representing YHWH to the world (Exodus 19.6).

The covenantal basis of all of this is clear. Possession of the land forever, and even the smallest becoming a mighty nation (60.21-22), as well as the inclusion of the other nations, recalls the promises made to Abraham (see also 63.16). YHWH's action through Moses and the exodus period (63.11-19) is also recalled as the basis for the action that he will take. As the long book of Isaiah moves towards its close, it combines continuing warnings of judgement to Israel with the promise of the renewal of creation that had always formed the ultimate objective of the covenant climaxing in coming of a new heavens and new earth in which the renewed Jerusalem will take its place (65.17-25). The description of birth occurring without labour pains forms an obvious reversal of Genesis 3.26 (66.7-9) and reinforces the message of the envisaged salvation bringing about the full undoing of the effects of humankind's disobedience upon creation.

## The Psalms

In the Psalms – the worship book of Second Temple Judaism – we also find a similar emphasis upon YHWH's commitment to fulfilling his covenant promises. Earlier we noted the significance of the covenant term 'righteousness' within Isaiah 40–55 and it has a similar profile within the Psalms (e.g. 5.8; 22.31; 33.5; 36.6; 51.14; 71.2; 15-16, 19, 24; 72.1; 88.12; 89.16; 98.2, 9; 103.6, 17; 111.3; 119.40, 142; 143.1, 11; 145.7). Whilst 'righteousness' can be used of Israel's response to the covenant, all of these references in the Psalms use the term to refer to the righteousness of YHWH meaning *his* commitment to fulfilling his covenant purpose.

It is this commitment that forms the basis of the approach to YHWH contained in the Psalms.[31] Some of the psalms emphasize YHWH's great covenant acts of the past such as Psalms 78, 105, 106, 118, 135 and 136 which recall his call of Israel and the victories that he gave them. Others, such as Psalms 46, 48, 76, 95–100, celebrate YHWH taking up his residence in Mount Zion. At a more foundational level, Psalms 19, 65 and 95 display an unshakeable belief in creation's power to praise its maker and be filled with his glory. All of this belief in YHWH's past actions then serves as the springboard for those other psalms which look to the future and YHWH's fulfilment of his promises. Thus the so-called royal psalms – Psalms 2, 18, 21, 72, 110 – have their focus upon the future when, through his anointed king, YHWH will fully establish his rule on the earth. Psalms 24, 46 and 134 likewise look ahead to YHWH one day extending his peace and presence to the whole of the earth. It is this framework – belief in YHWH's covenant acts of past and faith in those of the future – that then allows other psalms such as Psalms 74, 77, 94 and 137 to acknowledge the pain and desolation of the experience of exile and oppression with the refusal to believe that YHWH would abandon his people: 'Have regard for your covenant, because haunts of violence fill the dark places of the land' (Psalm 74.20). Psalm 89 provides a particularly stark combination of belief in YHWH's unbreakable promise to David of an everlasting kingdom, alongside a sober acknowledgement of the reality of exile. Many of the psalms encourage their fallible worshippers to keep the demands of the covenant (Psalms 25.10; 50.16; 55.20; 78.10, 37; 103.18; 132.12) but alongside the strong belief that, whatever appearances might suggest, YHWH will keep his covenant promises forever (Psalms 74.20; 89.3, 28, 34; 105.8, 10; 111.5, 9). The Psalms contain little explicit explanation for how the devastation reflected in so many of them would lead to the righteousness of YHWH they equally proclaimed. But again there are more hints that this will be brought about by suffering, not least in Psalm 22 where its expression of desolation, shame and suffering (22.1-2, 6-7, 16-18) eventually gives way to a shout of triumph (22.22-23, 27–28).

## Ezra

It was around a century after the rebuilding of the Temple that Ezra returned to Judah to continue the restoration of the covenant community. Following its first six chapters which cover the earlier period, chapters 7–10 focus upon Ezra's further restoration of the Temple and the people. This is set in a covenantal framework with an emphasis upon Ezra's descent from Aaron, his status as 'a teacher well versed in the Law of Moses' (7.1-10) and his instructions from King Artaxerxes of Persia to enquire in regard to 'the Law of your God' (7.11-14) and show particular 'diligence for the Temple of the God of heaven' (7.15-24, 27). This duly follows (8.1-36) with Ezra also taking action against the intermarriages that he discovered the Jews had established with their pagan neighbours (9.1–10.17). The actions taken signify the attempt to renew Israel's covenant commitment with a fresh covenant made before God to send away the women and their children (10.3). However the sober ending to the book with its list of descendants of the priests who had been guilty of intermarriage (10.18-44) conveys the clear sense that Israel's full restoration is still awaited.[32]

## Nehemiah

A similar emphasis is seen in the book of Nehemiah. Nehemiah, this time on request, receives authorization from King Artaxerxes to return and rebuild the ruined walls of Jerusalem. The prayer that Nehemiah says before he approaches the king is to YHWH as 'the God of heaven ... who keeps his covenant of love with those who love him and obey his commands' (1.5). Echoing Deuteronomy 28–30, it includes reference to Israel's disobedience towards the laws given through Moses, the consequence of this in exile, and the promise of restoration 'to the place I have chosen as a dwelling for my name', if the people return to YHWH (1.6-9). Nehemiah then returned to Jerusalem and, in the face of considerable opposition from enemies in the land, organized the rebuilding of the city wall and its gates (3.1–4.23; 6.1–7.3). In addition, Nehemiah took measures to support the poor amongst the Jewish people and to challenge any replication of the slavery from which the Jews were meant to have been freed (5.1-19).

The efforts of Ezra and Nehemiah culminated in a covenant renewal ceremony (Nehemiah 8–10). In a manner recalling King Josiah, Ezra read the book of the Law to the people (cf 2 Kings 22; 2 Chronicles 34), leading to a restitution of the Feast of Tabernacles instituted by Moses (8.1-18). This is followed in Nehemiah 9 by a review of Israel's covenant history covering creation (9.6), Abraham (9.7-8), the Exodus and Desert (9.9-21) and settlement in the Land (9.22-31). Throughout this account, the emphasis is upon the faithlessness of Israel in contrast to the constantly forgiving, gracious, compassionate and righteous God. This account ends with the plea for God to keep his covenant of love and reverse the present situation in which they are still slaves in the land given to their fathers, with its abundant harvest going to the kings placed over them (9.32-37). This forms perhaps the most explicit example of the belief that, though a geographical return to the land had occurred, the people of Israel were still very much 'in exile' and awaiting YHWH's return and rescue.

This is reinforced by the manner in which the book of Nehemiah ends. During Nehemiah's second term as governor of Judah, he confronted collaboration between the high priest Eliashib and Tobiah the Ammonite (13.4-9), neglect of the Temple and its Levites (13.10-14), neglect of the Sabbath (13.15-22) and the resurfacing of mixed marriages (13.23-28). Nehemiah invokes the example of similar sin by Solomon – loved by God and made king over all Israel – to indicate the people's continuity with the start of Israel's disastrous path to division and exile (13.26-27 cf 1 Kings 11). Purification is effected by Nehemiah but with the sense of something greater being needed from God to respond to the defilement of 'the priestly office and the covenant of the priesthood and of the Levites' (13.29).[33]

## Chronicles

Another writing responding to this context is the book of Chronicles. Within the unfulfilled context of 'post-exilic' Judah, Chronicles uses Israel's history to keep the covenant hope alive. The foundations for this are laid by the genealogies found in 1 Chronicles 1–9, written to show how the post-exilic community awaiting its redemption were descended from those to whom YHWH had made his covenant promises. From that point on Chronicles covers similar ground to that found in the books of Samuel and Kings, with its most obvious difference being the idealization of David and Solomon. This is done in order to demonstrate the location of Israel's hope in YHWH's promises to David and their implementation through his son. The heavy emphasis upon the Temple is made to draw out the reciprocal link between David establishing the cult of YHWH and YHWH establishing the kingship of David. The function of the Solomonic account (2 Chronicles 1–9) is that of assuring the reader that the eternal character of the dynasty has been secured. This is followed by much more critical accounts of the kings that followed (2 Chronicles 10–36). The focus here is almost entirely upon the kingdom of Judah with 'good' kings such as Asa, Hezekiah and Josiah appealing to 'all Israel' and attempting to redeem the northern tribes. Like Kings, the monarchs are evaluated by their dedication towards the Jerusalem Temple, with emphasis upon its ritual and organization combined with the importance of the inner quality of faith and 'seeking after YHWH' (1 Chronicles 16.11; 22.19; 28.9; 2 Chronicles 15.1-2; 30.18-20).[34]

Chronicles thus played a crucial role in conveying to the post-exilic community that YHWH would fulfil his covenant promises and bring a proper end to the exile. The emphasis is upon theocracy, the establishment of YHWH's rule, reinforced by the inextricable connection between the Davidic dynasty and the Temple. The concentration on temple building as linked with the purposes of the kingdom of God finds its theological conclusion in the restoration edict of Cyrus (2 Chronicles 36.22-23 cf Ezra 1.1-3). This parallels the end of Solomon's reign with the arrival of the Queen of Sheba to marvel at the wisdom and splendour of Solomon's court (2 Chronicles 9.1-12). In the bleak context of post-exilic Judah, the vision presented is that of a united Israel centred on YHWH's presence, with the Gentile rulers also coming to acknowledge him. The message is that YHWH would never withdraw from his covenant commitments and the Temple-structured society ruled by YHWH's anointed leaders is represented as the model for what would one day come. The right response from God's people in the meantime was a faithful and sincere response of the heart to YHWH and the place that symbolized his presence amongst them.[35]

### Esther

Other books produced during this 'post-exilic' period approach its issues from other directions. The book of Esther is set in the Persian capital of Susa and concerns those Jews who had not returned to Israel after the edict of Cyrus. Famously, the book fails to mention YHWH at any point, thus inviting its readers to look for how he is working through the events that it narrates to fulfil his purposes. Its story revolves around the way in which the plot of Haman the Agagite to destroy the Jews is foiled through the bravery of Esther and Mordecai, alongside some crucial providential events. The story is full of moral ambiguities, not least on the part of Mordecai and Esther. But its message appears to be that, however absent the covenant God might seem, YHWH had not abandoned his exiled people. YHWH is at work in the mess of human history – and using the faithfulness of even morally compromised people to take forwards his covenant purpose of redeeming the world.[36]

### Jonah

A rather different challenge is presented by the book of Jonah which also probably comes from this period. Through its story of a rebellious prophet who hates YHWH for loving his enemies and is thrown into the sea as a result, it demonstrates the folly and consequence of Israel's disobedience to her covenant calling. The folly is shown by the comic contrast made throughout the story between Jonah's selfishness and the surprising repentance and humility shown by it pagan characters – firstly the sailors on board the ship in which Jonah tries to escape his calling (Jonah 1.13-16) and later the wicked Ninevites, who are 'overturned' in a manner very different to that expected by Jonah (3.1-10). Jonah's anger at God's compassion towards Nineveh is clearly shown to be a rejection of the covenant when the prophet uses its language to declare: 'O YHWH, is this not what I said when I was still at home … I knew that you are a gracious and compassionate God, slow to anger and abounding in love, a God who relents from sending calamity. Now O YHWH, take away my life, for it is better for me to die than to live' (4.2 cf Exodus 34.6). The message is that Israel, like Jonah, will indeed have to be plunged back into the waters of chaos and undergo a submarine 'death' and 'resurrection' (2.1-9) and a withering of their vine (4.6-7), in order for the fullness of his covenant purposes, particularly for the nations and creation itself (4.10-11), to be realized.[37]

### Proverbs, Ecclesiastes, Job and the Song of Songs

The so-called Wisdom literature within the Old Testament is not usually considered in relation to the theme of covenant. Reference to YHWH's covenant is not found within its books and nor is any mention of the great events that formed the basis of Israel's covenant story. However, in the light of what has already been examined, the contents of the wisdom literature can be seen to fit extremely well within the covenant theme. This is because it is explicitly based upon a relationship with YHWH – 'the fear of YHWH is the beginning of wisdom' (Proverbs 9.10 cf 1.7; 15.33; Job 28.28). Taken as a whole, it can be seen as an exposition of the vocation to be God's genuine humanity.[38] Each of the wisdom books is addressing, in different ways, how to live well within the world that God has made.

Proverbs is practical wisdom based upon belief in YHWH's wise and just ordering of the world. Wisdom is presented as a personified attribute of God woven into the creation meaning that goodness and justice are objective, God-given realities that can and should be accessed and put it into practical action. Hundreds of proverbs sum up the best way to live if health and prosperity are to be achieved.[39]

Ecclesiastes balances this perspective through its frank acknowledgement that the world isn't always predictable and is often difficult to comprehend. This is summed up by the book's constant expression that 'everything is *hevel*'. Rather than 'meaningless', *hevel* refers more to vapour or smoke – something that may look solid but is elusive, confusing and cannot be grasped. The ultimate *hevel* of everything that people chase after means that the best approach to life is that of humility and enjoyment of God's gift of the simple, good things of life.[40]

The book of Job pushes this further by examining God's wisdom and justice in the light of human suffering. Job is a blameless, righteous man who honours God and yet endures terrible suffering. Unaware of this, Job's friends argue, in a series of speeches, that since God runs the world according to justice, Job must somehow be guilty (3–28; 32–37). Eventually Job gives up on his friends and demands an answer from God (29–31). God's response is to reveal the wonder and complexity of the world and how Job cannot possibly comprehend this and therefore pass judgement upon God's actions. The order and beauty of God's world is affirmed but also the way in which so much of this is beyond human understanding (38–41). Job's response is one of humility and repentance expressing the fear of YHWH, and his fortunes are eventually restored.[41]

The Song of Songs adds to this perspective through its reflections upon the mystery of the divine gift of love. Within its eight chapters of love poetry, it celebrates sexual love and attraction through a series of scenes in which a couple are separated and then search for one another. This points to the human desire to know and be known as the most transcendent and yet elusive experience of human life. Through this emphasis upon the elusiveness of love the book also points beyond itself to God's love that will one day be fully experienced as it permeates and transforms his beloved world.[42]

Taken together, the wisdom literature of the Old Testament thus provides greater depth to the calling to God's people to live out their response of faith to his covenant love. In their different ways, each of its books witnesses to trust in God's relationship of love with the world and faith in his commitment to justice is the best way of living within the world and navigating those aspects of it that bring suffering, loss and confusion. The great story of God's covenant from its beginning in creation to its consummation in the new creation forms the bedrock of the wisdom that it contains. This background is largely unstated, perhaps because a major aim of the wisdom literature is to direct YHWH's people to *the manner* in which they live as the primary means of showing their loyalty to the covenant God and fulfilling their calling to be his witnesses to the surrounding world. But it is also because delay in the fulfilment of YHWH's covenant promises brought much greater reflection upon what it meant to live by faith and, in particular, the role of the suffering of YHWH's people within this.

## Daniel

This continues in the book of Daniel. Whilst its setting is the Babylonian exile, most scholars believe the book to represent ancient stories reflected upon within the context of the Syrian oppression of the Jews during the middle of the second century BC (i.e. the Maccabean period). Through its first six chapters, the stories of Daniel and his friends represent the challenge to steady faithfulness to YHWH within a pagan land. Central to this challenge is the vision of the kingdoms of the world eventually being replaced by the everlasting kingdom of Israel's God (Daniel 2). In chapters 7–12, the stories about the individual fortunes of Daniel and his friends make way for more complex accounts of the national fortunes of Israel ahead of her final redemption. A particular feature of this is the apocalyptic imagery they employ. Grotesque beasts represent the oppressive kingdoms of the world, and the sea that they emerge from represents the chaos needing to receive divine order and 'one like a son of man' representing the humanity that the true king, having destroyed the beasts, will eventually vindicate and exalt (7.1-28). Much of this imagery has its foundations in Genesis 1–11, as well as the divine intention for human beings expressed in Psalm 8. The message is that divine order will be restored to the cosmos through the restoration of God's true humanity so that human beings can then fulfil the vocation and mandate given to them in creation.[43]

It is in chapter 9 of Daniel that these themes are explicitly integrated within that of the covenant. Daniel prays about the prophecy of Jeremiah that the desolation of Jerusalem would last seventy years, calling to YHWH as 'the great and awesome God who keeps his covenant of love with all who love him and obey his commands' (9.2-4).

This is then followed by a recital of Israel's covenant history and the appeal for God 'who brought your people out of Egypt' and 'in keeping with your righteous acts' to bring forgiveness and restoration to 'your desolate sanctuary' (9.15-19). As this happens, Gabriel comes to Daniel and reveals that *seventy weeks of years* will occur between the exile and the restoration of Jerusalem with the latter mysteriously connected to an 'anointed one' who will be cut off and the destruction of the city and its sanctuary by 'the people of the ruler' who will 'put an end to sacrifice and offering' and set up within the temple 'an abomination that causes desolation' (9.20-27).

At the heart of the book of Daniel is thus a further development of Isaiah 40–55's emphasis upon *the role of suffering within the fulfilment of God's covenant promises*. The emphasis in Isaiah 53.10 upon the suffering of 'the servant' being somehow sacrificial is reflected in similar sacrificial language within Daniel. The role of the extended exile and its suffering is to enable 'your people and your holy city to finish transgression, to put an end to sin, to atone for wickedness, to bring in everlasting righteousness, to seal up vision and prophecy and to anoint a most holy one' (9.24).

Another significant development within Daniel is its reference to *resurrection*. A time of distress and anguish will simultaneously be a time of deliverance when 'multitudes who sleep in the dust of the earth will arise: some to everlasting life, others to shame and everlasting contempt' (12.2). Earlier we noted how corpses coming back to life was used in Ezekiel as a vivid way of presenting the return from exile and consequent renewal of the covenant and creation. Tom Wright has argued that the context of further oppression and martyrdom caused the metaphor of resurrection to then develop into a more literal hope. Without losing its earlier sense of national vindication, this development of the hope of resurrection spoke more powerfully of the renewal of creation through the complete renewal of God's image-bearing creatures.[44] The book ends with Daniel seeing two men on either side of a river, particularly one 'above the waters', speaking of the time before these events are fulfilled (12.5-7). The period of suffering is described as a time when many are refined as the wicked continue in their ways, followed by a further time beyond the abolition of sacrifice and the establishment of the abomination that causes desolation (12.8-12). But Daniel and his readers are assured that following their patient wait, YHWH's salvation would finally come: 'You will rest, and then at the end of the days you will rise to receive your allotted inheritance' (12.13).

### The 'post-exilic' writings and the covenant

The greatest contribution of the 'post-exilic' literature towards the covenant theme, therefore, lies in its greater reflection on the role that the suffering of YHWH's people would have within its fulfilment. This built upon Isaiah 40–55's presentation of the Suffering Servant, intensified by perplexity over the seeming absence of YHWH during this period and the delay in his fulfilment of the covenant promises. However this only represented a deepening of the call to patient faith and trusting obedience that had always formed an essential part of Israel's response to the covenant. The link between patient faith and suffering, indeed, had already been established within the covenant story through Israel's time as slaves in Egypt (Exodus 2.23-25) and during the desert (Numbers 14), David's time being hunted by Saul (1 Samuel 18–30) and the hardships suffered by the prophets Elijah, Hosea and Jeremiah (1 Kings 19; Hosea 1–3; Jeremiah 11.18–12.6; 15.10-21; 17.14-18; 18.18-23; 20.7-18). In the 'post-exilic' period, this simply becomes more sharply focused as its various writers are forced to reflect more deeply and, from a number of different directions, on the role that such suffering has within the call to faithful obedience of YHWH's covenant people.

Much the same can be said about the greater development of the apocalyptic genre during this time. Greater wrestling with the role of suffering inevitably led to greater reflection upon the unseen spiritual realities standing behind the events being experienced by Israel. This is seen most obviously in Daniel and the apocalyptic sections of Zechariah but also includes the deeper understanding of the power of evil that developed during this time. 'The Satan' emerges as an accuser in the heavenly court (Job 1.6-12; Zechariah 3.1-2) but swiftly becomes an embodiment of the evil afflicting the world and leading its people into sin (1 Chronicles 21.1). The theme of apocalyptic has sometimes been set against that of covenant by biblical scholars keen to present a steady and unfolding understanding of YHWH's activity as being replaced during this period by the expectation of a more dramatic intervention on YHWH's part. This is both unnecessary and unhelpful, especially where it has led to over-spiritualizing of Israel's hope. This hope never became escapist or detached from YHWH's redemption of the created order. The covenant promises remained focused upon a forgiven and restored people possessing the land pledged to them and sustained by a spiritual relationship with YHWH based upon his presence on earth with them. The development of the apocalyptic genre merely reinforced the nature of the victory that needed to be won by YHWH for this fulfilment of the covenant to come about. 'Post-exilic' writings such as Daniel asserted that behind Israel's oppressors stood the real enemy in the form of the powerful spiritual forces of evil that needed to be disarmed and destroyed.[45]

The 'post-exilic' belief in resurrection naturally sprang from this since the greatest weapon possessed by the oppressive empires, and the shadowy powers behind them, was *death*. The defeat of death through resurrection, making possible both vindication and judgement, thus became a central expression of Israel's covenant hope during the bleak centuries under foreign rule that continued throughout this period. But this too was consistent with the earlier development of the covenant and not just because resurrection was anticipated in the ministries of the covenant prophets Elijah (1 Kings 17.17-24) and Elisha (2 Kings 4.8-37; 13.20-21) and Ezekiel 37. The hope of resurrection represented the ultimate form of the fulfilment of the covenant promises made to respond to the problems presented in Genesis 1–11: YHWH's renewed and united Spirit-filled people ruling over his renewed and restored creation.

A final aspect of the 'post-exilic' expression of the covenant faith was its treatment of the mighty empires who were oppressing Israel and their rulers. Earlier we saw that there were two streams of thought in regard to the nations within the prophets: one seeing their *destruction* as a sign of covenant fulfilment and another envisaging their eventual *inclusion* within the covenant blessings. Both streams occur within the same prophecies with little explanation of their reconciliation. This continues in 'post-exilic' writings with the certainty of YHWH's judgement upon the successive world empires (Daniel 2, 7), combined with episodes where their kings turn from their arrogance and folly to acknowledge the lordship of YHWH (Daniel 4.34-37; 6.25-27; Jonah 3.5-9). The latter are intended less as a historical account of what actually occurred than as an expression of the hope that, against all current appearances, YHWH's covenant promise to bless all peoples through Abraham would eventually, somehow, be realized.

## Malachi

Despite the physical return from exile, the covenant, in other words, still awaited fulfilment. This situation, however, would not last forever. The *Jewish* Scriptures end with Chronicles to reinforce the message that the fulfilment of YHWH's covenant promises, most obviously to David, was still awaited and that faithful obedience to the law and attentiveness to the place of YHWH's presence was the appropriate response by his people in the meantime.

The *Christian* ordering of the Old Testament concludes with the book of Malachi for a similar reason. Malachi's prophecy probably comes from the fifth century addressing the context of a covenant awaiting fulfilment. YHWH's continuing commitment to Israel/Jacob is affirmed (1.2-5) but also the continued corrupt response to the covenant from both Israel's priests and people. This is demonstrated by the unacceptable offerings brought to the Temple (1.6-14), the corruption of her priests who by their false teaching 'have violated the covenant with Levi' (2.1-9) and also the way in which the people's faithlessness to one another has profaned 'the covenant of our fathers'. This latter accusation focuses upon the way in which the marriage covenant has been profaned, with seeming reference to both the people's infidelity towards YHWH and within their human marriages (2.10-16). Malachi makes it clear that YHWH is wearied by the irony of their inability to tell good from evil whilst claiming to await the God of justice (2.17).

YHWH's response to this situation is then given: 'I will send my messenger, who will prepare the way before me. Then suddenly the Lord you are seeking will come to his temple; the messenger of the covenant, whom you desire, will come' (3.1). This coming will result in a purifying judgement (3.2-5; 4.1) aimed at continuing the covenant (2.4). In the meantime God's people are summoned to return to YHWH in faith that he will 'throw open the floodgates of heaven and pour out so much blessing that you will not have room enough for it' (3.10). This obedience will be expressed through the people remembering the law given to Moses at Horeb as they await the reappearance of the covenant prophet Elijah to turn the people back to faithfulness 'before that great and dreadful day of YHWH comes' (4.4-6). The book of Malachi, and the entire Old Testament, thus ends by looking ahead to YHWH's fulfilment of the covenant.

4

# God's covenant (part two)

## Covenant fulfilled – the Messiah

### A covenant seeking fulfilment

As the previous chapter shows, the Old Testament concludes with the long covenant story of Israel in search of an ending. This is the context in which we need to understand the words and actions of Jesus of Nazareth and everything that flowed from his ministry.[1] By the New Testament period, the majority of Jews were longing for YHWH, the covenant God, to act and bring about the new exodus that he had promised. This future event was understood to be the real return from exile promised by the prophets and would involve the defeat of Israel's enemies and the re-establishment of YHWH's presence amongst his people. By the first century, the fulfilment of these promises was understood by most Jews as involving the destruction of the nations that were oppressing them, most obviously Rome, and the restoration or renewal of the Temple in Jerusalem. Whilst understandings varied about the way in which YHWH would bring about this fulfilment of the covenant, there was widespread belief that it would involve a messianic figure, with these beliefs closely associated with the reestablishment of the Davidic monarchy. The diversity of belief about a coming Messiah (or Christ) is partly because it formed part of the more fundamental expectation that, when he acted to fulfil his covenant promises, YHWH himself would become king.[2]

As oppression of Israel grew under successive nations, the book of Daniel became a particularly popular source of hope, with its vision of the covenant being fulfilled through the kingdom or rule of YHWH finally triumphing over the kingdoms of the world. The apocalyptic nature of Daniel gave birth to the widespread use of this genre to sustain Israel's hope. The language and style of apocalyptic literature had nothing to do with presenting YHWH's rescue as an escape to heaven. It was instead used to unveil the present spiritual realities involved in Israel's current situation and what would happen as YHWH's rule was established *on earth*. The other significant development during this period, again with critical input from the book of Daniel, was belief in *resurrection*. Central to the hope of most Jews of this period was the belief that YHWH's fulfilment of his covenant promises would involve the raising of the dead, with this resurrection enabling the righteous to receive their vindication. This is the hope that Martha expressed to Jesus when she said of her dead brother Lazarus: 'I know he will rise again in the resurrection on the last day' (John 11.24).

Resurrection spoke particularly strongly of YHWH's justice in a context where savage death at the hands of foreign oppressors was a constant reality. Those who were invested in the status quo, such as the wealthy Sadducees, rejected any idea of resurrection. But for those who longed for YHWH to bring about the new exodus from slavery and real return from exile, belief in a future resurrection, became a major focus of their belief in YHWH's commitment to bring his kingdom rule and fulfil his covenant promises.[3]

It was for these reasons that symbols developed such importance for the Jews during this period. The land itself was an important symbol of YHWH's commitment to fulfil his covenant promises and at the centre of this was Jerusalem and, in particular, the Temple. Whilst most Jews believed the Temple required rebuilding, or at least renewal, when YHWH returned, regular pilgrimage to the existing Temple and participation in its sacrifices represented the commitment to YHWH that was necessary if his promises were to be received. Another crucial symbol was the Torah or Law with obedience to its commands seen as the sign of those whom YHWH would vindicate (or in the language of the covenant, 'declare righteous') when he finally acted to fulfil his promises. Of particular importance were those 'works of the law' such as circumcision, the Sabbath and adherence to food laws which expressed Israel's commitment to staying separate from the pagan nations and sinners whom they assumed would be the objects of YHWH's judgement when he returned to re-establish his presence and his rule. All of Israel's festivals played a role in reminding her of YHWH's covenant story and therefore his commitment to fulfil his promises. The most important of these was the Passover which remembered YHWH's rescue of Israel from slavery in Egypt. But the Passover also looked forwards as well – to YHWH repeating this rescue in a new and more permanent exodus that would finally bring the fulfilment of all the great covenant promises that YHWH had made.[4]

## The covenant fulfilled in the ministry of Jesus the Messiah

The New Testament is determined to show that the coming of Jesus of Nazareth represented the fulfilment of the covenant. This is apparent from its very first chapter which traces the genealogy of Jesus in generations of fourteen from Abraham to David and then on to the exile as a deliberate expression of this fulfilment (Matthew 1.1-17). Crucially, the genealogy includes reference to four Gentile women in Tamar, Rahab, Ruth and Uriah's wife or Bathsheba (1.3, 5, 6). Each of these women, as we saw in the previous chapter, had played a surprising but vital role in the covenant story and, in the light of the coming of Jesus, can be seen as signalling vital aspects of its fulfilment (cf Hebrews 11.31; James 2.25). The 'fulfilment formulae' employed by Matthew (1.22-23; 2.14-15; 2.17-18; 2.23) are then used to add further confirmation that, rather than fulfilling the odd prophecy, the whole of the covenant story was reaching its climax in Jesus the Messiah. Mark, Luke and John all have a similar emphasis with Zechariah declaring in Luke, for instance, that in the birth of his son John, the forerunner of the Messiah, God was remembering 'his holy covenant, the oath he swore to our father, Abraham' (Luke 1.68-79). Of equal importance, however, is the emphasis within the four gospels upon Jesus fulfilling the covenant in a cryptic and hidden manner that no one had expected. This is perhaps the reason why Jesus so rarely used the word 'covenant' during his ministry. Careful analysis of the words and actions of Jesus, however, culminating in his death on the cross, shows the way in which Jesus consciously intended to bring about the climax of the entire covenant story. The Gospels and the rest of the New Testament then seek to reinforce this through the way in which the resurrection of Jesus followed by his ascension into heaven, the coming of the Holy Spirit upon his followers and the calling of the church are represented as vital outcomes of Jesus's fulfilment of the covenant.

Before we turn to Jesus, however, we must comment on the role of John the Baptist. The baptism of John will be covered in more detail in the next chapter. But central to his ministry was John's prophetic role, in continuity with his Old Testament predecessors (Mark 1.2-3, 6; Matthew 3.3-4; Luke 3.4-5), in recalling Israel to the covenant. But John was also more than a prophet. Through gathering people in the Jordan wilderness, where Israel had first entered the land, and leading them through water, John was declaring that the new exodus (and by implication the new covenant) was now occurring. Proclaiming a baptism 'for the forgiveness of sins' announced that Israel's exile was now coming to an end because John was the messenger sent to prepare the way for the long awaited return of YHWH (cf Malachi 4.5f). By declaring that this baptism was one of 'repentance', John further indicated the fresh challenge to 'turn around' that was now being issued to Israel. This challenge, expressed through both John's preaching and his ministry of baptism, was for Israel to recognize that they were not automatically children of Abraham without bearing 'fruits worthy of repentance' (Matthew 3.7-10; Luke 3.7-9). Israel was now on the same level as the pagan nations, needing to repent in the same manner as a proselyte, if she wished to be included within the covenant people of YHWH. It is also significant that, through his baptism, John was offering a forgiveness that, previously, was only accessible through the Temple in Jerusalem. John's major point, however, was to point to the one coming after him and the deeper covenant renewal that he would achieve. This would include both deeper cleansing and fiercer judgement, since the one coming after John would baptize them 'with the Holy Spirit and with fire', as well as judge between those who belonged to God's covenant people and those who did not (Matthew 3.11-12; Mark 1.7-8; Luke 3.16-17).

Like John the Baptist, Jesus of Nazareth appears to have understood his ministry as being in continuity with and forming the climax of the great prophets of the Old Testament. Like the prophets, he proclaimed an urgent message to Israel from her covenant God and, again like the prophets, he lived out this message in symbolic actions. Jesus's own baptism will be discussed further in chapter 6 and there we will see his identification with the new exodus that John had announced as coming. This was reinforced by his period in the wilderness that followed (Matthew 4.1-11; Mark 1.12-13; Luke 4.1-13). After this, Jesus appeared in Galilee, proclaiming that the kingdom of God was at hand (Matthew 4.17; Mark 1.14). The kingdom of God summed up what it meant for the story of Israel to be coming to fulfilment: it spoke of evil being defeated, the covenant being renewed, creation being restored and YHWH returning as king.

It is this that explains Jesus's actions. His calling of the twelve apostles deliberately evoked memory of the twelve tribes and thus represented the reconstitution or restoration of Israel (Matthew 10.1-4; Mark 3.13-19; Luke 6.12-16). Several of Jesus's acts of power were clear recapitulations of earlier covenant episodes. The feeding of the five thousand, for instance, contained overtones of the period following the exodus (Matthew 14.15-21; Mark 6.35-44; Luke 9.12-17; John 6.1-13) and the stilling of the storm (Matthew 8.23-27; Mark 4.35-41; Luke 8.22-25) evoked, not only the exodus, but the earlier stories of Noah and creation itself. Jesus's healings pointed to the healing rule of YHWH at last returning to his people and gathering up those who had previously been excluded. This was also expressed through Jesus's table fellowship with tax collectors and sinners (e.g. Matthew 9.9-13; Mark 2.13-17; Luke 5.27-32). On these occasions, those previously excluded from Israel discovered that they were being accepted into YHWH's people, with Jesus using covenantal language to express this. He thus affirmed that the woman bent double, whom he healed on the Sabbath, was 'a daughter of Abraham' (Luke 13.16) and, after the acceptance and transformation of Zacchaeus, declared 'Today salvation has come to this house, because this man too, is a son of Abraham' (Luke 19.9).[5]

However Jesus did not simply affirm the expectations that Israel possessed. His words and actions brought the covenant story to a climax in a manner that no one had expected. This is the reason that Jesus did so much of his teaching through parables retelling the story of Israel in a manner that was designed to subvert the prevailing understanding of how the covenant would be fulfilled.[6] This also involved redefining the true enemy that needed to be defeated. In the early parts of the covenant story, as we have seen, the enemies of Israel were largely identified as those foreign nations oppressing the people of YHWH, such as the Pharaoh of Egypt. However, as the story continued, a simplistic perspective upon Israel's enemy breaks down. Evil was revealed to be just as present *within* Israel, within even her anointed leaders, most strikingly King David himself. Apocalyptic writings, such as Daniel, had further revealed the spiritual forces operating behind the oppressive enemies of Israel. As we have seen the understanding of Satan as the representation of this quasi-personal force of evil starts to develop towards the end of the Old Testament. This was developed in subsequent Jewish literature. But it was Jesus who decisively presented Satan and the evil running through all human beings, including YHWH's people, as the real enemy that needed to be defeated (Matthew 10.28; 15.1-20; Mark 7.1-23; Luke 12.5). This is the significance of Jesus's exorcisms which indicated the nature of the victory that needed to be won if YHWH's covenant promises were going to be fulfilled (Matthew 12.22-37, 43-45; 15.21-28; 17.14-21; Mark 1.21-28, 34; 3.23-30; 5.1-20; 7.24-30; 9.14-29; Luke 4.31-37, 41; 8.26-39; 9.37-43; 11.14-26).[7] By identifying the deeper enemy that needed to be vanquished, Jesus also signalled the way in which the tensions within the Old Testament concerning the judgement upon Israel's enemies and inclusion of the nations would find their resolution.

It is this which lay at the basis of Jesus's challenge to live as the renewed Israel. In the previous chapter we saw how Deuteronomy 30, and prophets such as Jeremiah and Ezekiel, had said that Israel's return from exile would be dependent upon a renewed heart. Much of the teaching of Jesus, particularly in the Sermon on the Mount, summoned Israel to this deeper faithfulness. This took the form of an intensification of the commandments to fulfil their intention of bringing about wholehearted obedience to YHWH. This was illustrated in the story of the Rich Young Man whom Jesus told that obeying the commandments entailed selling everything that he had and following him (Matthew 19.16-30; Mark 10.17-31; Luke 18.18-30). It is also seen in Jesus's conversation about the greatest commandment, with love of God and loving your neighbour as yourself presented as more important than burnt offerings and sacrifices (Matthew 22.34-40; Mark 12.28-34; Luke 10.25-28).

Two points need emphasis here. The first is the need to avoid understanding Jesus as coming to replace 'an outward approach to religion' with an inward, more spiritual one. It is this misreading that has resulted in many Christians failing to recognize the unity of the Bible's covenant theme and the consequent disjuncture that many have then seen between Jesus and the Old Testament. As we have seen, the covenant always aimed to integrate outward obedience with an inward and spiritual relationship with YHWH. Jesus came to make this integration possible with renewed hearts precisely intended to lead to a visible and outward (as well as inward) obedience. This was shown when Jesus was asked about divorce. Here he used Genesis 1.17 and 2.4 to show that what YHWH had always intended for marriage was becoming possible through the hardness of heart (which had necessitated Moses's permission of divorce in Deuteronomy 24.1-3) now being healed (Matthew 19.3-12; Mark 10.2-12). It was to ward off such misunderstanding of his ministry that Jesus declared: 'Do not think that I have come to abolish the Law and the Prophets. I have not come to abolish them but fulfil them' (Matthew 5.17). Rather than declaring that external obedience no longer mattered, Jesus came to bring that inner renewal of the heart that could result in a righteousness greater than that of the Pharisees and teachers of the law (Matthew 5.20).

The other important point is the need to remember the *aim* of this renewal. The whole purpose of the transformation that Jesus came to bring was to enable his followers to be renewed in that original vocation that YHWH had given to human beings in creation. Every stage in the covenant story had formed part of YHWH's plan to restore human beings as his image-bearers exercising his wise and just rule over creation. This reached its fulfilment in the command of Jesus to be 'the salt of the earth' and 'light of the world' (Matthew 5.13-16). Once again, we need to avoid the tendency to see Jesus as bringing a renewal that was purely inwards and therefore private. The inner renewal that Jesus came to bring to Israel was not only intended to transform his followers outwardly but to result in the renewed vocation of YHWH's people to reflect his sovereign rule over the *world*.[8]

It was this understanding of the covenant vocation that resulted in the challenge that Jesus issued to the manner in which keeping the covenant was understood. As we saw earlier, three of the key symbols of covenant membership for Israel were the Torah/ Law, the Temple and the Land. In each case, these symbols were relativized by Jesus. This was not because they were bad or erroneous, but because the way in which they were being used was working against the very love for God and neighbour that they were given to foster. This was the principal point of the healings that Jesus performed on the Sabbath (Matthew 8.14-15; 12.9-13; Mark 1.21-31; 3.1-6; Luke 4.31-39; 6.6-11; 13.10-17; 14.1-6; John 5.1-18; 9.1-14). He was powerfully demonstrating that the fullness of life to which Sabbath observance pointed was now being fulfilled and that to cling onto such covenant symbols as restrictive, boundary markers could only serve to stifle this life.

This challenge was particularly extended to the way in which Israel's covenant symbols had become symbols of national exclusivity. In the parable of the Good Samaritan (Luke 10.25-37), Jesus showed how apparent loyalty to the Temple and the Torah (represented by the priest and Levite) had ironically become the means of Israel evading the love of neighbour that lay at the heart of the Torah. A new way of being faithful to Torah was to be found instead through a radical love that involved the dramatic redrawing of Israel's boundaries (represented by the Samaritan) and the recognition that loving Israel's God was now to be fulfilled by loving him as the creator of all. Whilst Jesus's mission was to Israel (Matthew 15.24), the significant interactions that he had with Samaritans and Gentiles (Matthew 8.1-11; 15.21-28; Luke 17.11-19; John 4.1-26) signalled the way in which YHWH's covenant blessings were about to burst beyond Israel to the rest of the world (Matthew 8.11).

The most striking aspect of Jesus's ministry was the manner in which he replaced adherence to the covenant symbols of Judaism with loyalty to himself. This was shown when those hearing Jesus's teaching remarked upon its authority, in contrast to that of their scribes (Matthew 7.28). Rather than commenting on his tone of delivery, this was a recognition of the way in which Jesus's teaching was transcending that found in the Torah. Likewise, the forgiveness of sins which Jesus granted was given with an authority that superseded the normal practice of going to the Temple and offering sacrifice (Matthew 9.1-8; Mark 2.1-12; Luke 5.17-26). This was made explicit when Jesus declared that 'one greater than the Temple is here' (Matthew 12.6) and throughout the gospels, we see Jesus speaking and acting in a manner that showed that he was bringing the reality which all of these covenant symbols had been pointing to. This is particularly evident in the first half of John's Gospel with the seven signs performed by Jesus and seven discourses he then speaks, each carefully designed to show vital institutions and feasts associated with the covenant were reaching their fulfilment in him (John 1–10). On several occasions Jesus commended people for their faith (Matthew 8.10; 9.22, 29; Mark 5.34; 10.52; Luke 7.9, 50; 8.48; 17.19; 18.42) meaning their belief that Israel's covenant God was now acting climactically in him.[9]

All of these claims indicate that Jesus saw himself as the Messiah – the coming king whom the prophets had declared would be the means of YHWH fulfilling his covenant and restoring his people. This is most obviously shown by Jesus's entry into Jerusalem and subsequent act of judgement over the Temple (Matthew 21.1-22; Mark 11.1-25; Luke 19.28-48; John 12.12-19). However, cryptic statements of his messiahship can be seen within Jesus's Galilean ministry as well. The role of Jesus's baptism in this regard will be examined in Chapter 6. But the messiahship which Peter eventually confessed at Caesarea-Philippi was prompted by the self-referencing nature of Jesus's kingdom announcement and his exorcisms, which represented the central messianic role of defeating Israel's enemies. The parallel that Jesus made between himself and David pointed further towards this (Matthew 12.1-8; Mark 2.23-28; Luke 6.1-5). References to himself as 'one greater than Solomon' (Matthew 12.42; Luke 11.31) were also an implicitly messianic claim by Jesus, and the welcome that he extended into the people of YHWH is only explicable if Jesus was claiming the representative status of Israel's king.[10]

At a deeper level, the words and actions of Jesus fulfilled the covenant promise of YHWH himself returning to his people. As we saw in the previous chapter, a persistent claim of the prophets was that YHWH would return to Zion and do again what he had done at the exodus. However, whilst Israel's physical return from Babylon had occurred, there had been no point where YHWH's presence had returned in the manner of Exodus 40, Leviticus 9 or 1 Kings 8. Parables such as the Pounds (Luke 19.11-17) and Talents (Matthew 25.14-30) have often been interpreted, however implausibly, as Jesus providing long-distance teaching about his 'Second Coming'. They are better understood as *Jesus interpreting his arrival in Jerusalem as embodying YHWH's return to his people* and their failure to recognize it. This is made explicit when Jesus weeps for Jerusalem 'because you did not recognise the time of God's coming to you' (Luke 19.39-44). Once this is recognized, we again see the ways in which this is evident in Jesus's earlier ministry. Jesus's call of the disciples (Mark 1.16-20) is revealed as a recapitulation of YHWH's call of Abraham (Genesis 12.1) and references Jesus made to himself as, for instance, 'the bridegroom' (Matthew 9.14-15; Mark 2.18-20; Luke 5.34-35; John 3.29 cf Isaiah 54.5-8; 62.4-5; Jeremiah 31.31-33; Ezekiel 16; Hosea 1–3; Joel 1.8) and 'shepherd' (John 10.14 cf Isaiah 40.11; Ezekiel 34; Micah 7.14; Psalm 23.1f; 28.9; 79.13; 80.1; 95.7; 100.3), recognized as similar appropriation of YHWH language for himself. By giving instructions on his own authority, Jesus represented not only a new Moses but, more fundamentally, YHWH himself. It is particularly striking that, when interpreting the Ten Commandments, he felt able to replace the first three commandments concerning loyalty to YHWH, with command to 'follow me' (Matthew 19.16-30; Mark 10.17-31; Luke 18.18-30). This is the context in which to understand the deepest significance of Jesus's description of YHWH as 'Abba' or 'Father' (e.g. Matthew 11.25-27; Luke 10.21-22; John 14–17). Israel had been described as YHWH's son (Exodus 4.22) with this designation then focused, in a representative sense, on the Messiah (2 Samuel 7.14; Psalm 2.7, 12; 89.26-27). Without losing this messianic sense, Jesus's use of 'Father' for YHWH also spoke of his vocation to do and be for Israel what YHWH alone could do and be. As Tom Wright has commented, 'He would be the pillar of cloud and fire for the people of the new exodus. He would embody in himself the returning and redeeming action of the covenant God.'[11]

The result of Jesus's prophetic role, his messianic self-understanding and his calling to embody the return of YHWH to Zion was the judgement he proclaimed upon the city and Temple. In a similar manner to prophets such as Jeremiah, Jesus declared that Israel's covenant God would use the pagan nations to exercise his judgement upon his people. Again like the prophets, this message was not only spoken but symbolically enacted through his cursing of the fig tree and then his action in the Temple (Matthew 21.10-22; Mark 11.11-25; Luke 19.45-48 cf John 2.1-11). Following hints of it earlier in his ministry (Matthew 7.24-27), this judgement was then proclaimed in the parables Jesus told after he entered Jerusalem and made explicit in the extended discourses that he spoke (Matthew 24.1-51; Mark 13.1-37; Luke 21.5-36). The apocalyptic imagery in these discourses has convinced many that they were, at least in part, speaking about 'the end of the world'. This rests upon a mistaken interpretation of their genre. They were instead using standard Jewish apocalyptic language to draw out the spiritual significance of concrete political events. Such language had previously been used in Isaiah 13 to speak about the downfall of Babylon. Shockingly, Jesus now employed a metaphor previously used about the destruction of the greatest pagan city in the Old Testament to pronounce the destruction of YHWH's chosen city of Jerusalem. YHWH, as the prophets had declared, would return in judgement. This would not be, as expected, through judgement upon the pagan nations but through judgement on his own covenant people. Horrifically, the fourth beast of Daniel facing judgement at the hands of YHWH was being revealed to be Israel itself.

The reason for this judgement was connected with the earlier critique that Jesus had made of what Israel's covenant symbols had become. Instead of being a light to the Gentiles, Jerusalem and the Temple had become symbols of the idolatrous national assertion that eventually took Israel into its disastrous revolt against Rome in AD 66. This was what Jesus was referring to when he said, quoting Isaiah 56.7 and Jeremiah 7.11: 'It is written: My house shall be called a house of prayer but you are making it into a den of brigands' (Matthew 21.13; Luke 19.46). The fruit that Israel should have produced, and whole point of the covenant, was YHWH's blessings passing via Israel to the nations. However none of this was evident, hence Jesus's earlier curse upon the fig tree. This failure had been brought to a climax by Israel's rejection of Jesus and his message that the way to respond to pagan oppression and disarm evil was with love. This is why recognizing 'the things that made for peace' was coupled with Israel's failure to recognize 'the time of your visitation from God' (Luke 19.41-44). One of the functions of Israel's king was to restore the Temple by destroying its pagan influences in a similar manner to Josiah (2 Kings 23). Many expected the Messiah to achieve this in much the same way as Judas Maccabeus when he entered Jerusalem in 167 BC and cleansed the Temple of its defilement by the pagan Syrians. The kingship of Jesus the Messiah was expressed instead in judgement upon the collusion with pagan evil, particularly pagan violence, which the Temple had come to represent. It was this which would lead very soon, Jesus proclaimed, to its complete destruction at the hands of the very pagan nations from which Israel had become indistinguishable.[12]

Within the same discourses that Jesus proclaimed this judgement upon Jerusalem, he also spoke of YHWH rescuing those who were faithful to him. As the judgement upon Israel revealed her to be the fourth beast of Daniel, so Jesus would receive the vindication that revealed him to be YHWH's true humanity – the Son of Man (Matthew 24.26-44; Mark 13.24-27; Luke 17.22-37). Rather than describing Jesus's Second Coming, this language about 'the coming of the Son of Man' remains true to its original use in Daniel, describing the heavenly vindication that the Son of Man will receive from the Ancient of Days when the oppressive beasts are being destroyed. This vindication would include all those belonging to the Messiah/Son of Man who would form the renewed people of YHWH.[13] The counter-Temple movement that Jesus had formed around himself during his ministry was thus revealed to be part of the process by which the promises made about Jerusalem would be transferred to Jesus and his people. The presence of YHWH – previously encountered through the Temple – was to be gained through Jesus the Messiah and then God's Holy Spirit and would be with his people forever (Matthew 18.19-20). The forgiveness of YHWH – previously mediated through the Temple – was to be received through Jesus, his people (John 20.23) and their ongoing forgiveness of one another (Matthew 10.21-33). And the covenant love of YHWH – previously symbolized by the Temple – would be received through fellow members of the renewed people of YHWH showing that they were disciples of Jesus by loving one another (John 13.34-35). With the coming of Jesus the Messiah, all of the previous symbols of Israel's covenant relationship with YHWH were thus revealed to be obsolete. Partly because they had become so corrupted – but mainly because what they imperfectly foreshadowed had now arrived in its entirety.

This includes one of the greatest covenant symbols – the land. In contrast to the Torah and Temple, Jesus said little about the land. This has led many to assume that this is because the physical promises under the old covenant were replaced by Jesus with more spiritual ones. Specifically that the promise of the land was replaced by 'the hope of heaven'. This has had particularly unfortunate implications for understanding sacraments. It represents, however, a major misunderstanding. Like the other covenant symbols, the land was not discarded but relativized by Jesus as he indicated that it would be transcended by YHWH's rule being extended to the whole of the earth. Admittedly, the major emphasis of this is within the period following Jesus's ascension, as the Acts of the Apostles forms an enlarged version of the book of Joshua by recording the conquest of 'the whole world' by God's people. However we still see this development being signalled during Jesus's earlier ministry. Rather than being limited to the land of Israel, Jesus moves freely amongst 'Gentile' territory such as Decapolis, Tyre and Sidon (Matthew 8.28-34; 15.1-28; Mark 5.1-20; 7.24-31; Luke 8.26-39). He also visits Samaria (Luke 9.51-56; John 4.1-42). In the Beatitudes he speaks of 'the meek' inheriting, not the land of Israel, but 'the earth' (Matthew 5.5). In an ironic statement of truth, the Pharisees announced with concern that 'the whole world has gone after him' (John 12.19). Once again, it forms part of YHWH's covenant promises coming to fulfilment in Jesus in a manner that so transcended their earlier forms as to make them obsolete. Everything that the covenant represented was now reaching its fulfilment in the coming of Jesus the Messiah.

Not before, however, a final great battle took place. If one of the principal tasks of the Messiah was to restore or rebuild the Temple, the other great task was to defeat Israel's enemies. Earlier we saw how Jesus redefined the real enemy as the evil known as Satan running through all human beings, including Israel, and the way involved a different perspective upon her traditional enemies. The temptations near the start of Jesus's public ministry formed an initial victory over Satan (Matthew 4.1-11; Mark 1.12-13; Luke 4.1-13), as did the exorcisms that he performed. Jesus taught his followers that the way to combat evil was to 'love your enemies and pray for those who persecute you' (Matthew 5.43-48; Luke 6.27-28) and to go to the furthest distance possible to avoid returning evil (Matthew 5.38-42; Luke 6.29-30). Central to following Jesus was the calling to embrace the suffering that would result from this with the warning that this involved taking up your cross (Matthew 16.24-27; Mark 8.34-38; Luke 9.23-26) and undergoing a similar baptism of suffering to that which Jesus would undergo (Matthew 20.20-28; Mark 10.35-45).

It was through his own suffering and death that Jesus would fulfil his calling to be Israel's Messiah and win the decisive victory over evil. He himself would embody to the fullest degree possible the agenda that he had mapped out for his followers. No one had previously expected suffering, let alone death, to be part of the Messiah's role. Once Peter had acknowledged Jesus as Messiah (Matthew 16.13-20; Mark 8.27-30; Luke 9.18-21), however, Jesus began speaking about his death with attempts to deflect him from this vocation understood as part of ongoing battle against Satan (Matthew 8.21-23; 17.22-23; 20.17-19; Mark 8.30-33; 9.30-32; 10.32-34; Luke 9.22, 43–45; 18.31-34). Crucially, this suffering and death would involve Israel's religious leaders handing him over to be killed by the Gentiles. Jesus's use of the term 'Son of Man' when referring to his suffering, death and subsequent vindication indicates his belief that this would bring about Daniel's vision of the kingdom of God triumphing over the kingdoms of the world. Isaiah 40–55 appears to have been equally vital in shaping his call to fulfil the role of the servant whose suffering and death would bring about the new exodus, the end of Israel's exile and all the blessings of the new covenant associated with this. The anointing at Bethany provided another cryptic illustration of the link between his messianic role and approaching death (Matthew 26.6-13; Mark 14.3-9; John 12.1-8).[14]

As mentioned, actual references by Jesus to the covenant are infrequent, probably because of the gradual and cryptic manner in which he chose to reveal how it would meet its fulfilment through his ministry. This changed, however, on the night before he died when Jesus shared a Passover meal with his disciples and drew onto himself Israel covenant traditions by declaring: 'This is my blood of the (new) *covenant* which is poured out for many/you for the forgiveness of sins' (Matthew 26.28; Mark 14.24; Luke 22.20; 1 Corinthians 11.25). Through these words, Jesus made explicit reference to both the words of Moses at Sinai, 'This is the blood of the covenant' (Exodus 24.8), the 'new covenant' looked for by Jeremiah (31.31), and 'the blood of my covenant with you' in Zechariah 9.11. Jesus's reference to 'the forgiveness of sins' spoke of how Israel's long period of exile would be brought to an end through his death. This symbolic meal and Jesus's earlier action in the Temple were intended to interpret one another. Both indicated that Jesus was now superseding the Temple with his approaching death replacing its sacrifices. The significance of Jesus choosing the Passover festival rather than the Day of Atonement to illustrate this was that his death, like the exodus, would be a great, *one off* moment achieving the victory necessary for YHWH's people to move on and receive the inheritance that he had promised them.

The link between Israel's judgement and the suffering and death of Jesus is important in understanding the way in which the latter fulfilled the covenant. As we saw in the previous chapter, the whole purpose of the covenant was to undo the sin of Adam and enable YHWH's blessing to come to the world. Much of the mystery within the covenant story lay in YHWH's chosen people swiftly seen to be just as infected with sin as the rest of the world. From the prophets onwards, however, it starts to become evident that YHWH will somehow use judgement upon Israel as part of his covenant plan. As we saw in the previous chapter, Isaiah was commissioned by YHWH to preach precisely so that Israel would fail to understand and thus ensure that they would not turn and be healed (Isaiah 6.9-10). This problematic verse is quoted by Jesus in all three synoptic gospels when he explained why he spoke in parables (Matthew 13.10-15; Mark 4.10-12; Luke 8.9-10). The majority of commentators seek to avoid the most obvious sense of these words, seeing it as inconceivable that either Isaiah or Jesus could have intended to prevent Israel from repenting. However this starts to make sense once we recognize that, having failed to be a light to the nations, Israel was called to bear YHWH's judgement *precisely so that this judgement could then be carried by her Messiah.* This appears to have been Jesus's understanding of how he would fulfil his calling to be Israel's Messiah. Having pronounced YHWH's judgement upon Israel, Jesus believed that he was called to share in this judgement by fulfilling the role of the Isaianic servant. A number of Jesus's sayings expressed this organic link between his death and the fate of Israel such as his statement about judgement coming upon both the green tree and the dry (Luke 23.27-31). By sharing in the judgement that he had pronounced upon Israel, Jesus believed that he could be Israel for the sake of the world and defeat evil once and for all.

The gospels go onto describe the suffering and death of Jesus in a manner that reinforces this understanding. All four gospels place a major emphasis within their passion narratives upon the kingship of Jesus being fulfilled through his death on the cross. The notice declaring Jesus to be 'the King of the Jews' which provokes such great mockery is fulfilled precisely through his suffering and death. Two incidents at the moment that Jesus died are particularly used by the synoptic writers to show how his death formed the fulfilment of the covenant. The first of these is the Temple curtain being torn in two, symbolizing that the Temple was now obsolete (Matthew 27.51; Mark 15.38; Luke 23.45). The second is the confession of the Gentile centurion. Within Matthew and Mark, the centurion declares: 'Truly this man was God's Son' (Matthew 27.54; Mark 15.39), whilst in Luke he praises God and declares that Jesus was righteous (Luke 23.47). Somehow, the gospel writers are declaring, the death of Jesus had finally achieved what was necessary for YHWH's covenant blessings to flow to the Gentiles. The long story of YHWH's covenant had reached its fulfilment in the death of Jesus the Messiah.

The subsequent *resurrection* of Jesus was the event that showed that this had indeed occurred. The accounts of Jesus's resurrection within the four gospels are remarkably unvarnished in theological terms, pointing to their nature as carefully preserved primary accounts (Matthew 28.1-28; Mark 16.1-8; Luke 24.1-49; John 20.1–21.25). They reflect the surprise that what most of Israel had expected to happen to all of YHWH's people at the end of time had happened instead to one Israelite in the middle of time. However it was not long before Jesus's followers were understanding his resurrection as the evidence that he was indeed Israel's Messiah and the one through whom YHWH's covenant promises could at last be received. His resurrection represented the first day of God's new creation (John 20.1) and thus the goal of the whole covenant process. Reflection upon Jesus's ministry then made greater sense of his earlier words about his embodying of God's presence in a way that was greater than everything in the covenant story that had gone before. This is particularly evident in John's Gospel with its emphasis on the fullness of YHWH's glory being revealed through Jesus (John 1.14; 2.11; 8.54; 11.40-44; 12.23, 28, 41; 13.31-32; 14.13; 17.1, 4-5, 22, 24). At the end of Matthew's Gospel the risen Jesus issues the Great Commission to baptize and teach all nations in the context of his recapitulation and embodiment of YHWH's regular covenant promise to be with his people (Matthew 28.16-20). This recalls the description of Jesus earlier in the gospel as Immanuel, meaning 'God with Us' (Matthew 1.23 cf Isaiah 7.14).[15]

As they further unpack and explain the significance of Jesus, the subsequent New Testament writers unite in interpreting his ministry in covenantal terms – the covenant fulfilled. But the covenant theme very much continues. The new community brought into being through the death and resurrection of Jesus inherit through the Messiah (through being 'in Christ') the blessings of the covenant and are charged with bringing them to the world.

### The covenant fulfilled in the Acts of the Apostles

Inheritance of the covenant blessings by the followers of Jesus is very apparent in the Acts of the Apostles. Acts begins its account of the spread of Christianity during its first thirty years with the ascension of Jesus into heaven (1.1-12) followed by the coming of the Holy Spirit at Pentecost (2.1-13). The association of Pentecost with the giving of the law at Sinai suggests that this event was now being recapitulated with Jesus, like Moses, ascending into heaven so that he could return with a law that could now be placed within human hearts.[16] Peter's speech at Pentecost made it clear that the outpouring of the Holy Spirit and the preceding resurrection and ascension of Jesus represented the fulfilment of God's ancient promises, with the calling then made to his hearers to 'repent and be baptised' so that they could receive the covenant blessings of forgiveness of sins and the gift of the Holy Spirit (2.14-41). Following the healing of the man at the temple gate, Peter proclaims that the God of Abraham, Isaac and Jacob had glorified his servant Jesus (3.13) and declares his listeners as now 'heirs of the prophets and of the covenant God made with your fathers' (3.25). The communal life of the earliest Christians is presented as God's restored covenant community, with their oneness 'in heart and mind' fulfilling Jeremiah 32.39 and Ezekiel 11.19 (4.32), and there being 'no needy person among them' fulfilling the Jubilee legislation in Deuteronomy 15.4 (2.45; 4.34). The judgement that comes upon Ananias and Sapphira (5.1-11) recalls the earlier judgement upon the sons of Aaron (Leviticus 10.1-2), Achan (Joshua 7), Uzzah (2 Samuel 6) and Uzziah (2 Chronicles 26) and presents the community of Jesus's followers now functioning as God's Temple-like place of holiness.[17]

The claim that God's covenant promises were now being fulfilled through the community belonging to Jesus Christ posed a very direct challenge to the existing symbols of covenant membership. Acts depicts the early Christians maintaining reverence for the Temple (2.46; 3.1; 5.12), and respect for Jewish traditions, alongside words and actions that asserted that God was now acting in Jesus Christ in a way that superseded everything that had gone before. This explains the conflict between the followers of Jesus and the Jewish authorities from early on in Acts, as the latter recognized that the key covenant symbols that they upheld were being relativized by the Christian movement (4.1-31; 5.17-42).[18]

This conflict culminates in the arrest of Stephen, following accusations that he was speaking against the Temple and the law and saying that 'Jesus of Nazareth will destroy this place and change the customs Moses handed down to us' (6.9-14). The speech that Stephen makes in his defence takes the form of a retelling of the covenant story. Starting with the call of Abraham, Stephen affirms God's promise of the land to Abraham's enslaved descendants and his giving of the covenant of circumcision (7.1-8). He then focuses on the story of Joseph, highlighting the way in which Joseph was rejected by his brothers, only for God to use this as the means of making him ruler over Egypt and being able to feed them (7.9-16). A similar theme continues through Stephen's retelling of the story of Moses. Moses grows up outside of Israel, is rejected by his people and yet is still called by God to be their rescuer and deliverer (7.17-36). Even after the rescue from Egypt, the rejection of both Moses and God continued with the idolatry the Israelites committed in the desert (7.37-43) and which accompanied the Tabernacle being established under Moses and carried into the land from Joshua through to David (7.44-46). Stephen's speech then reaches its sudden climax as he declares that, rather than David, it was the ambivalent Solomon who built a house for God, despite the impossibility of the creator of heaven and earth being contained in one (7.47-50). He then rounds on the Israelites as 'stiff-necked people' with 'uncircumcised hearts and ears'. Just like their 'fathers' who had rejected the prophets, Stephen declares that his listeners have constantly resisted the Holy Spirit, betraying and murdering that one whose coming the prophets had predicted and, whilst receiving the law, they have not obeyed it (7.51-53).

Stephen's speech gives a great deal of insight into how the early Christians began to understand the covenant story and its symbols in the light of the coming of Jesus Christ. The theme of the speech is that the fulfilment of God's promises had to work through his people's constant opposition and distortion of his purposes. Whilst circumcision, the prophets and the law had all been from God, Israel's constant resistance to God's messengers had completely undermined the covenant they represented. Stephen's speech implied that the same was true of the Temple, with the truths that it was meant to point to about God's heavenly sovereignty over all the earth undermined by Israel's refusal to accept Jesus Christ. The Temple's relativized status as the place where the divine presence can be encountered becomes particularly clear as Stephen declares that he can 'see heaven open and the Son of Man standing at the right hand of God' (7.54-56). Already furious, this prompts his hearers to stone him to death (7.57-60). This, and his plea for their forgiveness (7.59), then makes Stephen a model of the godly suffering of Jesus's followers that becomes a key theme throughout Acts.[19]

As Acts continues, we see something similar with the other key covenant symbols of the land, the law and Jewish ethnic identity, as the covenant bursts out of the categories that had previously contained it. Back at the start of Acts, the disciples asked Jesus if, at this time, he was going to restore the kingdom to Israel. The answer they receive is that, whilst the time scale remains with the Father, the disciples would receive the Holy Spirit to be Jesus's witnesses 'in Jerusalem, and in all Judea and Samaria and to the ends of the earth' (1.6-8). Now that the covenant had been fulfilled through Jesus's death and resurrection, in other words, it was time for the ancient promises about the expansion of God's blessings to be fulfilled as his rule was brought from Israel to the nations. The choice of Matthias to replace Judas within the Twelve then completes the reconstitution of Israel, which forms the necessary preliminary before this expansion can occur (1.12-26). This takes places in stages.

At Pentecost, the effects of the Tower of Babel begin to be reversed as the Holy Spirit enables Jews 'from every nation under heaven' to hear God's wonders proclaimed in their own native languages (2.1-12). Following the death of Stephen, the expansion begins in earnest as the followers of Jesus are scattered and proclaim his word. The first place that this happens is Samaria as Philip wins converts and they are baptized into the name of Jesus, although initially without the reception of the Holy Spirit that the baptized Jews had received at Pentecost (6.1-13). This duly takes place once Peter and John arrive and place their hands on the Samaritans, with the unusual delay in their reception of the Spirit seemingly to ensure that this expansion of God's people is understood to be growing out of the Twelve, rather than separately from this symbol of the reconstituted Israel (6.14-25). Further expansion then takes place through the ministry of Philip as an Ethiopian eunuch is told the good news of Jesus and is also baptized (8.26-40). As with the crippled beggar in 3.1-9, this represents the inclusion of those that the covenant had previously excluded. This is signalled by the eunuch's focus upon the suffering servant in Isaiah 53. As we noted earlier, the sacrifice of the servant in Isaiah 53 leads to the renewal of the covenant in Isaiah 54 and the renewal of creation in Isaiah 55. This process is now extended with the inclusion of the previously excluded foreigners and eunuchs spoken of in Isaiah 56, so that they too can now 'hold fast to my covenant' (Isaiah 56.1-8).

All of this forms the prelude to the momentous process by which the Gentiles were finally incorporated into God's people, chiefly through the ministry of Paul. Paul's conversion is narrated three times in Acts (9.1-19; 22.1-21; 26.1-23), with a major emphasis upon his calling to take the good news of Jesus to the Gentiles, as well as the people of Israel (9.15; 22.21; 26.17-18). Before that takes place, however, we hear about the conversion of the Gentile centurion Cornelius through the ministry of Peter, following the latter's dramatic vision of God overturning the food laws that separated Jews from Gentiles (10.9-16). Peter's conviction that 'God does not show favouritism but accepts men from every nation who fear him and do what is right' (10.34-35) is reinforced by Cornelius and his associates receiving the Holy Spirit as Peter preaches to them. This causes Peter to recognize that no one should keep them from being baptized with water (10.44-48). Once this is reported back to the other apostles, they accept that 'God has granted even the Gentiles repentance unto life' (11.1-18). The key role of Peter, rather than Paul, at the beginning of this process is probably emphasized to stress that, whilst most Gentile mission was undertaken by those outside of the Twelve and the Jerusalem church, these leaders were still central to its establishment. As with the Samaritan believers in 8.14-25, Luke sees it as crucial to emphasize that the Gentiles were being incorporated into the one, covenant family of God, rather than forming a separate entity. This is again emphasized through the key role that Peter and James later have in the Council of Jerusalem in 15.1-35, which further ratifies the Gentiles' membership of the church.

It is nonetheless from the church at Antioch in Syria, rather than Jerusalem, that the expansion to the Gentiles mainly proceeds through the three missionary journeys that Paul and his companions undertake (13.1–14.28; 15.36–18.22; 18.23–21.16). In each town that they visit, they generally first proclaim the good news to the Jews, turning to the Gentiles once the Jews have rejected their message. It is in the former context that Paul speaks on the Sabbath in the synagogue at Pisidian Antioch, giving an exposition of how the covenant story of Israel reached its fulfilment in the coming of Jesus Christ.[20] Starting with the election of Israel, Paul speaks of God's successive provision during the exodus, the wilderness period, the conquest, the judges and finally the monarchy in order to show how the culmination of this was God bringing Jesus, descended from David and witnessed to by John, to be their promised saviour (13.16-25). He appeals to his 'brothers' as 'children of Abraham' to recognize how the actions of those in Jerusalem who condemned and killed Jesus represented the fulfilment of the prophets (13.26-29). God's action in raising Jesus from the dead is then presented as the fulfilment of the promise made to their fathers and, in particular, those scriptural statements made in the Psalms and Isaiah about David (13.30-37). The climax of his speech is Paul's exhortation to his hearers to recognize that, through Jesus, the forgiveness of sins had been proclaimed and the opportunity to 'be justified from everything you could not be justified from by the law of Moses'. He finishes with the danger, spelled out by the prophet Habbakuk, of rejecting the unexpected action of God (13.38-41 cf Habakkuk 1.5). Following the dismissal of the congregation, we are told that many Jews and converts to Judaism were urged by Paul and Barnabas 'to continue in the grace of God' (13.43). Whilst this could mean the exhortation to maintain the interest that they had just shown, it is more likely that it means that these Jews were being urged to continue in the grace that God had constantly displayed through the covenant story that Paul had narrated and which had now been brought to its surprising climax in Jesus Christ.

It was the following Sabbath that the Jews reacted strongly against Paul and Barnabas's message, causing them to pronounce that, in fulfilment of Isaiah 49.6, they were now turning to Gentiles. The Gentiles make a positive response to this and a pattern begins in Acts whereby acceptance of the good news of Jesus by many Gentiles is accompanied by jealousy and anger about this from many Jews. Once again this anger is prompted by a relativization of a key covenant symbol; in this case, the special status accorded to Jewish ethnic identity. Twice during his speech at Pisidian Antioch, Paul distinguishes between 'Men of Israel'/'Children of Abraham' and 'you Gentiles who worship God'/'you God-fearing Gentiles' (13.16, 26). This was probably to highlight the ethnic distinction that was being abolished as people were now declared righteous through Jesus Christ rather than keeping the law of Moses (13.39). Two key symbols of Jewish separation from Gentiles within the law were now particularly giving way. One of these, highlighted particularly in the Cornelius episode, was the regulations regarding food laws and table fellowship with Gentiles, and the other was the requirement for those joining the People of God to be circumcised. The abolition of these symbols as signifying membership of the covenant was deeply contested by many Jewish Christians (11.2-3; 15.1) with some declaring that 'unless you are circumcised, according to the custom taught by Moses, you cannot be saved'. Dispute about this results in the council held in Jerusalem at which the different views are expressed. Peter declares that since God made no distinction between Jews and Gentiles when he gave the Holy Spirit and purified their hearts by faith, it would be wrong to impose upon the Gentiles 'a yoke that neither we not our fathers have been able to bear' (15.7-11). Following testimony from Barnabas and Paul about what God had done amongst the Gentiles, James then uses a quotation from Amos 9.11-12 to endorse the full acceptance of Gentiles into God's people (15.12-18). James's judgement, conveyed by letter to the Gentile churches, is that their turning to God should not be made difficult by burdens placed upon them (15.19, 28). Whilst not specifically stated, this clearly referred to full adherence to the law, and most obviously circumcision, not being required from Gentile converts to Christianity.

However Luke is still keen to portray the early Christians as full of respect for Jewish traditions. The same judgement of James told the Gentile Christians to abstain from food polluted by idols, from sexual immorality, from the meat of strangled animals and from blood (15.20, 29). Various explanations have been offered for these elements of the law being retained. But the most convincing is that which takes note of the reason that James himself gave: 'For Moses has been preached in every city from the earliest times and is read in the synagogues every Sabbath' (15.21). Now that keeping the law and particularly circumcision were no longer the markers of who was within the covenant, maintenance of these four stipulations formed the way in which Gentile Christians could express their love and respect for their Jewish brothers and sisters and therefore hold the one church together. The principle of Christians being justified (i.e. declared righteous) through faith in Christ, rather than works of the law, had not been compromised. But concessions had nonetheless been made to express respect for the ancient versions of the covenant that the Jews so valued and, by so doing, to express the deep value of the Jewish Christians themselves within the one church.

As Acts continues, this emphasis is maintained, particularly in the portrayal of Paul. In fact we see Paul going out of his way to express his solidarity with his fellow Jews. This involves him circumcising his travelling companion Timothy (16.3) to avoid giving offence to the Jews, going first to synagogues (13.14; 17.2-3; 18.4-5) or other places where Jews prayed (16.13) and continuing himself to observe Jewish rituals (18.18), festivals (20.16) and respect for the priesthood (23.2-4). The last section of Acts details Paul's imprisonment, near misses with assassination and the various trials that endured following the accusations that he was seeking to undermine the law of Moses amongst the Jews and desecrate the Temple. Luke, however, is careful to record that the very incident that precipitated this was Paul seeking to show respect for his Jewish heritage and that there was no basis in the accusation that he had taught Diaspora Jews to turn away from the Mosaic law and not circumcise their children or that he had offended against Temple custom (21.20-29). Throughout the various hearings, Paul is concerned to show how everything that he had done was consistent with the law and prophets rather than in any way undermining them (24.10-21). Rather than abandoning the faith of 'our fathers', Paul is proclaiming the resurrection that brings this to fulfilment. The climax of the book is Paul reaching Rome and summoning the Jewish leaders to make a similar defence of his actions as 'he declared to them the kingdom of God and tried to convince them about Jesus from the law of Moses and the from the Prophets' (28.17-23).

Despite this, Acts also contains a strong emphasis upon how closed the Jews generally are to the message that the covenant has come to fulfilment in Jesus. Some Jews respond positively but, like the earlier preachers, Paul receives consistent opposition from his Jewish hearers (13.45; 14.2, 19; 17.5; 18.6; 28.24-25). The overall rejection of his message by Israel is symbolized by the Temple gates being immediately shut after Paul is dragged out of the building (21,30). These emphases are partly to explain the judgement that Luke sees as inevitably approaching for the Temple and nation of Israel. However quotation of Isaiah 6.9-10 near the end of Acts (following its similar prominence in the Synoptic Gospels: Matthew 13.10-15; Mark 4.10-12; Luke 8.9-10) suggests that something more significant in the covenant process is also at work, with God actually closing the hearts, eyes and ears of Israel. Like Paul in Romans 9–11, Luke appears to be implying that Israel's inability to hear the gospel and consequent rejection of her Messiah is paradoxically vital to the fulfilment of God's covenant.

This links to another prominent feature of Acts in the continuing calling of God's people to suffer as the process by which God's fulfilment of the covenant is implemented through the good news of Jesus Christ being taken to the ends of the earth. This is made clear by not only the constant imprisonments (5.17; 12.3), martyrdoms (7.54-60; 12.1-2) and other afflictions (14.19; 16.22-24) but also the explicit message about the necessity of suffering for Jesus's followers that is proclaimed (9.16; 14.22; 20.23). This is particularly drawn out in the last section of Acts as the powers of evil combine in all of their various forms as they seek to thwart Paul's intention to proclaim the gospel in Rome. These take the form of assassination attempts on Paul (21.31; 22.22; 23.12-22; 27.42), the corruption and incompetence of officials (24.26; 25.9) and then, climactically and recalling the earliest chapters of Genesis, the waters of chaos threatening to engulf him (27.6-44). In a final flourish he is even confronted with a serpent (28.3-5 cf Genesis 3.1f)! It is in the midst of the storm that Paul receives a divine revelation that he and his companions will endure to stand trial before Caesar (27.23-24), and in its very last line, Acts presents Paul in Rome preaching the kingdom of God and teaching about the Lord Jesus Christ 'openly and unhindered' (28.31). The clear message is that just as earlier parts of the covenant story had seen God's people passing through water to safety, so the advance of the gospel 'to the ends of the earth' requires a similar process from God's new covenant people.[21]

## The covenant fulfilled in Paul's letter to the Romans

Nowhere in the New Testament is the fulfilment of the covenant in Jesus Christ set out more clearly than in Paul's letter to the Romans. As Tom Wright has shown, the letter forms Paul's fresh and detailed exposition of the Old Testament covenant story showing how all of its apparent tensions and problems met their surprising resolution in the coming of Jesus Christ.[22] If, as Wright claims, the presenting cause for the letter was the Gentile Christians in Rome sitting lightly to their Jewish heritage and disparaging their Jewish brothers and sisters, it shows that the tendency to detach Christianity from its covenantal moorings began very early indeed. Paul's response is to show how authentic Christianity, including the key issues of *holiness* and *unity*, is completely grounded in a carefully worked-out covenant theology, drawn from a thorough and daring reinterpretation of the Scriptures. This is signalled near the start of the book when Paul declares that 'in the gospel, a righteousness from God is revealed, a righteousness that is by faith from first to last, just as is written "The righteous will live by faith"' (Romans 1.17).

The early sections of Romans particularly focus upon the problem of how God could fulfil his 'righteousness'/'covenant faithfulness', once Israel, as the supposed bearer of his solution to the plight of the world, failed to live up to this calling. The basic problem was that Israel turned out to be as caught up in sin as the rest of the world and a large part of this failure was Israel's desire to establish a 'righteousness' *exclusive to Israel* (the meaning of the phrase 'a righteousness of their own' that Paul later uses in 10.3). As a result the nations intended by God to be blessed through Israel actually blasphemed God because of her (2.24). Added to this, Israel's possession of the covenant law simply confirmed her true status as uncircumcised, since the circumcision that mattered and made someone a Jew inwardly was a circumcision of the heart (2.25-29). The law revealed that, just as much as the pagan nations, Israel was trapped under sin (3.9-20, 23 cf 1.18-32). Paul is therefore totally frank about the unresolved nature of the covenant story by the end of the Old Testament. Given that Israel had so grievously failed in her vocation, how could God's righteousness – understood as both his commitment to work through his chosen people of Israel to rescue the world and his impartiality in regard to the other nations – possibly be upheld?[23]

From this point, Romans reveals God's surprising solution. God's righteousness had been upheld, Paul moves on to proclaim, and the tensions in the covenant story finally resolved, by God revealing this 'righteousness' through the faithfulness (to his covenant purpose) of Jesus as Israel's Messiah (3.21-22a). Paul's explanation of the relationship between the events surrounding Jesus and what had gone before is very carefully expressed. Whilst this righteousness revealed in Jesus the Messiah is thus 'apart from the law', Paul states that the law and the prophets nonetheless testified to it. The firmly covenantal nature of the rescue is reinforced by the terms he uses to describe it. Jesus's death has brought about redemption (i.e. freedom from slavery) and atonement, implying that Jesus is the reality to which the Exodus and the Temple had been signposts (3.24-25a).

Wright has described the death of Jesus the Messiah as 'the climax of the covenant' since, according to Paul, it both dealt with the problem of sin and finally enabling Gentiles, as well as Jews, to enter the single people of God (3.25b-31). None of this, Paul says, nullified the Law because the gospel of Jesus Christ had revealed that God had always intended it to be fulfilled, not by works, but through the faith that declared Jews and Gentiles to be part of God's people on a completely equal basis.[24]

The covenant theme then continues in Romans 4 with Paul's exposition of the story of Abraham to show that God's intention in making the covenant was always to bring in the nations by faith. Paul's major point is that, according to Genesis 15.6, Abraham was declared righteous by God on the basis of his faith, with the sign and seal of circumcision only following later in Genesis 17 (4.1-10). This means that circumcision cannot be necessary to belong to Abraham's family and that Abraham is the father of all, both circumcised and uncircumcised, who have faith (4.11-12). Paul understands the promise to Abraham regarding the land of Canaan as merely an advanced picture of God's blessing, asserting that Abraham's offspring will actually inherit the whole world (4.13). He also draws out the continuity between Abraham's faith that God would give his 'good as dead' body a son, which God credited to him as righteousness, and the same righteousness that is credited to those who believe that God raised Jesus Christ from the dead (4.17-25).[25]

From this foundation, Romans proceeds to build a picture of the Christian life in which all of God's covenant promises are coming true. Temple language is used to speak of the access to God and hope of his glory that suffering Christians have by faith (5.1-5). God's love is seen as revealed to its fullest extent in his sending of the Messiah to die for those who were still sinners, reconciling them to God and guaranteeing their future salvation (5.6-11). The whole purpose of the covenant is then recalled as Paul shows how the trespass of Adam which brought sin and death received its solution in the righteousness of Jesus the Messiah which brought grace, righteousness and life to those who received it (5.12-19). Many of Paul's Jewish contemporaries would have seen the arrival of the law under Moses as the decisive covenantal solution to sin. Paul, however (anticipating his discussion in chapter 7), declares that the law merely intensified Israel's sinful state, preparing for God's grace in Jesus the Messiah to abound even more (5.20-21).[26]

The theme of covenant fulfilment continues in Romans 6–8 as Paul retells the story of the exodus, the receiving of the law and the inheritance of Canaan in the light of the death and resurrection of Jesus. In response to the question of whether God's abounding grace encouraged its recipients to sin, Paul invokes the language of the exodus to picture baptism into the Messiah's death and the hope of resurrection as bringing about a similar passage from the slavery to sin that must not be returned to (6.1-23). Paul then deals in Romans 7 with the law that Israel received after the exodus and its mysterious role in God's covenant plan. Wright has argued that the 'I' in this chapter is Israel as Paul describes the role that the law played in intensifying sin within her (7.13 cf 5.20). Paul exonerates the law calling it holy, good and just and affirming its intention to give life. Israel is also exonerated (7.17, 20). The problem lay instead in *sin* which, in a similar manner to Adam in Eden, seized the opportunity provided by the commandment to bring death. Israel may have delighted in God's law (7.22 cf Psalm 19, 119) and wanted to obey it, but she found that the law only served to accuse her of sin and even kindle it within her (7.5, 7–8, 23). Rescue from this predicament finally came, however, through God sending Jesus the Messiah to die 'in the likeness of sinful man' so that sin could be condemned and the righteous requirements of the law met within those no longer living according to the sinful nature but according to the Spirit (8.1-4). From Paul's perspective, the Jewish law thus had a terrible but necessary role in God's covenant plan. It locked up his chosen people of Israel under sin *but precisely so that this sin could then receive its proper condemnation in Israel's Messiah.*[27]

The rest of Romans 8 then describes how, in consequence of this, all of God's ancient covenant promises have found, and will find, their fulfilment in the Messiah and the Spirit. Having died to sin in the Messiah, God's people now have the very same Spirit that raised Jesus from the dead living within them. It is this which enables the requirements of the law to be fulfilled within them bringing the life that the law always promised to give (8.5-13). God's covenant promise to dwell amongst his people and make them his children (Exodus 4.22; Hosea 11.1) is also fulfilled by his Spirit of sonship coming within them and enabling them to cry 'Abba, Father' (8.14-16). It is this status as God's children that leads to their promised inheritance, with their present shared suffering with the Messiah (similar to the Israelites time in the wilderness) leading to their sharing in his glory through their future resurrection and victorious rule over totally liberated creation (8.17-39).[28]

Paul's interpretation of the covenant continues in Romans 9–11, prompted by the need to explain the rejection of Jesus Christ by the majority of Israel and the role of this rejection within the covenant plan. His first move is to state his love for his brothers and the uniqueness of the revelation that Israel had received (9.1-5). From that point on, however, Paul uses the covenant story to show the deeper complexities involved in God's election. This involved choice *within* Abraham's family as well, demonstrated by Isaac and Jacob being 'children of the promise', rather than Ishmael and Esau (9.6-13). The story of Moses gives further indication of God's sovereign choice to harden some for wrath and others for mercy (9.14-24) and this is reinforced by Hosea and Isaiah's pronouncements about God's people (9.25-29).

Paul then applies this to his contemporary situation as Gentiles flooded into God's family by faith in Jesus the Messiah, whilst Jews largely turned their back on this. The problem, according to Paul, was that the Jews had tried to make their unique possession of the law, rather than faith, into a badge of righteousness/covenant membership. This, he then argues, had made the Messiah into the stumbling block for Israel spoken of by Isaiah and made Israel miss the righteousness/covenant membership from God that he came to bring and the Messiah's nature as both the goal of the law and the end of the temporary role that it had possessed (9.30–10.5). Paul then states how Deuteronomy 30, with its great covenantal promises of the end of exile and a fresh act of grace bringing God's word to people's mouths and hearts, had been demonstrated by people through confessing with their mouths that Jesus is Lord and believing in their hearts that God raised him from the dead. Using Isaiah 28.16 and Joel 2.32, Paul reinforces how this saving faith is open to everyone because the same Lord is Lord of both Jews and Gentiles and blesses all who call on him (10.5-13).[29]

From this point, Paul goes into more detail in Romans about the actual role of Israel's failure to believe within God's covenant purposes. He starts by using Isaiah 52.7 to show how his preaching to the Gentiles wasn't being disloyal to Israel's traditions but fulfilling them (10.14-16). Paul then deals with Israel's relative failure to respond using a succession of Old Testament passages to build towards the remarkable point that *God's hardening of Israel was all part of the mystery of the covenant plan of enabling God's salvation to come to the Gentiles*. This, in turn, would arouse Israel to envy, leading to the salvation of some of them (11.7-15). Illustrations like the olive tree are then used to show that God's purposes in this regard are yet to be completed (11.16-24). Paul's point is that the Gentile Christians in Rome must not be arrogant. They need to recognize God's enduring love for Israel, continue in the faith that is for everyone rather than slide into their own version of elitism and accept with gratitude the mysterious wisdom of God binding Israel for a time so that 'all Israel' (i.e. God's complete Jew plus Gentile family) might receive mercy (11.25-29).[30]

The practical application of this covenant theology in the remaining chapters of Romans centres upon Paul drawing out the implications of all of this for how the one covenant community of Gentiles and Jews now needed to live in response. Much of this involves encouraging the Jewish and Gentile Christians in Rome with their differences of conviction and practice to accept and bear with one another (12–16). Paul then concludes the main section of the letter with a number of Old Testament quotes to back up his declaration on the vital point of the entire covenant process that he has been expounding: 'For I tell you that the Messiah has become a servant of the Jews on behalf of God's truth to confirm the promises made to the patriarchs so that the Gentiles may glorify God for his mercy' (15.8-9).[31]

Others of Paul's letters contain a similar emphasis upon Jesus as the fulfilment of the covenant. The Corinthian correspondence is seemingly directed to largely Gentiles churches but Christ is still described as 'the Passover lamb' (1 Corinthians 5.7) and the Israelites of the exodus as 'our fathers' (1 Corinthians 10.1). In his second letter to Corinth Paul declares that all God's promises are given their 'Yes' (i.e. their fulfilment) in Christ (2 Corinthians 1.20). Within Ephesians, perhaps the most panoramic theological perspective provided by Paul, those 'excluded from citizenship in Israel and foreigners to the covenants of the promise, without hope and without God in the world', have now 'been brought near through the blood of Christ' (Ephesians 2.12-13).

In chapter 2 the striking parallels across the New Testament between baptism into Christ and the Old Testament covenant episodes were noted – with respect to Noah, to Abraham and circumcision, and to Moses. We also saw the parallel use of Old Testament covenant imagery of washing, sealing, anointing, promise, inheritance, redemption and the marriage metaphor. It seems overwhelmingly clear that the new covenant is strikingly similar to, and continuous with, the old. The supreme benefit for its people is their being brought by God's grace, through election, redemption and adoption, into a community that is progressing towards God's purpose for his image-bearing creatures of ruling over his new creation. The conditions are that this promise is accepted and worked out in a life of Spirit-led faith and obedience that declares that Jesus is Lord and is particularly marked out by a similar pattern of redemptive suffering. All of this is a wonderful amplification and fulfilment of the covenant within the Old Testament rather than any sort of radical departure away from it.

However, there are passages in the New Testament that speak of striking contrasts and discontinuity between the old and new covenants. We have already looked in detail at Paul's letter to the Romans and how its examples of this should be understood. But there are other examples as well which need to be carefully studied and understood.

## Discontinuity between the old and new covenants explained: Paul's second letter to the Corinthians

2 Corinthians 3 is perhaps the most striking example of this. In this passage Paul declares that the old covenant is of the letter and brings condemnation and death, but the new covenant is of the Spirit and brings righteousness and life (3.6). At first glance these comments can appear rather dismissive and derogatory about the old covenant. Paul's overall purpose here, however, as throughout 2 Corinthians, is to show how openly God's glory is displayed through the human weakness of his ministry. As part of his argument, Paul refers to Exodus 34 and the glory that was present in Moses when he came down from Sinai but which had to remain veiled because of the condition of the Israelites' hearts (3.7, 12–14 cf Exodus 34.29-34). The same condition meant that

the old covenant was equally veiled for Jews in Paul's day when the law was read in the synagogue (3.15). This is why it brought death rather than life. As we saw earlier Paul makes a similar point in Romans 7 when he talks about the law/commandment being holy, righteous, good and spiritual but leading to death because of Israel's sinful nature. Whilst Paul does see the glory of the new covenant as surpassing the fading glory of the old, the primary reason for this is because, through Christ, the veil separating the people from God's glory has now been removed (3.16). The difference between the old and new covenants is that the Spirit has now brought the change necessary for human hearts to receive God's glory (3.17). Paul's point is that this glory is supremely revealed in the strength through weakness that he is able to display quite openly in his apostolic ministry and which is evident in all human beings being further transformed into God's likeness through his Spirit (3.18).[32] This provides further witness to the central role that the suffering of God's people has under the new covenant, an emphasis that grows very obviously from the Old Testament and is also strongly present in the Acts of the Apostles, Philippians, 1 Peter and Revelation.

### Discontinuity between the old and new covenants explained: Paul's letter to the Galatians

Paul's letter to the Galatians is another part of the New Testament that can also be seen as emphasizing major discontinuity between the old and new covenants. Within it, Paul makes a passionate argument and appeal for Gentile Christians not to have to submit to the Jewish law, particularly circumcision. The epistle is full of strong language with Paul contrasting this 'yoke of slavery' with the freedom found in the gospel (5.1) and declaring that 'a man is not justified by observing the law but by faith in Jesus Christ' (2.16). From the Reformation onwards, Galatians has often been interpreted as Paul's opposition to those seeking to contribute towards their own salvation, rather than relying on the grace of God received through faith alone. Even when earning salvation through obeying the law is recognized as a major distortion of the Old Testament's teaching, this understanding has still contributed to a sense of strong disjuncture between the old and new covenants. The gospel of Jesus Christ has been understood as replacing 'the wrong kind of religion' rather than something growing organically from the faith of Israel.

With the advent of the so-called New Perspective on Paul, the recognition has come that much of this interpretation is mistaken.[33] Rather than facing a situation similar to that of the sixteenth-century reformers, the issues Paul faced in Galatia were those insisting that ethnic boundary markers, such as circumcision, were still needed to mark out the covenant people of God. At the heart of the gospel for Paul, by contrast, was the conviction that, because of the death and resurrection of Jesus and the coming of the Spirit, membership of the people of God was now open to everyone with baptism/faith in Christ now being the sole markers of those justified (declared righteous) as part of God's one covenant people.

However, it is crucial to note the way in which Paul locates this development within a very coherent Old Testament covenant theology. Central to his argument here are the original covenant promises made to Abraham that 'all nations will be blessed through you' (3.8), Abraham himself being declared righteous through believing/placing his faith in God (3.6) and particular importance being attached to the promise being made to Abraham 'and his seed' (3.16, with the single 'seed' rather than 'seeds' indicating God's future purpose to make one single covenant people in Christ). Paul then goes on to say that, rather than setting any of this aside, the introduction of the law (through Moses), 430 years later, possessed a particular role in enabling the promises of the Abrahamic covenant to go forwards. Part of this was through the law acting as a temporary guardian or child-minder but also, more mysteriously, through its role in actually bringing the covenant curses upon Israel (3.10-12). This process was crucial in enabling her Messiah to then redeem Israel from this curse through taking it upon himself (3.13), meaning that the blessing given to Abraham could then be given to the Gentiles (3.14). Here Paul's thinking is similar to that we saw in Romans where he describes the law as being given 'to increase the trespass' (Romans 5.18) resulting in Israel's plight under the law (Romans 7) but which then enabled sin to be passed onto the Messiah and condemned (Romans 8.3).[34]

Paul in Galatians therefore sees the Mosaic law as having a vital but temporary role in the covenant process. But that role had now been completed, and any attempt by Christians to maintain the ethnic boundary markers such as circumcision was to turn their back on the freedom they had gained through Jesus and return to slavery.[35] Once again Paul's thinking here is completely grounded in Old Testament covenant story as he uses the story of Abraham's two sons to compare the two covenants (4.21-31 cf Genesis 16, 21). Jews at that time would have seen themselves as very much descendants of Sarah's son Isaac and thus as inheritors of the covenant promises that Isaac carried.

Paul argues instead that it is actually the slave woman Hagar and her child Ishmael who represent the Sinai covenant. This is because Ishmael was born 'according to the flesh' rather than through any promise of God and into a slavery similar to that which Paul has already shown being brought about by the law (4.23-25 cf 3.23–4.3). Hagar in the covenant story, Paul declares, stands for Sinai in (pagan) Arabia and corresponds to the present city of Jerusalem 'because she is in slavery with her children' (4.25).

Sarah, by contrast, as 'the free woman' represents 'the Jerusalem that is above' with her son Isaac, unlike Ishmael, born 'as the result of a promise' (4.23). This means that all those marked out by faith in the Messiah are, like Isaac, 'the children of promise' (4.28). Within the original story, Isaac was mocked by Ishmael, and Hagar and Ishmael were eventually sent away by Abraham so that the inheritance could belong to Isaac alone (Genesis 21.8-20). Paul uses this to parallel the Galatian situation when he says, 'The son born in the ordinary way persecuted the son born in the power of the Spirit' (4.29). But his major point is that, like the expulsion of Ishmael, those in slavery to the law cannot share in the inheritance that comes to the children of the promise (4.30-31).[36]

In the rest of the letter, Paul shows being 'children of the promise' leads to the growth of God's fruitful covenant community. Now that the Messiah has brought freedom, marks of the flesh such as circumcision (or indeed non-circumcision) have no value, with any continuing emphasis upon them only leading to a fall from God's grace and also divisiveness within the Christian community. Faith, on the other hand, leads to the fruit of the Spirit within those who, through belonging to the Messiah, have crucified their sinful nature (5.22-26). This will then show itself in meaningful and practical Christian care for one another as an expression of the new creation they have become part of (6.1-18).[37]

Overall, therefore, Paul's letter to the Galatians rests upon a completely coherent theology of the covenant theme within the Old Testament and its fulfilment in Jesus Christ. Paul's treatment of it is highly sophisticated, particularly when it comes to the mysterious role of the Sinai covenant and the law in enslaving Israel so that sin could be dealt with through her Messiah. But this happened, he believed, precisely in order to allow the promises of the Abrahamic covenant to proceed to fulfilment. This is summed up when he declares: 'You are all sons of God through faith in Christ Jesus, for all of you who were baptised into Christ have clothed yourself with Christ. There is neither Jew nor Greek, slave not free, male nor female, for you are all one in Christ Jesus. If you belong to Christ, then you are Abraham's seed and heirs according to the promise' (3.26-29).

## Discontinuity between the old and new covenants explained: The letter to the Hebrews

Another New Testament book making a strong contrast between the old covenant and the new covenant is the letter to the Hebrews. The occasion of the letter appears to have been the temptation facing Jewish Christians to retreat back into the rituals and practices that had characterized their Judaism before they came to faith in Jesus Christ. They were particularly drawn to those expressing their connection with the sacrifices being offered in the Temple in Jerusalem. This is probably because these Christians were facing the threat of persecution from their fellow Jews unless they did so. Hebrews responds with a sustained exposition of the superiority of the new covenant over the old. In section after section the writer seeks to show how what came before Jesus was partial, incomplete and now obsolete in the light of what the death and exaltation of Jesus had achieved. Hebrews uses the term 'better' more than all the other New Testament books put together and, in every case, it is in order to draw a contrast between the ministry of Jesus through the new covenant and what had gone before.

It is nonetheless important to recognize that this is because, like the rest of the New Testament, the writer of Hebrews sees the old covenant as brought to fulfilment and completion in Jesus Christ. The most obvious sign of this is the number of Old Testament quotations throughout the letter and, in particular, the way in which these are used. The writer is not unaware of the stories regarding Jesus's earthly ministry (e.g. 4.14; 5.7-8; 13.12) but prefers to use quotations from the Old Testament Scriptures to speak about what Jesus represented and accomplished. This shows his belief in the continuity of the covenant story. Its earlier stages are rendered obsolete, not because they were wrong or misguided, but *because their role in anticipating the fuller revelation of God in Jesus Christ had now been superseded by his coming.*

This is evident from the very start of Hebrews. Whilst God had spoken to their forefathers, through the prophets, in 'many and various ways', this process had now reached its climax with him speaking by his Son (1.1-2). Jesus is described as 'the radiance of God's glory' and 'exact representation of his being' (1.3) to contrast him with the more partial revelations that had gone before, and a sustained contrast is then made between the Son and the angels to emphasize Jesus's superiority over the law that the angels had revealed (1.4–2.18). A similar contrast is made between Jesus and Moses, making it clear that Moses's ministry as a servant in God's house was preparatory for that of the Son over God's house (3.1-6). The writer then uses Psalm 95 to make it clear that the promise of rest after Israel's time in the wilderness was a hope still being sought and only to be found through holding firmly to Christ (the second Joshua/Jesus) and obeying his word (3.7–4.13).

The major theme through the next section of Hebrews is that of the high priesthood of Jesus (4.14–8.6). The exhortation to persevere in the Messiah continues (5.11–6.12) with the letter encouraging its recipients to copy Abraham's patient faith (6.13-15). But the basis for this now extends to God fulfilling his ancient promise to send a priest to achieve in perpetuity the mercy and grace that Israel's Levitical priesthood symbolized but could only bring about in part and imperfectly. The priesthood of Jesus achieved this through his being fully human (and therefore sympathetic to human weakness like the Levitical priests), yet without sin, and through the obedient suffering that made his priesthood perfect/complete and thus the source of eternal salvation (4.14–5.10). The writer then proceeds to reflect upon the mysterious Old Testament figure of Melchizedek to show that God had always intended to provide a better priesthood (5.6, 10 and 6.20; 7.1-28). The reason that this was needed was because the Levitical priesthood, established by the law, was unable to bring perfection/completion, hence its description as 'weak and useless' (7.11, 18–19). The priesthood of Jesus, however, is far better. Partly because it was established by God's oath but also because the indestructible life of Jesus means that his is a permanent priesthood, able to save completely, because he lives forever to intercede for his people (7.15-25). Rather than offering sacrifices day after day for his own sins, and then for the people's sin, this holy and blameless priest sacrificed once and for all when he offered himself (7.26-28). Jesus's priesthood is also superior because it is served in the true Tabernacle, established by God in heaven, rather than the copy and shadow of this, established on earth by Moses (8.1-6).

This leads into the next section of the letter and its sustained emphasis upon the superiority of the new covenant over the old or first covenant (8.7–10.18). Jeremiah 31.31-34 is quoted in full to back up the assertion that the coming of the new covenant was necessary because of the faults within the first covenant, which was now obsolete and about to disappear (8.7-13). The writer then describes the regulations for worship in the earthly sanctuary established by the old covenant, using the separation of its outer and inner rooms as an illustration of its weakness. The high priest entered just once a year into the inner room, alone and never without blood offered for his sins and that of the people. These sacrifices, however, were not able to cleanse the conscience of the worshippers, representing external regulations applying only until the time of the new order (9.1-10). This time had arrived with the coming of the Messiah who not only entered into the greater and more perfect heavenly Tabernacle but entered by his own blood, rather than that of goats and calves, thus achieving a cleansing of consciences that had not been possible before (9.11-15).

As the writer unpacks the significance of Jesus's death, we see further emphasis upon his fulfilment of what the sacrifices under the old covenant had pointed to, but been unable to effect. Just as a will requires the death of the person making it to come into effect, so the first covenant was not put into effect without the blood constantly used to cleanse everything within the Tabernacle, and without which there was no forgiveness (9.16-22). However, if the earthly copies needed such purification, the heavenly sanctuary required something better with the Messiah appearing before God's presence and offering his own blood once and for all to do away with sin (9.23-28). From this, the writer then extrapolates that the law was only a shadow of the good things to come, rather than the realities themselves. The need for its sacrifices to be repeated, and their inability to remove guilt from the worshippers, pointed to their nature as a reminder of sin, rather than something that could actually remove it (10.1-4). Psalm 40.6-8 is then quoted to show that, rather than the sacrifices and offerings required by the law, it was a human life doing the will of God that represented the real thing that God wanted and which was found in the bodily sacrifice that Jesus made (10.5-10). The exposition of the new covenant concludes by showing the contrast between the priests standing day after day to offer the sacrifices that could never take away sins and Jesus the priest who, having offered for all time, one sacrifice for sin, now sits down at the right hand of God. Jeremiah's prophecy is then quoted again to reinforce the deep, internal change within God's people that the new covenant has brought (10.11-18).[38]

All of which forms the basis of the appeal that then follows to the Hebrews in 10.19-39 to display full commitment to Jesus and to continue to persevere in faith. The basis of this appeal is the blessings that the new covenant has brought: the full entry into God's presence, a great priest over the house of God (i.e. the church), complete assurance of faith, hearts sprinkled to cleanse them from an evil conscience, and bodies 'washed with pure water'. The Old Testament terminology used to describe these blessings shows the writer's belief that the new covenant represented the fulfilment of the ancient covenant story, rather than a radical departure from it. Critical language is used of the old/first covenant, not because the writer regards it as a bad thing but because *it was always intended to be provisional and a signpost to the realities that it symbolized*. The negative statements are made even more necessary by the pressure upon the letters' recipients to revert to these imperfect models when the reality to which they pointed had now arrived. The writer is not saying that before Jesus came, God's grace was ineffective and that no one knew or trusted God. He is declaring that the grace experienced by God's people was reliant upon what their covenant practices imperfectly foreshadowed. As with Paul in Galatians 4, the full arrival of God's grace in Jesus Christ has now changed everything, meaning that ongoing reliance upon the earlier, provisional models of the covenant was now a rejection of God's grace. This is the reason for the severe warnings about the dangers of falling away found within Hebrews (5.11–6.12; 10.26-31).

This is reinforced by chapter 11 and the account of 'the ancients' commended for their faith. The writer is encouraging the Hebrews to pursue a similar faith in what they do not see. But in the process, we see an emphasis upon the faith of all of these Old Testament characters heading towards the same hope which awaits the letter's recipients. This is most obvious in the case of Abraham who is described as 'looking forward to the city with foundations whose architect and builder is God' (11.10). However the writer says that all of those who responded with faith to God – Abel, Enoch, Noah, Abraham and those that followed – were 'longing for a better country – a heavenly one. Therefore God is not ashamed to be called their God, for he has prepared a city for them' (11.16). The writer develops this further by presenting Abraham's offering of Isaac as faith in God's power to bring resurrection (11.17-19) and reasserts the hope of resurrection, particularly in reference to those who went through appalling suffering for their faith (11.35). This leads into an emphasis on the suffering of Jesus (12.1-3) and an encouragement to the recipients of the letter to persevere through their own suffering (12.4-13) in order to inherit that same hope that all the people of God down the ages had been seeking.

The hope established by the covenant will be examined in the next section. But another contrast between the first/old covenant and the new covenant is established by the writer in 12.18-28. In a similar manner to Paul in Galatians 4.24-27, the writer distinguishes between the Israelite's experience of Mount Sinai and the hope of Mount Zion, the heavenly Jerusalem. Referring to Exodus 19, the holiness of Mount Sinai is presented as terrifying and unapproachable (12.18-21), in contrast to the joyful, cleansed assembly enjoying the presence of God on Mount Zion (12.22-24). The point being made is that the blood of Jesus Christ has achieved an access to God that was not possible through the Mosaic covenant. A contrast is then drawn between the sprinkled blood of Jesus (achieving forgiveness) and the blood of Abel in Genesis 4.10 (crying out for vengeance) implying, in a similar manner to Paul in Galatians and Romans, that the law had served to trap Israel under sin rather being able to actually deal with it. Another comparison then follows as rejecting the warning on earth (under the old covenant) is compared to the even greater danger of rejecting him who warns from heaven (under the new) (12.25-29).

As the letter reaches its conclusion, we see further indications of the context of Hebrews with its recipients urged to be strengthened by grace rather than ceremonial foods (13.9). The latter probably refers to Jewish meals expressing solidarity with the Temple in Jerusalem and its sacrifices. The recipients are instead urged to follow Jesus who 'suffered outside the city gate' and bear a similar disgrace by going to him 'outside the camp', because rather than having an enduring city here 'we are looking for the city that is to come' (13.11-14). The destruction of Jerusalem spoken of by Jesus is clearly in mind here, with the city itself included within the earlier, provisional parts of the covenant which were now passing away, as it reached its fulfilment in Jesus Christ. The unity of the covenant however is emphasized in the final statement made in Hebrews about the death of Jesus when the writer refers to it as 'the blood of the eternal covenant' (13.20). The message of the letter is that God always planned creation and covenant to meet their fulfilment in Jesus Christ. If the creation itself is now revealed to have been effected through him (1.2), the implication is that God's previous acts of grace through the covenant were through him as well, with their apparent forms now revealed as merely signposts pointing to Jesus Christ. It is this unity of the covenant that is expressed as the writer declares that 'Jesus Christ is the same yesterday, today and forever' (13.8).[39]

But the blessings and conditions of the covenant are not changed as the old becomes the new. The partial merely gives way to the complete and promise to fulfilment. It is particularly important not to read Hebrews through a Platonic lens that sees the letter as disparaging the old covenant for being too physical and promoting in its place a non-physical understanding of salvation. There is no doubt that the letter has often been read that way, leading to the view that the new covenant of Jesus Christ is completely different in its nature from the old covenant, replacing the former's concept of an earthly salvation with the more spiritual 'hope of heaven'. This a serious misunderstanding which ignores its references to the thoroughly *physical* hope of resurrection (6.2; 11.19, 35). The explanation for the earthly versus heavenly contrast in Hebrews lies instead in the letter's incarnational emphasis upon Jesus as the Son of God bringing the full life of heaven to earth, rather than the incomplete and partial versions of the old covenant that only pointed towards this joining of heaven and earth.[40]

## The mystery of Jesus Christ as the fulfilment of the covenant

The new covenant is new because after centuries of 'promise', there is now 'fulfilment' through the coming of Jesus Christ. In his letter to the Ephesians, Paul does present the gospel of Jesus Christ as a mystery 'which was not made known to men in other generations as it has now been revealed through the Spirit to God's holy apostles and prophets' (3.5). The following verse explains, however, that 'this mystery is that through the gospel the Gentiles are heirs together with Israel, members together of one body, and sharers together in the promise in the Messiah Jesus' (3.6). The newness of this mystery of Christ therefore refers not to a *new* promise made by God but rather to everyone now being welcomed through Jesus the Messiah into a single people that could inherit his ancient promises. Gentiles, previously in the main excluded, were now able to become, through Jesus, as fully members of God's covenant community as Jews. This then takes its place, alongside the permanent assurance of forgiveness and permanent reception of the Spirit, as the 'new' aspects of the covenant.

However, the nature and benefits of the eternal covenant, which reaches its fulfilment in Jesus the Messiah, remain the same. It retains its sole basis in the initiative of God's grace and the sole means of response to this grace is in trusting faith issuing in loving obedience. At its centre is an intimate relationship with God enabling the restoration of the vocation to rule over the world that he entrusted to human beings as his image-bearing creatures.

There certainly are discontinuities within the covenant story. But these are to be understood as part of the frequently surprising process by which the covenant theme is introduced, clarified, developed, broken, renewed, awaited and eventually fulfilled. In telling the story of the covenant, the Bible presents one great narrative, and in our understanding of how the Old and New Testaments relate to one another, we should not insist on a full stop where God only intended a comma. To suggest, as George Beasley-Murray did, that the covenants before and after Christ represent death versus life, condemnation versus righteousness and flesh versus spirit is seriously to misconceive the relation of Old and New Testaments.[41] To assert, as he again did, that circumcision had no relation to moral renewal can only be explained by concern at some possible inference of infant baptism rather than a consideration of the actual evidence.[42] Any simplistic contrasts between Old and New Testaments in terms of carnal versus spiritual, national versus universal, letter versus Spirit and law versus grace are seriously misleading. Promise and fulfilment is the best contrast because it expresses the nature and purpose of the covenant story. However, even after the death and resurrection of Jesus Christ and the outpouring of the Spirit at Pentecost, there is yet unfulfilled promise.

## Covenant completed/consummated – the new creation

The goal of God's entire covenant project is the final coming of the new creation and the resurrection of God's people so that they can rule over it. It is here, however, that generations of Christians have managed to miss this completion of the biblical story, preferring to understand the Christian hope as 'going to heaven' rather than resurrection to a new creation. This has had very serious consequences for Christian belief and practice, not least in understanding and appreciating the value of the sacraments. Even when Christians have spoken of receiving new bodies in heaven, understanding their hope as located in a different place has produced a concept of salvation largely unrelated to creation and the vocation given to human beings within it. This has contributed to many of the popular misconceptions of a disjuncture between the old and new covenants challenged in the last two chapters, with many of the covenant promises contained in the Old Testament being seen as foreign to the faith of the New Testament and, at best, a provisional, inadequate and 'worldly' illustration of the more spiritual and 'heavenly' truths that replaced them.

### Revelation 21–22 and the New Jerusalem

The error of this is shown when we examine the New Testament passages that describe the *Christian hope*. The vision contained in Revelation 21–22, in particular, could hardly be more grounded in Old Testament covenantal imagery. Using the terminology of Isaiah 65, John describes the coming of a new heaven and a new earth to replace the first heaven and first earth (21.1a). The sea – used from Genesis to the Psalms to Daniel as a picture of anti-creation chaos plus, of course, the factor necessitating salvation in the story of Noah and the Exodus – will no longer exist, revealing that both creation and covenant have reached their final goal (21.1b). The marriage imagery employed by Hosea and Jeremiah to speak of the covenant is also evoked as the writer speaks of the Holy City coming down out of heaven from God, 'prepared as bride beautifully dressed for her husband' (21.2). The central covenant promise is also proclaimed when it is declared that 'they will be his people, and God himself will be with them and be their God'. This in turn leads to the completion of the whole reason for the covenant: the banishment of all the death, mourning, crying and pain that has spoilt and defaced God's creation (21.3-4, 7).

The strongest covenant imagery in Revelation 21–22, however, is that drawn from the Temple with its emphasis upon the new creation as a new Jerusalem and holy city. The language of God dwelling amongst his people is used to show that what had previously been the case with the Tabernacle/Temple and more fully with Jesus Christ (e.g. John 1.14) would now be extended on a cosmic scale (21.3, cf Ephesians 1.10). Much of the content within the previous chapters of Revelation has built up to this point by recapitulating the story of Exodus with the great plagues, the lamb who was slain, the redeemed people singing by the sea and the great apostasy, all occurring before God's dwelling place is finally established. The vision of the new Jerusalem shining with the glory of God recalls the vision of God's future temple contained in Ezekiel 40–48 with the cubic structure of the city recalling the holy of holies in Solomon's Temple (21.15-16 cf 1 Kings 6.20). No actual temple will be found within the city, however, because 'the Lord God Almighty and the Lamb are its temple' (21.22). Both the earlier temple on earth and the corresponding temple in heaven (11.19; 15.5) are thus revealed to be advance signposts of the new creation and the promise contained in Habakkuk 2.14 and Isaiah 11.9 of that future when God's glory would fill the entire earth. The vision goes still further as it declares that the sun and the moon will not be required to shine upon the city, since the glory of God will give it light and the Lamb will be its lamp (21.23). Even the original creation is thus revealed, like the Tabernacle and Temple, to be an advance sign of the full reality of God's glory that will be revealed with the coming of the new Jerusalem.

The centrality of the covenant to this process is shown, however, by the twelve gates of the city upon which are written the names of the twelve tribes of Israel, alongside the twelve foundations of the city's wall, which bear the names of the twelve apostles of the Lamb (21.12-14). Unlike the gates in the original temple, these gates will never be shut (cf Acts 21.30) 'for there will be no night there' (21.23). It is through these open gates and in fulfilment of Psalm 72.10-11, Isaiah 49.6-7, Zechariah 14.16-17 and particularly Isaiah 60 that the nations will come, bringing their glory and honour. For most of Revelation, the nations and their kings have been portrayed as hostile and Babylon-like in their idolatry and resistance to God. This will now cease as they walk in the city's light and bring their splendour to it (21.24-26), although the city's holiness will also entail the exclusion of all those who are impure (21.8, 27). A similar theme continues into Revelation 22. This time the imagery of Eden in Genesis 2 and Ezekiel 47 is invoked as the angel reveals to John the river of the water of life flowing from the throne of God and the Lamb down the middle of the great street of the city. As in Ezekiel, the river irrigates fruit trees on its banks which are now revealed to be 'the tree of life' from Genesis 2 bearing twelve crops of fruit and whose leaves 'are for the healing of the nations' (22.1-2). With all the curses from Genesis 3 to those afflicting Israel and the nations finally removed, God's presence will be fully revealed to the servants who bear his name and who will then reign for ever and ever (22.3-5).[43]

### Resurrection to the new creation

The prelude to the coming of the new creation, according to the New Testament writers, will be the return/appearance of Jesus Christ and the resurrection of those who have died 'in Christ' to reign with him. Once again it is covenant imagery that is used to

*God's Covenant (Part Two)* 127

convey this, such as when 1 Peter speaks of this living hope as 'an inheritance that will never perish, spoil or fade' (1 Peter 1.4). This inheritance is 'kept in heaven for you' – not because Christians will one day go to heaven to receive it, but because it is in heaven that this inheritance is being safeguarded ahead of being brought to earth in the new creation.

1 Thessalonians 4 is perhaps the earliest passage where Paul speaks of the return of Jesus and the resurrection of those in the Messiah. The passage is full of metaphor with much of it drawn from language used at that time of a Roman emperor being received into a city by its citizens. However, alongside this is use of the covenant language used in Exodus 19 to describe YHWH's descent from heaven to meet with Moses on Mount Sinai and the trumpet and voice of YHWH that accompanied the giving of the law. Jesus is described as coming down from heaven accompanied by 'a loud command' and 'the trumpet call of God'. 'The dead in the Messiah will rise first' (4.16) and this will be followed by those who are still alive being 'caught up together with them in the clouds to meet the Lord in the air' (4.17a). Rather than describing a rapture to heaven, this verse is using imagery drawn from Daniel 7.13-14 to describe the vindication of all those who will be caught up with the Son of Man to share in the sovereignty and dominion given to him by 'the Ancient of Days'. This will signal the consummation of the covenant relationship as they 'will be with the Lord forever' (4.17b).[44]

Similar covenant language is used by Paul in 1 Corinthians 15 to speak of the return of Jesus and the resurrection of those who belong to him. This is again most obvious in the reference to 'the final trumpet' that will sound as the dead are raised and clothed with their resurrection bodies (15.52). But it is also seen in the reference to the Messiah, because of his earlier resurrection, as the 'first-fruits' (15.20, 23). As well as its association with the earliest part of the annual harvest, this term appears to be an allusion to the episode in Numbers 13 where Moses sent spies into the Promised Land to explore it and bring back some of its fruit in anticipation of its later conquest. The return of the Messiah and the resurrection of those belonging to him are thus represented as completing the process of inheriting God's covenant promises that was anticipated through the resurrection of Jesus. The whole reason the covenant was needed is also recalled as Paul speaks of how 'in Adam all die' only to follow this by declaring 'so in the Messiah all will be made alive' (15.22). This is followed by use of the Psalms and Daniel as Paul speaks of the reign of the Messiah until 'he has destroyed all dominion, authority and power' and finally hands over the kingdom to God the Father (15.24-28).[45]

It is in Romans 8 that Paul speaks most fully of the fulfilment of all those Old Testament passages that spoke of the redemption of creation through God's completion of the whole covenant project. He speaks of the creation being 'subjected to frustration' and 'in bondage to decay' but also of how it 'waits in eager expectation for the sons of God to be revealed' and to be 'brought into the glorious freedom of the children of God' (8.19-21). These latter references illustrate the intrinsic covenantal connection between the perfection of human beings and the bringing to completeness of the creation that they were commissioned to care for and rule over. This time it is the Holy Spirit who is described as the 'first-fruits' of the new creation as those who possess the Spirit groan like the creation as we await 'our adoption as sons, the redemption of our bodies' (8.23). The covenant story is again invoked as Paul employs the language of the conquest of the Canaan to describe followers of Jesus as 'more than conquerors through him who loved us' (8.37). The present suffering of both God's people and the creation itself will be brought to an end when God's covenantal love triumphs in the resurrection of those in the Messiah to a new creation.[46]

## Priests and rulers in the new creation

Central to the hope set out in the New Testament is thus its emphasis upon God's people reigning with Christ in the new creation. The significance of this is often missed, perhaps because its clearest expression is found in Revelation where John makes repeated reference to the destiny of God's people as both priests and rulers (1.5-6; 3.21; 5.9-10; 20.4-6; 22.3-5). The basis of this lies in God's covenant promise back in Exodus 19.4-6 to make Israel into 'a kingdom of priests and a holy nation'. Central to the covenant was Israel's priestly calling to lead creation back to God, alongside the commission to exercise the sovereignty over creation that formed the original mandate given to those made in God's image and expresses what it means to be human (see also Psalm 8). Humankind had failed in this vocation, hence its concentration upon Israel and, following its failure in Israel, its concentration in the Messiah. This explains the 'royal' strand of Jesus's ministry as he proclaimed and embodied the arrival of God's kingdom rule and the 'priestly' strand as Jesus was revealed as the new Temple, the one through whom God's glory had finally returned to his people. The Sermon on the Mount formed the summons to Israel to become this renewed humanity. This was finally made possible through the death and resurrection of Jesus which, with the coming of the Holy Spirit, enabled the vocation of being priests and rulers to be re-established amongst those 'in the Messiah'. The New Testament is clear that it is this goal – God's people being priests and rulers in the new creation – that represents the completion of God's entire covenant project.[47]

The clarification of this hope is extremely significant for Christian living in the present which is called to anticipate this future and display this priestly and royal vocation. 1 Peter uses strongly covenantal language to describe followers of Jesus 'a chosen people, a royal priesthood, a holy nation that you may declare the praises of him who called you out of darkness into his wonderful light' (2.9). Earlier it speaks of the renewed people of God as 'living stones ... being built into a spiritual house to be a holy priesthood, offering spiritual sacrifices acceptable to God through Jesus Christ' (2.5). Hosea's words about the renewal of the covenant are then quoted as 1 Peter declares: 'Once you were not a people, but now you are the people of God; once you had not received mercy, but now you have received mercy' (2.10 cf Hosea 1.10; 2.23). The theme of 1 Peter is how Christians are to live within a pagan culture, and central to this is the priestly calling to display God's holiness so that the surrounding pagans are drawn further towards God. This vocation involves a particular role for suffering as the means by which this holiness is displayed. Paul employs similar language and ideas when he speaks of his ministry as 'the priestly duty of proclaiming the gospel of God, so that the Gentiles might become an offering acceptable to God, sanctified by the Holy Spirit' (Romans 15.16). Earlier he also uses priestly language when he urges the Roman Christians to 'offer your bodies as living sacrifices, holy and pleasing to God – this is your spiritual act of worship' (Romans 12.1).

Elsewhere in Paul's writings, it is the vision of God's people being the world's future rulers that is more prominent. In Romans 5 he contrasts the effect of Adam and Jesus, with the obedience of Jesus leading to human beings not only being rescued and renewed but placed in authority over God's new world: 'how much more will they reign in life through the one man, Jesus the Messiah' (5.17). In 1 Corinthians 6, Paul rebukes the Corinthian Christians for taking their cases against one another to secular courts. The basis of this rebuke is the future sovereignty over the world that they should be modelling: 'Do you not know that the saints will judge the world? And if you judge the world, are you not competent to judge trivial cases? Do you not know that we will judge angels? How much more the things of this life?' (1 Corinthians 6.2-3). The *current* expression of this sovereignty is within the Christian community, rather than the wider world, hence the commands to obey the rulers given authority over the world by God (Romans 13.1-7). 1 Peter commands the same obedience to external authority and makes the additional point that the suffering this involves is an intrinsic part of following the Messiah who also suffered (1 Peter 2.13-25). This links back to the gospels and the emphasis of Jesus upon both his rule and that of his followers being expressed through loving and suffering service, rather than the expression of power and domination (Matthew 20.20-28; Mark 10.35-45). But it is an anticipation, nonetheless, of the future rule of his followers expressed in the previous chapter of Matthew's Gospel when Jesus declares: 'I tell you the truth, at the renewal of all things, when the Son of Man sits on his glorious throne, you who have followed me will also sit on twelve thrones, judging the twelve tribes of Israel' (Matthew 19.28). This perspective is further reflected in part of the 'trustworthy saying' that Paul endorses to Timothy when he says, 'If we endure, we will reign with him' (2 Timothy 2.8-13).

Understanding the destiny of those who follow Jesus to be priests and rulers in the new creation is very different from that which understands the Christian hope as one of eternal rest in heaven. It presents a picture of the promised future for Christians which is dynamic and active rather than static and passive. As Tom Wright has said, resurrection life in the new creation will involve new tasks and opportunities, hence the lasting role of faith and hope within it, as well as the supreme virtue of love (1 Corinthians 13.13). Crucially, this also leads to a completely different understanding of the Christian's role and identity in *the present*. The Westminster Confession famously states that 'the chief end of man is to glorify God and enjoy him forever'. A more biblical and covenantal perspective sharpens this into the rather more specific calling of those 'in the Messiah' to be a royal priesthood, reflecting creation's praise back to God and implementing his just rule over that same creation.[48]

## The role of the Holy Spirit in bringing new creation into the present

The Holy Spirit is given to bring some of this promised future into the present. Paul says, 'If anyone is "in Christ" – new creation!' (2 Corinthians 5.17) and elsewhere he describes the Holy Spirit as a deposit or down payment 'guaranteeing our inheritance/ the future to come' (2 Corinthians 1.22; 5.5; Ephesians 1.14). The Greek word for deposit, 'arrabon', is used today of an engagement ring and, as mentioned earlier, the Holy Spirit is also described by Paul as 'the first fruits' of the promised new creation. It is through the Holy Spirit that those who are 'in the Messiah' can begin to practise in the present those ways of life that will characterize their future as priests and rulers in the new creation. As Tom Wright puts it, 'The practice and habit of Christian virtue is about learning in advance the language of God's new world.' However, given that the resurrection of Jesus has brought the breaking in of God's new age, living Spirit-filled lives in the present is not just anticipating the new creation but actually implementing it.

The application of this destiny of being priests and rulers in the new creation is not found in followers of Jesus attempting to establish themselves as present rulers over the world. Its primary application is found instead in the calling to holiness, unity and suffering for the gospel. In Romans 6 Paul uses covenantal language to describe those in the Messiah as no longer slaves to sin. This is because they have been united with the Messiah in his death precisely so that the body of sin would be done away with. And if they have been united to the Messiah in his death, Paul adds, they will also be united with him in his resurrection. As a result of this, they need to count themselves dead to sin but alive to God in the Messiah and reflect their new status by offering their bodies in 'slavery' to righteousness leading to holiness. In 1 Corinthians 6, Paul also uses the future resurrection of believers as the vital stimulus to holiness, since the Corinthians' bodies are now part of the Messiah himself (6.13-17). In Colossians, he goes further, describing those in the Messiah as already raised with him 'through your faith in the power of God, who raised him from the dead' (2.12). Since they have been raised with the Messiah, his followers are to set their hearts and mind above, with the goal that when the Messiah appears, they will appear with him in glory (3.1-4).

It is the Holy Spirit who draws this future into the present by effecting this union with the Messiah and living within his followers. Once again it is covenantal language that is used to describe the Spirit's work. Within Romans 8, Paul says that those who are led by the Spirit are sons of God, heirs of God and co-heirs with Christ as they await the redemption of their bodies. In 1 Corinthians 6 he describes the believer's body as 'a temple of the Holy Spirit who is in you' (6.19). The Spirit's role, like the temple under the old covenant, is therefore to establish the presence of God amongst his people ahead of the day this is made complete in the new creation. It also represents the inward renewal and cleansing that Jeremiah 31.31-34 and Ezekiel 36.25-27 had declared would be a vital part of the new covenant.

However, whilst all followers of Jesus possess the Holy Spirit, there is nothing automatic about the Spirit's effect. The calling of the Christian is to make a constant effort to submit to the Spirit's guidance and prompting. The fact that the Spirit occupies the bodies of those in the Messiah has particular implications for holiness and, in particular, the avoidance of sexual immorality (1 Corinthians 6.12-18). Paul says, 'Since we live by the Spirit, let us keep in step with the Spirit' (Galatians 5.25) and part of what this involves is constantly putting to death, by the Spirit 'the misdeeds of the body' (Romans 8.13, see also Colossians 3.1-8). As Tom Wright has emphasized, considerable moral effort is required to conform our will to that of the Spirit, with a particular importance laid upon the renewal of our minds so that they can direct our bodies appropriately (Romans 12.2; Philippians 1.9-11). Priestly language is used to describe the offering of these bodies 'as living sacrifices, holy and pleasing to God' and a 'spiritual act of worship' (Romans 12.1).[49]

This submission to the Spirit very much extends to the development of positive gifts and characteristics. Paul's letters include four lists of gifts of the Spirit (Romans 12.6-8; 1 Corinthians 12.8-10,28; Ephesians 4.11) with the variation between these lists suggesting that they provide examples of such spiritual gifts rather than aiming to be exhaustive. Some of these gifts such as prophecy and speaking in tongues are more mysterious than others but all of them are seen as ways in which the Holy Spirit brings the life of heaven to earth, ahead of the day when this process is made complete in the new creation. However, whilst Paul values gifts such as prophecy and speaking in tongues, he is also clear that these are only a temporary provision and will no longer be needed when the new creation comes to completion (1 Corinthians 13.8-12).

What instead deserves the greatest value and what Paul regards as the greatest mark of the Holy Spirit is love. This is the virtue that heads up his list of the fruit of the Spirit in Galatians followed by joy, peace, patience, kindness, goodness, faithfulness, gentleness and self-control (Galatians 5.22-23). When Paul exhorts the Colossians to clothe themselves in very similar virtues, adding compassion and forgiveness, it is love that is once again supreme and seen as binding the rest together (Colossians 3.12-14). And in 1 Corinthians 13, Paul lists the cardinal virtues as being faith, hope and, once again and above all, love.

The reason for the priority of these three virtues and the supremacy of love is that, unlike gifts such as speaking in tongues and prophecy, faith, hope and love will abide in the new creation. Earlier we saw how the continuance of these virtues with the new creation indicates the active rather than passive nature of this destiny. The priority of love is because it provides the greatest anticipation of that complete humanness that God's people are promised in the new creation. At an even deeper level, this is because love represents the very essence of the God revealed in Jesus Christ. From the perspective of the coming of Jesus and the Holy Spirit, the whole of the covenant story – and especially the giving of the law – can be seen as pursuing this goal. This is why Paul regards the entire law as summed up by the command in Leviticus 19.18 to 'love your neighbour as yourself' (Galatians 5.14). He makes a similar point when he declares that 'love is the fulfilment of the law' (Romans 13.8-10). Before the coming of the Spirit, the law brought condemnation because, despite its contents, it led to the opposite of love. This was not because there was anything bad about the law but simply because it lacked the power to change those who received it. Paradoxically it was those who insisted on clinging to the law as the marker of God's people and thus living by the flesh rather than the Spirit, who were stuck in this loveless and divisive state (Galatians 5.15) and thus condemned by the law. Those, in contrast, led by the Spirit, are enabled to display the love that the whole of the covenant story, including the law, aimed to produce in God's people. Faith expressing itself in love and new creation thus form two ways of talking about the same single reality which, in contrast to temporary signs (or indeed non-signs) of the flesh, is the one that really counts (Galatians 5.6; 6.12-16).[50]

It is the priority of love that points us to the seamless link between the call to holiness under the new covenant and its call to unity. Almost all of Paul's letters place a major emphasis upon the critical importance of unity between Christians. In Philippians 2.1-4, unity is presented as the vital outcome of union with the Messiah and fellowship with the Holy Spirit. A similar emphasis is found in 1 John. 1 Corinthians forms a sustained appeal for unity to the church at Corinth including the exhortation to its members to use their individual gifts of the Spirit in a manner that builds up their community, rather than doing anything to divide it. Tom Wright has emphasized that Paul's famous description of the church as 'the body of the Messiah' (Romans 12; 1 Corinthians 12; Ephesians 4) is more than simply a metaphor to emphasize the need for a diversity of gifts within a unity of purpose. It instead represents a vision of the church as God's renewed humanity, with Christians – both individually and corporately – called to be the place where genuine human life continues within the present world. Ephesians 4, in particular, identifies unity in the faith with spiritual maturity and growing further into the head of the body which is the Messiah. The risen Jesus thus represents the fully human being with those belonging to him growing further into this fullness of the Messiah though striving to build up their common life through love (Ephesians 4.1-16).

Such Spirit-inspired unity was obviously made into an even more of a challenge from the single Jew plus Gentile community that was created under the new covenant. Paul speaks in Ephesians of how the Gentiles were previously 'excluded from citizenship in Israel and foreigners to the covenants of promise' now being brought near through the blood of the Messiah (2.12). Once again the goal is described as restored and unified humanity with God's purpose 'to create in himself one new man out of two, thus making peace' (2.15). Earlier we noted how Paul described the individual body of someone belonging to the Messiah as a temple of the Holy Spirit and this forming the basis of his appeal for holiness (1 Corinthians 6.18-20). In Ephesians he describes the entire Jew-plus-Gentile church as a holy temple 'built on the foundation of the prophets and apostles, with the Messiah, Jesus himself as the chief cornerstone' and 'a dwelling in which God lives by his Spirit' (2.20-22). It is the revelation of this mystery that 'through the gospel the Gentiles are heirs together with Israel, members together of one body and sharers together in the promise in the Messiah Jesus' (3.6) that leads to Paul's great prayer that, 'being rooted and established in God's love', the Ephesian Christians would be able to 'know this love and be filled to the measure of all the fullness of God' (3.14-21). These truths then form the basis of the practical exhortations to loving unity in the Messiah that form much of the rest of the letter (4.1-6.9).

Alongside holiness and unity, another major aspect of the church's call to live by the Spirit is its calling to suffering. This is chiefly because followers of Jesus are called to live as members of God's new creation within a world that is still part of the old order. Within the Farewell Discourses in John's Gospel, Jesus spoke to the disciples about the hatred from the world that his followers must expect (John 15.18–16.4). We have already seen the way in which the theme of suffering is present within the rest of the New Testament with the message that sharing in the Messiah's suffering is the path to sharing in his resurrection and the inheritance promised to God's people. However, rather than presenting this suffering as something to be simply endured ahead of that resurrection, the New Testament writers present it, like holiness and unity, as another way in which God's people actively anticipate their role as priests and rulers in the new creation. Paul, in particular, sees his calling to suffer for the gospel as the means by which God advances his rule over the world understanding his life as being 'poured out like a drink offering' (Philippians 2.17; 2 Timothy 4.6) ahead of receiving the 'crown of righteousness' (2 Timothy 4.8). Rather than being restricted to the apostles, the call to suffer is one that belongs to all of those who belong to Jesus Christ.

Part of this suffering will arise from the commitment to holiness rather than conforming to the pattern of the world (Romans 12.1-2). Another source of suffering is the commitment to unity and ongoing love towards Christian brothers and sisters, as seen in the pain shown within Paul's second letter to the church at Corinth. But at the basis of all Christian suffering is the proclamation by words and deeds that Jesus Christ is Lord and the reaction against this by the human powers within the world and, even more, the shadowy powers of evil lying behind them. As Paul declares: 'For our struggle is not against flesh and blood, but against the rulers, against the authorities, against the powers of this dark world and against the spiritual forces of evil in the heavenly realms' (Ephesians 6.12). Recalling Isaiah, Paul therefore urges the Ephesians to don the full armour of God including 'the breastplate of righteousness', 'the helmet of salvation' and 'sword of the Spirit' (Ephesians 6.13-18 cf Isaiah 59.17).

Another crucial weapon given to Christians is prayer (Ephesians 6.18-20). Within Romans, Paul makes an explicit connection between the creation 'groaning as in the pains of childbirth' for the new creation to arrive, followers of Jesus 'groaning inwardly' as they await their adoption and resurrection, and the Holy Spirit interceding for us 'with groans that words cannot express' (Romans 8.18-27). Recalling Moses's intercession for the rebellious Israelites in the wilderness, the implication is that a major part of the Christian life is the equally painful calling to partner the Holy Spirit in prayer at precisely those points where he is engaged in the struggle of bringing God's new creation into the world. Many of the references to Paul's tears for his fellow believers appear to have this ministry as their context (Acts 20.19, 31; 2 Corinthians 2.4; Philippians 3.18).

## The centrality of the covenant to understanding the New Testament

The Bible's covenant theme has been unpacked in detail over the last two chapters because it is indispensable for understanding Christian baptism. Many of the misunderstandings connected to baptism are due to the failure to recognize its nature as a covenant sign and, at a deeper level, a failure to understand the nature of the covenant itself.

The covenant, to repeat, is God's plan for rescuing and restoring the world with the key role within this plan accorded to the human beings that God created to bear his image. It is, from start to finish, a covenant of grace on God's part and a covenant of vocation on the part of his people, as they are called to display his rule to the world. The connection between God's grace and this vocation is the consistent call to God's people to live by faith in God's covenant promises in order to receive and then display his blessings. This call to faith exists from the start of the covenant but finds its maturest form after the death and resurrection of Jesus Christ in the call, assisted by God's Spirit, to holiness, unity and suffering for the gospel. This is because the covenant is centred upon God's Son, Jesus Christ, with the difference between its two phases, BC and AD, best understood in terms of promise and fulfilment. However, throughout the development of the covenant within the Bible, every aspect of it remains centred upon God's grace received by faith. The blessings of this grace and faith as the means of appropriating this grace remain the same. From its very first chapter, the whole of the New Testament is written precisely in order to show how the coming of Jesus Christ represented the climax and fulfilment of the covenant story that is in the Old Testament and cannot be understood outside it. Jesus summed this up when he said, 'Your father Abraham rejoiced at the thought of seeing my day; he saw it and was glad' (John 8.56). So did Paul when he declared, 'The Scripture foresaw that God would justify the Gentiles by faith and announced the gospel in advance to Abraham: "All nations will be blessed through you"' (Galatians 3.8). This is the context in which the New Testament writers understood the nature and meaning of Christian baptism.

Before we turn back to baptism, it is perhaps helpful to reflect briefly upon some of the reasons why the covenantal reading of the Bible presented over the last two chapters has been widely avoided. This is a delicate subject with the potential to cause offence, especially to those Christian traditions that pride themselves on being biblical. But it is dealt with here because it is perhaps the crucial factor in shedding light on the crucial but often unacknowledged presuppositions that are often at work when baptism is debated.

The most obvious factor behind a covenantal reading of the Bible being avoided or missed is distaste for the Old Testament and a good deal of incomprehension about how much of its contents can relate to the gospel of Jesus Christ. This feeling can be very conscious but is perhaps more powerful when there is less awareness that such a reaction is present. Stories of violence, bizarre occurrences and the details of obscure laws and practices within the Old Testament often appear more unhelpful than illuminating to the development of Christian faith. This reaction developed very early on in the history of Christianity, most obviously through the influence of the second-century heresies of Marcionism and Gnosticism which actively sought to detach Christianity from its Old Testament basis. As noted earlier, opposition to an early form of this is seen in the letter to the Romans and the need that Paul felt to ground God's action in Jesus Christ within such a lengthy exposition of the covenant. In its modern form, this tendency is more often seen in a practical rather than official denial of the authority of the Old Testament. In churches where the Anglican lectionary is used, the Old Testament is still read but with the sermon that follows often based solely upon the New Testament and normally Gospel reading. Where the Old Testament is preached upon and officially valued, it is still commonly used as a book of illustrations for doctrines drawn from a truncated reading of the New Testament or the source of isolated prophecies concerning Jesus Christ, rather than as a connected, exciting, complex and surprising narrative finding its fulfilment in him.

A further, more subtle, factor at play is the modern tendency towards a privatized, individualized and depoliticized form of Christianity. This has its roots in the eighteenth-century Enlightenment with its very clear agenda of placing Christianity in a box called 'religion' and thus safely away from areas such as politics and economics that it might otherwise challenge. The result of this is a form of Western Christianity that struggles to relate to almost every aspect of the covenant presented in the Old Testament and, even in the most devout contexts, tends to read it as primitive in its failure to separate faith from the world of kings, nations, societies and politics. The New Testament is then read in a manner that screens out most of the political and social implications of its proclamation that Jesus is Lord in favour of various forms of the more privatized 'accepting Jesus as your personal Lord and Saviour'. The biblical hope of resurrection to a new creation gives way, almost without anyone noticing, to the sub-biblical hope of 'going to heaven when you die'. This results in a vocational understanding of God's renewed, multi-ethnic people called to anticipate their future rule over the world through courageous and prayerful acts of faith, hope and love giving way to an essentially escapist understanding of salvation. The Old Testament, as already noted, is then selectively used to illustrate this 'spiritualised' reading of the New Testament and all of this serves to reinforce the practical separation of New Testament Christianity from the covenant context against which it needs to be understood.

All of this must be recognized and avoided if a biblical doctrine of baptism is to be established. As this chapter has sought to demonstrate, every single part of the New Testament is saturated with quotations from and allusions to the Old Testament which, if taken seriously, force a covenantal reading of the New Testament and everything in it. Fortunately, many strands of contemporary Christianity are already starting to wake up to the inadequacy of a privatized, individualized and escapist form of their faith in search of something with much greater relevance to the world in which we live. Recent biblical scholarship has, as mentioned in Chapter 1, provided many of the tools required for this task. The time is completely right, therefore, for a rediscovery of the covenantal context of baptism that will allow the fullness of its importance and its relevance to be similarly discovered.

# John the Baptist and baptism

An important antecedent to Christian baptism is obviously the baptizing ministry of John the Baptist. John's use of water to symbolize washing had its own antecedents, almost certainly including the baptism of those converting to Judaism. Before these important factors are studied, the word itself needs consideration.

## The meaning of the word 'baptism'

The meaning of any word is determined not only by its derivation but, more significantly, by its actual usage within a particular context. Complex discussions about, and examples of, the use of the word in classical and secular Greek, or in the Greek Old Testament, are not actually very helpful. We shall instead look at how it is used in the New Testament.

The verb 'baptize' is used in three ways:[1]

(a) Of Jewish ritual washing (also the noun, *baptismos*). For example, in Mark 7.4 the verb and noun occur, also Luke 11.38 and possibly Hebrews 9.10.
(b) Of the religious ceremony of washing with water (also the noun, *baptisma*), performed by John, by Jesus's disciples during his ministry, and by the early church.
(c) Figuratively, e.g. 'into Moses in the cloud and in the sea' (1 Corinthians 10.2) and 'in the Holy Spirit (and fire)' (Matthew 3.11). Also (with the noun, *baptisma*) of martyrdom (Mark 10.38; Luke 12.50).

Baptize/baptism may mean to dip, or to use water with some special effect, or (metaphorically) to be overwhelmed. The usage of the word does not offer a conclusive answer to the question of the manner of Christian baptism, whether dipping, pouring or sprinkling.[2] Dipping may be appropriate to the imagery of burial, pouring to the imagery of washing or being overwhelmed with the Spirit, whilst sprinkling with water or with the blood of the covenant was used of consecration in the Old Testament and may be appropriate to the imagery of anointing or sealing.

Neither is the question of the mode of Christian baptism settled by the use of the words 'to go down into' and 'to come up out of'. Although this may indicate an immersion, it could just as well indicate going into a river or lake prior to the minister scooping up water to pour it over the candidate's head, i.e. affusion.

# Washing with water in the Old Testament

As already noted, the covenant law of God required frequent washing with water to establish purity. When the prophets pleaded for a cleansing in the heart, they were expounding what was always the intention of the ceremonial system in Israel – 'Be holy for I am holy,' says YHWH (Leviticus 19.2 cf 11.44; 20.7). Isaiah thus preached, 'Wash and make yourselves clean. Take your evil deeds out of my sight! Stop doing wrong, learn to do right' (Isaiah 1.16). Ezekiel 36.25 and Zechariah 13.1 have a similar message. The psalmist, too, prays, 'Cleanse me with hyssop, and I shall be clean; wash me, and I shall be whiter than snow' (Psalm 51.7).

Within the context of God's covenant promise of grace, and covenant expectation of loyal love, it is absurd to interpret the washings with water as 'merely' ceremonial or ritual. There is, of course, a tendency in all religious life towards mere externalism and this occurred all too frequently in Israelite history. But the story of the covenant demonstrates clearly that from the outset the covenant purpose acknowledged the distinction between, but maintained the closest relationship between, the outwards and inwards, the ceremonial and spiritual, the ritual and moral, the sign and the reality. It is there in the covenant with Abraham and Moses. It is then reinforced by prophets and psalmists – 'Who may stand in God's holy place? He who has clean hands and a pure heart' (Psalm 24.3-4).

The tendency to externalism was one which Jesus ruthlessly attacked, not least amongst the Pharisees. 'Woe to you, hypocrites! You clean the outside of the cup and dish, but inside they are full of greed and self-indulgence … first clean the inside … then the outside also will be clean' (Matthew 23.25f). 'Blessed are the pure in heart' (Matthew 5.8). Yet Jesus didn't thereby indicate disapproval of outward rites or ceremonies. On the contrary, he not only identified himself with the baptizing ministry of John but also challenged the chief priests and teachers of the law towards acknowledging that John's baptism was 'from heaven' and with the authority of God (Mark 11.30f).

The ceremonial washings of purification were used repeatedly and throughout life, and so, in that respect, are quite distinct from a single washing which marked a distinctive, unique and once-for-all initiation into a new relationship and way of life. This concept only emerged later.

Around the middle of the second century BC groups within Judaism developed strong traditions of very frequent washing with water which clearly combined concern for ceremonial and moral purity. *The Manual of Discipline* from the Dead Sea Scrolls demonstrates the pattern in the Qumran community, and other Essene groups had similar practice. In general these are frequently repeated, although there are clear signs of a development towards an initiatory washing which 'admits to the covenant of the community for ever'.[3]

# Jewish baptism of proselytes

From the very beginning of the covenant with Abraham, those outside of the physical family of Abraham/Israel could be brought within the covenant and receive the sign of circumcision. Originally this provision appears to have been directed towards household slaves (Genesis 17.12f). The provision is reinforced in Exodus 12.48 which explains how foreigners can share in the Passover.

At some point these God-fearing Gentiles were required to submit also to a special washing or baptism. The date of this development is unclear, but it is widely accepted that although detailed evidence dates from the second century AD, there is clear evidence for proselyte baptism in the first century AD (and probably pre-70) as an already well-established custom.[4] Flemington argues the likelihood for this Jewish baptism being widely known before the ministry of John because, in the Gospels, the baptism of John is introduced without any explanation of its meaning.[5] Also, in view of the later bitterness between Jews and Christians, it is highly unlikely that the Jews would have borrowed baptism from the Christians or even from John. It is very likely, then, that Jewish proselyte baptism was the major influence on John's ministry.

This washing with water was increasingly seen (especially in the rabbinic school of Hillel) as the decisive mark of conversion to Judaism. After confessing faith in the God of Israel in the presence of witnesses the convert experienced the baptism-washing and so became 'a child of the covenant'. The Rabbis used the language of regeneration – the convert is 'like a child newly born'. It was an initiation into a new life to be lived according to the law of the living God.

It is not clear how and why this requirement became established and even dominant in conversion to Judaism. There was the strong tradition that Gentiles were 'unclean' (both morally and ceremonially), and the law of God provided regulations of washing for purification, as seen in the last section. Furthermore, women converts increased in number and often came into Judaism independently of their husbands. Thus the initiatory washing with water became increasingly appropriate. The rabbinic traditions of the second century AD indicate that it was taken for granted that children, including the very young, would share the baptism-washing and be received into the Jewish faith, into the covenant.

## The Baptism of John

The ministry of John the Baptist was clearly of very great significance. Mark describes John's preaching and baptizing as 'the beginning of the good news', a perspective which the other gospel writers appear to share, given the major profile that John receives near the start of all of their accounts. Jesus endorsed John's ministry and even requested his baptism. Both Jesus and the Synoptic Gospel writers (partly signalled by their description of his clothing, see Matthew 1.4; Mark 1.6 cf 2 Kings 1.8) regarded John as the promised Elijah of Malachi 4.5f who was to 'turn the hearts' of people before 'the great and terrible day of the Lord' (Mark 9.13; Matthew 11.14; Luke 1.17 although cf John 1.21). More generally, John the Baptist is clearly understood by the Gospel writers to form the vital connection between Jesus and the Old Testament prophets as a whole. Even after the ministry, death and resurrection of Jesus, it is significant that some of the earliest apostolic preaching recorded in Acts still presents John's baptizing ministry as the vital start of the message they have to convey (Acts 1.22; 10.37; 13.24). Quite clearly the baptism of John forms the most crucial antecedent to Christian baptism.

Some scholars have gone further than this and consider that John's baptism was itself the commencement of Christian baptism.[6] However there are very significant differences between John's baptism and that of the early church which need to be noted: (a) John's baptism was not explicitly 'in the name of Jesus'; (b) It was not a baptism of the Spirit, and John himself sharply contrasted his baptizing and the subsequent baptizing of the Messiah on this very point (Matthew 3.11-12; Mark 1.7-8; Luke 3.16-17; see also Jesus's words in Acts 1.5); (c) The apostles clearly regard Christian baptism as deriving its key significance from events that happened *after* John's time – chiefly Jesus's death, resurrection and pouring out of the Spirit at Pentecost; (d) In line with this, Acts records the story of 'the disciples' at Ephesus who had received John's baptism but did not know the Holy Spirit. After instruction by Paul they were baptized 'into the name of the Lord Jesus' and the Holy Spirit came on them (Acts 19.1-7). On the other hand we have no record of the original disciples being baptized with water after Jesus's death, resurrection and gift of the Spirit. Nor are we told of Apollos, who knew only the baptism of John (18.25), receiving another baptism into Christ. However, these points scarcely overthrow the weight of the earlier arguments. Jesus's own comments on John the Baptist combine a strong endorsement of John's ministry with contrast to membership of the kingdom of heaven/God that Jesus himself was bringing (Matthew 11.7-19; Luke 7.24-35). A more precise understanding is needed of the relationship between the baptism of John and Christian baptism.

All three of the Synoptic Gospels record John the Baptist appearing 'in the wilderness' of Judea/around the Jordan and proclaiming 'a baptism of repentance for the forgiveness of sins' (Matthew 3.1-2; Mark 1.4; Luke 1.3). All of these details have major significance for understanding both the nature of John's baptism and the crucial legacy that it passed on to Christian baptism.

## 'The forgiveness of sins' – the covenant context of John's baptism

Earlier statements in the Gospels (most obviously Zechariah's song in Luke 1.67-79) make it clear that the principal significance of the ministry of John the Baptist lay in its announcement of the imminent covenant renewal of Israel. This was reinforced by its location and nature. The Judean wilderness around the Jordan was the area in which the people of Israel had first entered the land (Joshua 3.1-17). By leading God's people once again through water in this region, John was very deliberately recalling the key covenant episodes of Israel's salvation: the exodus and her subsequent receipt of the Promised Land.[7] As we have seen in Chapter 3, Israel passing through water in the exodus itself looked back to God's earlier salvation through Noah and the flood and his act of creation itself. In the hands of the prophets, particularly Isaiah 40–55, the exodus was then used to look forwards to God's future renewal of the covenant and fulfilment of his purposes for creation. John's baptism was thus indicating that all of God's ancient promises of covenant renewal were now being fulfilled through the coming of that great new exodus spoken of by the prophets.This is the context in which we need to understand John's baptism as bringing 'the forgiveness of sins'. Rather than simply holding out the offer of personal forgiveness to those baptized, John's baptism was proclaiming that, through this new exodus, Israel's long period of exile was coming to an end. 'The forgiveness of sins' was thus acting as a shorthand summary for Israel's liberation from everything that had been thwarting her reception of the covenant promises that God had made to her.[8] Israel's sin was now, somehow, going to be dealt with meaning that all of its damaging consequences would finally be undone.

Israel, however, was not merely being affirmed where she stood. The blessings of the covenant were not automatic. John's announcement that the covenant promises were about to be fulfilled was accompanied by severe warnings about the need to be part of the true people of God when this great moment arrived. The right response was crucial if God's covenant promises were to be received.

## 'Repentance' – the ethical and moral context of John's baptism

John's baptism was about cleansing. This fitted with the message of his preaching which urged his listeners to 'bear fruit worthy of repentance' (Matthew 3.8; Luke 3.7) and indeed John's baptism is described as 'a baptism of repentance' (Mark 1.4; Luke 3.3). Repentance means a change of heart and mind (literally a 'turning around' or conversion). The baptism of John involved the outward use of water, an obvious and historic symbol of washing and purification, and the inward spiritual and moral appeal for a turning from sin to God's way of living. There was therefore the closest possible connection between the symbol and the reality with God giving John both the verbal message and the visual message (John 1.33). When the people of Jerusalem and Judaea came to John for baptism they simultaneously confessed their sins and were presumably assured by him of their forgiveness (Matthew 3.5-6; Mark 3.5).

It is certainly true that John emphatically contrasted his baptism with water and the Messianic baptism with Spirit that was to come. However careful questions must be asked about the point of the contrast. As has already been noted with regard to the relation between 'old' and 'new' covenant, superficial contrasts are all too easily made that neglect the full evidence. For instance, it is frequently asserted that John's baptism was merely outwards as opposed to Jesus's inward baptism through and with the Spirit.[9]

However it is clearly wrong to describe a baptism of repentance, conversion, confession and forgiveness as merely outwards and the point of the contrast is to be found elsewhere, as will be seen. It is certainly not to be found by making John's baptism into an external ritual and ceremony with water alone. Such a view contradicts his entire message and purpose. John's ministry was spiritual through and through – in its initial call for repentance, in its warning of divine judgement, and in its careful and detailed teaching of the practical implications of repentance in daily life (Luke 3.10-14). It was a baptism of purification and cleansing of the heart and mind confirmed by the sign of water-washing.

## 'Baptism' – the 'ecclesiological' context of John's baptism

But perhaps the most distinctive and significant feature of John's ministry of baptism was its administration to *Jews*, to those who considered themselves already part of God's covenant people. Judaism, as we have seen, had almost certainly by this stage established proselyte baptism – the custom that God-fearing Gentiles who wished to become children of the covenant and members of God's people needed to mark this step by a ritual washing. John now made the scandalous proposal that the people of Israel themselves were 'unclean' and needed cleansing and that they were outside of the covenant through their faithlessness and needed decisive renewal if they were to (re)join it. John was therefore claiming for his baptism the status of *the* new initiation rite for joining the people of God.

Once again the prophetic sign of baptism that displayed this was accompanied by words providing this with further explanation. Having summoned his hearers to 'produce fruit in keeping with repentance' John asserted, 'Do not think you can say to yourselves "We have Abraham as our father". I tell you that out of these stones, God can raise up children for Abraham. The axe is already at the root of the trees, and every tree that does not produce good fruit will be cut down and thrown into the fire' (Matthew 3.9-10; Luke 3.8-9). The very ceremony devised for those outside the covenant was thus now being required of those who prided themselves on already being the covenant people. John's baptism was declaring that to be racially Jewish was (in the final analysis) spiritually irrelevant unless there was decisive spiritual change.

John's baptism was, to our knowledge, administered only to Jews. A number of aspects, however, suggest John believed that his statement about God going beyond the physical family of Abraham to raise up children was more than theoretical. One aspect hinting at this was John's provision of cleansing and forgiveness of sins outside of the Temple system. As mentioned, the Temple in Jerusalem was one of the foremost symbols of Israel's status as YHWH's covenant people. By breaking the Temple's monopoly on the provision of forgiveness, John's baptism was suggesting (in a manner that Jesus's ministry extended) that the covenant was about to burst beyond the national categories that had previously contained it. Another hint of this comes in the unique details that Luke includes of John's ministry (Luke 3.10-14). This not only includes mention of tax collectors (who worked for the pagan Romans) coming to be baptized but John's interaction with soldiers as well. Whilst these may have been Jewish soldiers, both the location of Judea and the time frame make it more likely that they were Roman soldiers.[10] Although we aren't told whether he baptized any of these soldiers, their presence adds to the elements in John's baptism that strongly recall the story of the prophet Elisha and the pagan soldier Naaman and the way in which the latter's washing in the River Jordan led to his cleansing, membership of God's covenant people and 'the land' being carried beyond Israel (see 2 Kings 5).

All of these form important hints that a critical new point in God's covenant plan was now being reached. With hindsight, John's baptism signified the start of what later became *the* really distinctive feature of Christianity: the decisive ecclesiological truth that everyone, regardless of race or any other previous impediments, could now become part of the People of God. This is surely why the apostles in Acts (where the inclusion of the Gentile is such a central theme) give such prominence to the baptism of John and why it is seen as the beginning of the gospel or good news of Jesus Christ. Anticipated by the role of Gentiles such as Ruth and Rahab, as well as Naaman, within the Old Testament covenant story (one of the major points of the genealogy with which Matthew starts his Gospel 1.1-17) the baptism of John still only made this inclusion potentially rather than actually present. Other vital factors would need to be added before *Christian baptism* would be present but the baptism of John can be seen as the decisive beginning of arguably its most important and distinctive characteristic.

## 'He will baptise with the Holy Spirit and fire' – the preparatory context of John's baptism

John was clearly a great prophet. Indeed Jesus described him as 'more than a prophet' declaring 'among those born of women there has not risen anyone greater than John the Baptist' (Matthew 11.9-14). We have already seen how John's ministry developed some crucial aspects of what later became Christian baptism.

However, on the other hand, John, Jesus and the New Testament writers were equally clear that John's ministry was essentially *preparatory*. All three of the Synoptic Gospels introduce his ministry with the words of Isaiah/Malachi concerning the one sent to 'prepare the way of the Lord' (Matthew 3.3; Mark 1.3; Luke 3.3) and, pointing to Jesus, John himself declared, 'He must become greater; I must become less' (John 3.30). In regard to baptism the key contrast that John made (and Jesus later echoed in Acts 1.5) was:

> I baptised you with water for repentance. But after me will come one who is more powerful than I, whose sandals I am not fit to carry. He will baptise you with the Holy Spirit and with fire. His winnowing fork is in his hand, and he will clear his threshing-floor, gathering his wheat into the barn and burning up the chaff with unquenchable fire. (Matthew 3.11-12 cf Mark 1.7-8; Luke 3.16-18)

It is easy to explain the Messianic baptism of the Spirit as a reference to the coming of the Holy Spirit upon Jesus's disciples from the Day of Pentecost onwards. The reference to 'fire' is rather less clear. It possibly refers to the 'tongues of fire' which came to rest upon the disciples on that occasion (Acts 2.3). Matthew and Luke, however, who (unlike Mark) refer to this 'fire', immediately go on to speak of the judgement as well as salvation that Jesus would bring (Matthew 3.12; Luke 3.17). This has led some to suggest that the baptism 'of Spirit and fire' refers to two baptisms – one of the Spirit upon Jesus's followers and one of fiery judgement upon the wicked.

It is more likely that the reference is to one fiery Spirit baptism which involves both blessing and judgement at one and the same time.[11] Spirit and fire are linked together by Isaiah as a judgement in the context of washing and cleansing.

Those who are left in Zion, who remain in Jerusalem, will be called holy, all who are recorded among the living in Jerusalem. The Lord will wash away the filth of the women of Zion; he will cleanse the bloodstains from Jerusalem by a judgement of spirit and a judgement of fire. (Isaiah 4.3-4)

A similar sense is found in Malachi after its reference to a messenger preparing the way for YHWH.

'See, I will send a messenger, who will prepare the way before me. Then suddenly YHWH you are seeking will come to his temple, the messenger of the covenant, whom you desire, will come' says YHWH Almighty. But who can endure the day of his coming? For he will be like a refiner's fire or a launderers soap. He will sit as a refiner and purifier of silver; he will purify the Levites and refine them like gold and silver. Then YHWH will have men who will bring offerings in righteousness, and the offerings of Judah and Jerusalem will be acceptable to YHWH, as in days gone by, as in former years. (Malachi 3.1-4)

The surrounding context of both passages is God bringing both judgement upon the unrepentant and a cleansing and restorative judgement upon those shown to be his true people, purifying them to be able to serve God. The baptism 'with fire' that John spoke of probably referred to both, but with a particular emphasis on the power that would work through the redemptive suffering of those who receive this, perhaps through being caught up in some of the wider judgement coming upon the world. If this is along the right lines then it provides a link to the relationship between baptism and suffering that Jesus spoke of (Mark 10.35-45) and points ahead to what, as we shall see, became another crucial part of Christian baptism. The coming great baptism referred to by John may therefore incorporate all of the crucial salvation-judgement complex of events from Calvary to Pentecost. The baptism of blood and judgement fire of the cross is intimately linked to the baptism of the Spirit at Pentecost, and both will reach their consummation at the Parousia, the return of Jesus Christ as Lord and Judge.

A good degree of care and nuance is therefore needed for the significance of John's baptism to be appreciated and the nature of its relationship to Christian baptism to be properly understood. It is clear that several crucial aspects of fully Christian baptism were not present within the baptism of John and indeed John himself was quite explicit about this. Having praised John as 'more than a prophet' and declared that 'among those born of women there has not risen anyone greater than John the Baptist', Jesus also declared 'yet he who is least in the kingdom of heaven is greater than he' (Matthew 11.9-11; Luke 7.26-28). Through these words, Jesus was making it clear that John, despite his greatness, still belonged to the Old Testament era of 'promise' which needed to be differentiated from the Messianic era of 'fulfilment' under the new covenant. He brings down the curtain on the Old Testament era of promise by pointing beyond his own ministry to the supreme salvation events of the cross, Pentecost and ultimately the Parousia of the Messiah.

However, as we have seen, it would be quite wrong to see John's baptism as merely outwards and ceremonial since, like the prophets that preceded him, his ministry sought to recall Israel to a spiritual and moral conversion of the heart. Indeed his status as 'more than a prophet' was based upon the clarity with which his verbal and visual message declared that initiation into the renewed covenant community precisely did not rest upon outwards or racial factors but solely in the inwards and spiritual conversion that would lead to a radically different lifestyle. Whilst many of the implications of this still lay ahead plus the coming of the power that would make it possible, John's baptism can thus be seen as the start of the gospel of Jesus Christ. John's was a baptism of real purification (by God's grace) and real initiation (into God's covenant life), whilst still having the nature of the partial and temporary because it was a *preparation* for the baptism of completion and permanence fulfilled in Jesus Christ.

# 6

# The baptism of Jesus

The most notable baptism by John was when Jesus himself came from Nazareth and was baptized in the River Jordan. We have already seen that John's baptism was, in one respect, preparatory and looking forward to a greater one who would exercise a mightier baptism. Having referred to Jesus as 'the Lamb of God, who takes away the sin of the world', John declared, 'the reason I came baptising with water was so that he might be revealed to Israel' (John 1.29-31). This revelation occurred at Jesus's baptism.

The actual descriptions of Jesus's baptism are found in Mark 1.9-11, Matthew 3.13-17 and Luke 3.21-22. The fullest account is in Matthew's Gospel:

> Then Jesus came from Galilee to the Jordan to be baptised by John. But John tried to deter him, saying, 'I need to be baptised by you, and do you come to me?' Jesus replied, 'Let it be so now; it is proper for us to do this to fulfil all righteousness'. Then John consented. As soon as Jesus was baptised, he went up out of the water. At that moment heaven was opened, and he saw the Spirit of God descending like a dove and lighting on him. And a voice from heaven said, 'This is my Son, whom I love; with him I am well pleased'.

The other accounts have minor variations. In Mark and Luke, the words from heaven are addressed to Jesus. Luke's Gospel reports characteristically that Jesus was praying immediately after the baptism when he receives the vision. John's Gospel does not describe the actual baptism of Jesus at all (nor the following temptations). However, the writer presupposes his readers know about Jesus's baptism, and John 1.29-34 is very relevant in its reflections upon it. In each gospel the account immediately follows the description of John's general ministry of preaching and baptizing.

Some have sought to draw a line between Jesus's baptism with water in the Jordan and the subsequent anointing with the Spirit and words from heaven. This is not only pedantic but contrary to the integration of all of these elements within the Synoptic accounts.[1] Rather than imposing a divorce upon them, our task is to try and understand the relationship between the different features of Jesus's baptism and the theological issues that they point to. But before that, we need to ask why the event itself took place?

# Why was Jesus baptized?

It is not surprising that through the centuries Christians have been perplexed by this question. The first and clearest characteristic of John's baptism was that it summoned Israel to repentance and the forgiveness of sins. Alongside and contained within John's call of God's people to national repentance were very personal charges to groups and individuals to turn from their specific sins (Luke 3.10-14). Did Jesus's baptism include repentance for his own personal sin? The apostolic witness gives no indication that this is so and many indications to the contrary. Jesus is described in the gospels as one who is totally obedient to the Father and for whom the fulfilment of Scripture was his utmost priority. He was consistent in his opposition to the Evil One, and his greatest concern was for the glory of God, the kingdom of God and the will of God. The biblical testimony to the reality of his humanity and yet the sinlessness of his character is summarized in Hebrews 4.15: 'We do not have a high priest Jesus who is unable to sympathise with our weaknesses, but we have one who has been tempted in every way, just as we are – yet was without sin.' The answer to why Jesus was baptized must clearly be sought elsewhere.

It is found in Jesus's response to the questioning of John the Baptist. Matthew alone records John's anxiety about Jesus's request for baptism (3.14). Presumably, even before the revelation in the baptism itself, John had a strong understanding that Jesus was (at the very least) a greater prophet for whom he was preparing the way. Jesus replied to his attempt at dissuasion by declaring, 'Let it be so now: It is proper for us to do this to fulfil all righteousness' after which, we are told, 'John consented' (3.15). 'Righteousness', as we have seen, is a strongly covenantal term, used in the Old Testament to refer to both God's commitment to his project of redeeming creation and the response required from his covenant people. Both senses of righteousness were expressed in Jesus's baptism and reveal central truths about his identity and role. The events that occurred immediately after Jesus's baptism, and especially the words of the voice from heaven, are crucial to understanding this.

# Jesus's identification with Israel

This is the most obvious emphasis of the accounts of his baptism recorded in the Synoptic Gospels. Just as the Israelites passed through the water of the Red Sea before proceeding to a period of temptation in the wilderness, so these events were recapitulated in the baptism of Jesus and his subsequent temptations (all answered by Jesus using quotations from Deuteronomy). It was during the period of the Exodus that God particularly referred to Israel as his 'son' (Exodus 4.22; Hosea 11.1) and the reference to both this and God's love by the voice from heaven is clearly intended to echo and reflect the covenant relationship that God made with Israel. Israel came through the water of the Red Sea and was given the law confirming their status as God's Son. Jesus came up from the water of baptism and received God's Spirit or breath declaring him, in a new and deeper way, to be God's Son or Israel-in-person.

However, Jesus's baptism went further than simply representing his recapitulation of the ideal relationship with God intended for Israel. His baptism was quite specifically an identification with Israel in her state of sin. John the Baptist had called upon Israel to repent and express this through baptism and, though sinless, Jesus also underwent baptism to express his solidarity with Israel in its fallen and sinful state. The words from the heavenly voice 'with him I am well pleased' are a clear reference to Isaiah 42.1, evoking the mysterious figure of 'the Servant' and its representation of both Israel and a distinct figure who would be 'numbered with the transgressors' (Isaiah 53.12). This aspect of Jesus's baptism was then strongly demonstrated in his public ministry as he went out of his way to befriend outcasts, sinners and those who were unclean. Time and again he challenged the self-righteousness of the Scribes and Pharisees and emphasized that he came for the sick, the lost, the outsiders, the poor and those who mourn. The supreme example of this was in Jesus's death. Having prophesied that Israel's faithlessness would lead to her destruction at the hands of Rome, Jesus then shared in the consequences of this. Although innocent (a particularly strong theme of Luke's account), Jesus shares in the typical fate of a Jewish rebel, being crucified between two brigands.

Without making specific reference to Jesus's own baptism, this emphasis on his identification with Israel and humanity itself is very much continued within the rest of the New Testament. Paul speaks of Jesus taking the very nature of a servant (Philippians 2.7) and John declares that 'the Word became flesh and made his dwelling among us' (John 1.14). The writer to the Hebrews says that because Jesus came to help Abraham's descendants 'he had to be made like his brothers in every way' (Hebrews 2.16-17) and identified with, and representative of humanity, he was called 'the last Adam' (1 Corinthians 15.45).

Here, in the baptism for sinners, Jesus unambiguously affirms his identification with rebellious and covenant-breaking Israel and, by extension, all humanity – an identification planned in eternity, prophesied in the Old Testament, unveiled in the incarnation, demonstrated in his public ministry and fulfilled in his crucifixion.

## Jesus's anointing with the Spirit as Israel's Messiah/the Son of God

As we have already noted, the term 'Son of God' was used not only of Israel in the Old Testament but also of her kings. The similarity of the words of the voice from heaven to Psalm 2.7's 'You are my Son' shows that the latter sense is the one being most strongly evoked here. Whatever deeper significance is recognized within Jesus's identification as Son of God, it is important to recognize that it was, most obviously, a royal term referring to Israel's king whose vocation was to keep or restore the covenant.[2]

This is reinforced by the emphasis within all four gospels upon the coming down of the Spirit upon Jesus at his baptism and the consequent description of him through the New Testament as 'the anointed one' (*Messiah* in Hebrew, *Christos* in Greek). Throughout the Old Testament period, the Spirit of YHWH was at work, coming upon specific people for special responsibility or service. In Chapter 2, we saw that anointing was associated with the outpouring of the Spirit, particularly on kings, prophets and priests. As the messianic hope of a covenant-restoring ruler in the line of David developed, so did the prophetic understanding that he would be uniquely the recipient of the Spirit of the Lord with his graces and gifts. This was particularly evident in Isaiah 11.1-2 and 61.1-3, which was read by Jesus in the Nazareth synagogue after which he said, 'Today this Scripture is fulfilled in your hearing' (Luke 4.16-21).

Throughout the Old Testament, anointing with the Holy Spirit (being 'Christ-ed') has the double significance of (a) consecration, being set apart for a holy purpose, and (b) being empowered and equipped or gifted for the divine task. So, here in the baptism, in an obvious and dramatic way Jesus consecrates himself to the will of God, and God consecrates him for his public ministry and supreme vocation. The Father had already set him apart as his very own and sent him into the world, and Jesus nearing the cross was to say, 'For them (the disciples) I sanctify myself, that they too may be truly sanctified' (John 10.36; 17.19).

This was how the gospel writers understood the coming of the Holy Spirit at Jesus's baptism. We have seen something of the significance of 'sealing' with respect to both baptism and the Holy Spirit. So when Jesus says of the Son of Man 'on him God the Father has placed his seal of approval' (John 6.27), the sentiment is true generally but focused upon the ordination to public ministry enshrined in Jesus's baptism. The early Christians also spoke of Jesus as God's holy servant who was anointed with the Holy Spirit and power (Acts 4.27; 10.38).

Following Jesus's resurrection and ascension and the coming of the Holy Spirit, the early Christians were forced to rethink their understanding of God. Remaining fiercely monotheistic, they redefined their monotheism by incorporating Jesus and the Spirit within the most emphatic statements of God's oneness from the Old Testament (e.g. 1 Corinthians 8.4-6; cf. Deuteronomy 6.4-5). Without losing any of its original messianic and representative sense, 'Son of God' took on a deeper layer of meaning signifying Jesus's unique status as God's 'second self' and ultimate self-expression as a human being.[3] Outside of the Gospels, the other New Testament writers make no mention of Jesus's baptism. However, it is beyond doubt that, from very early on, the church understood Jesus's baptism as the crucial moment when the full range of meanings and significance contained within his designation as the Son of God was divinely affirmed.

## Anticipation of the new creation

A renewed and widespread work of the Holy Spirit had long been part of the prophetic hope of new creation (Isaiah 63.7ff, especially 10–14; Ezekiel 36.26f; 37.1-14 noting that the Hebrew word *ruach* means Spirit and breath; Joel 2.28). The presence of YHWH, limited in the Old Testament to particular places, most notably the Temple, and particular people on a temporary basis, would one day be everywhere filling his people in a new and permanent manner.

This new creation was decisively inaugurated through the resurrection of Jesus Christ on Easter Day and the coming of the Holy Spirit at Pentecost. But both were anticipated through Jesus's public ministry in his healings, his raising of the dead and other signs indicating the renewal of creation. Luke, in particular, constantly describes Jesus as able to do the things he did because he was full of the Holy Spirit. The arrival of this resurrection/new creation power and Jesus's initiation into it are decisively linked by the gospel writers to Jesus's baptism.

This is partly through their vital references to the heavens being 'opened' (Matthew 3.16; Luke 3.21) or 'torn apart' (Mark 1.10) following Jesus baptism, allowing the Spirit of God/the Holy Spirit to descend (see also John 1.32, 50–51). Isaiah 64.1 used very similar language in asking God to 'rend the heavens and come down' as the path towards the renewal of creation spoken of in its surrounding chapters. Later in the New Testament, both the risen Jesus (1 Corinthians 15.20, 23) and the Holy Spirit (Romans 8.23) are described as 'the first fruits' of the new creation, and both of these senses are reflected in the accounts of Jesus's baptism. Anticipation of the resurrection of Jesus is particularly apparent in Matthew and Mark with their emphasis upon these events occurring as Jesus 'was coming up / came up out of the water' (Matthew 3.16; Mark 1.10).

The simultaneous reference to the Holy Spirit descending on Jesus 'like a dove' at this point is also vital here and referred to by all four gospels (Matthew 3.16; Mark 1.10; Luke 3.22; John 1.32). Scholars have debated whether this symbol derives from 'the Spirit of God hovering over the waters' at the very beginning of creation (Genesis 1.2) or Noah's use of a dove to establish the ending of the flood and the beginning of the new era after the catastrophic judgement (Genesis 8.8-12). Given the close connection between these narratives it is surely both. As we noted in Chapter 2, the story of the restoration after the Flood is deliberately written to present this event as an act of new creation. In both events the separation of the waters is the vital first stage to the coming of life/new life to the earth. This sense is also present within the stories of the dividing of the Red Sea and River Jordan so that the Israelites could proceed to 'a land flowing with milk and honey' (e.g. Exodus 3.8; Jeremiah 11.1-5; Ezekiel 20.6). The story of the Flood was used to symbolize and illustrate Christian baptism in 1 Peter 3.20f, and a major contributing factor here was clearly the way in which the baptism of Jesus himself was understood as a decisive part of the process by which God's new creation was entering the world through his Holy Spirit.

## The commitment to suffering and a sacrificial death

The New Testament is clear that the coming of resurrection/the new creation is only possible through the defeat of evil that occurred when Jesus died on the cross. This too forms a central part of what was being symbolized through the baptism of Jesus. Earlier we saw how Jesus's baptism also represented his identification with Israel and specifically his anointing as her representative Messiah. Both of these motifs are also strongly interlinked, through his baptism, with Jesus's calling to suffer and die so that God's covenant purposes through Israel could reach their fulfilment.

This is initially signalled by the way in which the voice from heaven, as already noted, uses words about Jesus which were originally used in Isaiah in reference to 'the Servant' ('with him I am well pleased', Isaiah 42.1). As the central chapters of Isaiah proceed, it becomes clear that the vocation of 'the Servant' was to be 'stricken by God', 'pierced for our transgressions' and bearing 'the punishment that brought us peace' through his carrying 'the sin of many' and because 'he poured out his life unto death' (Isaiah 53.4, 5, 12). The baptism of Jesus was thus understood by Jesus himself, and confirmed by the voice of God, as a symbol of the overwhelming experience of death as a sacrifice for sin. The one more powerful than John who 'will baptise with Spirit and fire' had to first be led by that same Spirit into a baptism of fire – a baptism of the holy wrath of God – through which God would win the decisive victory over sin and evil.

This emphasis is implicit rather than explicit within the accounts of Jesus's baptism because the startling message that Israel's Messiah came to suffer and die is one that is only gradually revealed within the Synoptic Gospels. But it becomes more explicit within the references, admittedly opaque, that Jesus later made to 'his baptism'. When James and John asked for special positions in his glory, Jesus replied, 'You don't know what you are asking. Can you drink the cup I drink or be baptised with the baptism I am baptised with?' (Mark 10.35ff). The 'cup' is a much used Old Testament symbol of the wrath of God in judgement against sin (see Psalms 75.8; Isaiah 51.17-23; Jeremiah 25.15-28; Habakkuk 2.16). In the Garden of Gethsemane, Jesus prayed, 'Take this cup from me' (Mark 14.36) referring to his death at Calvary and the abandonment from God that he was about to experience. A little earlier at the Last Supper he had taken the cup and explained its significance in terms of blood poured out for many for covenant renewal.

Being overwhelmed or engulfed in the waters of baptism is thus used by Jesus in Mark 10.35-35 (though not in Matthew's account in 20.20-28) as a parallel image to the cup of the suffering that both he and his followers were called to endure. Once again the Isaianic image of the suffering servant is being evoked and combined with the message of suffering followed by vindication in Daniel 7 when Jesus says, 'For even the Son of Man did not come to be served but to serve, and to give his life as a ransom for many' (Mark 10.45). As we shall see, the strong association of baptism with suffering is one that very much continued within the theology of the early church (see particularly 1 Peter 3). Some see its presence within this story from Mark's Gospel as further representation of the church's reflection on the significance of baptism. However, particularly given the opaque and allusive nature of this passage, it is more likely to be an original saying of Jesus and indicative of the use to which he put his baptism in both understanding and explaining his path to suffering and death.

Another passage is which Jesus refers to 'his baptism' in these terms is Luke 12.49-51: 'I have come to bring fire on the earth, and how I wish it were already kindled. But I have a baptism to undergo, and how distressed I am until it is completed!' The baptism Jesus spoke of here was clearly a coming ordeal which was consuming his mind and governing all his thought and action and must refer to his death on the cross. Baptism is thus used by Jesus here to represent a flood of unimaginable pain and suffering. The primary reference here is to the pain and suffering of Jesus. But its placement alongside Jesus's sayings about the division that he came to bring suggests the intention (either by Jesus or by the gospel writer) to make the link between the baptism his followers would undergo and suffering (Luke 12.51-53). Baptism and fire had already been linked by John the Baptist in his prophecy of Jesus's new kind of baptism (Matthew 3.12; Luke 3.17). It was suggested earlier (and this passage supports the interpretation) that 'the baptism of Spirit and fire' represented the complex of salvation-judgement events from Calvary to Pentecost. However, before the refining and judgement fire could be truly kindled and have its effects, Jesus had to be plunged in the flood of pain and sorrow.

Although John's Gospel does not have a baptism narrative comparable to the Synoptics, its writer in John 1.29-34 clearly presupposes knowledge of the event and refers to its theologically significant aspects. The passage is set within an obviously baptismal context with three references to baptism and clear references to the descent of the Spirit and the heavenly affirmation of Jesus's sonship. Within this context, it is surely significant that John the Baptist's first words are 'Look, the Lamb of God, who takes away the sin of the world' (1.29). Why does John use the description 'Lamb' (*amnos*) of God'? Many think instinctively of the Passover lamb with which Jesus was later identified (1 Corinthians 5.7). This might have been in John's mind if, like the gospel writers, he also saw Jesus as leading a second and greater exodus. But the Greek word used for this is *pascha* rather than *amnos*. Other suggestions are the lambs of the daily Temple sacrifice or the God-provided lamb that took the place of Isaac in Genesis 22.8. This story was highly significant in Judaic thought, but the lamb was not obviously 'taking sin', although it was sacrificial. In view of the voice from heaven introducing the suffering servant idea from Isaiah, it again seems most likely that John had in mind the imagery of the lamb used in the Servant songs, notably Isaiah 53 – 'he was led like a lamb to the slaughter' (Isaiah 53.7). John thus recognized that, as well as being the mightier one, Jesus was to fulfil the role of the Servant of the Lord, involving a sacrificial suffering that would effect a baptism of infinitely more significance than his washing in the Jordan, and yet of which that very washing was a prophetic sign.

Thus, through the symbolism of baptism itself in Jesus's own consciousness, and through the confirming words from heaven and the similar understanding of John the Baptist, it becomes apparent that in his baptism Jesus was committing himself to sacrificial death for both Israel and, by extension, the sin of the whole world. Having begun his earthly ministry with this sign, Jesus very obviously ended with another, which pointed even more clearly to his sacrificial death, in the Lord's Supper.

## Baptism within the earthly ministry of Jesus

As noted previously, Jesus and his disciples practised a baptizing ministry themselves. The Synoptic Gospels are silent about this with the only references to this contained within John's Gospel (John 3.22ff; 4.1ff). Even here the details are very sparse with reference to this baptism taking place in the Judean countryside and being administered by his disciples rather than Jesus himself (4.2). The Fourth Gospel has a particularly strong emphasis upon John the Baptist's acknowledgement that Jesus was greater than him and the details about Jesus baptizing more disciples than John are given in that context. According to John 4.1, it was when Jesus learned that the Pharisees had heard that he was gaining and baptizing more disciples than John the Baptist that he left Judea and went back once more to Galilee. Given the Pharisees rejection of the baptism of John the Baptist (Matthew 21.23-27; Mark 11.27-33; Luke 7.29-30; 20.1-8), it appears that Jesus withdrawal from Judea (and seemingly any further ministry of baptism) was prompted by the desire to endorse rather than undermine John's ministry (reflected strongly in Matthew 11.7-19; Luke 7.24-35).

This would explain the absence of any reference to Jesus and his disciples having a ministry of baptism within the Synoptic Gospels. The Synoptics' focus upon Jesus's ministry within Galilee rather than Judea (a greater focus in John's Gospel) may also explain this. But perhaps it was also prompted by Jesus's desire to draw a clearer line between the baptism of John and that baptism 'with the Holy Spirit and fire' that his disciples would receive in the future. This would fit with his assertion that great though John the Baptist was, 'yet he who is least in the kingdom of heaven / God is greater than he' (Matthew 11.11; Luke 7.28). Rather than practising baptism, Jesus appears to have decided to restrict himself to speaking about its significance in the light of his own baptismal experience (the passages in Mark 10.35-45 and Luke 12.49-51) because of his awareness that the vital events that would give baptism its full significance had yet to occur. These vital events were eventually revealed to be the death and resurrection of Jesus followed by his ascension and the coming of the Holy Spirit at Pentecost. It is after the resurrection that we receive the clearest instructions ascribed to Jesus about baptism in the so-called 'Great Commission' where Jesus appears to his eleven disciples in Galilee and says,

> All authority in heaven and on earth has been given to me. Therefore go and make disciples of all nations, baptising them in the name of the Father and of the Son and of the Holy Spirit, and teaching them to obey everything I have commanded you. And surely I am with you always to the end of the age. (Matthew 28.18-20)

It is customary for scholars to attribute the wording of this saying to the theological reflections of the early church rather than ascribing them to Jesus himself, particularly because of the Trinitarian reference contained within them. However, even if some later theological reflection is evident within them, these words clearly represent the belief of the early church that the risen Jesus wished his followers to baptize those who were becoming his disciples. Since baptism seems to be almost instantly established as the sign of entry into the early church (Acts 2.38-41), it makes most sense to understand Jesus as having directly commanded this practice, once the vital events had been completed for it to have its full significance, including his disciples' baptism with the Holy Spirit at Pentecost (Acts 1.4-5; 2.1-4ff).

# The contribution of the baptism of Jesus to the development of Christian baptism

Whilst to some extent unique in its significance, the baptism of Jesus was quite decisive in its influence upon the nature of Christian baptism. The following features, all of which we have noted as central in regard to Jesus's baptism, also form central aspects of the understanding of baptism 'into Jesus Christ' as it was administered by the early church.

- The anointing with the Holy Spirit
- The assurance of divine sonship
- The commission to serve God
- The calling to suffer

It is to Christian baptism, as understood and administered by the early church, that we now turn.

# 7

# Baptism in the Early Church

From the earliest records of the Christian church, baptism appears as the rite of passage through which people become part of the renewed covenant community of God. After the coming of the Holy Spirit at Pentecost in Acts 2, Peter speaks to Jews from the Diaspora about God's promises being fulfilled through the crucified Jesus being raised from the dead and thus declared by God to be 'both Lord and Christ'. When the people respond and ask what they should do, Peter replies:

> Repent and be baptised, every one of you in the name of Jesus Christ for the forgiveness of your sins. And you will receive the gift of the Holy Spirit. The promise is for you and your children and for all whom the Lord our God will call. (Acts 2.38-39)

It is possible that baptism wasn't established so instantly as the church's rite of passage and that the account of Pentecost represents a projection of later practice onto the earliest days of the movement. But, in line with the argument at the end of the previous chapter, it makes greater sense to understand baptism as one of the earliest developments in primitive Christianity. The profile of John the Baptist at the start of all four gospels is more remarkable than is sometimes recognized, given the evidence that many at the time seem to have understood John's and Jesus's movements rather separately. This understanding is reflected in some sections of the gospels (e.g. John 4.1-3, Matthew 11 and Luke 7) and Acts (18.25; 19.1-7), as well as the separate treatments given to John the Baptist and Jesus by the Jewish historian Josephus.[1] The strong overall connection that the gospels make between John and Jesus is explained, however, by the strong belief of the early Christians that John's ministry of baptism had represented the beginning of the good news of Jesus Christ. This was particularly true after the resurrection of Jesus and the instructions the risen Jesus gave to his followers to 'go and make disciples of all nations, baptising them in the name of the Father, the Son and the Holy Spirit, and teaching them to obey everything I have commanded you' (Matthew 28.19-20). It is sometimes doubted whether this passage represents the actual words of Jesus. However, whether this is the case or not, these words, at the very least, represent the strong conviction of the early Christians about the mandate that the risen Jesus Christ had given the church in regard to baptism.

It was only after the resurrection (and probably Pentecost as well) that, as with so many aspects of Jesus's ministry, the earlier cryptic words that he had previously spoken about baptism suddenly made sense to his disciples. The same perhaps goes for their understanding of the significance of the ministry of John the Baptist and the deeper baptism that John had spoken of Jesus bringing. This may have been through conversations with the risen Jesus but also because of the new context that now explained them. Easter and the new creation which had broken into the world in the risen Jesus convinced his disciples that Jesus was indeed the Messiah that Israel had been waiting for and the events surrounding him had formed the climax of God's covenant plan for redeeming the earth and his chosen people. More specifically, Jesus's disciples realized that, in the actual body of the Messiah, God had defeated evil through his death and brought his new creation into the world through his resurrection. The ascension of the risen Jesus into heaven was then understood as establishing Jesus's Lordship over the whole world and enabling the Holy Spirit, as the first fruits of the new creation, to come down at Pentecost upon Jesus's followers and join them to his body. These foundational events – Good Friday, Easter, Ascension and Pentecost – are thus crucial to understanding what now completed the establishment of Christian baptism. Particularly once Pentecost and the coming of the Holy Spirit had occurred, all the components of the more powerful baptism, that both John and Jesus himself (in Acts 1.5) had said that Jesus would bring for the renewed people of God, were now present.

Just as earlier Judaism contained key symbols and praxis that reinforced Israel's identity as YHWH's covenant people, so baptism and the Lord's Supper swiftly became the community-defining symbols of the new covenant people. Tom Wright argues that baptism wasn't, first and foremost, a statement about the individual being baptized but a communal statement of identity. It was an encoded narrative proclaiming the covenant story into which the person being baptized had been incorporated. Baptism declares that followers of Jesus Christ are the true exodus people, the place of God's presence, defined and set free by the death and resurrection of the Messiah and on their way to inheriting the true 'promised-land' of the whole renewed creation.[2]

Another important aspect of baptism is its *oneness*. Ephesians 4.5 declares that there is 'one baptism'. The major implications of this one baptism are for Christian unity, which will be explored shortly. However, it also means that there can only be one true theology of baptism. In recent times, for instance, some have sought to develop a separate and distinctive theological understanding of household or infant baptism, alongside a different theology of adult baptism. This is a grave error and completely counter to the witness of the New Testament. The New Testament writers know only one theology of baptism and questions about the appropriateness or otherwise of any forms of baptism need to be posed in these terms alone. It is also a reminder that baptism does not belong to any one Christian tradition – Catholic, Orthodox, Anglican, Baptist or any other. The New Testament is clear that it belongs to the one Lord, one Spirit and one God and Father, 'who is over all and through all and in all' (Ephesians 4.6).

## Baptism 'into Christ/the Messiah'

Understanding why Jesus's followers are described as being 'in Christ/in the Messiah' or 'Christians' (a name developed early on and first reported in Acts 11.26) is vital to understanding baptism. Too often, scholars have downplayed the messianic significance of 'Christ' within Paul's theology treating it as a term he used with little reference to its original derivation. This has contributed to a similar approach at a popular level with many Christians seeing 'Christ' almost as surname for Jesus. Tom Wright, by contrast, has emphasized how appreciation of the full messianic significance of Christ is critical to understanding Paul's thought.[3] Key to this is an understanding of the representative nature of Israel's anointed kings, with their people, for good or bad, incorporated within their roles and actions. Very often within Israel's history this incorporation had been for bad (see particularly 1 and 2 Kings), echoing the way in which human beings' status 'in Adam' had similarly left them cursed and afflicted (Genesis 3.16-19; Romans 5.12-19). But, after the events of Easter, Ascension and Pentecost, the early Christians were aware that it was through being 'in the Messiah'/'in Christ' and members of his crucified and risen body that they could assume a similar status as God's children, receive his Holy Spirit and participate in the new creation which he had brought (see particularly Romans 5–8).

This is where baptism 'into (Greek *eis*) the name of Jesus Christ' (Acts 2.38; Romans 6.3) gains its full significance. Being identified with Christ/the Messiah meant, in particular, participating in Jesus's death and resurrection. As Paul described it, 'all of us who were baptised into Christ Jesus' have been 'baptised into his death', 'buried with him through baptism into death', 'united with him ... in his death' with the result that 'our old self was crucified with him' (Romans 6.3-6). It is as a result of this baptism into Christ Jesus that Paul also speaks of Christians being 'united with him in his resurrection'. This is both a future event that Christians have to look forward to (Romans 6.5) and a present reality (Colossians 2.12). Elsewhere Paul uses different language to speak of this identification with Jesus the Messiah, saying, 'for all of you who were baptised into Christ have clothed yourself with Christ' (Galatians 3.27).

It is from this basis that the New Testament speaks of the blessings that come upon the followers of Jesus as a result of being baptized into Christ. These blessings are accompanied by significant responsibilities for the baptized as well. Both are detailed below. Several are very obvious recapitulations of those features of the baptism of Jesus that we noted at the end of Chapter 5. This is because being 'baptized into Christ' means that what is true of Jesus the Messiah becomes true of all those who belong to him.

## 1. The blessings of being united with Christ in baptism

### (a) Forgiveness and cleansing

At Pentecost Peter declared, 'Repent and be baptised ... so your sins may be forgiven' (Acts 2.38). After Paul's experience of the risen Jesus on the Damascus road, Ananias said to him, 'Get up, be baptised and wash your sins away, calling on his name' (Acts 22.16). Much the same is expressed in 1 Corinthians 6.11, Ephesians 5.26, Hebrews 10.22 and Titus 3.5.

The letter to the Hebrews makes it clear that whilst forgiveness and cleansing were available under the old covenant, this forgiveness and cleansing were only temporary. As well as meaning that sacrifices constantly had to be made in the Temple, this was also reflected in the ritual washings that Judaism developed having to be regularly repeated. The water used in baptism and particularly the references to it 'washing' its recipients show such cleansing lay at its heart and the non-repetitive nature of baptism enshrines the new covenant truth that the forgiveness it conveys is, like the death of Jesus itself, 'once and for all'. Whilst the New Testament exhorts Christians to continue confessing their sins (James 5.16; 1 John 1.9), the single nature of their baptism forms the assurance that the fundamental forgiveness and cleansing that establishes their status before God has already occurred. This is also surely related, however, to the stern warnings given in Hebrews concerning those who deliberately turn away from the God who has found them in Jesus (Hebrews 6.4-6; 10.26-31 with the latter passage occurring soon after the probable references to baptism in 10.22).

An important passage in this regard is 1 Peter 3.18-21, which describes baptism as 'the pledge of a good conscience towards God'. Some have interpreted this pledge or promise as made by the person being baptized and expressing their faithfulness towards God.[4] This, however, is problematic, given that the pledge expressed in baptism is described as what 'saves you by the resurrection of Jesus Christ'. The rest of the New Testament presents baptism as representing promises or pledges *made by God to us, rather than from us to God*. It is therefore consistent with the rest of the biblical witness to see this admittedly complex passage as asserting that baptism is a pledge from God of the good standing that followers of Jesus have before him. Rather than representing an outward cleansing ('the removal of dirt from the body'), baptism represents God's solemn promise of an inward cleansing of our conscience, brought about by Jesus dying for our sins and being made alive by the Spirit.

### (b) The gift of the Holy Spirit

We have seen that John the Baptist contrasted his water-baptism with the coming Messiah's Spirit-baptism (Matthew 3.11; Mark 1.8; Luke 3.16). The risen Jesus said something very similar when he told the disciples to wait in Jerusalem for the coming of the Holy Spirit (Acts 1.4-5). This might have led one to expect that after the Messianic baptism with the Spirit at Pentecost, water-baptism might be discontinued. However, Jesus's receipt of the Holy Spirit at his own water-baptism and the command he gave concerning baptism after his resurrection clearly indicated otherwise. Peter said, 'Repent and be baptised … and you will receive the gift of the Holy Spirit' implying that water-baptism symbolizes Spirit-baptism. The pouring of the water dramatizes the outpouring of the Spirit (Acts 2.38; 1.5; Titus 3.5). This gift of the Spirit is a seal, a deposit, a guarantee assuring the inheritance of God's people until the final day of redemption (2 Corinthians 1.21f; Ephesians 1.13f; 4.30). Baptism is thus the mark of both the present experience of God's indwelling presence and the hope of its future consummation in the new creation.

The Acts of the Apostles lays a great emphasis upon the coming of the Holy Spirit which it regularly identifies with baptism 'into Christ'. However, as noted in Chapter 2, there were exceptions to this and part of the significance of these exceptions will be examined in Chapter 13. As a whole, however, the New Testament seems to assume that a close connection between baptism and receiving the Holy Spirit is the norm and certainly a crucial part of what Christian baptism represents. Once again we must not lose the vital corporate nature of the Spirit, alongside its personal indwelling in followers of Jesus: 'For we were all baptised by one Spirit into one body – whether Jews or Greeks, slaves or free – and are all given one Spirit to drink' (1 Corinthians 12.13).

### (c) New birth and adoption as children of God

Another feature of the baptism of Jesus that we noted in Chapter 5 was the affirmation of his status as God's Son. Earlier we noted how, under the old covenant, not only the Davidic king but the whole of Israel was described as God's Son (Exodus 4.22; Hosea 11.1). The disobedience of Israel towards the covenant, however, resulted in Israel's loss of this status (Hosea 1.9). Hosea also made it clear, however, that when God's covenant promises were fulfilled, those previously stripped of this status would become 'sons of the living God' (Hosea 1.10).

This new birth and adoption of God's children occurs within Christian baptism. It is in the context of baptism into Christ that Paul declares, 'You are all sons of God through faith in Christ Jesus' (Galatians 3.26f) and God 'saved us through the washing of rebirth' (Titus 3.5f). Many assume that Jesus also refers to Christian baptism when, in his conversation with Nicodemus about the importance of being 'born again', Jesus declares 'no one can enter the kingdom of God unless he born of water and the spirit' (John 3.5). The status of Christians as God's sons (and daughters!) is hugely significant within the New Testament. This is presented most clearly in Romans 8.12-17 where the 'Spirit of Sonship' enables them, like Jesus, to call God 'Abba, Father' (8.16) and to assume an identical status to Jesus – 'heirs of God and co-heirs with Christ' (8.17). This blessing of divine son and daughtership, with all its assurance of eternal relationship with God, lies at the heart of Christian baptism.

### (d) Incorporation into the one people of God

One of the most obvious symptoms of the failure of the old covenant was the division and enmity between its people. After the failure of the first 'son of David' to maintain the covenant (1 Kings 11), the result was the division of Israel (1 Kings 12) recapitulating the division within the people of the world following their building of the Tower of Babel (Genesis 11). When they spoke of the renewal of the covenant, however, the prophets spoke not only of the reunification of the people of Israel and Judah under one appointed leader (e.g. Hosea 1.11) but of a future day when the Gentiles would also be incorporated into the single people of God (Isaiah 19.23-25).

The unity of the people of God, and specifically the incorporation of the Gentiles alongside believing Jews into the one united people of God, is one of the most important themes of both Acts and several of the Pauline Epistles (particularly Romans, Galatians and Ephesians). It is also one of the most important themes associated with baptism with Paul declaring:

> As a prisoner of the Lord, then, I urge you to live a life worthy of the calling you have received. Be completely humble and gentle; be patient, bearing with one another in love. Make every effort to keep the unity of the Spirit through the bond of peace. There is one body and one Spirit – just as to one hope you were called – one Lord, one faith, *one baptism*, one God and Father of all, who is over all and through all and in all. (Ephesians 4.1-6)

Earlier in Ephesians, Paul speaks of how the Gentiles were once 'called uncircumcised' and 'separate from Christ, excluded from citizenship in Israel and foreigners to the covenants of the promise, without hope and without God in the world' (2.11-12). All this had now changed, however, since 'in Christ Jesus you who once were far away have been brought near through the blood of Christ' (2.13). Paul sees this peace as achieved through Jesus's abolishing 'in his flesh, the law with its commandments and regulations' (2.14) and is clear that 'through the gospel, the Gentiles are heirs together with Israel, members together of one body and sharers together in the promise in Christ Jesus' (3.6). All of this radical equality was based on Paul's conviction that the one God through the one Body of his Son and through the one Spirit was creating one single people to belong to him. Central to this was there being one baptism and one faith through which both Jews and Gentiles joined this one family on completely equal terms.[5]

The same point forms the basis of the anger that Paul shows in Galatians at the attempt of some Jewish Christians to insist that Gentile converts be circumcised in order to be fully part of the people of God. Paul insists that this is a denial of the gospel itself since, in Jesus the Messiah, God had revealed that the sole marker of those whom God will one day justify (or declare righteous/part of his covenant people) is faith in Jesus Christ. To attempt to re-establish obedience to 'works of the law' (Jewish boundary markers such as circumcision and food laws) as the sign of those whom God would justify was to reintroduce an exclusivity which had been completely swept away in Jesus. And when Paul makes his fullest statement of the radical inclusivity of the covenant people that Jesus had established, baptism 'into Christ' is once again present, alongside faith.

> You are all sons of God through faith in Christ Jesus, *for all of you who were baptised into Christ have clothed yourself with Christ*. There is neither Jew nor Greek, slave nor free, male nor female, for you are all one in Christ Jesus. If you belong to Christ, you are Abraham's seed, and heirs according to the promise. (Galatians 3.26-29)

The precise relationship between baptism and faith will be explored later in this chapter and the next. But for now we can see how one of the major blessings associated with baptism in the early church was the completely equal basis that baptism and faith in Jesus provided for anyone and everyone to become part of the covenant family of God.

A similar message about the radical equality of members of the church is expressed in different manner within Paul's first letter to the Corinthians. Here Paul focuses upon Christians being members of the one body of Christ with the different gifts of each member of the body being equally important. And once again, the means by which this equality is brought about is baptism.

> The body is a unit, though it is made up of many parts; and though all its parts are many, they form one body. So it is with Christ. *For we were all baptised by one Spirit into one body* – whether Jews or Greeks, slave or free – and were all given the one Spirit to drink. (1 Corinthians 12.12-13)

One of the unique features of early Christianity and a major reason for its explosive growth was the way in which the movement welcomed anyone and everyone to become part of the people of God on precisely the same terms. In a world that was deeply segregated this call to 'oneness' was unheard of and lay at the heart of the good news of Jesus Christ which many found so attractive.

## (e) Resurrection life

Mention of this blessing of baptism has already been made. It is repeated, however, because of the regularity with which the Christian hope of resurrection is replaced by the (at best) inadequate shorthand of 'going to heaven when you die'. When this occurs, much of the significance of baptism is then missed. According to Paul, baptism unites Christians with Christ in his death so that they can then be *raised* with him. This bodily resurrection of Christians belongs in the future (Romans 8.10-11; 1 Corinthians 15) but, crucially, union with the dying and risen Christ in baptism and faith is what enables Christians to possess this risen life in the present: 'All of us who were baptised into Christ Jesus were baptised into his death. We were therefore buried with him through baptism into death in order that, just as Christ was raised from the dead through the glory of the Father, we too might live a new life' (Romans 6.3-4).

This point is re-emphasized because of the way that it leads so naturally from the blessings of baptism to the calling and responsibilities within it. We have seen already that baptism is frequently used by the New Testament writers to encourage the churches to live out the right response to God in their lives. Paul, in particular, consistently encourages the Christians to whom he is writing to think through their response to God on the basis of their baptism. Within all the letters in which he mentions baptism – Romans, 1 Corinthians, Galatians, Ephesians and Colossians – Paul urges these Christian communities to live out the death to sin and resurrection to eternal life that their baptism represents. As we saw in Chapter 2, the principal ways that they are called to express this response to their baptism is through working out their holiness and unity.

## 2. The calling and responsibilities of baptism

### (a) The call to holiness

In 1 Corinthians 8–10, Paul is engaged in advising the Christians at Corinth about how they should interact with the pagan culture which surrounded them and dealing, in particular, with the question of whether Christians should eat food that had previously been offered to idols. Paul asserts, on the basis of Christian monotheism, the Corinthians' right to eat anything (8.4-6; see also 10.26). This is immediately qualified, however, by the need to exercise this freedom with love and consideration for fellow believers for whom the issue was more problematic (8.7-13). But when he moves on to speak of the dangers of actual idolatry, Paul's approach is to retell the story of exodus through the lens of baptism and the Lord's Supper:

> For I do not want you to be ignorant of the fact, brothers, that our forefathers were all under the cloud and that they all passed through the sea. They were all baptised into Moses in the cloud and the sea. They all ate the same spiritual food and drank the same spiritual drink; for they drank from the spiritual rock that accompanied them, and that rock was Christ. Nevertheless, God was not pleased with most of them; their bodies were scattered over the desert. Now these things occurred as examples to keep us from setting our hearts on evil things as they did. Do not be idolaters, as some of them were; as it is written "The people sat down to eat and drink and got up to indulge in pagan revelry." We should not commit sexual immorality as some of them did – in one day twenty-three thousand of them died. We should not test the Lord, as some of them did – and were killed by snakes. And do not grumble as some of them did – and were killed by the destroying angel. (1 Corinthians 10.1-10)

Paul's point is that Israel's equivalents of baptism and the Lord's Supper were not enough to save most of her people from disaster and God's judgement. This was because Israel's 'baptism' and 'communion' were followed by behaviour that denied her status as God's people. Paul makes it clear that he understood baptism and the Lord's Supper as intrinsically connected with the earlier covenant story of Israel. He is also clear that baptism and the Lord's Supper define the community of God's people as the place of God's presence in Christ. It is precisely because of this that the Corinthian Christians need to avoid any temptation to fall back into idolatry. The fellowship or participation (Greek *koinonia*) that they enjoy with Christ, through baptism and the Lord's Supper, means that the fellowship with demons that idolatry creates is completely off limits. A major implication of baptism and the Lord's Supper, therefore, is the calling to live in a way that is consistent with the fellowship with God in Jesus Christ that baptism has established and the Lord's Supper maintains. The need to preserve holiness by avoiding the dehumanizing effect of idolatry is the major point here. But it is significant that much of this holiness finds its expression in concern for others, as Paul returns to the question of whether to eat food offered to idols and stresses the importance of concern for unbelievers, as well as those within the Christian family (10.23-33). Paul wants the baptized Christians at Corinth to be so defined by Jesus Christ, and particularly his saving death, that their behaviour is shaped by a similar denial of self for the sake of others.

A similar emphasis is found in Paul's treatment of baptism in *Romans*. In Chapter 4 we saw how Romans is structured around a Christian recapitulation of the covenant story, all the way from the call of Abraham (Romans 4) to the inheritance awaiting God's renewed people (Romans 8.17-30). In the midst of this, Paul does the reverse of what he has done in 1 Corinthians 10, using the exodus story as the template for what has happened to the Christian community. This includes presenting them as 'slaves' rescued by coming through water (Romans 6), ahead of travelling through the 'wilderness' towards their promised inheritance, accompanied by God's presence through the Holy Spirit (8.9-16). The baptized are therefore the true exodus people, defined by the death and resurrection of the Messiah and who must now live in an appropriate way. Central to this is the need to recognize that they were buried with Christ through baptism into death, so that just as Christ was raised from the dead, they too could live a new life. Previously the Romans were in slavery to sin which could only result in death. Now that they have been rescued through their baptism into the Messiah, they need to become 'slaves to God', with the very different result of holiness and eternal life. As Romans continues we see that this involves being led by the Spirit to put to death the misdeeds of the body (8.13), as well as being prepared to share in Christ's sufferings (8.17) and live in love and unity with other believers (12–16).

An important aspect of this is Paul's instruction to 'offer the parts of your body … as instruments of righteousness' (6.13) and 'become slaves to righteousness' (6.18). The use of term 'righteousness' points to Paul's conviction that the holy lives of those who belong to God form part of his ongoing covenant plan for the redemption of the earth. The end goal of the covenant project is that restored human beings will rule the renewed creation on behalf of God. This future rule is anticipated in the present, not by domination of others but by a pattern of living based on our baptism into Christ: death to sin resulting in the experience of resurrection life.

In Colossians 2–3 we see a similar emphasis. Paul once again uses covenantal imagery by saying that the Colossians have received a 'circumcision done by Christ' when they were 'buried with him in baptism and raised with him through your faith in the power of God who raised him from the dead' (2.12). As a result of this, followers of Jesus have received both forgiveness of their sins and freedom from the Torah which had condemned them. The response to this is twofold. First, resistance to any pressure to submit to the regulations of the law, which possessed only human power and lacked any real value in restraining sin (2.16-23). Second, the development, instead, of practical holiness based upon the powerful truth of their union through baptism in the death and resurrection of the Messiah.

> Since then, you have been raised with the Messiah, set your hearts on things above, where the Messiah is seated at the right hand of God. Set your minds on things above, not on earthly things. For you died and your life is now hidden with Christ in God. When the Messiah, who is your life, appears, then you will also appear with him in glory. Put to death, therefore, whatever belongs to the earthly nature. (Colossians 3.1-4)

Developing this holiness involves strenuous effort to rid oneself of the evil behaviour that belonged to our formerly earthly nature, such as sexual immorality, greed, anger and dishonesty (3.5-11). In its place, and based upon their status as 'God's chosen people, holy and dear loved', believers are instead to 'clothe themselves' with compassion, kindness, humility, gentleness, patience, forbearance, forgiveness and love (3.12-17). Whilst baptism is only mentioned in Colossians 2.12, everything that follows in terms of the challenge to develop holiness is based upon living out the truth of what has been proclaimed in that baptism.

### (b) The call to unity

As we have seen, all the passages that exhort Christians to holiness on the basis of their baptism go on to include within this the development of love for others. This particularly includes fellow members of the one covenant family that have joined through their baptism. Rather than being simply a sub-branch of Christian virtue, however, giving meaningful and practical expression to Christian unity stands at the heart of the response that the New Testament calls believers to make to baptism.

We have already seen in this chapter how both Galatians and Ephesians emphasize that a major blessing brought about by baptism is incorporation into God's one, multi-ethnic family. Galatians, in particular, goes on to assert that any apartheid between Christian believers is therefore a straightforward denial of the gospel. The situation in Galatia means that most of Paul's letter contains examples of behaviour to be avoided, such as Peter's withdrawal from eating with Gentile Christians at Antioch (2.11-14) and any continued promotion of circumcision and the law in the new age of the Spirit. But in the final part of the letter he speaks of the practical ways in which the Galatians should seek to serve one another in love (5.13-14; 6.1-10).

However, it is in 1 Corinthians that we see Paul provide the fullest explanation of how baptism should lead to the priority of unity. This begins in 1.13-17 as Paul disassociates himself from factionalism by pointing to what a travesty it would be if baptism were associated with either himself or any other Christian leader. With all the divisions that exist amongst the Corinthians, Paul states how thankful he is that he didn't baptize more than a handful of them. The point that he is making is baptism can only ever be 'into the name of Jesus the Messiah'. Given the impossibility of the one Messiah being divided and the truth that the Messiah alone was crucified for them, the divisions amongst the Corinthians only served to show how much they are still dominated by the false wisdom of the world, rather than being shaped by the gospel of Christ crucified. The implication is that baptism into the name of the one crucified Messiah should make nonsense of all the petty ideas of importance and status that so frequently divide the church.

This message is reinforced in Chapter 12 as Paul deals with divisions within the Corinthian church over spiritual gifts. The problem appears to have been that those with more obviously spectacular gifts were being seen as superior to others. Paul begins by asserting that there are different kinds of 'gifts', 'service' and 'working' but one Spirit, one Lord and one God behind them (12.4-6). The message is that just as the

Father, the Son and the Spirit are one, so the Corinthian church, with all of its diversity of people with different kinds of spiritual gifts, should be one as well. This is reinforced a few verses later by baptism. Paul speaks of the body being a single unit though it is made of many parts and then says:

> For we were all baptised by one Spirit into one body – whether Jews or Greeks, slaves or free – and we were all given one Spirit to drink. (1 Corinthians 12.13)

It is from this basis that Paul asserts the folly of any sort of rivalry and that the different gifts of the Corinthians should, like the different parts of a human body, be seen as equally valuable and work in harmony with one another. This leads him on to speak about the paramount importance of love over any other gift (13.1-13) and the very practical ways in which this love needed to be worked out in the life of the church at Corinth (14.1-40).

The final reference to baptism in 1 Corinthians provides further testimony to the oneness that it represents. In Chapter 15, Paul is engaged in arguing for the indispensable importance of the resurrection. As part of this, he asks:

> Now if there is no resurrection, what will those do who are baptised for the dead? If the dead are not raised at all, why are people baptised for them? (1 Corinthians 15.29)

The lack of detail is frustrating but also telling because it shows that by the mid-50s, it was common practice for Christians to undergo a baptism on behalf of those who had died.[6] Since Paul then speaks about facing danger and death, it may be that such proxy-baptisms were particularly used for believers who had been martyred before they had the chance to be baptized. In the absence of any other evidence for the practice, this is speculation. But the existence of Christians being 'baptized for the dead' is further evidence of the communal nature of baptism and the unity that it represented.

The interrelationship that we see in 1 Corinthians between messianic monotheism, baptism and the unity in diversity of the church helps us to appreciate more of the significance of Matthew 28.19-20. The same three elements are contained here as the risen Jesus commands his followers: 'make disciples of all nations, baptising them in the name of the Father, the Son and of the Holy Spirit and teaching them to obey everything that I have commanded you'. Monotheism, as stated in 'the Shema' of Deuteronomy 6.4-5, had been crucial to the faith of Israel for centuries. Its central application was in there being one people of YHWH gathered around one place of worship to love God with all their heart, soul and strength. Now, as monotheism was freshly revealed through the work of Jesus the Messiah and the Spirit, the one people of God was also freshly revealed as one worldwide, multi-ethnic family called to be one body possessing one faith, one hope united in love for God and one another.[7] And, as Paul states in Ephesians 4.3-5, since there was one baptism providing entry into this family, it was imperative for Christians to do everything that they could to maintain this unity and make it really meaningful.

Make every effort to keep the unity of the Spirit through the bond of peace. There is one body and one Spirit – just as you were called to one hope when you were called – one Lord, one faith, one baptism. (Ephesians 4.3-5)

It is following this reference to baptism that Paul, as in 1 Corinthians, goes on to list some of the diverse gifts that the ascended Messiah had given 'to prepare God's people for works of service, so that the body of Christ may be built up until we all reach *unity* in the faith and in the knowledge of the Son of God and become mature, attaining to the whole measure of the fullness of the Messiah' (Ephesians 4.12-13).

Once the relationship between baptism and the calling to holiness and unity is recognized, it becomes clear how much of Paul's message to the churches that he writes to can be seen as an appeal to work out the implications of their baptism. All the practical instructions that he gives in his letters can be understood within this context. The collection that Paul organized amongst the Gentile churches for their Jewish brothers and sisters in Jerusalem (Romans 15.25-27; 1 Corinthians 16.1-3; 2 Corinthians 8–9), to give just one example, was an opportunity for the early Christians to give practical expression of the truth that they were all baptized by one Spirit into one body.

### (c) The call to suffer

In Chapter 5 we noted the emphasis upon the calling to suffer within the baptism of Jesus himself. We also saw this in his teaching about the baptism of suffering servanthood that his followers would also have to undergo (Mark 10.35-45). Before that, in Chapter 4 we also saw that John the Baptist's reference to the baptism 'with fire' that Jesus would bring probably referred, at least in part, to the suffering that his followers would be called to endure (Matthew 3.11; Luke 3.16). The question is whether this emphasis was also made in the early church and whether the call for followers of Jesus to suffer was understood as just as vital within baptism as the calling to holiness and unity already examined.

Those who see the gospel accounts as largely a projection of the thinking of the early church onto the person of Jesus will already be able to affirm this. But this perspective on the nature of the gospels, popular for a long time, has increasingly been found wanting. There is simply too much within the gospels, not least in the references of John the Baptist and Jesus to baptism and suffering, which is too opaque to be understood as theological thinking of the early church projected back in this manner. In fact the allusive, puzzling and uncomfortable nature of these sayings on baptism, in particular, gives every indication of their authentic nature as strange words of John and Jesus that were remembered long before they made full sense to their hearers.

But did these sayings nonetheless feed into and inform the understanding of baptism in the early church? At first sight, this is less obvious, particularly in the case of Paul. Back in Chapter 2 and again in this chapter, we have seen the explicit connections that Paul makes between baptism and the call to holiness and unity. There are no passages in which he makes a similarly explicit connection between baptism and the call to suffer. However, when we pay attention to the *narrative* structure of Paul's letter to the Romans, a different picture emerges. As noted, Tom Wright has shown how much of Romans is a very deliberate retelling of the significance of Jesus the Messiah through the template of the exodus narrative.[8] Baptism into Jesus being presented as making his followers slaves set free by coming through water in Romans 6 is only the start of this. Through Romans 7 we see them travelling, like Israel, to Sinai to grapple with the role of the Torah, before Romans 8 covers their 'journey to the Promised Land'. This includes the construction of a 'tabernacle' as God comes to dwell, through the Holy Spirit, in their midst (8.9-11) and, from that point, the renewed people of God continue through the 'wilderness' (8.12-16) ahead of glimpsing their promised inheritance (8.17-30). It is within this narrative structure that Paul shows how the call to suffer is a crucial part of the journey that starts with baptism. Throughout Romans 8 we see two of the most prominent blessings associated with baptism – assurance of divine sonship and possession of the Holy Spirit – helping and sustaining the 'freed slaves' through the suffering that they have endured on their way to the glorious inheritance that God has promised them.

> For those who are led by the Spirit of God are sons of God. The Spirit you received does not make you slaves, so that you live in fear again; rather, the Spirit you received brought about your adoption to sonship. And by him we cry, "Abba, Father." The Spirit himself testifies with our spirit that we are God's children. Now if we are children, then we are heirs – heirs of God and co-heirs with the Messiah, if indeed we *share in his sufferings* in order that we may also share in his glory. I consider that our present *sufferings* are not worth comparing with the glory that will be revealed in us. For the creation waits in eager expectation for the children of God to be revealed. For the creation was subjected to frustration, not by its own choice, but by the will of the one who subjected it, in hope that the creation itself will be liberated from its bondage to decay and brought into the freedom and glory of the children of God. (Romans 8.14-21)

The rest of Romans 8 continues the theme of how God's promises to his chosen people and their possession of his Spirit can assure them that not even the very worst forms of suffering will be able to separate them from the love of God. Quite the opposite, in fact, because sharing in the suffering of the Messiah is central to sharing in his glory. It couldn't, therefore, be clearer that Paul understands the calling to God's people in baptism to include suffering just as much as the calling to develop their holiness and unity.

Once this is seen in Romans, it becomes clearer elsewhere in Paul's letters. Paul's letter to the Philippians nowhere mentions baptism. But its key theme is the fellowship or participation (Greek *koinonia*) that lies at the heart of what it means to belong to the Messiah and the call to 'work out' what this salvation means in the Christian life. Much of this fits with what we saw earlier about the call to holiness and particularly unity arising from union with the Messiah in baptism:

> Therefore if you have any encouragement from being *united with the Messiah*, if
> any comfort from his love, if any common sharing in the Spirit, if any tenderness
> and compassion, then make my joy complete by being like-minded, having the
> same love, being one in spirit and of one mind. Do nothing out of selfish ambition
> or vain conceit. Rather, in humility value others above yourselves, not looking to
> your own interests but each of you to the interests of the others. (Philippians 2.1-4)

But an equally important part of this fellowship with the Messiah for Paul is sharing
in his suffering.

> I want to know the Messiah and the power of his resurrection and the fellowship
> of sharing in his sufferings, becoming like him in his death, and so, somehow, to
> attain to the resurrection from the dead. (Philippians 3.10-11)

The tone of Philippians indicates that Paul would probably have placed the call to
suffer within the blessings of baptism rather than the responsibilities arising from it.
Being buried with the Messiah in baptism and thus sharing in his death very clearly
involved the understanding that this involved the calling to suffer ahead of receiving
the promised resurrection.

Something similar is then seen in Acts where the suffering of God's renewed people
is a major theme. After Paul's meeting with the risen Jesus on the road to Damascus,
the disciple Ananias is summoned by God to minister to him. As well the recovery
of his sight, this results in Paul being filled with the Holy Spirit and being baptized
(Acts 9.17-19). But as Ananias is commissioned for this task, he is told not only about
Paul's ministry to the Gentiles and Israel but also about his suffering 'I will show him
how much he must *suffer* for my name' (Acts 9.15-16). Paul's subsequent teaching in
Acts is consistent with this. On the return leg of the First Missionary Journey, Luke's
focus is upon one aspect of Paul's message to the new (and presumably newly baptized)
Christians of Lystra, Iconium and Derbe: 'We must go through many *hardships* to
enter the kingdom of God' (Acts 14.22).

The passage within the epistles where baptism is explicitly mentioned in the context
of the calling of Christians to suffer is 1 Peter 3. Parts of the passage are difficult to
fathom but as its writer speaks of the calling of believers to suffer for doing good, he
invokes the example of not only Christ being 'put to death in the body but made alive
by the Spirit' but also Noah and his family. The water that saved those in the Ark, Peter
says, 'symbolises baptism that now saves you also' (1 Peter 3.21). The clear implication
of this, admittedly complex passage, is that a large part of being baptized into Christ
is accepting the calling to be submerged in a similar suffering that will then lead to
salvation through this identification with the risen Jesus Christ.

More broadly, it is clear that the New Testament regards the faithful suffering of
Jesus's followers as one of the major ways in which his victory is implemented within
the world. This is one of the central themes of Revelation. Explicit connection between
baptism and this calling of Christians to suffer is not as plentiful in the epistles as
we might expect, given the example of Jesus's baptism and his own teaching on this
connection. However, there are simply too many parallels between the symbolism of

dying with the Messiah in baptism and the widespread teaching about Christians being called to suffer (not to mention the regular experience of this in the early church) not to recognize this as a fundamental aspect of how the early Christians understood baptism.

Interestingly, there is evidence beyond the New Testament period that some saw *martyrdom* as a valid form of baptism. This idea was articulated by Cyril of Jerusalem (*c.* 313–386) and based on Jesus's words in Mark 10.38-39 and Luke 12.50. Baptism was understood, as we have seen, to bring about an identification with Christ in his death and therefore with his resurrection. By the third and fourth centuries, preparation for baptism was taken very seriously, and sometimes people on such a programme were martyred for their faith in Christ before their baptism had occurred. In this case, Cyril argued, this 'baptism of blood' was an equally valid form of identification with Christ as baptism by water.[9] Rather than being a denial of the biblical principle of there being 'one baptism', 'baptism by blood' was seen as expressing the same truths expressed in more normal baptism. As suggested earlier, it is possible that the practice of 'baptism for the dead', mentioned by Paul in 1 Corinthians 15, arose from a similar context.

## Baptism as 'the ordination of the laity'

In the first part of this chapter, we saw how every blessing of the gospel is contained within baptism. In the second half, we have seen how this is also true of every calling that God makes to his people as well. Human beings, back in Genesis, were created to represent God to creation by ruling it on his behalf and to represent creation to God by reflecting its praises back to him.[10] Each of the different stages in the covenant story was working towards the final defeat of sin and evil in Jesus Christ so that this vocation could be renewed and re-established. Baptism thus represents the re-establishment and restoration of this vocation. By living as the rescued and renewed people of God, the little groups of baptized believers scattered around the Mediterranean formed the living temple in which God was now dwelling. Faith, love and hope found their major application in the baptismal call to the churches to live in holiness, unity and patient suffering as advanced signs of the time when the whole world would be filled with God's glory. It is for this reason that baptism is sometimes called 'the ordination of the laity'. It conveys all of God's blessings to his people and both equips and commissions them to live for God in the world.

## The connection between baptism and faith

The examination of this will continue into the next chapter. All nine references to baptism in the Acts of the Apostles occur explicitly within the context of the proclamation of the gospel or good news of Jesus Christ and the vital reception of this gospel with faith.

This is linked to the crucial emphasis within the New Testament upon justification by faith. 'Justification' is a covenantal term referring to God's declaration of a person's righteousness. It is also eschatological, referring to the declaration that God will make on the future day of resurrection. Vitally, however, this future declaration is also signalled in the present by God marking out those who belong to his people. Paul strenuously argues in Galatians and Romans that rather than being justified by 'works of the law', the sign that people are members of God's covenant family, justified or declared righteous by him, is *faith* in Jesus Christ.

It is of the greatest importance to recognize that each of the blessings signified in baptism that we examined earlier in this chapter is similarly attributed by the New Testament writers to the proclamation of the good news/the word of God and its acceptance by faith.

*Identification with Christ by sharing in his death and resurrection* – 'raised with him through your faith' (Colossians 2.12; Galatians 2.20) 'that Christ may dwell in your hearts through faith' (Ephesians 3.17).

*Forgiveness and cleansing* – 'He purified their hearts by faith' (Acts 15.9; see also Acts 13.38f; Romans 3.21ff).

*The gift of the Spirit* – 'so that by faith we might receive the promise of the Spirit' (Galatians 3.14; 3.2; Ephesians 1.13).

*New birth, Adoption and Divine Sonship* – 'you are all sons of God through faith in Christ Jesus' (Galatians 3.26; John 1.12; James 1.18; 1 Peter 1.23f).

*Incorporation into God's One Covenant People* – 'Is God the God of the Jews only? Is he not the God of the Gentiles too? Yes of the Gentiles too, since there is one God who will justify the circumcised by faith and the uncircumcised through that same faith' (Romans 3.29-30; Galatians 3.6-9).

These references make it clear that in the New Testament, the word of the gospel received by faith and the sign of baptism are seen as a unity. The same effects are attributed to both without contradiction or difference of meaning. Baptism into Jesus Christ and faith in Jesus Christ clearly have the closest possible relationship. Scholars of widely different traditions have affirmed this. The Presbyterian James Denney said, 'Baptism and faith are but the outside and the inside of the same thing'[11] and the Roman Catholic Rudolf Schnackenburg wrote that 'baptism without faith in Christ is unimaginable for the thinking of the primitive church'.[12]

The crucial factor is that both baptism and faith point beyond themselves to God's grace and gift of salvation through Jesus Christ. It is not that faith makes human beings worthy of such blessings or that baptism has an intrinsic power to produce them; it is God who enables faith and gives baptism – and all the blessings are his alone. The blessings are only secondarily baptism-blessings or faith-blessings; primarily they are God's blessings, embodied in baptism and received by faith. As George Beasley-Murray neatly put it, 'Baptism is the divinely appointed rendezvous of grace for faith.'[13]

Another fundamental factor uniting baptism and faith in Jesus Christ is their inclusive nature. Previously, symbolized by 'works of the law', membership of the people of God was understood as being generally restricted to Israel. Baptism and justification by faith both proclaimed that through the work of Jesus the Messiah, membership of the people of God had now become open to everyone. The crucial text here is Galatians 3.26-29:

You are all sons of God through faith in Christ Jesus, for all of you who were united with Christ in baptism have been clothed with Christ. There is neither Jew nor Gentile, neither slave nor free, nor is there male and female, for you are all one in Christ Jesus. If you belong to Christ, then you are Abraham's seed, and heirs according to the promise.

These common emphases are important for understanding the relationship between baptism and faith. Too often the contrast drawn between the Old Testament and the New Testament is one between the supposedly external nature of the former, with all its rituals and ceremonies and its replacement by a more inward relationship with God. Justification by faith and an emphasis upon the Holy Spirit can appear to fit with this understanding. But, far less, the ritual and ceremony of baptism. To many it is unconceivable that the same Paul who proclaims justification by faith and opposes circumcision could replace the latter ritual with another in baptism.

However, as we saw in Chapters 3 and 4, this contrast between the Old Testament and the New Testament is a major misunderstanding. The story of the covenant in the Old Testament is just as strongly about God's grace being received by faith as the New Testament. The difference, as we saw, is not that of 'outward religion' being replaced by 'inward faith' but the temporary and passing provisions that brought God's covenant grace to Israel being fulfilled (and therefore replaced) by the person and work of Jesus Christ so that this same covenant grace could come to everyone.

Baptism is thus the outward and visible sign of justification by faith. Justification by faith brings God's future verdict in to the present, declares that the whole of the Christian life is dependent upon the death and resurrection of Jesus Christ and that everyone confessing that Jesus is Lord is part of the single sin-forgiven family promised by the covenant God to Abraham and called to the obedience of faith. Baptism proclaims all of this and, in the words of Tom Wright, 'is the action that turns that declaration into visible, concrete, symbolic praxis'.[14] It displays, and the following chapter will argue, effects, God's future verdict of resurrection coming into the present, the union with Jesus's death that makes this possible, the cleansing from sin and incorporation into God's single family that this brings and the call to faithful obedience.

In the light of the close association between the blessings associated with baptism and those arising from faith in Jesus Christ, it is inevitable that baptism of converts involves a confession of faith. However, it is important to note that the New Testament writers nowhere indicate the significance of the baptism-event in terms of the convert's witness to others. Rather it is *God's* witness or seal to the convert. It is the baptized life that is understood as a witness to others rather than the baptism-event itself. This will be crucial when we examine the issues surrounding infant baptism and the 'baptist view' in Chapters 9 and 10.

# 8

# Baptism as a sacrament

So far in this book (other than in the Introduction), one of the key terms often used when referring to Christian baptism has not been used – the word 'sacrament'. Sacraments are usually defined as divinely authorized vehicles of God's grace. Within the Roman Catholic Church, baptism is understood to take its place alongside six other such sacraments – Confirmation, the Eucharist (or Holy Communion or the Lord's Supper), Penance, Extreme Unction, Ordination and Marriage. The sixteenth-century Reformers were anxious to only give the title of sacrament to those signs specifically commanded by Jesus and so most followed Martin Luther in restricting the term's use to baptism and communion, hence their frequent description as 'dominical sacraments' (i.e. authorized by the Lord).

Today Eastern Orthodox and more Catholic churches (be they Roman Catholic or Anglo-Catholic) continue to make very strong use of the term 'sacrament' in speaking of baptism because of their conviction that the action actually conveys the blessings from God that it symbolizes. Despite the Reformers' maintenance of the term 'sacrament' to describe baptism and Holy Communion, this is less common within more Protestant, evangelical and charismatic traditions of Christianity. The major emphasis of the Reformation was upon the word of the gospel needing to be received 'by faith alone', with the result that churches more shaped by this have tended to have much greater reticence about using the term 'sacrament'. This is partly because the term is not used in the Bible. It is even more because of the dangers regularly associated with such an understanding of baptism and Holy Communion. Acknowledging that God works through anything physical is, for some, the swift road to idolatry rather than encouraging a true faith in Jesus Christ. Likewise the emphasis upon any actions by worshippers runs the danger of trying to earn favour with God rather than accept his grace. As noted in Chapter 1, these sorts of thoughts have resulted in many Christians denying, either explicitly or implicitly, that baptism or communion convey any spiritual blessings at all. If this view is taken, then the term 'sacrament' is usually regarded as inappropriate. Baptism and the Lord's Supper are 'bare signs' which helpfully point believers to the spiritual realities of God's forgiveness of us through the death of Jesus but do not actually convey these blessings.

It will hopefully be clear already that the authors disagree with this understanding. A sacramental understanding of baptism both can and must be combined with the vital importance of a response of faith. The basis of this understanding will be outlined below before the issue of baptismal efficacy (i.e. whether baptism actually conveys the blessings it symbolizes) is addressed.

## Word and action in explaining sacraments

A way into understanding sacraments is when we recognize the way that the most important words that human beings use are frequently reinforced by actions. This has been true in the daily life of all cultures and countries throughout history. It is particularly true when those words involve a solemn promise or commitment. So the final part of a modern business deal, once the terms have been agreed and the contract signed, will often be a handshake. Another example is the marriage vows made at a wedding service being followed by an exchange of rings. In these cases and many others, a symbolic action adds an extra power and depth to the words that are spoken. The Latin word 'sacramentum' was used of the oath of loyalty taken by a soldier to his emperor and this too would have been accompanied by various symbolic actions, most obviously a salute. Examples can also be found in the Old Testament. In the account of Boaz becoming the kinsman-redeemer to Naomi and Ruth, the storyteller explains that 'for the redemption and transfer of property to become final, one party took off his sandal and gave it to the other. This was the method of legalising transactions in Israel' (Ruth 4.7). The more significant the words that we speak, the more likely we are to reinforce them with a symbolic action.

Symbols or symbolic actions also play a crucial role in communities, usually giving vital expression to their shared values. Obvious examples of this are the importance of the flag or national anthem of a country and the shared assumptions about the appropriate response its citizens should make to them. Such symbols have been described as 'portable narratives' because of the way in which they can capture and represent, frequently in an unspoken manner, the story through which a community understands itself. The potency of these symbols lies in the way that they often speak, far more powerfully than words, to reinforce the worldview of the community that they represent. This is most obviously demonstrated in the fierce reaction that occurs when these symbols are challenged or abused. The response to the burning of a nation's flag, for instance, will usually tell us everything about the importance attached to that particular symbol.

We have seen the significance associated with symbols as we have traced the development of the covenant story in Chapters 3 and 4. Right from the start, the solemn words of promise declared by God were accompanied by signs. The covenant promises made to Noah were accompanied by the sign of the rainbow, those made to Abraham by the sign of circumcision and those made to Israel, through Moses, by the Passover and the Tabernacle. When the prophets such as Hosea, Isaiah, Jeremiah and Ezekiel spoke on behalf of God, they also frequently used dramatic signs to reinforce 'the Word of YHWH'. We also saw how many of the symbols associated with the covenant – particularly circumcision, the food laws, the Sabbath, the Temple and its festivals and the land itself – then became crucial for defining the people of Israel by encapsulating the narrative by which they understood themselves.

Much of Jesus's ministry was characterized by the deeply symbolic actions that accompanied the words that he spoke. John's Gospel draws particular attention to this by referring to Jesus's miracles as 'signs'. But across all four gospels, Jesus announces his message through words and symbolic actions working together – not least to challenge the existing narrative of Israel, which is why his actions caused such controversy. These actions included Jesus eating with sinners, healing on the Sabbath, entering Jerusalem on a donkey and driving out those buying and selling in the Temple area. These were symbolic actions that went beyond merely illustrating the words that Jesus spoke. They embodied his words in a tangible form that conveyed something of the reality of which they spoke. Jesus's actions didn't convey all of this reality, because much of the rule of God of which he spoke was yet to come. But they conveyed enough of it for his hearers to experience its reality and respond with faith in the fulfilment of the covenant that Jesus proclaimed.

It is within this context that we need to understand the role of baptism and the Lord's Supper. In both cases, we see words of covenant promise from God, reinforced by tangible signs, establishing a narrative for the renewed people of God to live within. Those who have studied early Christianity from a sociological perspective have identified how central these repeated rituals were for the early church.[1] They were practised by all Christians and, as we have seen, swiftly became a theological given from which the answers to matters of less clarity could be inferred. The centrality that such studies have given to sacraments in the early church has caused Tom Wright to comment that it is an example of where 'sociologists run in where Protestants fear to tread'![2]

So far, so good. All of us are able to see how an action can reinforce a word or promise and provide it with greater power and clarity. We can also see the power that such shared symbolic actions have for a community. If the explanation ends here, however, it is not really enough to justify an understanding of sacraments as vehicles of God's grace. This is partly because the assumption can still exist that the disembodied word of God remains its purest form. This reduces any signs accompanying this word to a strictly secondary or supporting role, rather than being essential. The tell-tale of this is when evangelical Christians who want to endorse a sacramental understanding describe such signs from God in a manner that make them sound like a concession to our human frailty. The original edition of this book could have been understood as implying this when it declared: 'God's word is always declared by the biblical writers to be totally dependable, and yet, in his condescending mercy, God repeatedly adds a confirming and dramatic sign to his words.'[3]

The problem with this approach to sacraments is that it could be taken to suggest that the embodiment of God's Word is something that, ideally, would not be necessary. But for our human frailty, it implies, we would simply be able to hear God's words of promise and respond in faith. However, a moment's thought reveals the impossibility of this within orthodox and biblical Christian faith. The physicality of the incarnation, the crucifixion of Jesus and his resurrection were not of secondary importance to the words that proclaimed what God was doing through these events but vital to their significance. 'The Word became flesh and made his dwelling amongst us', John's Gospel declares, with this embodiment of God's Word

in the physical form of Jesus Christ presented as the climax of God's long plan
of salvation (John 1.14). In recent times some liberal Protestants have, of course,
dispensed with the need to believe in the physical reality of these gospel events and
perhaps a low-church anti-sacramentalism has contributed more to this than has
sometimes been recognized.

## The role of a biblical cosmology and eschatology in explaining sacraments

The vital factor in making full sense of sacraments is when we allow a biblical
cosmology (understanding of the relationship between heaven and earth) followed
by an equally biblical eschatology (understanding of how God is going to make
everything end up) to replace the less than biblical viewpoints that often stand in
their place.

The common, but nonetheless sub-biblical, understanding of heaven and earth is
one that understands these spheres of existence as being completely separate from
one another. This is usually accompanied by the escapist understanding of salvation,
popularly summarized as 'going to heaven when you die'. Earthly things, from this
perspective, have little value since the people God rescues through Jesus Christ are/
will be taken off to heaven, leaving the world to its ultimate fate of destruction. Within
this paradigm, with its rejection of any real and lasting value for the earth and matter
itself, sacraments make little sense. In fact, unless they are seen as 'bare signs', baptism
and the Lord's Supper are seen as running the serious risk of becoming idols and
endangering the spiritual nature of the Christian faith.

A biblical understanding of the relationship between heaven and earth is quite
different. Heaven and earth are understood as overlapping and interlocking
dimensions of creation with the great theme of Scripture being the rescue and renewal
of this creation. The ultimate result of this renewal will be heaven and earth being
purged of evil (where fire and destruction have their place), so that they can then
be fully and finally united. God's glory and presence, rather than remaining partial,
will flood the whole of creation. The resurrection of God's people will enable them
to finally fulfil the mandate God gave them as his divine image-bearers: to rule the
creation on his behalf and reflect its praises back to God.[4]

It is this understanding that fits with the story of the covenant covered earlier in
Chapters 3 and 4. There we saw that every stage of the covenant story was working
to this purpose with a crucial part of this story being the establishment of God's
presence on earth, most obviously during the Old Testament period through the
Temple, which provided the meeting point of heaven and earth. The covenant story
reaches its climax in Jesus Christ as the one in whom heaven and earth supremely
overlap and the resurrection of Jesus on Easter Day formed the start of the long
awaited process of integration between heaven and earth and the coming of the
new creation. Jesus's ascension marks the life of earth entering into heaven, whilst
the coming of the Holy Spirit at Pentecost and the church becoming God's Temple

represent the life of heaven coming on earth. The end goal is the day when Jesus finally returns to earth and the final integration of the new heavens and the new earth becomes complete.

## Space, time and matter

Once this biblical cosmology and biblical eschatology are adopted, sacraments take on an entirely different perspective. Earth and heaven are understood as made for each other, rather than being mutually exclusive, and an understanding that the very earthly realities of space, time and matter were created to be God-bearing provides the basis for a sacramental theology.

We have already seen how this is true in terms of space. Heaven and earth have become joined together in the risen body of Jesus Christ. The Holy Spirit works through both baptism and the Holy Communion to join us to the risen body of Christ meaning that the church becomes, through these sacraments, the place of God's special presence on earth. It forms an anticipation of the day when Jesus Christ will return to earth and, through him, God will become all in all.

This links to the role that time plays within the sacraments. Tom Wright has particularly drawn attention to this.[5] Creation is not static but, from the very beginning, a project that is moving forward. Time is also positive – part of the overall creation that God declares to be good in Genesis 1. However, rather than being simply linear, the way in which time works within the biblical story is somewhat more mysterious, particularly when it comes to the great moments of covenant salvation. At these moments, both the significance of past events comes powerfully into the present and part of the future comes forward into that present as well.

We saw this when we traced the story of the covenant in Chapter 3. The exodus, for example, was not just YHWH freeing the Israelites from slavery in Egypt. A key part of this was him remembering his covenant with Abraham, Isaac and Jacob and bringing the significance of this past event powerfully into the present. The way that the exodus story is told implies that the earlier events of the Flood and Creation were similarly recapitulated as God divides the waters of the Red Sea to save the Israelites. But the future is brought forward into the present as well, as the exodus anticipates God's ultimate rescue of the world. Part of this is shown by the episode when the spies enter the Promised Land and bring back its food for the Israelites to eat as an anticipation of its possession. All of this is reflected in the celebration of the Passover, as subsequent generations of Israelites recalled the exodus in a way that not only brings this past event powerfully into the present ('This is the night that God freed us from slavery') but also brings some of the reality of God's future liberation forwards into the present to sustain them as well.

We see the same in the New Testament with all of its writers keen to show how Jesus Christ gathers up the past of Israel in his person. But his signs, culminating in his own resurrection, bring God's future powerfully into the present as well. We have already seen how this is represented in Paul's theology as well with his insistence that God's work in Jesus Christ incorporates the entire story of Israel within it and the Holy Spirit brings God's promised future powerfully into the present as well.

The sacraments repeat this pattern. Those who are baptized into Jesus Christ are incorporated into the past event of his death as well as his present risen life and also find that their own future resurrection and hence the final renewal of the cosmos comes forward to meet them. Baptism sums up the entire narrative of God's covenant project of redemption from the past, present and future and incorporates both the story of the person who is being baptized and the community defined by baptism within this narrative.

A final aspect of understanding the sacraments is understanding God's presence within the matter of creation. A tension exists within those parts of the Bible that describe the whole earth as already full of God's glory (e.g. Isaiah 6.3) and those parts that picture this as a future reality (Isaiah 11.9; Habakkuk 2.14). Protestant Christians can often, as mentioned already, be nervous about the idea of God working through anything physical because of the danger of idolatry this brings. Idolatry is worshipping created things instead of God and the Bible is completely consistent in its rejection of this (Exodus 20.4; 1 Thessalonians 1.9).

However, as big a danger as idolatry is the opposing error of dualism. Dualism, most obviously represented by the heresy of Gnosticism, is a rejection of the biblical cosmology outlined earlier in favour of the belief that earth and heaven are completely separate from one another. For Gnostics, salvation was unapologetically about escape from the earth, and matter was understood as irredeemably evil. This meant that they had no time at all for sacraments.

None of this finds any basis in the Bible which, just as consistently as it opposes idolatry, depicts God's presence being experienced through his creation. The Burning Bush (Exodus 3) is an obvious example of this, as is the Ark of the Covenant and the bronze snake that Moses made so that those Israelites who had been bitten by poisonous snakes could look at it and be healed (Numbers 21). Potential abuse of these 'sacraments' is constant. When the Israelites try and use the Ark of Covenant as a magic charm, the result is complete disaster as they are defeated and the Ark is captured by the Philistines (1 Samuel 4). However, when those same Philistines express their disrespect for YHWH through the Ark that represents him, they discover that it still possesses a terrible power (1 Samuel 5). Centuries after the exodus and wilderness period, the writer of 2 Kings records, with approval, King Hezekiah's destruction of the bronze snake that Moses had made because the Israelites had been burning incense to it (2 Kings 18.4). If created things are put in place of God, they become idols bringing his curse down on those abusing them in this way. If, by contrast, created things are placed in their proper place *below God*, they become capable of bearing his transforming presence.[6]

Gaining this clarity about the difference between idolatry and the God-bearing potential of matter is crucial to understanding the sacraments. It enables us to accept the plain sense of what Paul is saying when he declares:

> Is not the cup of thanksgiving for which we give thanks, a participation in the blood of Christ? And is not the bread that we break a participation in the body of Christ? (1 Corinthians 10.16)

The basis for understanding the sacraments is recognizing and accepting the cosmology and eschatology presented within the Bible together with a clear understanding of what idolatry is and what it isn't. It is not just human beings that God is concerned to redeem but the whole cosmos. In fact, as Paul says in Romans the two objectives are inextricably entwined:

> For the creation waits in eager expectation for the children of God to be revealed. For the creation was subjected to frustration, not by its own choice, but by the will of the one who subjected it, in hope that the creation itself will be liberated from its bondage to decay and brought into the freedom and glory of the children of God. (Romans 8.19-21)

Once we understand the goal of God's salvation as being to flood the whole of the world with his presence, it becomes totally consistent with this for God to take parts of that creation to fill with his presence now. All of creation is capable of bearing God's presence and one day this will be the case. For the moment, and because of its fallen nature, this is generally not the case. The basis of sacraments, however, lies in the acknowledgement that God has chosen to institute baptism and the Lord's Supper as the means by which the renewed people of God can be incorporated in Jesus Christ and thus within the story of his redemption of the world.

## The effect of baptism

The blessings signified by, and associated with, baptism cannot be exaggerated. We have seen that they comprise the whole gospel of Jesus Christ and the covenant promises of God. We have also seen the vital nature of *faith* in receiving the promises of God and the call to a *transformed life* that comes with baptism.

Before we embark on an examination of what the act of baptism brings about, it is important to remember the biblical claim that human life is lived in one or other of two realms which are in dramatic and vivid contrast. We may be members of the old creation or the new creation, either in Adam or in Christ, in darkness or in light, living according to the sinful nature or living by the Spirit, in death or in life, belonging to the world or belonging to God. These contrasts are found in 2 Corinthians 5.17; 1 Corinthians 15.22; Ephesians 5.8; Colossians 1.13; Romans 8.5f; 1 John 3.14; John 17.6-19. Conversion from one realm to the other is critical and theologically the contrast that cannot be exaggerated. Nevertheless, from the human point of view, that conversion may be a long, gradual and almost imperceptible process, rather than a single, dramatic event. The New Testament writers nowhere require a sudden conversion experience, but they do require convertedness — 'Unless you change (literally "turn") and become like little children, you will never enter the kingdom of heaven' (Matthew 18.3).

Conversion means to turn around, to face the right direction, to be following Christ. The significant issue is not when or how but whether a person is going in the right direction i.e. is converted (Acts 3.19; 26.18). The metaphor of 'being born again' (John 3.3) is more to do with the decisively new character of life with God than with the suddenness of its arrival in human experience. Baptism is, by its very nature, a single definite event, but the human experience of conversion is not always (or even often) like that. Hence the relationship in time between baptism (the outward sign) and conversion (the spiritual reality) is not always a simple, obvious and straightforward one – as we shall see.

What, then, is the actual effect of water-baptism? There have been four main answers to this question through the centuries:

- It is unnecessary – it has no effect, and Christians need not bother with the physical sign if they experience the spiritual grace.
- It is desirable as an expression of obedience to Jesus but not essential. It is not considered in terms of effect, and the sign merely symbolizes the spiritual reality.
- It is essential – a sign which actually conveys the blessings and grace of God. This description of its effectiveness often makes the whole process seem to be automatic.
- It is God's gift and normal Christian practice – a sign and seal of God's grace effecting what it signifies in the context of faith.

This issue of the 'efficacy' of baptism underlies many bitter divisions and controversies. These have been between Catholics and Protestants, between those who only baptize confessing believers and those who baptize households, and amongst the latter between those who look for a credible faith-response and those who appear to be virtually indiscriminate in their practice of baptism. The debates and writings through the centuries have been sadly disfigured by caricature and misrepresentation of other positions. Far too often theologians begin with a confessional position or ecclesiastical practice and then select or bend the biblical evidence to suit the predetermined goal. This has had disastrous effects in the disciplines of biblical and systematic theology, in ecumenical relationships and in terms of pastoral practice. We shall examine the four answers listed but in the reverse order:

## 1. Baptism effects what it signifies, in the context of faith

Labels can often be misleading and mean different things to different people. Nevertheless, broad classifications are necessary in historical and theological study. This view is often broadly described as 'Reformed' or 'Covenant'. It is the confessional position in both the Anglican 39 Articles of Religion and the Presbyterian Westminster Confession of Faith. However, both those theological confessions explicitly require that the Holy Scriptures be the final authority for faith and practice, and so the question must be pressed with complete integrity as to whether the biblical witness points to this theological answer.

Three major truths relevant to the issue have emerged from the enquiry into the baptism texts and contexts. Firstly, *the New Testament writers use the language of efficacy repeatedly and without embarrassment*. Baptism effects what it signifies. The outward sign is described in terms of the spiritual reality it signifies. 'We were buried with him through baptism', 'we were all baptised by one Spirit into one body', 'baptism now saves you' (Romans 6.4; 1 Corinthians 12.13; 1 Peter 3.21). 'Be baptised and wash your sins away', 'all who were baptised into Christ have been clothed with Christ' (Acts 22.16; Galatians 3.27). This language of efficacy is not occasional or idiosyncratic. It is normal and characteristic of the biblical thought-world and varying types of literature. This is reinforced by the tradition that we have observed of adding a confirming sign or action to a solemn word of promise.

Secondly, the apostolic writers unanimously and explicitly speak of the context of the *gospel met by faith*. We have seen how the very blessings signified in baptism are also in the same apostolic writings indissolubly linked to the word of God received by faith. Thus, the blessings are not attached to water-baptism just as a mere ceremony – there must normally be the accompanying (in fact, preceding) words of interpretation, the gospel proclamation and the accompanying context of a faith-response. The New Testament writers look for some evidence of the work of the Spirit through the gospel. 'You must be born again. The wind blows wherever it pleases. You hear its sound, but you cannot tell where it comes from or where it is going. So it is with everyone born of the Spirit' (John 3.7f). There is much we do not know about the Spirit's work, but we do 'hear its sound' i.e. experience its effect in people's lives. The people of Samaria 'believed Philip as he preached the good news of the kingdom of God and the name of Jesus Christ, they were baptised... Simon himself believed and was baptised'. Nevertheless, later on, Simon tried to purchase the ability to lay hands on people to receive the Spirit, and Peter sternly rebuked him: 'You have no part or share in this ministry, because your heart is not right before God. Repent of this wickedness and pray to the Lord' (Acts 8.9-24). Here we see that even baptism with a profession of faith does not effect a truly Christian life – there must be a continuing baptized life of repentance and trusting commitment.

As we saw in the previous chapter, the vital importance of this continuing faith-response to the covenant signs of God is spelled out vividly by Paul in 1 Corinthians 10. All the Israelites experienced the sign of the baptism 'into Moses in the cloud and in the sea. They all ate the same spiritual food and drank the same spiritual drink... Nevertheless, God was not pleased with most of them'. Paul is clearly warning that participation in the outward covenant signs or sacramental actions is not effectual unconditionally; they must be received with faith and obedience. As Richard Hooker said, 'All receive not the grace of God which receive the sacraments of his grace'.[7] The gospel, faith and baptism must be kept closely bound together both in theological thought and in pastoral practice if we are to be true to the New Testament. Baptism is efficacious, i.e. it effects what it signifies, in the context of faith. The evidence will be seen in the fruit of the Spirit and his gifts.

As we have seen, Paul lays a major emphasis on justification by faith. The sign of those whom God has declared righteous are those who place their faith in Jesus (Romans 3.27-30; Galatians 2.15ff; Ephesians 2.8f; Philippians 3.4-9). However, we must guard against any impression that faith is the cause or basis of salvation. God's grace and God's covenant sign of his grace do not derive their power and effect from the faith of the recipient; they derive their power from God himself. Faith does take the grace that God offers, but faith does not make that grace.

Thirdly, the apostolic writers unitedly and naturally speak of baptism in the context of *the covenant plan of God*. The clear implication is that baptism is a covenant sign. Thus, it is essentially a gift from God witnessing to what he has done and intends to do, rather than a human action witnessing to the faith-response. It may actually imply such a witness to faith, but this is not part of the New Testament theology of baptism and is not its primary significance. But, to repeat, the covenant promises of God and covenant signs of God must be received by faith. It has always been so, and there is no other way to benefit from or enjoy them.

There has been a historic polarization between a Protestant type of pietism which has placed almost its entire emphasis on the inward reality of regeneration/conversion through the work of the Spirit and seen the outward sign of baptism as having very minor importance, and the Catholic type of sacramentalism which appears to place almost its entire emphasis on the outward sign and to place very little on the word of the gospel, conversion and the response of faith. In contrast to this dichotomy, a biblical theology gives strong emphasis to both the efficacy of baptism and the necessity of faith in the context of God's covenant.

Baptism is a pledge from God which confirms his word of promise. It is backed up by God's righteousness, his own covenant faithfulness. This promise and confirming sign need (in normal circumstances) to be received by faith. However, as we have seen, baptism is more than just a symbol. It is God's covenant sign that:

(a) *confirms the promises* – adding solemn action and sign to the word of promise concerning forgiveness and the gift of the Spirit;
(b) *confers a status* – as an adopted child of God. The new nature of the child of God may well develop gradually, but the new status is signified and sealed in baptism. Naturalization in a new country brings a new citizenship status, but adopting the lifestyle of that new nation may take a longer time;
(c) *conveys an inheritance* – the kingdom of God. This is conveyed by baptism in a way analogous to the legal deed of conveyance used for transfer of land or property.[8]

Note that the promise must be received, the status adopted and the inheritance claimed by faith.

Another way of similarly describing the relation of baptism to God's covenant plan and promise of salvation is to say that baptism:

(a) *pictures it* – as washing, as anointing, as burial and resurrection;
(b) *promises it* – the sign which dramatizes and confirms the word;
(c) *presents it* – in the context of gospel and faith, baptism embodies and effects the salvation it pictures and promises.[9]

The faith which takes this promise and sign of God's salvation involves repentance, trust and obedience. It is not just a single act (a turning, a change, a conversion) but a continuing attitude (being turned to Christ, remaining changed and converted). This is the continuing character of the baptized life, the life that is baptized into Jesus

Christ. As it was suggested earlier, the relation in time between the reception of the sign and the reception of the blessings signified is not always straightforward. Quite apart from the question of household (infant) baptism which will be considered in the next chapter, in the baptism of an adult the ideal may well be conversion followed immediately by baptism. This seems the normal pattern in the early church. However, baptism may be delayed for many reasons until years after conversion because of antagonism of husband or family, or because of inadequate instruction. On the other hand, someone may be baptized before (even long before) conversion. This may be through family, peer or other pressures, or again because of inadequate instruction. Now, although when this happens in the case of an adult baptism it may be regarded as irregular and unfortunate, none of the major churches (including those with baptist theology who emphasize that personal confession of faith should precede baptism) will offer 'another' baptism. The original baptism is regarded as valid initiation which (by definition) can only, and must be, 'once-for-all'. It may be improper and irregular but is regarded as 'valid'.

Although the concept of a valid or real baptism is not dealt with explicitly in the New Testament, from the earliest centuries Christian churches of all types have had to answer the question, 'When is a baptism a real baptism?' Although the spiritual reality or efficacy of the baptism depends on God's promise of grace being met by faith, the reality of the outward sign cannot be made to depend on an inward and spiritual response. Ultimately, only God can judge the reality and sincerity of repentance, faith and obedience. Christians with tender consciences could repeatedly be anxious about their previous spiritual condition and apply for 'another' baptism. Christians who receive some fresh (even dramatic) experience of the reality and blessing of God are often unsure whether it is an initial conversion or a subsequent and further step in their pilgrimage.

What, then, makes a valid or real baptism in terms of the outward sign? Most churches agree that two elements are required. Baptism must be:

(a) an administration of water;
(b) in the name of God, the Father, Son and Holy Spirit or in the name of Jesus Christ.

In the earliest days of Christianity, both of these forms were accorded validity because of their equal scriptural basis. Jesus's words in Matthew 28.19 instruct baptism to be in the name of the Father, the Son and the Holy Spirit but many more references speak of baptism 'in/into the name of Jesus Christ' (Acts 2.38; 8.16; 10.48; 19.5; 22.16). This changed once the Arian controversy took place in the fourth century. With the followers of Arius (256–336) denying the full divinity of Christ, use of the Trinitarian formula for baptism became seen as crucial for maintaining orthodoxy.[10] Some churches still conduct baptisms 'in the name of Jesus Christ' but a greater number see Christian baptism as needing to be 'in the name of the Father, the Son and the Holy Spirit'. Some (though not all) baptist churches add a third requirement:

(c) following a personal confession of faith in Jesus as Saviour and Lord

However, as we noted above, even churches which baptize only adults and young people following a profession of faith find the necessity of distinguishing (spiritual) efficacy from (outward) validity. If validity of sign is made to depend on a spiritual state that only God can truly know, there will be perpetual potential for feelings of insecurity about its reality. We may sum up by saying that the outward sign of baptism as defined above is complete in terms of (outward) validity but conditional in terms of (spiritual) efficacy, i.e. it will require (in normal circumstances) the response of faith.

An example of the distinction between outward sign or ceremony and existing reality is to be found in the relationship between a monarch inheriting the throne and being formally crowned. Queen Elizabeth II inherited the throne on the death of her father but it was some months later that the existing reality of her monarchy was declared, confirmed and celebrated in the service of coronation. In one sense she really became queen on her accession, in another sense she was 'made queen' in the coronation ceremony. In this example, the reality precedes the ceremony or sign. However, in another case, the new monarch may be a child. In this situation, although on the one hand inheriting the throne and experiencing the ceremony of coronation, on the other hand the full enjoyment of rights, privileges and powers will follow later at an appropriate age of majority. This is not cited as an example to justify infant baptism. At this stage it is simply an example of how the outward sign or ceremony could precede the full enjoyment of the reality of the thing signified. This can and does happen in 'believer-baptism only' situations.

C. S. Lewis wrote, 'Don't bother at all about that question of a person being "made a Christian by baptism." It is only the usual trouble about a word being used in more than one sense. Thus we might say a man "became a soldier" the moment he joined the army. But his instructors might say six months later, "I think we have made a soldier of him."'[11]

We conclude then that the biblical theology of baptism is this: Baptism is a covenant sign that God gives to confirm and seal his promise of salvation. It effects what it signifies, in the context of faith. The language of efficacy which the New Testament writers use with respect to baptism is sacramental language, covenant language. It is not unconditional for it presupposes the context of faith – the sacramental language used of baptism must always be faith language as well.

However, there are other views which need to be considered.


## 2. Baptism always conveys the blessings of salvation

This view presents God's blessings coming with the act of baptism in a way that appears almost automatic. It has been held in order to safeguard the sovereignty of God's work of salvation, the divine initiative in both covenant promise and covenant sign and the power of Christ's sacrifice. It takes very seriously the vigorous New Testament sacramental language of efficacy.

This view is broadly termed the 'Catholic' or *ex opere operato* view (a Latin phrase meaning 'by the deed performed', i.e. 'by the performance of the ceremony'). There was an exception to this automatic conveyance of the divine grace in baptism if an adult recipient placed a barrier (*obex*) or obstacle to it through mortal sin (e.g. impenitence or hypocrisy). However, the *ex opere operato* view gained supremacy during the later Middle Ages and was endorsed by the Council of Trent in 1547: 'If anyone shall say that grace is not conferred ex opere operato, but that belief in the Divine promise alone suffices to obtain grace, let him be anathema.'[12]

Because of the obvious dangers of a magical and superstitious use of baptism, many Catholic theologians have much modified this view in the direction of the Reformed position whilst still seeking to retain the emphasis that the grace is conferred by virtue of the action of the Saviour God rather than by any virtue of the recipient's merit. We noted earlier that faith should not be understood as a meritorious action or attitude which offers a basis for deserving or even enabling the grace of God to operate.

Nevertheless, this view does not do justice to the careful biblical balance between the effective sign and the context of faith. We have seen that the blessings of baptism are equally and indissolubly the blessings accorded to those who believe. Some are saved without baptism (the thief on the cross in Luke 23.39-43 perhaps, those amongst the Society of Friends and Salvation Army today); some are saved before baptism (Cornelius received the Spirit-baptism before the water-baptism); and some are not saved although they have been through baptism (as Paul warns in 1 Corinthians 10). As has been said, many of those inside (the church) are outside; and some of those outside are inside.[13]

Secondly, this view does not do justice to the biblical contrast between the outward and the inward. The outward sign is a precious covenant sign from God and is not to be in any way despised. But there is no automatic or unconditional identification with what it signifies. So Paul writes, 'A man is not a Jew if he is only one outwardly, nor is circumcision merely outward and physical. No, a man is a Jew if he is one *inwardly*; and circumcision is circumcision of the heart, by the Spirit, not by the written code' (Romans 2.28f).

Thirdly, whilst Paul speaks equally of baptism-blessings and faith-blessings, they are ultimately grace-blessings that come through the gospel of the Lord Jesus Christ. Whilst as bold as any in using the sacramental language of baptismal efficacy, when Paul is faced with the divisions in the church at Corinth, and the horrendous speculation that anyone could possibly be a follower of, or baptized into, himself, Paul asserts strongly that he, personally, rarely performed baptism 'for Christ did not send me to baptise, but to preach the gospel of the cross of Christ' (1 Corinthians 1.15-17). Whilst fully acknowledging that Paul is here responding sharply to a scandalous situation and that baptism is a confirming sign of that very gospel of Christ crucified, nevertheless, Paul is pointing out that, in the last analysis, it is the word of the gospel received by faith that is the absolute priority. Without that context the sacrament, the covenant sign, loses its significance and power. 'Faith comes by hearing, and hearing by the word of God' (Romans 10.17).

An important controversy surrounding this issue took place in the mid-nineteenth century. The Bishop of Exeter, Henry Philpotts (1778–1869), refused to institute the Reverend George Gorham (1787–1857) to a parish in Devon because he took exception to Gorham's view that baptismal regeneration was conditional. Gorham's view was eventually upheld with the final judgement in 1850 stating:

That baptism is a sacrament generally necessary to salvation, but that the grace of regeneration does not so necessarily accompany the act of baptism that regeneration invariably takes place in baptism; that the grace may be granted before, in or after baptism; that baptism is an effectual sign of grace, by which God works invisibly in us, but only in such as worthily receive it — in them alone it has a wholesome effect; and that without reference to the qualification of the recipient it is not in itself an effectual sign of grace ... that in no case is baptism unconditional.[14]

The *ex opere operato* view, then, does not fully meet the balance of the biblical teaching. It does not recognize sufficiently the covenant context of proclamation of the divine promise in the gospel and the necessity of a faith-response. The power of the covenant sign is entirely from God as is the covenant gospel itself, but it must be accepted. It is not unconditional. Faith does not *make* the grace present in baptism, but faith must *receive* it.

### 3. Baptism is desirable as a symbol of the blessings but does not convey them

This view has been held to safeguard the essential condition of faith as the only and necessary way to receive God's offer of forgiveness and salvation. Baptism is certainly a symbol of salvation, but no integral link is seen between the symbol and the reality symbolized in terms of any effectual nature of the symbol.

The view is often described as 'Zwinglian' (after Huldrych Zwingli, the Swiss Reformer, 1484–1531) or 'Baptist'. The latter description, however, is unfortunate. Although very many 'Baptist' churches (including probably the majority of Pentecostal, Brethren, Independent Evangelical and Restorationist 'House' churches) do teach this view, there are an increasing number of baptist theologians who have moved towards a sacramental view which is much closer to the 'Reformed', even though they still consider baptism of infants either improper or irregular.

Baptism is generally seen as proper and significant for the confessing believer for the following reasons:

(a) It is a step of obedience to Christ's direct command, and, therefore, part of discipleship.
(b) It was the normal practice of the early church as seen in the New Testament and was used by the apostolic writers as a basis for their appeal to living in Christ, in holiness and in unity.
(c) It is a picture and symbol of the meaning of the gospel. This is seen in its identification with Jesus. Most (though not all) proponents of this view use immersion as the normal mode of baptism and see its symbolism of burial and resurrection as the most significant characteristic of baptism.
(d) It is an opportunity (even the decisive opportunity) to witness to one's faith in Christ, to confess the faith in the waters of baptism. It is also an act of identification with the Christian community. However, many of the churches which take this view of baptism either do not require baptism for or do not closely link baptism with church membership and/or Holy Communion.

Those who take this view of baptism usually place their whole emphasis on the preaching of the gospel of salvation. This must be received by faith and conversion. The born-again believer is then summoned to bear witness to his faith and conversion by the act of obedience in baptism. These churches are often marked paradoxically by a high degree of personal commitment to Christ along with a rather loose and voluntary view of church membership and even, sometimes, of baptism itself.

The emphasis on receiving the gospel with an understanding faith was a vigorous reaction to the late medieval views in the Catholic Church which seemed to have an almost magical view of the sacraments allied to widespread carelessness about preaching the gospel of God's grace and summoning people to lives of trusting obedience. In this reaction, the 'missionary' adult baptisms of the Acts of the Apostles were taken as the model. Unlike the major Protestant Reformers they denied validity (as well as any kind of efficacy) to infant baptism. Upon a profession of faith, people who had been through a baptismal rite in infancy were 'baptized again'. This is why they gained the title 'Anabaptists', the re-baptizers. It is important to realize that those conscientiously holding this view do not agree with, and are aggrieved by, the terms 'Anabaptist' and 're-baptism'. On their understanding, it is not 'another baptism'; since infant baptism is theologically improper and invalid, it is only 'believer's baptism' which is true and valid baptism at all. This question of 're-baptism' will be examined more carefully in Chapter 12.

However, there are some serious weaknesses in this view in the light of the whole of the biblical testimony:

Firstly, it interprets the frequent passages which indicate the efficacy of baptism in a 'spiritual' sense, so that instead of referring to the outward sign they refer to the inward and spiritual reality that is signified. This results constantly in tautology, i.e. senseless repetition. For example when Paul says 'baptised into his death', it is interpreted as 'converted, born again into, sharing the significance of the death of Jesus of which water-baptism is a picture' (Romans 6.3). When Peter says 'Baptism now saves you', it is interpreted as 'conversion (being saved) now saves you, of which the water-ceremony is a witness and symbol' (1 Peter 3.21). But this is not what the passages say, and the exegesis becomes tortuous and artificial. Certainly the language of baptism-efficacy must always be interpreted in its unfailing context of faith in the gospel. Nevertheless, the apostolic writers appear to have a much more dynamic understanding of the nature of the sacraments than those who take this view.

This is because, secondly, this theology effectively associates baptism much more closely with the human response than with the divine promise, gift and sign. Proponents of this view draw a sharp contrast between the old covenant and its rite of circumcision and the new covenant in Christ and its rite of baptism in the name of Christ. The discontinuities are emphasized and the continuities interpreted in terms of spiritual typology. The sacraments, then, are seen not so much as God's covenant signs but rather as tokens and symbols of discipleship and Christian commitment. One popular and typical book representing this view has a major section called baptism and its meaning.[15] Its significance is summarized as 'in baptism we actively and openly make declaration of certain facts'. These are fivefold – obeying, owning, dedication to, identification with and continuing with Jesus Christ. Now this is all true and implicit in baptism, but the New Testament writers say much more about God owning us in baptism, dedicating himself to us and having identified himself with us he now identifies us with himself. He puts us into Christ, into his death and resurrection; he anoints us with the Spirit and washes us with rebirth. In the New Testament, baptism, like the salvation it signifies, is Christo-centric, God-initiated and Spirit-endowed. It loses so much of its rich and powerful assurance when not interpreted in its covenant contexts. It must certainly have its faith context too, but the apostolic writers even saw believing faith as ultimately 'the gift of God' (Ephesians 2.8; Philippians 1.29; Acts 18.27).

Finally, the heavy emphasis on witness to others in baptism is not according to the balance of New Testament teaching. Certainly, baptism may be a fine and effective witness to one's faith and testimony to believers and unbelievers alike. But the apostolic writers do not make the point, let alone emphasize it. Rather, they expound baptism as primarily God's witness to us, his confirming sign of his covenant promise, the dramatic portrayal of his salvation and of the seal of his gift of the Spirit. The convert's witness emphasis is not biblical and, when taken out of the biblical covenant context, it is in grave danger of making baptism (and even salvation itself) man-centred. It is often too close to Pelagianism (the heresy that the human will is capable of choosing God without divine aid) for comfort.

This view is diametrically opposed to the *ex opere operato* interpretation, but like that, it fails to maintain the biblical covenant balance between word and action, promise and sign, outward ceremony and inward reality.

### 4. The ceremony of water-baptism is unnecessary – it has no effect – but Spirit-baptism is its fulfilment

This view asks why bother with an outward symbol with water when one is daily enjoying the experienced reality with the Spirit? Outward forms have become outmoded now that living realities are present.

This view is described as the 'Quaker' or 'Spirit-baptism' doctrine. The Society of Friends (the proper name for Quakers) are not so much opposed to water-baptism as indifferent to it. They say it is irrelevant because they continually seek to practise 'a sacramental life through the living presence of Christ'.[16]

The Salvation Army do not use the sacraments of baptism and Holy Communion either, but here it was originally due to their desire to be an evangelistic and mission agency rather than another church or denomination. There are other groups with a particular charismatic and Pentecostal emphasis who omit water-baptism in favour of the practice of Spirit-baptism. Such groups are not a large proportion of world Christianity. However, even amongst the major churches which practise baptism, there will frequently be found an undervaluing or misuse of it which virtually amounts to a denial of its importance.

Like the development of the Zwinglian view, this doctrine of Spirit-baptism emerges as a strong reaction against a sacramentalism which appears to give all its emphasis to outward forms and ceremonies, formal orthodoxy and such doctrinal and legal questions as efficacy and validity.

It is urged that there is a strong contrast between baptism-with-water and Jesus's promise of baptism-with-Spirit. Pentecost ushers in the new era of the Spirit, and the direct personal experience of his power and illumination seen in fruit of character and gifts of service renders the outward ceremonies redundant. Furthermore, it has been, and is, patently clear that God's grace and saving power cannot be confined to channels whether ecclesiastical, ministerial or sacramental. God's Spirit blows where it wills. People enter God's kingdom without baptism and receive the baptism of Spirit without the benefit of water-baptism. God's salvation is supremely a spiritual matter of grace and faith. Signs and ceremonies quite clearly are ineffective in certain situations, and where there is spiritual reality it is not because of the signs but because of the grace, faith and Spirit signified.

This can be presented as a very effective case. Any Christian should warm to an emphasis on spiritual realities as opposed to outward ceremonies and forms. There is a widespread feeling that ecclesiastical hierarchies and sacramental restrictions and formalities have 'quenched the Spirit'.

However, this view is far from the overall testimony of the New Testament writers. They see the closest relation between outward sign and spiritual reality, between water and Spirit, between Old Testament and New. Certainly the church and ministry must be continually alerted to the dangers of constraining and quenching the Spirit, but the covenant signs and sacraments are regarded as 'means of grace' whereby God's promises are confirmed, clarified and conferred – in the context of faith. In spite of the contrast between water and Spirit, water-baptism was undergone by Jesus, commanded by him and consistently practised by the early church. The references to baptism in the epistles cannot systematically be interpreted as Spirit-baptism – the water symbolism cannot be ignored. The examples of people spiritually alive apart from baptism and spiritually dead with baptism can be acknowledged. There are exceptional situations on the one hand and there is the necessity of faith-response on the other. This view, however, ignores the unity of the rich covenant scheme running throughout the Scripture with its pattern of promise and sign, word and confirming action. It misses a source of assurance and strength. It is always in danger of losing touch with the historical, the objective and the corporate dimensions of the sacraments in favour of the mystical, the subjective and the individualistic aspects. The Scriptural testimony unites the water-baptism and the Spirit-baptism in positive and creative harmony – the covenant sign and the covenant seal in God's saving purpose, both to be received by faith and worked out in a separated life of holiness. The sign of washing and seal of the Spirit belong together – 'Repent and be baptised and you will receive the forgiveness of sins, and the gift of the Holy Spirit' (Acts 2.38).

The biblical theology of Christian baptism is an immensely rich mine as it draws together the whole of God's eternal covenant plan of salvation with the simple yet profound and varied symbolism of water-washing. As with other Christian doctrines, the whole biblical material must be studied and in its contexts. The blessings of baptism embrace the entire gospel of God's grace, but it can only be known in the context of the covenant pattern and in the context of the word of the gospel received by faith. Efficacy there is – as a sacrament, a covenant sign from God, it is a gift of loving grace; unconditional it is not – as a sacrament, a covenant sign from God, it is to be received with faith. 'Baptism is the divinely appointed rendezvous of grace for faith.'[17]

# Baptism and the Christian family

We have established the biblical theology of baptism as a covenant sign (or sacrament) of God's grace, which is to be received in faith, and is used as a continual motivation for a life of holiness and service within the united people of God. The New Testament writers clearly expect adult believers in Christ to be baptized. In the early years of the church, delay in baptism seems to have been unknown, so that it is all who have been baptized who are 'in Christ', 'clothed with Christ', washed, adopted, recipients of the Holy Spirit and members of the church, the body of Christ. Later in the history of the church, as in many countries in this century, reasons for postponement (for teaching or testing or through persecution and social factors) appeared convincing, but the apostolic writers seem not to envisage this in their teaching. The baptized are the Christians; the Christians are the baptized.

We turn now to the question of the children of believers, children of the Christian family. On the basis of the biblical theology of baptism, is there any justification for the covenant sign of baptism being given to infants? On this issue there has been long and sad division in the Christian Church. This division has been exacerbated by a failure to hear properly what is the best case of the other side and also a frequent appeal to inadequate theology and inadequate authority for that theology.

The polarization we have already noted appears again strongly. Those with a predominantly 'catholic' viewpoint strongly defend infant baptism, but very frequently on the basis of church tradition or selective texts of Scripture. Those with a predominantly 'baptist' view deny the propriety of infant baptism at all, urging that infants cannot exercise repentance and faith. But they usually look to the Acts of the Apostles and selective texts in the Epistles without an awareness of the covenant contexts. This polarization has been seriously debilitating to Christian theology and mission. In the previous chapter we argued that the 'Reformed' or Covenant view most fully embraces the total biblical teaching on God's covenant sign of baptism. However, very sadly, the application of this view to the question of household and infant baptism has frequently been spoiled by the development of alternative theologies of adult and infant baptism or the appeal to biblical texts that cannot bear the weight of the superstructures built upon them. It is of the greatest importance to the development of biblical and ecumenical theology that these inadequate approaches be avoided.

## Inadequate approaches to infant baptism

It would be the task of a major research (and very tedious) to detail the range of inadequate approaches. However, they must be examined in broad outline because of their damaging consequences for both practical pastoral work and inter-church relationships and discipline.

An inadequate theology of baptism is adopted by some proponents of infant baptism. We have seen that a biblical theology of baptism must hold together both the language of efficacy of God's covenant sign of his grace and the necessity of the faith-response. Time and again, theologians have sought to justify infant baptism by seriously reducing the significance and reality of one or other of these two dimensions with regard to an infant.

On the one hand, many reformed theologians of an evangelical standpoint have largely evacuated the full significance of efficacy language in the case of infants and spoken rather of 'the language of potential' or 'hypothetical language'. Where this is an alternative theology to that of adult or believer's baptism, it is quite unacceptable from the standpoint of biblical theology. Quite simply there is no biblical support for two theologies of baptism, one for adult and another for infant.

On the other hand, many reformed theologians on the more 'catholic' side have seriously undervalued the significance and requirement of faith – both in the infant and in the family. The practice of virtually indiscriminate infant baptism is regrettable and will be considered in detail in Chapter 11. Where an alternative view of a 'seed' of faith or a 'potential' or 'hypothetical' faith is developed, without the context of a living faith and the nurture of faith, this view is again seriously unacceptable in the light of the biblical theology. Inadequate authority being cited to support infant baptism is equally damaging. Too often the case for infant baptism, particularly within Roman Catholic and Anglo-Catholic churches, has been based solely on church tradition. Those of the Reformed tradition can do something similar, often complacently referring back to the Protestant Reformers of the sixteenth century, to Luther and Calvin, to the Thirty Nine Articles of the Church of England and Presbyterian Westminster Confession. But this will not do in forming biblical or ecumenical theology. An appeal to church tradition can only be supportive of, and must never be regarded as foundational and constitutive of, Christian doctrine.

Another form of arguing from inadequate authority has been the use of select biblical passages to bear the weight of a theological superstructure that they cannot securely support. The following passages may well be agreeable to the baptism of infants but by themselves they cannot be held to require it. Such passages are, for example, Mark 10.14 in which Jesus said, 'Let the little children come to me, and do not hinder them'; the 'household' (Greek *oikos*) formula used repeatedly in the 'Acts' and in 1 Corinthians 1.16; the holiness of a child of a believing parent in 1 Corinthians 7.14; and finally, the parallel drawn between baptism and circumcision in Colossians 2.11f. All these are significant passages which will be examined later. However, they simply do not, as such, demonstrate the propriety of baptizing infants, and it is futile to imagine or to argue that they do. Such arguments have, over the years, lulled paedo-baptists into a quite false sense of theological security and caused those of baptist conviction to suspect the biblical and theological integrity of the paedo-baptist case. It is one of the greatest tragedies of the history of Christian doctrine that so many theological debates have been conducted, not only with acrimony but on the basis of an inadequate authority and with careless attention to biblical exegesis and the full context.

## The biblical case for Christian family baptism

The apostolic writers of the New Testament give us no explicit and unambiguous evidence about the baptism of the children of the Christian family. There is no explicit account of an infant baptism or teaching about this matter. But neither is there any account of or teaching about the adult baptism of a child born into a Christian family. So the case is not a matter of unambiguous biblical precedent or instruction. This should immediately warn all engaged in the debate to be cautious, careful and respectful to other carefully presented positions.

As with other issues where there is no explicit biblical command or example, biblical theology proceeds on the basis of legitimate inference. It will be a matter of judgement how strongly or otherwise the general weight of the biblical theology renders such an inference, but it will be a matter of the general pattern of biblical theology and not a matter of looking for proof texts that settle the issue one way or the other. The classic example of legitimate inference with no direct biblical command or example is the matter of women sharing in Holy Communion. Most Christians are quite unembarrassed by the lack of explicit evidence but regard the issue as settled by the general New Testament teaching about the unity of the body of Christ and the lack of any instruction to the contrary. But an appeal to proof texts would be a very dangerous expedient in this case. It would be a very tempting short cut to appeal to Paul's great claim that 'there is neither male nor female, for you are all one in Christ Jesus' (Galatians 3.28). But it would be a short cut, for the passage is not speaking about Holy Communion explicitly. The point is, that with respect to many matters of church life we do, and can only, work on this basis of legitimate inference rather than direct instruction. In passing, we might add that even apparently direct instruction will need to be carefully interpreted in the light of its historical and literary contexts. Thus, there is no need for embarrassment at this point – whatever conclusion we may feel the biblical theology points to in the end. The question we ask is: in the light of the general teaching of the Bible, and more especially the New Testament, is it more agreeable to the apostolic witness to bring the infants of Christians to baptism or not?

There are three main lines of evidence:

*The covenant principle*
*The family principle*
*The sacramental principle*

We immediately agree that none of these matters are explicitly baptismal, but remind the reader that there is no incontrovertible evidence one way or the other on the specific issue of the baptism of infants of a Christian family. In each case we shall examine the general biblical theology and then look at certain passages in the New Testament and ask whether or not they make better sense if the apostolic writers were assuming Christian family baptism. Much of the evidence has already been expounded in previous chapters and so in order to prevent tedious repetition there will inevitably be references back to those passages.

## The covenant principle

This as a recurring biblical pattern was followed through the Scriptures in Chapters 3 and 4. We noted that the marks of this covenant principle included the primacy and initiative of God's grace, the supreme spiritual blessing of God's presence amongst his people, the necessity of receiving God's covenant promise with faith that issues in obedience, the use of covenant signs which signify, seal and embody God's covenant grace and the pattern of promise and fulfilment. We noted the continuity of the essential elements of this covenant pattern in the 'new covenant' – especially in terms of the initiative of grace and the necessity of responding faith.

In Chapter 2 we considered each of the references to baptism in the New Testament epistles and saw that the apostolic writers naturally and regularly thought of baptism in terms of covenant situations, covenant imagery, covenant blessings and covenant response. The use in these passages of Abraham, Moses and Noah is remarkable. It is in the light of this great pattern of biblical theology that the parallel of circumcision and baptism in Colossians 2.11f must be interpreted. In view of the baptismal and eucharistic language that Paul uses in reference to the Israelites in 1 Corinthians 10, it is not in the least surprising that he asserts that the same spiritual realities are signified in circumcision and baptism. There is no proof of infant baptism here, but the inference seems clear.

It is against this background and in this context that the crowd at Pentecost heard Peter issue his call to baptism and then proclaim: 'The promise is for you and for your children and to all that are afar off' (Acts 2.39). The word 'promise', as we have seen, is very rich in covenant associations. We have to be careful with the mention of 'children' here because a strong part of its reference is to the descendants of those he was speaking to. Peter is asserting that the gift of the Holy Spirit will be the permanent possession of God's people rather than just those who were present at Pentecost. But given that actual children were included by circumcision within God's covenant people in the Old Testament, it would be strange and misleading for Peter to have used this language if they were now meant to be excluded from the new covenant sign of baptism. No proof again, but yet another indication of the covenant principle.

## The family principle

Already it is evident how closely this is associated with the covenant pattern. God's initiative of grace comes to a *people*, rather than simply individuals, and within this there is a special emphasis on the family unit. Balance is important here. Whilst each individual stands responsible before God for disobedience and unfaithfulness to the covenant, nevertheless, there is a strong element of family solidarity running through the Scriptures. Noah was called to take his whole family with him into the ark, the promise to Abraham was also to his descendants after him. Once the people of Israel grew out of the family of Abraham, this became the major collective unit to whom God related. Israel, as a people, receive God's promises and covenant sign, even if 1 Corinthians 10 insists that this 'baptism' was in no way automatic or unconditional in its benefits but instead required the response of faith and obedience.

Within God's covenant relationship with Israel, however, there continues to be an emphasis upon the solidarity of the smaller family unit (see Deuteronomy 29.10-12; Psalm 103.17f; Isaiah 65.23; Jeremiah 32.38-41). On numerous occasions in the Old Testament, we see both blessings and curses from God shared by families. The latter is seen in the impact of the rebellion of Korah (Numbers 16), the dishonesty of Achan (Joshua 7) and apostasy of Ahab (1 Kings 21.21-29; 2 Kings 9–10). Blessings shared by families include the way that YHWH blessed Obed-Edom the Gittite 'and his entire household' when the Ark of the Covenant was kept in his house (2 Samuel 6.11; 1 Chronicles 13.14).

On those occasions when the expansion of God's people beyond Israel is anticipated, we again see this family principle at work. This is most obvious in the story of Rahab where her family are included within her rescue from the destruction of Jericho (Joshua 2 and 6).

It is within this overall context that we see a strong emphasis upon the duty of Israelite parents to bring up their children within the covenant community. The Shema is one of the most emphatic statements of Israelite belief and having affirmed the oneness of YHWH and the wholeness of love needed in response, it immediately commands the inclusion of children within this:

> Hear, O Israel: YHWH our God, YHWH is one. Love YHWH your God with all your heart and with all your soul and with all your strength. These commandments that I give you today are to be on your hearts. Impress them on your *children*. Talk about them when you sit at home and when you walk along the road, when you lie down and when you get up. Tie them as symbols on your hands and bind them on your foreheads. Write them on the doorframes of your houses and on your gates. (Deuteronomy 6.4-9)

When the Jews later adopted baptism for the initiation of Gentile converts or proselytes to be 'children of the covenant', it is therefore not surprising that they baptized both the adult converts and the children of their families too. It does not matter about the exact date of the introduction of this practice, although it seems to have been established before the baptizing ministry of John. The point is that when converts were admitted into the covenant people, it was considered appropriate that their family, especially the small children, would join too. The family principle was an integral and natural part of their thought patterns with respect to conversion and the covenant people of God.

Most of this understanding of the Old Testament is uncontroversial. The vital question is whether this family principle continues under the new covenant? Some have argued that it very much doesn't, with Jeremiah 31.29-34 cited as evidence of this. Within this passage, which of course includes the promise of a new covenant, Jeremiah says that people will die for their own sins, rather than children sharing in the sin of their fathers (31.29-30). A few verses later, the prophet again appears to indicate the passing of the principle of family solidarity when he says that 'a man' will no longer need to teach 'his brother, saying "Know YHWH", because they all will know me, from the least of them to the greatest' (31.34). At the start of the New Testament, John the Baptist warns his hearers not to presume that having Abraham as their ancestor will ensure their inheritance of God's blessing (Matthew 3.9-10; Luke 3.8-9). Most tellingly of all, Jesus appears to overthrow the family principle very directly when his mother and brothers arrive to see him and 'pointing to his disciples, he said, 'Here are my mother and my brothers! For whoever does the will of my Father in heaven is my brother and sister and mother' (Matthew 12.46-50; cf. Mark 3.31-35; Luke 8.19-21). Doesn't all of this indicate that with the coming of the Holy Spirit, the New Testament sees the beginning of individual responsibility before God, rather than any continuation of family solidarity? Instead of being born into God's family, people instead need to be 'born again' by responding with faith to God's gift of Jesus Christ.

Many of the emphases made within such interpretations are important. They reinforce the point that we have sought to make throughout the book that God's promises require the response of faithful obedience. The popular saying that 'God has no grandchildren' is helpful in asserting the need for every individual to make a personal response to God, rather than rely upon their spiritual pedigree. Children growing up in Christian families do need to make a personal response to God as they grow up. The main emphasis within these passages, however, is upon the expansion of God's people under the new covenant to include all those responding to his grace with faith and obedience. A major function of the Holy Spirit coming on 'all flesh' is to enable this response to God to be made. At the end of Chapter 4, we observed that simplistic contrasts made between the Old and New Testaments, in this case between corporate and personal response to God, are deeply misleading. Both a corporate and a personal response to God were essential under the old covenant and remain essential under the new. In fact, if anything, the indwelling of the Holy Spirit amongst the people of God and its supreme manifestation in love bring with it a deeper sense of the corporate relationship to God of the church as the body of Christ.

It is against this background that we now examine New Testament references to families and little children. Detailed exegesis of these passages will not be attempted nor the baptist objections to the use of them. As already made clear, none of these passages by themselves demonstrate or require infant baptism. However, the reader is asked to judge whether or not they are best interpreted as a continuation of the biblical tradition of the family principle. One of these in Peter's reference to 'the promise is for you and your children' in Acts 2.39 has already been examined. But there are a number of others as well.

(a) Children were addressed as members of the church – 'children obey your parents *in the Lord*' (Ephesians 6.1; cf. Colossians 3.20; 1 John 2.13 – although John often uses the term 'children' metaphorically, here it is likely to be literal). The significance of children growing up 'in the Lord' can scarcely be exaggerated for the phrase is baptismal and enshrines all the blessings of the covenant and salvation. This reminds us of the angel's prophecy to Zechariah about John: 'He will be filled with the Holy Spirit even from birth' (literally 'from his mother's womb') (Luke 1.15).

(b) There are several references to *'the household'* in connection with baptism – with Lydia, with the jailer of Philippi, and with Stephanas (Acts 16.15; 16.33; 1 Corinthians 1.16) and probably with Cornelius (Acts 10.48, cf. 11.14). See also Crispus (Acts 18.8). There is no proof that these households contained infants, though perhaps in the context of an extended family pattern it is highly likely. It is the family principle clearly in operation once again. This is also seen (without any mention of baptism) in the story of Jesus and Zacchaeus, where the latter's 'house' is included within his salvation and the declaration that Zacchaeus is 'a son of Abraham' (Luke 19.9).

(c) In 1 Corinthians 7 Paul deals with questions concerning marriage. In 7.14 he speaks about an unbelieving partner being 'sanctified' by the believing partner who has been converted after marriage. As part of his argument for this he adds, 'otherwise *your children* would be unclean, but as it is, *they are holy*'. It seems best to interpret this passage in the light of covenant 'separation' and family solidarity. It is unlikely to refer to civil legitimacy, nor is it likely to mean moral holiness of character. The words 'unclean' and 'holy' are covenant status words, which speak first of God's consecration of things or people and then of their subsequent life of moral and spiritual separation to God's service. The unbelieving partner must embrace the gospel by faith in order to be saved (7.16), and the children must grow up 'in the Lord' to make this holy status a living reality of faith and obedience. But, alongside this is the definite emphasis upon the conversion of a parent drawing the whole family into the covenant privileges (and responsibilities) of God.

(d) Jesus's attitude to little children is quite striking. 'If anyone causes one of these little ones who believe in me to sin, it would be better for him to have a large millstone hung around his neck and to be drowned in the depths of the sea' (Matthew 18.6). Jesus said, 'Let the little children come to me, and do not hinder them, for the kingdom of heaven belongs to such as these.' He placed his hands on them with his blessing (Matthew 19.13f). In the parallel passage at Mark 10.13f there is the addition 'I tell you the truth, anyone who will not receive the kingdom of God like a little child will never enter it.' Little children can believe, and be led astray, they can be brought to Jesus, be members of the kingdom of God, and their simple trustfulness is an example to all. The question that we should ask in the light of these passages is not so much what are the grounds for children's inclusion within God's covenant sign as the grounds of their exclusion from it?

None of these passages are *proof* texts for infant baptism, but, when understood in the covenant context, they provide grounds for a legitimate inference that is a matter of biblical and spiritual integrity and not just a case of special pleading.

## The sacramental principle

This has been explored in the previous chapter. To summarize, the sacrament of baptism is an action or sign which confirms God's word of promise. It represents God's gift to us, rather than what we do for him. Baptism is a sign of grace rather than a witness to faith but it is a sign that, nonetheless, must be received with faith.

God's grace is secure and his promise utterly dependable. However, although faith is also a gift of God, it is worked out in human response, and this response is not always easy to evaluate. When an adult confesses repentance, faith and conversion, some church leaders will offer baptism immediately, as seems the practice in the earliest days of the church. Other leaders, however, will offer further instruction, make further enquiry into the reality of the faith and test it in various ways. Quite often someone baptized as an adult will appear to fall away from faith. Similarly, with the child of a Christian family, the response may be erratic, complex, sometimes inconsistent or even hostile.

However, in spite of these inevitable uncertainties (which are paralleled in adults), it appears appropriate:

(a) *To bring up children of a Christian family in the grace of God.* Thus, we teach them to know and pray to God as Father and, therefore, to consider themselves as his children; to know Jesus as their friend and saviour from sin; to know the Holy Spirit as their comforter and the church as their fellow brothers and sisters in Christ. These are the full blessings of the gospel, of salvation, of the covenant, of baptism and of faith in God's promises.

(b) *To bring up children of a Christian family responding to this grace in repentance, faith and obedience to God.*

Thus, we teach them about knowing and obeying God's commands in the Bible, the importance of confessing our sins and trusting God's offer of forgiveness, and to work at growing in grace and in the knowledge of the Lord Jesus. In these circumstances, both knowing the grace of God and responding to this grace in trusting obedience can and do develop from the earliest times in a child's life. They very often become part of an infant's experience alongside (ideally) the love, care and protection of their parents (or guardians) and also others within the body of Christ. In fact there are no grounds for making knowledge of, and love for, God a matter of intellectual understanding and some hypothetical age of discretion, when no such criterion could be applied to knowledge of, and love for, a mother and father.

In the light of (a) and (b), it also seems fully appropriate:

(c) *To offer such a child the covenant sign, or sacrament, of God's grace in baptism.*

Baptism is initiation into Christian life. It marks the beginning (not a further stage) of discipleship to Jesus. It should then be worked out, whether in adult convert or Christian child, in a baptized life – being cleansed and living in Christ through the Spirit as a child of God and member of the church. Baptism has past, present and future dimensions with respect to God's covenant plan of grace; it also has past, present and future dimensions with respect to the faith-response. The deepest concern and most earnest prayer of every Christian parent should be that, from the very beginning of life, the child that has received the promise of God's grace will live their new life 'in the Lord' and so grow in grace and in the Spirit of God.

# Issues related to infant baptism

We shall now consider four related issues arising from the consideration of the propriety of baptizing the children of Christian parents. These are:

- The issue of indiscriminate baptism
- The liturgical language in the services of baptism
- The question why baptism replaced circumcision
- The question whether the salvation of infants depends on baptism

There are many thoughtful Christians who will follow the biblical argument up to this point, but for whom the issues of indiscriminate baptism and the liturgical language are highly significant obstacles. This is well understood and the topics require careful attention.

## The issue of indiscriminate baptism

This is distressing to many Christians and the major reason why many of baptist convictions are doubtful of the theological integrity of those who defend Christian family baptism. Indiscriminate baptism of infants occurs primarily in countries which have established or state churches and where, over the centuries, there have been close links with or even identity between church and state. In these situations the baptism of infants becomes a social or cultural norm or custom, and there may be little or no understanding of the gospel, little or no credible confession of faith, membership of the church or likelihood of real Christian nurture. In terms of the theology of Christian baptism that has been developed in these chapters, such a ceremony can be seen more as a rite of folk religion than 'christening' or being baptized into Christ. The pressure of this folk religion is historically deep-seated and profoundly subtle, but must be withstood if infant baptism is to carry credibility.

The issue of a proper discipline over infant baptism which preserves the context of living faith in the gospel of Jesus will be examined in Chapter 11. Suffice to say at this moment that the biblical theology of infant baptism can only be argued with integrity in the context of a proper discipline of practice. Even where the biblical theology of infant baptism is not inadequate, the pastoral practice can leave much to be desired. However, it needs to be said that too great a gap between theological position and pastoral practice can be a problem in baptist churches too. Faulty practice should make us ask searching questions about the theology behind such practice. But if we are satisfied about the legitimate inference of the propriety of Christian family baptism, it is the faulty pastoral practice that needs reform and not the biblical theology of covenant sign and sacrament.

## The liturgical language used in the services of baptism

This frequently causes widespread embarrassment and misunderstanding. *The Book of Common Prayer* (1662) states after the baptism:

Seeing now…that this child is regenerate and grafted into the body of Christ's Church, let us give thanks unto Almighty God for these benefits, and with one accord make our prayers unto him.…We yield Thee hearty thanks, most merciful father, that it hath pleased Thee to regenerate this infant with thy Holy Spirit, to receive him for thine own child by adoption, and to incorporate him into thy Holy Church.[1]

Similarly the baptism service within the Church of England's *Common Worship* (2000) declares in the prayer over the water:

We thank you, Father, for the water of baptism. In it we are buried with Christ in his death. By it we share in his resurrection. Through it we are reborn by the Holy Spirit. Therefore, in joyful obedience to your Son, we baptise into his fellowship, those who come in faith. Now sanctify this water that, by the power of your Holy Spirit, they may be cleansed from sin and born again.[2]

It later declares in the welcome to those newly baptized:

We welcome you into the fellowship of faith; we are children of the same heavenly Father; we welcome you.[3]

Many sincere Christians are hostile to, or at least uneasy about, such expressions. They feel that when applied to an infant, they undermine the New Testament emphasis on the necessity of faith. A similar problem could be felt with regard to an adult baptism candidate for we cannot be totally sure that the fruit of spiritual regeneration will mature following an initial profession of faith. However, we assume the sincerity of the profession of repentance and faith, and, in addition, may require some evidence in terms of instruction received and a sharing in church life. On some such basis, we speak of the baptized person in terms of all the realities which baptism signifies – born again, a child of God, etc.

Similarly, in the case of the Christian household baptism of an infant, we cannot be totally sure that the fruit of spiritual regeneration will mature following nurture in the faith of Christ. However, we assume the grace of God at work in terms of the covenant and family principles, and the sincerity of the parents' promises to bring up the child in the Lord and in faith, and, in addition, may require some evidence on the part of the parents in terms of instruction received and sharing in church life. On this basis, we speak of the baptized child in terms of all the realities which baptism signifies – born again, a child of God, etc.

This is the language of baptismal efficacy the New Testament writers use – but, as emphasized, it is always faith language. It is not unconditional efficacy. For the language of covenant and sacrament always requires the context of faith. So the BCP continues after the thanksgiving quoted above:

And humbly we beseech thee to grant that he being dead unto sin, and living unto righteousness, and being buried with Christ in his death, may crucify the old man, and utterly abolish the whole body of sin; and that, as he is made partaker of the death of thy Son, he may be partaker of his resurrection; so that finally, with the residue of thy holy Church, he may be an inheritor of thine everlasting kingdom.[4]

and *Common Worship* continues:

Renewed in your image, may they walk in the light of faith and continue for ever in the risen life of Jesus Christ our Lord; to whom with you and the Holy Spirit be all honour and glory, now and for ever. Amen.[5]

Once the baptism has taken place in *Common Worship*, a Commission then follows which includes the following words:

In baptism God invites you to a life-long journey. Together with all God's people you must explore the way of Jesus and grow in fellowship with God, in love for his people, and in serving others. With us you will listen to the word of God and receive the gifts of God.[6]

This language of expectant faith is categorical in form (i.e. describing the sign in terms of the realities signified) but it is hypothetical or conditional in effect (i.e. it depends on the living response of faith). It is intriguing to remember that the Anglican Reformers such as Cranmer and Ridley who are sometimes criticized for underplaying faith in their baptism liturgy actually died at the stake for the principle of justification by faith in their communion liturgy. The baptism liturgies of the Church of England are designed to express the two New Testament factors of baptism – the efficacy of the covenant sign of God's grace and the necessity of its right reception with faith. The language of one factor must be seen and interpreted in the context of the other factor.

The use of language to speak of a reality which is categorical in one sense but conditional in another sense has parallels in other situations of daily life. Take the wedding ceremony, for example. The bride and groom make their vows, give and receive the ring, and are solemnly pronounced to be 'man and wife'. This categorical assertion is never questioned by the guests at the wedding, but it is in actual fact conditional on their consummating their marriage and living together as man and wife. If this expectation is unfulfilled, then, vows and ring notwithstanding, the marriage can be null and void. We cannot be totally sure it will be a proper marriage. However, we assume the sincerity of their professions of love and, in addition, may well have seen evidence in terms of instruction about marriage and sharing in courtship and engagement.

Another example is to be found in the handing over of a cheque. The cheque is made out for (let us say) a thousand pounds, with the recipient's name, and handed to him. We then regard the beneficiary as one thousand pounds better off. No one dreams of questioning the categorical assertion that the beneficiary has received one thousand pounds, but it is in actual fact conditional on their taking the cheque to a bank and paying it into their account. If this expectation is unfulfilled, and the cheque is forgotten, lost or left in a drawer, the order's promise and payment notwithstanding, it fails to benefit the recipient. We cannot be totally sure the cheque will be used. However, we assume the grateful acceptance and use of the gift on the part of the recipient and, in addition, may have some evidence in terms of his knowledge about cheques and use of the bank to pay them in.

The ring and the cheque both make a very powerful statement but their full significance is nonetheless conditional on the context and subsequent action. So too with baptism. It powerfully expresses the gift of God's grace to adult or infant but the full significance of this is conditional on the context of faith and the subsequent action of a life of faith.

The liturgical language, similarly, is categorical in form (expressing the biblical teaching of the efficacy of baptism), but it is conditional in effect (requiring the response of faith for its full effect). This language is the Scriptural language of covenant sign and sacrament. It expresses the totality of the covenant promise as well as the necessity of the faith-response. The assertions of efficacy are a matter for joy and encouragement in the assurance of God's initiative of grace, whilst the petition for growth in Christian life is a matter for earnest prayer, faith and dedicated nurture. The diminution of either factor would impair the liturgical expression of the biblical doctrine.

## The question why baptism replaced circumcision

This has not yet been answered in this enquiry. The New Testament writers seem to assume the priority of baptism as Christian initiation, and Jesus's words in the Great Commission, Matthew 28.19, clearly express the convictions of the early Christians. The first Jewish Christians did not immediately and obviously detach themselves from Judaism, its customs and ceremonies. They continued to attend the Temple and synagogue (Luke 24.53; Acts 3.1f) and to use the covenant sign of circumcision alongside the new covenant sign of baptism (Acts 16.3). There are several factors that gradually led to the complete replacement of circumcision by baptism.

The most important of these was the incorporation of the Gentiles into the church. Circumcision formed one of the foremost 'works of the law' by which Jews demonstrated that they were the covenant people and those whom YHWH would vindicate when he at last brought his restoring justice to the earth. As we have seen, circumcision was far more than simply a physical or external sign, carrying deep spiritual significance and requiring the response of faith and obedience to God. But, crucially, *circumcision was also exclusive* acting as a boundary marker between Israel as God's covenant people and the uncircumcised Gentiles. At the heart of the Gospel, however, was the proclamation that because of the death and resurrection of Jesus the Messiah and the coming of the Holy Spirit, belonging to God's people was now open to everyone. It was this that made Paul so concerned in his letter to the Galatians about those who were trying to force Gentile converts to Christianity to be circumcised. Doing this was a straightforward denial of the gospel message that 'there is neither Jew nor Greek, slave nor free, male nor female, because you are all one in Christ Jesus' (Galatians 3.28).

But any re-establishment of circumcision was also, Paul declared, the path back to slavery and away from the freedom that the Galatians had found in Jesus. The background here is Paul's understanding of the mysterious role of the Torah in trapping

Israel under sin but precisely so that this sin could then be carried by her Messiah and dealt with when he died. Jesus had thus released Israel from the curse of the law (3.13) and to go back to it now, by insisting on the continuation of circumcision, was to return to the slavery that Jesus had released them from (5.1f). Paul was not advocating removal of the mark of the circumcision or even its discontinuation for Jews. He was simply declaring its redundancy as the covenant sign of God's new multi-ethnic people and the real dangers in trying to reimpose it as such. Near the end of the letter he declares, 'For in Christ Jesus, neither circumcision nor uncircumcision has any value. The only thing that counts is faith expressing itself in love' (5.6) and again 'neither circumcision nor uncircumcision means anything, what counts is a new creation' (6.15).

It was overwhelmingly this context and the agreement within the early church on this matter (Acts 15) that led to baptism replacing circumcision. Paul stops short in Galatians of an explicit comparison between the two preferring to contrast 'works of the law' with faith in Christ Jesus. But his description of baptism and faith in Colossians as 'the circumcision done by Christ' (2.11-12) is clear evidence that Paul regarded baptism as the covenant sign that had replaced its predecessor. Circumcision 'done by the hands of men' spoke of exclusion. Baptism, by contrast, spoke particularly powerfully of Gentile incorporation into the church given that the path that had once been required of Gentile converts to Judaism was now the single rite by which Jews and Gentiles alike entered on completely equal terms into the one covenant family of God.

An additional factor in the replacement of circumcision with baptism was probably the bloodless nature of baptism and appropriateness of this under the new covenant. Both the major signs of the old covenant, circumcision and Passover, involved the shedding of blood. This reminded God's people that 'without *the shedding of blood* there is no forgiveness' of sins (Hebrews 9.22). However, the major theme of Hebrews is how the sacrificial death of Christ and the shedding of his blood to deal with sin had fulfilled such signs and made them redundant: 'When this priest had offered for all time one sacrifice for sins, he sat down at the right hand of God' (Hebrews 10.12). Whilst it was the Temple sacrifices that Hebrews was concerned to show had become obsolete, the wider application of this would not have been missed by the early Christians. New covenant signs were now appropriate which did not involve the shedding of blood but which instead pointed back to the perfect sacrifice of Christ and the church recognized that it possessed these in baptism and the Lord's Supper.

It has often been asserted that another reason baptism replaced circumcision as a covenant sign is because it is offered *to women* as well as men. There is some weight in this point although it is partly based on underestimation of the full significance of circumcision within the Old Testament faith. Although it is the male sex organ's foreskin that is removed, circumcision ensured that at the moment of supreme expression of sexual love and the essential moment of conception, the covenant sign of God's grace was at the centre and shared in joyful solemnity by man and wife. In the context of a world full of sexual decadence, circumcision made a very strong statement of the importance of holiness within the 'one flesh' that YHWH had established between husband and wife. Having noted this, it is important to add that the number of Gentile women converting to pre-Christian Judaism was almost certainly part of what caused baptism to assume its profile as the key initiatory rite for proselytes. Considerable numbers of Gentile women joining the Christian movement (often without their husbands) continued as a major factor within the early church and this was another factor reinforcing the replacement of circumcision by baptism as God's covenant sign.

## The question whether the salvation of infants depends on baptism

This must surely be answered with a firm negative. We have seen that the blessings of salvation are all linked to baptism and that the identical blessings are linked to receiving the gospel by faith. However, behind both of these truths is the ultimate and primary truth that the blessings of salvation come from the grace of God alone. Those who hold a baptist theology often dedicate their infants to God and seek his blessing of salvation for them from the day of birth. Believers can entrust their infants (whether living or dying) to the mercy of God with utter confidence in his loving mercy and covenant grace. It is as they grow up that the children must, in an age-appropriate manner, affirm their desire to be in the Lord, converted to Christ, and thus confirm their baptism.

The biblical language of covenant signs and the liturgical language of the sacraments are always the language of faith. Infant baptism has precisely the same theological significance as adult baptism. It is God's covenant sign of his saving grace. It effects what it signifies, not automatically, but within the context of living faith.

The basis for this conviction is founded on appeal to Scripture alone. Just as indiscriminate adult baptism would be a denial of the necessity of faith, so indiscriminate infant baptism is destructive of the true nature of the sacrament. That is why infant baptism is better termed 'Christian family baptism'. It must be emphasized again – there is only one theology of baptism and that is believer's baptism. It is God's covenant sign to adult believers and to their children who are brought up in the grace and the faith of the Lord.

# The 'Baptist' view

Those who hold a 'baptist' view regard the case for Christian infant baptism expounded in the previous chapter as unconvincing. The title of this chapter is slightly misleading but avoids being pedantic. The fact is that there is no one 'baptist view'. Just as at the beginning of the previous chapter it was acknowledged that there have been various and inadequate expositions of infant baptism, so now we note that there are various views amongst those who disagree with infant baptism. It would be all too easy to quote copiously from quite unbiblical and incoherent passages of baptist writers and let them cancel out each other's positions. This approach has been repeatedly adopted against the family-baptism doctrine.[1] However, this is no way to conduct serious debate about biblical theology. It should be the best presentation of the opponents' case which is answered. Division about the defence of a theological position or the abuse resulting from such a position may properly form a part of theological debate, but the best answer to abuse may not be disuse but *right use*.

However, a major division amongst baptist scholars must be noted. Probably the majority still hold to the Zwinglian or 'symbolic' view of baptism, which was examined in Chapter 8. A growing number, though, recognize some of the biblical criticisms of that position and have adopted what is often called a 'sacramental' view, i.e. that baptism is a sign (and effective sign) of grace and not merely a symbol of faith in the gospel.

## Arguments against Christian family baptism

The first and major objection to infant baptism is:

### 1. Baptism should follow faith and be an expression of faith

All 'baptists' are agreed that baptism should follow a conscious profession of faith on the part of the candidate. They argue that this is the clear pattern of the Great Commission by the risen Jesus in Matthew 28.18-20, in the accounts of the Acts of the Apostles and in the theological implication of the Epistles. Baptism is an expression of the convert's faith and a witness or testimony to it. An infant cannot make a decision to confess faith in the waters of baptism.

There is a major problem with this doctrinal position. The apostolic writers, as noted earlier, do not explain baptism as a witness to faith, but rather as God's witness to his grace that is received in faith. This is a distinctly different approach. We saw earlier that Victor Jack explains the whole significance of baptism in terms of the convert confessing Christ and in terms of the believer's response.[2] Even Beasley-Murray, who held a sacramental baptist view, wrote, 'It is universally recognised that in the primitive Church baptism was the occasion par excellence for the confession of faith in Christ.'[3] In support he cited four texts (Acts 8.36ff; Romans 1.9; Ephesians 5.26; 1 Peter 3.18ff), none of which explicitly link baptism and witness, and concludes that they 'provide sufficient evidence on this point'.

Now as we said earlier, baptism of adult converts obviously involves a declaration of faith in Christ, but the New Testament writers nowhere speak of it in terms of witness to others – believers or unbelievers.

The crucial point is that the baptist doctrine puts the emphasis in the wrong place. Certainly baptism must be in the context of gospel proclamation received by faith, but essentially and primarily, the apostolic writers declare it to be God's covenant sign of his grace. This is the correct doctrine of all baptism – adult as well as infant. A child should only receive the sign if he or she is to be nurtured by parent or guardian in the Lord, in the knowledge of his grace and in trustful dependence on him. Baptism marks the initiation or beginning of Christian discipleship. For an adult convert, that will be at some point near his conversion, but for a child of Christian parents discipleship should, can and does start from the very commencement of life. This is God's ideal for the Christian family. Baptism may prove unfruitful – both in the professing adult convert and in the child of the Christian home. Nevertheless, when this occurs in an adult who is later genuinely converted to spiritual renewal, no responsible Baptist ministers offer a 'second' baptism. This is an example which indicates that the principle 'baptism must follow conscious faith' can have its exceptions, even amongst adults.

## 2. Baptism does not convey salvation automatically

This is entirely agreed. The *ex opere operato* view was criticized in Chapter 8. It was argued that the biblical doctrine combines both strong sacramental language of efficacy along with a clear emphasis on the necessity of faith-response. God's covenant promise of grace and God's covenant sign which confirms that promise are not automatically enjoyed or offered unconditionally – they must be received by faith. The same problem occurs with an adult as with the child of a Christian family. We can never be absolutely sure that the faith will develop and persist, but we presume the sincerity of the faith-context and that the right conditions for spiritual growth will continue. When Beasley-Murray criticized the explanation of infant baptism as a promise with a condition, he declared, 'observe what a drastic change has been wrought in the nature of baptism so administered. Baptism has been reduced from a sacrament to a sermon, from a gift to an offer, from an event of eternal consequence to an uncertain possibility'.[4] The basis of this criticism, however, is unsustainable. Unless we are to believe in an invariable baptismal regeneration in adult baptism (let alone infant), we are bound to acknowledge that the sacrament is an acted and confirmed sermon from God, a gift that is offered by God and an event of eternal consequence which nevertheless has a real element of uncertainty in the sense that we can never presume on God's mercy and must ever emphasize the responsibility of responding with faith.

This is precisely why the Anglican liturgies combine the two distinct elements that we observed in the previous chapter. The assertion of baptismal efficacy in terms of the gracious promise of God is strongly present but there is also the heartfelt prayer that the candidates (adult and infant) will grow in the faith and show fruit worthy of repentance and life in Christ.

### 3. Salvation and faith is an individual matter, not hereditary

It is agreed that in the final analysis everyone will stand before God responsible for their own attitudes and actions. This was true in Old Testament times as well as in the time of the new covenant in Christ. However, in both testaments, this responsibility is set within the context of the people of God – Israel in the Old Testament and the church in the New – and God's commitment to dwell amongst his people as a collective unit. And within this, as we have seen, there is a particular and continuing role for the family principle within God's covenant plan of grace. There are inestimable privileges in being brought up 'in the Lord'. Paul is unembarrassed about stressing this when he says to Timothy, 'I have been reminded of your sincere faith, which first lived in your grandmother, Lois, and in your mother Eunice and, I am persuaded, now lives in you also' (2 Timothy 1.5). Rather than Timothy's faith being seen as individual, Paul clearly views this faith as something owned by the family together. Part of the way in which this faith was nurtured in Timothy by Eunice and Lois is indicated later on in the letter when Paul speaks to Timothy of how 'from infancy you have known the holy Scriptures, which are able to make you wise for salvation through faith in Christ Jesus' (3.15). With the enormous benefits of such nurture, however, come equally great responsibilities. Alongside both references to his pedigree and nurture, Timothy is reminded of this, being instructed to 'fan into flame the gift of God that is within you through the laying on of my hands' (1.6) and to 'continue in what you have learned and have become convinced of' (3.14). His personal response to God's grace and the means by which he has been privileged to receive this is crucial. Likewise any child brought up within the grace of God in a Christian family is not automatically saved irrespective of the response of faith and commitment.

Thus, we find that these three objections fail to show Christian infant baptism to be unbiblical. Firstly, baptism is primarily a covenant sign of God's grace given to his people at the very beginning of their life of discipleship. It is to be received and lived out by faith, but is not itself essentially a witness to faith. Secondly, baptism does not convey its blessings of salvation automatically either to adult or to infant. The salvation is conditional upon the promises being truly received in living and continuing faith. Thirdly, salvation and faith are certainly not hereditary, in spite of the clear family principle in the Scriptures. A Christian family does bring great blessing but not automatically, and not by natural birth. The blessings of salvation are conditional upon the new birth in Christ effected by baptism being lived out through their faith and obedience to the Spirit living within them.

We now move on to consider:

## Problems of the baptist doctrine

These are considerable and not often recognized. It is usually baptists who are most interested in baptism and on the attack, whilst most members of churches which practise infant baptism often know little theology of baptism and are insecure and defensive. Those who have sincerely followed the development of the biblical case for Christian family baptism need not feel their position is threatened by criticisms aimed at either inadequate arguments for infant baptism or indiscriminate baptism. Neither are necessary, and both are abuses of the biblical teaching. It is the best and biblical case for infant baptism and the proper administration of it in the truly believing family that must be answered.

There are three serious weaknesses of biblical theology in the baptist doctrine. The first two have been considered already in this chapter.

### 1. Baptism is seen as a symbol of faith rather than as a sign of grace

This leads inevitably to a human-centred ceremony rather than a Christ-centred sacrament, which is given by God and involves the seal of the Spirit. This is a serious distortion of the biblical doctrine which some baptist theologians have sought to correct by developing a more sacramental theology.

### 2. Baptism is given an emphatic importance as witness to others

Baptism may well be a powerful witness, especially when an adult is converted but this is not a significant part of apostolic doctrine. Witness to Christ is vital but is focused on the continuing baptized life of holiness, unity and suffering for the gospel rather than the initial baptismal event. Once again, the perceived direction is wrong. Baptism is primarily not something a person does either for God or as a witness to others; it is something God gives to him or her. It is God's witness to his promise of saving grace.

### 3. Baptism is not acknowledged as essentially a covenant sign

This is the fundamental weakness of biblical theology, which underlies the first two problems. The essential covenant nature of the sacrament is not generally recognized by baptist theologians – the covenant language, imagery, contexts and illustrations so clearly seen in Chapter 2 where we considered each baptism reference in the Epistles. This was the essential pattern of apostolic understanding, and failure to recognize it leads inevitably to a whole range of erroneous exegesis. The covenant continuity is seriously undervalued and the discontinuities exaggerated (as worked out at the end of Chapter 5). This means that most baptist theologians gravely misjudge the nature of the covenant with Abraham and its developments with Moses and David. Repeatedly it is described as outward rather than inward, concerned with natural birth rather than spiritual life, racially exclusive rather than a universal promise and with circumcision seen a mere mark of the flesh rather than a sign of spiritual grace. Much of this is based on a major misunderstanding of the (admittedly mysterious) role of the law. This proceeds to play itself out in a negative reading of the entire covenant before Christ and which, despite Jesus's specific words in Matthew 5.17, he is seen as coming to abolish rather than bring to fulfilment.

Finally, there is a serious practical and pastoral problem:

## 4. How to bring up a child within a Christian family

Quite simply the question is this – should Christian parents bring up their children as 'in the Lord' and needing to grow in grace and in the knowledge of Christ, or assuming that they are outside of Christ and his kingdom and needing to be converted at some age of understanding? This is a very personal and sensitive matter and there is no desire to cause any offence. However, the baptist theology points to the latter of the two options, and both Davies and Watson are quite explicit that children of Christian families should be assumed to be unconverted until showing clear evidence to the contrary.[5] In practice, many baptist parents do bring their children up as Christians in much the same way as parents who have baptized their children with the covenant sign. Many such children have never known a time when they did not trust God as Father, Jesus as saviour and friend and the Spirit as guide and strengthener. All speculations about ages of discretion or conscious understanding are subjective and fruitless. One might just as well ask when a child starts to love and trust her parents. It is a nonsensical question which betrays an intellectual approach to a matter which is far more to do with 'infant-like' trust and the emotional response of love than it is to mental understanding. We have noted that John was Spirit-filled from his birth and that Timothy had from his childhood known the Scriptures which taught him of God's salvation. This is surely God's ideal for children – never to know a time when they are outside God's kingdom, a stranger to God's love, without his Spirit's power.

If Christian parents do believe God can bring spiritual life when he chooses (since all regeneration in adult or infant is a miracle of God's grace and a new birth only God's Spirit can effect), at what point will they give the covenant sign of that grace? When the two-year-old says 'I love Jesus', or the three-year-old says 'Our Father in heaven', or the four-year-old says 'Dear God, I'm sorry, please help me'? Such prayers cannot be lightly dismissed. Some baptists do offer 'believer's baptism' to children of five and upwards, but it is a hazardous pastoral matter assessing conscious faith at such an age.

However, if Christian parents do not believe God can bring new spiritual life until a child reaches an age when she is capable of a conscious and 'meaningful' profession of repentance, faith and conversion, they live in a very difficult position with regard to Christian nurture. Before the supposed time of possible conversion, the child will exist outside of God's family and unable to call God their Father or Jesus their saviour and friend. Many baptists are uncomfortable when these questions are raised and evasive in their response. In fact, at a popular level and when pressed, they often fall back on something that sounds very like an acknowledgement of the family principle covered in the previous chapter with their children being, somehow, covered by God's grace.

But the question of the status of these unbaptized children before God needs to be gently but firmly pressed: Are they part of his family or not? If they are, then what are the grounds for denying to them God's sign of this?

These problems of nurture for baptists indicate that something may be wrong with their premise. Surely it is biblically and pastorally more appropriate in a Christian family to bring up our children in the Lord, in glad and confident awareness of his saving grace and in trusting and obedient response which matures with the years. Knowing that, if they are responding to God's love, they already belong to him rather than this only being acknowledged when they are older. We must not expect an 'adult' faith in a two-year-old – the response will be appropriate to their age and development and indeed contain much that the adult members of the church family need to note and learn from (Mark 10.13-16).

The question may well be asked, 'How, then, do we know if and when a child is regenerate?' Once again, the answer must be the same with regard to adult and infant. The answer is that we can never be totally sure (in the sense that 5 + 5 = 10), but we can have a real faith in her or his regeneration on the basis of God's promise of grace and the context of faith. In the adult convert, God's promise has been given in the gospel and we presume the sincerity of the response of faith in the context of Christian nurture; in the child of a Christian family too, God's promise has been given in the gospel and we presume the sincerity of the response of faith in the context of Christian nurture. It is not automatic or hereditary or a matter of natural birth. It is conditional, spiritual and a matter of birth from above. Nevertheless, in baptism (adult and family/infant) we thank God in confident anticipation and pray to him on the basis of his sure promise of grace. Why is the faith-response vital? Not to achieve salvation (only God does that) but to receive it; not to make it but to show it forth in daily life.

The writers number many baptist Christians amongst their closest family and friends, and have the very highest respect for and gratitude towards them. This present exposition could be wrong. The aim is not really to persuade people to change churches. It is hoped to show that the case for Christian family baptism is sincerely founded on biblical theology alone and provides a more appropriate way to evangelize and nurture the child of the Christian family.

# 11

# Discrimination in baptism

To clarify biblical theology is one thing, to apply it consistently in practice is another. Differences come to the surface, and tensions are inevitably felt, when Christian teaching comes to be applied in concrete circumstances. At this point the context in which theology is learned, worked out and applied is of considerable (though often underestimated) influence. Moreover, there is a psychological and methodological contrast between those who see theology as primary and the cultural context significant but subservient and those who see the circumstances of the context in society as primary whilst the biblical theology is significant but subservient. The contrast has been drawn quite sharply, but there is, in fact, an entire spectrum of views between the two poles, particularly in regard to baptism. Deep feelings of emotion and security (or insecurity) are touched on here with regard to Scripture, tradition, church and nation, and it is not surprising that the regular bursts of correspondence on the subject in both the secular and church press are marked by considerable heat, even when there is a doubtful amount of light.

The idea of discrimination concerning the candidates for baptism raises deep feelings of bewilderment and resentment – more particularly when the discrimination concerns babies. Babies are lovely and innocent and deserve the best! To set conditions, let alone to refuse baptism to parents, especially in the emotional aftermath of pregnancy and first childbirth, is a path that is likely to lie fraught with misunderstanding, pain and anguish. The issues need to be considered with care and judgement.

It is worth noticing at the outset, however, that pastoral discrimination is a concept that is acceptable in other areas. Where adults are baptized, confirmed and admitted to Holy Communion, they are expected to declare their faith, receive instruction and share in church life in such a way that the declaration is credible. In ordination there are stringent procedures of discrimination. Everyone would agree that the most careful procedures of discrimination are appropriate in cases of application for '(re-)baptism'. Personal anguish and emotional expectation are significant but are clearly not the only (or even the major) factors in the pastoral situation. In all these pastoral situations judgement will be made (one way or the other) on the basis of a mixture of theological understanding and pastoral insight against a background of the rules and traditions of the church. All three of these dimensions are open for critical re-examination.

Discrimination in baptism is no longer the preserve of a few idiosyncratic individuals, nor of small reformist pressure groups nor of any particular theological tradition. Clergy and committed lay people alike are increasingly concerned that there should be proper baptism policies and anxious about indiscriminate baptism. We remind ourselves again that the highly influential World Council of Churches report *Baptism, Eucharist and Ministry* of 1982 said that those who practise infant baptism must reconsider certain aspects of their practice and 'must guard themselves against the practice of apparently indiscriminate baptism and take more seriously their responsibility for the nurture of baptised children to mature commitment to Christ'. Again, the report declared, 'It is appropriate to explain in the context of the baptismal service the meaning of baptism as it appears from Scripture (i.e. the participation in Christ's death and resurrection, conversion, pardoning and cleansing, gift of the Spirit, incorporation into the body of Christ and sign of the Kingdom).'[1]

As in all situations of theological debate we must try to hear the best case of the other side and beware of imputing motives which are insincere or disreputable. Phraseology like 'rigorist' and 'judgemental' on the one hand or 'careless' and 'slap-dash' on the other may well be justified in a particular situation here or there and (if widespread) be a significant feature in theological interpretation, but it is very difficult to evaluate in any objective fashion and can so easily generate more annoyance than illumination.

## The case for discrimination in infant baptism

This issue must be carefully developed. No one objects to the principle of discrimination as such, as has been noted in the contexts of adult baptism, Confirmation, Holy Communion and ordination. But what are the arguments for discrimination in regard to the baptism of infants? They are threefold:

### (a) Theological integrity

The meaning of baptism in the Scriptures must be kept crystal clear. It is not (primarily) a rite of passage, a naming ceremony, an opportunity for thanksgiving after childbirth nor even dedication (of a child) to God and asking for his blessing. It is God's covenant sign of salvation. It signifies sharing in Christ's death and resurrection. It signifies conversion, cleansing, the gift of the Spirit and incorporation into the body of Christ, the church. It conveys what it signifies not automatically or unconditionally but in the context of repentance and faith in the gospel of Jesus Christ. The general baptism of children whose parents are Muslim, Hindu or atheist by conviction is as utterly incongruous as the baptism of adults with these religious convictions. The same argument applies where parents are agnostic or indifferent. Baptism is into Christ through the Spirit. It is in the name of, by the authority of and with the significance given by Almighty God, Father, Son and Spirit. There is one baptism and only one biblical theology of baptism. If baptism sets the visible boundaries of the church, as in biblical theology it does, then there must be some credibility about those boundaries. Otherwise baptism falls into disrepute and can virtually cease to be Christian baptism at all.

## (b) Evangelistic and pastoral opportunity

In the early church, baptism was always in the context of gospel preaching and the response of 'What shall we do?' (Acts 2.37; 16.30). The answer was, 'Be baptised in the context of repentance and trust in Jesus Christ.' Baptism clarifies conversion whether it follows or precedes conscious understanding of it. It does not insist on a stereotype of conversion experience but does point to the necessity of convertedness, of being turned to Christ and changed to newness of life. The manifold imagery of baptism is a supreme opportunity for evangelistic proclamation and challenge and pastoral teaching and nurture. The increasing number of adult baptisms of those who have grown up in homes of other religious faiths or of no religious faith at all is a significant feature of the evangelistic and pastoral scene. When baptism – whether it is that of an adult or an infant – is conducted in the context of response to the good news of Jesus Christ and a living faith, it proclaims very clearly what the gospel is all about. Baptism becomes an exciting and powerful event for everyone present. Correspondingly, where Christian faith is not present in baptism or even expected, it simply creates confusion about the nature of Christianity and the gospel of Jesus Christ.

## (c) Pastoral consistency

There is an important concern that the mission, message and disciplines of the church will be coherent and consistent. The preaching of the gospel, the encouragement to conversion, the assurance of forgiveness and the administration of the sacraments should be all of a piece. The declarations made by candidates for baptism, and by parents and sponsors of infants, are identical to those of the Service of Confirmation and speak clearly of repentance, conversion and faith. It would plainly be unsatisfactory if adults when baptized did not become communicant members of their church. It is similarly unsatisfactory if parents and godparents of baptized children have no concern to practise their faith in public worship. The mission, message and sacraments are seen to be at odds with each other. The clergy know it and lose their nerve, and the laity know it and are perplexed and confused.

# The case against discrimination in infant baptism

The case against pastoral discrimination in the baptism *of adults* has not been made, at least not since the cessation of the use of force in conversion. The arguments for general, open or non-discriminating baptism of infants are still sometimes advanced, though with an increasing lack of confidence.

A major defence of general baptism entitled *Forbid Them Not* was written by R. R. Osborn and published in 1972. The title was drawn from Jesus's rebuke to the disciples when they sought to prevent people from bringing children for him to touch and pray for (Matthew 19.13-15; Mark 10.13-16; Luke 18.15-17). Osborn argued that baptism is essentially a sign of God's grace and effective in conveying God's love, forgiveness and life to the recipient. It provides the means and opportunity for the response of faith.

England was the supreme example of the phenomenon of Christendom, the fusion of church and nation. This meant that Englishmen by birth share a repentance for the death of Christ and breathe the atmosphere of godliness. To require explicit or credible profession of faith from parents presented a threat to the incoherent but nonetheless real and important substratum of Christian life in the nation. Such, in brief, is a summary of Osborn's thesis. It was a curious mixture of incoherent theology, evangelistic naivete, idiosyncratic exposition of church history and sentimental English nationalism.[2]

Even in 1972, Osborn's case was anachronistic and represented a great deal of wishful thinking in its presentation of Christian England. Even repeating his arguments can appear rather like setting up 'a straw man' to be easily knocked over. The reason for doing so, however, is because many of the ongoing arguments made for general or open baptism continue to rest, albeit more subtly, on similar thinking.

*Open Baptism* was produced by Mark Dalby in 1989. Partly in response to the first edition of this book, Dalby set out a vigorous case against any attempt to make infant baptism dependent upon the active faith of the parents or parent. Dalby argued that baptism expressed God's prevenient grace (i.e. this grace preceding any response of faith) and the welcome that Jesus gave to all the children brought to him. But the foundation of his argument was belief in infant baptism being administered in the faith of the church rather than simply the faith of the parents. For Dalby, godparents were more significant in baptism than that of parents because of their role as ministerial agents of the church.[3]

Dalby backed up his case with an extensive and careful appeal to church history. However, almost all of this history was drawn from time when almost everyone in England (the Jews being a notable exception) were regarded as Christian. The key role that he accorded to godparents in representing the faith of the church was particularly anachronistic with no acknowledgement of the infrequency with which non-churchgoing parents select churchgoing godparents for their child. Dalby understood his position as preventing an outward facing church turning into an inward facing sect. In reality it represented, in a less obvious manner than Osborn, a similar attempt to hang onto the vestiges of Christendom.

The attraction of general or open baptism lies in the generosity of spirit that it seeks to display. It enables the first words that the church speaks to people approaching her for baptism to be seemingly positive and affirming ones. It asks no difficult questions and sets no conditions. At its best, open baptism seeks to reflect the open and loving attitude of Jesus which is why it accords the story of Jesus and the children such central importance. The intention behind this is the laudable one of sharing the love of God and the hope of providing a starting point for Christian pilgrimage, pastoral care, Christian education and maintaining the influence of a national church upon the national culture.

However, the truth is that general or open baptism very rarely leads to the effective development of living faith, in either the child baptized or the parents. In fact, it could be argued that it directly works against this because of the manner in which it communicates the church's lack of belief in the truths that the service of baptism proclaims. During the time that Osborn was writing, this was displayed in the prevalence of 'private' baptisms often conducted with just the family present on a

Sunday afternoon. Whilst this has become less common, the practice still occurs and even when open baptism is administered within the main Sunday service, it continues to have minimal instruction and very little expectation of the family becoming regular members of the church.

However, the main objections to 'general baptism' are to be found not only in its inherent problems of theological and pastoral incoherence but also in the positive theological and pastoral grounds for discrimination outlined earlier. As we will see, the positive motives that underlie open baptism can be expressed far more appropriately when a discriminate approach to baptism is set within a missional context. This is faithful to the practice of baptism that we see in the New Testament and also appropriate to the reality of the culture in which we now live. To understand this further, we need to trace the developments in pastoral practice in regard to baptism and the changes that have brought this about.

## The developing pastoral practice in regard to baptism

This has been an area of controversy and confusion for over a century. The central authorities of the Church of England, the Bishops and the General Synod have on several occasions debated the subject or closely related issues. However, both the liturgical provisions and Canon Law are interpreted in widely differing ways when it comes to pastoral practice. Strong protests took place against unconditional and indiscriminate baptizing, notably in 1896 by Hensley Henson (later Bishop of Durham) and in 1907 by Roland Allen who resigned his appointment as vicar of Chalfont St Peter. However, until the middle of the twentieth century such protests made little headway against the general image of the Church of England's gentle but vague liberal Catholicism. The Mason-Dix school of Anglo-Catholics downgraded baptism by asserting that the gift of the Holy Spirit is (primarily) given in Confirmation (see Chapter 13). Evangelicals, meanwhile, were generally anti-sacramental and often embarrassed by infant baptism resulting in a largely untheological approach to its practice, with conversion and Confirmation seen as much more significant.

The fresh thinking on baptism in recent decades has emphasized the necessity of faith and a more complete theology of baptism as the single and complete sacramental rite of Christian initiation. Those developments are sheer gain. However, thinking has also become confused on at least two counts. As we have already seen, the defence of infant baptism has often been on the basis of highly debatable evidence from early church history or a reliance on biblical texts which cannot alone bear the weight, instead of a coherent understanding of biblical theology and of God's covenant plan and promise. This has, in turn, led to a widespread acceptance of the maxim that 'adult baptism is the norm' with infant baptism then accorded a derived and lesser status. Such an understanding only leads to confusion and faulty pastoral practice. True, adult baptism is the primary feature of a missionary situation. However, right from the beginning the reference to 'households' was emphatic historically, and the legitimacy and propriety of the baptism of Christian infants was strong theologically. It is therefore equally true then that in the Christian family adult baptism will be exceptional and infant baptism the norm. To give any impression of an uncertain theology of, or second-class character to, infant baptism in a Christian family is to invite even further misunderstandings about the nature of conversion and Christian nurture and exacerbate the divisiveness over 'rebaptism'. To repeat, there is one baptism and therefore one theology of baptism.

Before examining suggestions for pastoral procedures which cohere with the biblical theology, we do need to have a careful and sympathetic understanding of the context. This context includes the historical background touched upon earlier and the contemporary situation we now face.

## The historical background of Christendom

England inherited the concept of Christendom – a christened kingdom – from the Roman Empire. Following the conversion of the Emperor Constantine in the early fourth century, Christianity became the official religion of the Roman Empire. This rapidly led to universal infant baptism within 'Christian nations'. This social movement was reinforced by the theological teaching of St Augustine of Hippo (354–430) who taught that children who die unbaptized were in some sense 'lost'. The infant mortality rate was, of course, high and children were therefore baptized very swiftly after their birth.

A great deal changed in the wake of the Protestant Reformation in England but with continuity in terms of the nation being understood as Christian. If anything this was reinforced by a monarch who was now 'Head' or 'Supreme Governor' of the Church of England and with church law now passed through Parliament. The Prayer Books and Acts of Uniformity were designed to keep the whole nation together in the way of Christ and this included the universal nature of baptism. The 1552 Prayer Book thus included the instruction that 'the pastors and curates shall oft admonish the people that they defer not the baptism of infants any longer than the Sunday, or other holy day next after the child be born'. Burial in consecrated ground was only for the baptized, so the pressure was almost total.

Whilst the political-religious situation is now very different, the legacy of this thinking can still be evident in attitudes to 'christening'. Such attitudes are becoming less and less common but still underlie the folk-religion and superstition that, in certain areas, still identify danger in a child remaining unbaptized.

## Changing features in the life of the nation and church

It is these that have resulted in growing convictions about the possibility of discriminating procedures in infant baptism. Some have been described already in Chapter 1 and so only the headings will be noted again: the Western world is increasingly seen to be a largely secularized mission-field needing evangelism rather than part of a Christendom needing pastoral care; the growing influence of biblical theology has led to a decisive shift from a pragmatic (or merely 'traditional') to a principled viewpoint of baptism; there is ever-mounting pressure for agreed baptismal policies within co-operative and ecumenically shared ministry; teaching about and experience of a 'baptism of the Holy Spirit' is widespread and must be integrated into the theology and practice of initiation; and, finally, the issue of 'rebaptism' throws the issues of merely nominal Christianity and indiscriminate baptism into sharper focus. The involvement of lay people in church leadership, evangelism and baptismal preparation and the ecumenical dimensions have prompted many clergy to a radical reappraisal of their pastoral practice.

## Changes in pastoral procedures

This can still take many and varied forms. However, there are an ever-decreasing number of parishes where the parents simply complete an application form, arrive on a Sunday afternoon for a very brief service with none of the usual congregation present and are never seen again. That always was scandalous and indefensible. The baptism should always, at the very least, be accompanied by pastoral engagement, teaching and systematic attempts at Christian nurture.

Moreover, it is not possible to obey the Church of England's Canon Law without undertaking responsible pastoral procedures which contain an important and necessary element of discrimination. This Canon Law has undergone thorough revision by the General Synod in recent years and thus expresses the present discipline and rules of the church. However, it is not widely known by the clergy, scarcely known at all by lay people and inconsistently applied by the bishops.

The relevant Canons are here set out in full.[4]

### B 21 Of Holy Baptism

*It is desirable that every minister having a cure of souls shall normally administer the sacrament of Holy Baptism on Sundays at public worship when the most number of people come together, that the congregation there present may witness the receiving of them that be newly baptised into Christ's Church, and be put in remembrance of their own profession made to God in their baptism.*

1. *Due notice, normally of at least a week, shall be given before a child is brought to the church to be baptised.*
2. *If the minister shall refuse or unduly delay to baptise any such infant, the parents or guardians may apply to the bishop of the diocese, who shall, after consultation with the minister, give such directions as he thinks fit.*
3. *The minister shall instruct the parents or guardians of an infant to be admitted to Holy Baptism that the same responsibilities rest on them as are in the service of Holy Baptism required of the godparents.*
4. *No minister shall refuse or, save for the purpose of preparing or instructing the parents or guardians or godparents, delay to baptise any infant within his cure that is brought to the church to be baptised, provided that the due notice has been given and the provisions relating to godparents in these Canons are observed.*

5. *A minister who intends to baptise any infant whose parents are residing outside the boundaries of his cure, unless the names of such persons or of one of them be on the church electoral roll of the same, shall not proceed to the baptism without having sought the good will of the minister of the parish in which such parents reside.*

6. *No minister being informed of the weakness or danger of death of any infant within his cure and therefore desired to go to baptise the same shall either refuse or delay to do so.*

7. *A minister so baptising a child in a hospital or nursing home, the parents of the child not being resident in his cure, nor their names on the church electoral roll of the same, shall send their names and address to the minister of the parish in which they reside.*

8. *If any infant which is privately baptised do afterwards live, it shall be brought to the church and there, by the minister, received into the congregation of Christ's flock according to the form and manner prescribed in and by the office for Private Baptism authorised by Canon B 1.*

9. *The minister of every parish shall warn the people that without grave cause and necessity they should not have their children baptised privately in their houses.*

## B 23 Of godparents and sponsors

1. *For every child to be baptised there shall be not fewer than three godparents, of whom at least two shall be of the same sex as the child and of whom at least one shall be of the opposite sex; save that, when three cannot conveniently be had, one godfather and godmother shall suffice. Parents may be godparents for their own children provided that the child have at least one other godparent.*

2. *The godparents shall be persons who will faithfully fulfil their responsibilities both by their care for the children committed to their charge and by the example of their own godly living.*

3. *When one who is of riper years is to be baptised he shall choose three, or at least two, to be his sponsors, who shall be ready to present him at the font and afterwards put him in mind of his Christian profession and duties.*

4. *No person shall be admitted to be a sponsor or godparent who has not been baptised and confirmed. Nevertheless the minister shall have power to dispense with the requirement of confirmation in any case in which in his judgement need so requires.*

## B 24 Of the baptism of such as are of riper years

1. *When any such person as is of riper years and able to answer for himself is to be baptised, the minister shall instruct such person, or cause him to be instructed, in the principles of the Christian religion, and exhort him so to prepare himself with prayers and fasting that he may receive this holy sacrament with repentance and faith.*

2. *At least a week before any such baptism is to take place, the minister shall give notice thereof to the bishop of the diocese or whomsoever he shall appoint for the purpose.*

3. *Every person thus baptised shall be confirmed by the bishop so soon after his baptism as conveniently may be; that so he may be admitted to the Holy Communion.*

## B 25 Of the sign of the Cross in baptism

*The Church of England has ever held and taught, and holds and teaches still, that the sign of the Cross used in baptism is no part of the substance of the sacrament: but, for the remembrance of the Cross, which is very precious to those that rightly believe in Jesus Christ, has retained the sign of it in baptism, following therein the primitive and apostolic churches.*

## B 26 Of teaching the young

1. *Every minister shall take care that the children and young people within his cure are instructed in the doctrine, sacraments, and discipline of Christ, as the Lord has commanded and as they are set forth in the holy Scriptures, in the Book of Common Prayer, and especially in the Church Catechism; and to this end he, or some godly and competent persons appointed by him, shall on Sundays or if need be at other convenient times diligently instruct and teach them in the same.*
2. *All parents and guardians shall take care that their children receive such instruction.*

All pastoral practice should be 'pastoral', i.e. shepherd-like, gentle and caring. Practice of discrimination in any area of church life should never be harsh or unloving, and it is tragic if that impression is ever given. There are situations, however, where an element of pastoral judgement by Christian leaders cannot be avoided. This cannot be forbidden by Jesus's warning 'Do not judge, or you too will be judged' (Matthew 7.1). This command is closely followed by two others which require the exercise of critical discernment and discrimination – 'Do not give dogs what is sacred; do not throw your pearls to pigs' (7.6) and 'Watch out for false prophets' (7.15). The attitude Jesus forbids is harsh censoriousness which is destructive and condemning.

The Canon Law lays down four practical disciplines:

Firstly, ministers are to respect one another's baptism practices. This is achieved by the important stipulation (Canon B 22.5) that a minister, if requested to baptize a child from another parish, will seek the goodwill of the minister of that parish. In this way the undermining of a carefully constructed parish baptism practice is avoided. Of course 'to seek goodwill' for a Christian minister means far more than a cursory letter of information. No Christian minister will baptize against the wish of the parish minister except after very careful thought and (it is suggested) consultation not only with the parish minister involved but also with the bishop.

It is vitally important that bishops support those clergy who are seeking to fulfil these principles and prevent other clergy from baptizing children indiscriminately from neighbouring parishes.

Secondly, baptism should normally be at a main Sunday service (B 21). This enables the new members to be welcomed properly into the Christian family and for the whole congregation to be reminded of the sacrament and its rich significance for them all. Practical problems should not be allowed to lead to a regular ignoring of this Canon which has such clear and obvious theological justification. Rather, any practical problems should lead to a critical reconsideration of the parochial practice of worship, initiation, evangelism and nurture of young people in the Christian faith.

Thirdly, godparents or sponsors should be baptized, confirmed (and thus communicant) Christians. This is strongly asserted in B 23.4 and the permitted power to dispense with the requirement should be used sparingly. The permission to use discretion would be of value when suitable godparents are members of another denomination which does not practise confirmation, e.g. Baptist, Pentecostal or Brethren. The crucial role of godparents is detailed in B 23.2 and includes 'the example of their own godly living'. Discipline is needed to restore the spiritual character of this custom.

Fourthly, parents and guardians need to receive adequate instruction. It is not good enough briefly to describe the mechanics of the service and give them a leaflet or letter about the meaning of baptism. B 22.3 says unequivocally that the 'same responsibilities' rest on parents as on godparents. This clearly implies baptism, confirmation and 'the example of godly living' (B 23.2, 4). B 26 requires parents to ensure continued Christian instruction.

Within *Common Worship*, the section called 'Presentation of the Candidates' makes this clear when it says:

> *Parents and godparents, the church receives these children with joy.*
> *Today we are trusting God for their growth in faith.*
> *Will you pray for them, draw them by your example into the community of faith and walk with them in the way of Christ?*
> (Answer) *With the help of God, we will.*
> *In baptism these children begin their journey in faith. You speak for them today. Will you care for them, and help them to take their place within the life and worship of Christ's Church?*
> (Answer) *With the help of God, we will.*[5]

There is no ambiguity either in the part of the service called 'The Decision'. The minister says:

> *In baptism, God calls us out of darkness into his marvellous light. To follow Christ means dying to sin and rising to new life with him.*
> *Therefore I ask:*
> *Do you reject the devil and all rebellion against God?*
> (Answer) *I reject them.*
> *Do you renounce the deceit and corruption of evil?*
> (Answer) *I renounce them.*
> *Do you repent of the sins that separate us from God and neighbour?*
> (Answer) *I repent of them.*
> *Do you turn to Christ as Saviour?*
> (Answer) *I turn to Christ.*

*Do you submit to Christ as Lord?*
(Answer) *I submit to Christ.*
*Do you come to Christ, the way, the truth and the life?*
(Answer) *I come to Christ.*[6]

An alternative form of the Decision is provided in *Common Worship* accompanied by the rubric that it may be used 'where there are strong pastoral reasons'. Whilst it is less sustained and emphatic and regrettable in its omission of Jesus as Saviour, Lord and 'the way, the truth and the life', it still requires from parents and godparents a clear expression of their Christian commitment.

*Therefore I ask*
*Do you turn to Christ?*
(Answer) *I turn to Christ*
*Do you repent of your sins?*
(Answer) *I repent of my sins*
*Do you renounce evil?*
(Answer) *I renounce evil*[7]

Another central part of the service is the Profession of Faith or Creed where the parents and godparents, alongside the whole congregation, affirm and proclaim their Christian faith.[8] Once again an alternative Profession of Faith is made available for 'where there are strong pastoral reasons'. In this case it is thinner in its content but scarcely less emphatic in the response of faith that it requires.[9]

It is therefore clear that both the law and the liturgy of the Church of England require the parents bringing a child to be baptized to be confessing, practising Christians themselves. Even the concessions that have been made within the alternative forms of liturgy fail to endorse an indiscriminate approach to baptism. In fact their failure to do this is very telling and recognition of the truth that for any liturgy for infant baptism to be credible, it must include both affirmation of the Christian faith by those bringing a child for baptism and affirmation of their desire to bring up the child within that same faith.

Furthermore, for these affirmations to be credible they must be accompanied by practical actions that display this commitment. It is frequently a cause of public controversy when a church leader requires the parents to attend church worship before the baptism of their baby. But to participate in Christian worship and congregational life is clearly a most important part of the Christian life. The *Canons of the Church of England* say that no ministers may refuse or delay baptism 'save for the purpose of preparing or instructing the parents or guardians or godparents'. All good instruction should be *experienced* where possible and not just cerebral. Baptism is 'into Christ' and into 'the body of Christ' the church. It is a nonsense to divorce it from the congregational life. If the parents are promising a 'godly example', there must be some credibility to their profession and promise. Worship and church membership are not *optional aspects* of Christian life, parenthood and nurture. The church does grave disservice to God and his gospel to leave any grounds for people thinking they are.

A Service of Thanksgiving for the Gift of a Child is also available in *Common Worship*.[10] This involves acknowledgement of God's gift and love, and prayer for his blessing, but neither is based on confessed Christian commitment nor implies the fullness of the covenant relationship of blessing and obligation. It can be used as an element of teaching-evangelism hopefully leading into family-conversion, covenant-commitment and household-baptism.

## Other issues and factors surrounding the request for baptism

These also need to be considered alongside those points already made about the integrity of baptism. Chief amongst them is a proper engagement with why non-churchgoers, in a post-Christendom culture, are still requesting baptism for their child. The numbers doing this have hugely declined in recent decades but are still quite sizeable. Very often advocates of discriminate infant baptism put this down to simple superstition and an unfortunate legacy of the historical factors that we looked at earlier. The influence of these factors is undeniable. However, there is also very frequently more to it than this.

The truth is that the birth of a child often brings parents much closer to engaging with the Christian faith. Several factors are at work here. In the first place, for many new parents, finding *local community* suddenly becomes much more important. With families living further apart than once would have been the case, many new parents are far more open to joining a church where they will receive support and friendship as they approach the daunting task of raising their child. Another factor at play is the concern of many new parents to locate *values* with which to bring up their child. Where churches have good and accessible provision for children this provides a source for these values that many will take seriously and engage with, at least for their child. It also manifests itself in the attractiveness of church schools, which still make up a third of the primary schools within Britain. Where church affiliation is amongst the admissions criteria of these schools, it is common for there to be deep cynicism about the genuine faith of any new parent starting to attend church. Care, however, needs to be taken with such judgement (a very proper application of Matthew 7.1-2). Acknowledgement should be given to both the mixed motives within all of us and the genuine attraction that a Christian environment for their child has for many parents. But a third factor making new parents more open to engaging with Christianity is the most crucial one. This is the *'God-moment'* that confronts many parents particularly when their first child enters the world. Casual atheism or agnosticism is quite difficult to maintain when people witness new creation arriving right in front of them. It is, almost by definition, a deeply spiritual experience and whilst the initial response to this God-moment may be vague and confused, it is vital that the church acknowledges rather than dismisses the reality underlying this. This factor has been magnified in recent years by the fact that it is now almost universal for the father to be present at the birth. Men hardened by the world of work and ambition are frequently softened quite considerably by the arrival of their child and, whilst sometimes loath to admit it, often need and want something that will speak into the profound experience they have had.

This softening may not last long but sometimes provides an openness to Christianity that is dangerous and wrong for the church to scorn.[11]

The acknowledgement of these factors in no way undermines the case for discriminate household baptism that has been advanced in this chapter. What it does, however, is provide a really exciting missional context for its implementation which contains some parallels to the institution of baptism at Pentecost in Acts 2. On that occasion people witnessing the coming of God's Spirit were met with proclamation of the gospel by Peter and the summons to respond with repentance and baptism. Those experiencing God's Spirit through the birth of their children need to be met with a similar proclamation of the gospel of Jesus Christ and the way in which this provides the fulfilment of the joys and answer to the aspirations and anxieties in their lives. And if they then show the desire to repent and begin the journey of Christian discipleship, then household baptism becomes precisely part of a response of faith to the gospel of Jesus Christ that the church should encourage. A related factor that we need to bear in mind is how Christian baptism very much emerged in the context of newcomers entering God's people. The fulfilment of the covenant in the coming of Jesus Christ and the new age of the Spirit meant that the Gentiles – formally outside of God's people for centuries and generally not expecting entry to it – were suddenly being welcomed into his family. Many of those already in God's people had a problem with this and wanted the old boundary markers maintained. But central to Christianity was the joyful proclamation that belonging to the covenant God of Israel was now open to everyone and the controversial acknowledgement that traditional outsiders were in some cases closer to the kingdom of God than long-term insiders. Jesus's two most famous parables essentially make this point (Luke 10; 15) as does Paul's painful acknowledgement of the plight of his fellow Jews in Romans 9. A great deal of churchgoing is habitual with not as much active faith connected with it as is sometimes imagined. Even worse, this is sometimes accompanied by a very regrettable desire to maintain the status quo in regard to those inside and those outside of the church. At the heart of every church must be the expectation that God is in the business of bringing those who were previously outsiders into his covenant family and the active desire to do everything to facilitate rather than hinder their response to the gospel. This is in no way an undermining of the paramount necessity of those previously outside of God's people making the response of faith to Jesus Christ. It is simply an acknowledgement that churches are frequently part of the problem rather than the solution to encouraging this response of faith and that any policy of discriminate infant baptism needs to be built into an overall approach that is totally missional and a conscious rejection of the tribalism that the gospel of Jesus Christ came to dismantle.

## The importance of child-friendly and newcomer-friendly church

This is another critical factor that needs to form part of any policy in regard to baptism. When the term 'baptismal integrity' is used, its sole reference is usually to the parents and godparents and whether they can say the promises made at their child's baptism with integrity. If it is used of the church, it is usually in terms of whether it has integrity over its practice of baptism in terms of its expectations of the parents and godparents. Much of this chapter has been concerned with the importance of this. However, there is another crucial part of the baptism service in *Common Worship* that requires equal integrity. This is 'the welcome' where the minister declares:

> *There is one Lord, one faith, one baptism: (the child's name), by one Spirit we are all baptised into one body.*

and the congregation respond by saying:

> *We welcome you into the fellowship of faith; we are children of the same heavenly Father; we welcome you.*[12]

The question that needs to be addressed is whether the church can say these words with integrity if it then makes little or no provision for the Christian nurture and support of the child. Parents seeking baptism for their child might do this for many reasons of varying legitimacy. But if they do hear the gospel and resolve to respond with faith expressed in household baptism, are churches properly geared up to really welcome them into the fellowship of faith?

The answer in many cases is no. In too many churches there is either no provision at all for the Christian nurture of young children or what is provided is inadequate. In churches where a colouring table and books are placed at the back of the church, for instance, or a room is provided for parents to take children, this is usually done so that a service unsuitable to that child's needs can continue undisturbed. When children who have been baptized are brought to church by their parents, they are the ones showing integrity and these children must be met with appropriate Christian teaching and nurture. The excuse is often given that churches lack the resources to provide for children. The truth, however, is more often that the resources that do exist in terms of money, energy, buildings, creativity and time are simply being deployed elsewhere. Children shouldn't be given *more* of these resources than established adults but, if their welcome into the fellowship of faith is to be genuine, they should receive an *equal measure* of them. The responsibility for the provision of appropriate nurture for baptized children lies with the leader of church. Many clergy abdicate this responsibility all too willingly with the excuse that 'it is not my gift'. But it is their duty to ensure that such provision is made and they need to encourage and champion it with all their might.

The tragedy is that many young children want to come to church and their parents are more than happy to facilitate this. Children are naturally spiritual with few of the problems or embarrassment about faith that often afflict adults. They understand prayer and are usually very keen to learn about Jesus and the Bible. They also know when an effort is being made for them and will often respond to this with an enthusiasm and joy that can light up a church and help to reinvigorate its congregation. It is obviously more complex when these children grow older although the same principles about the allocation of resources and commitment to their nurture remain. But there is very little excuse for churches failing to supply any meaningful Christian teaching and nurture for young children, and a mixture of accessible 'all-age' church services and Sunday school groups is usually the best response. Ironically, it is often churches operating the most open baptism policies that are the least assiduous in offering appropriate teaching and nurture for those children they baptize. The welcome and generosity of spirit that open baptism claims to represent is then seen as more apparent than real and perhaps part of avoiding any real commitment to those baptized. It is also disappointing when some of the fiercest advocates of discrimination in infant baptism place little emphasis upon the church's responsibility, alongside the parents, for the Christian nurture of children. A responsible attitude towards household baptism and any responsible baptism policy will always include a resolute commitment to providing appropriate Christian teaching and nurture for those children who have been baptized and welcomed into the fellowship of faith.[13]

The provision of relevant and accessible church for adult newcomers is equally important. If our hope is that parents of those seeking baptism will hear the gospel message and respond with faith, churches have to be realistically set up for their support and nurture as well. This will involve a frank review of those aspects of church that are unnecessarily inaccessible and a positive effort made to translate the unchanging gospel into language and forms that make sense to newcomers. Too often it is newcomers that are expected to make all the cultural concessions to the church's existing members if they are to enter the fellowship of faith. Once again, it is important to remember that Christian baptism was established at precisely the moment when belonging to the People of God became open to everyone, with the abolition of all those boundary markers that had become redundant in the light of the coming of Jesus Christ. At the heart of Paul's doctrine of justification was the refusal to allow anything to define the people of God other than 'faith expressing itself through love' (Galatians 5.6). For any baptismal policy to be effective, it must be based upon the establishment of a church community that is ready, willing and able to incorporate those for whom household baptism represents their response of faith, however faltering, to the grace of God in Jesus Christ.[14]

No church is perfect and what has been written above is not intended to establish an impossible ideal. Every church will fail regularly in its effort to be accessible to children and newcomers. But the key word – and the one germane to this aspect of baptismal integrity – is *effort*. Too often debates about infant baptism take place at a safe distance from any discussion of the nature of the church we are expecting parents and children to come to. Household baptism, and any policy concerning it, should instead go hand in hand with the provision of child-friendly and accessible church that is suitable for everyone.

## The implementation of a policy of discriminate baptism

When churches are established that are child-friendly and accessible, it is quite common to find that parents and children come along to them before they request baptism for their child. Where an enquiry about baptism is the first point of contact, it should be met with warmth and congratulations (if the baby has arrived recently) and the request that the family start coming along to church as part of exploring what baptism is all about. If this is questioned, it is good to be clear from the start that baptism only makes sense in the context of Christian commitment and their enquiry provides the perfect opportunity for exploring whether this is a step they want to take. If the parents decline (and there is not a good reason such as health issues or other complications), then it is vital that they are politely told that baptism cannot take place. This is perfectly in line with Canon B 21.4 because the refusal to engage with the preparation and instruction cited there necessitates delay until this occurs. At this point the parents will often approach another church with a more compliant minister and this is the reason for Canon B 21.5. Churches have to decide their own baptism policies, but it is wrong when one church undermines another church's effort to show integrity over baptism and it is vital that bishops support the clergy to whom they have given responsibility for the care of souls in that parish.

Happily, it is becoming more common for families seeking baptism for their child to agree to come along to church, even if this is seen as simply a hoop they need to jump through. This is where the preparation and instruction about baptism begin. A home visit is often the best place for explaining the commitment that baptism involves usually by looking at the service together and the promises made within it. This should be placed within the context of the overall vision of the church, what it is seeking to do and specifically its desire to partner the parents in seeing their child flourish and grow into the person that God made them to be. This will make more sense if the family have already come along for several weeks because they will have witnessed some of the things that are discussed and hopefully the love, support and care that the church wants to extend to them and their child. At this meeting it should be explained that if baptism will involve the parents making promises they will not want or be able to fulfil, the church will be delighted to offer a service of Thanksgiving for the gift of a Child, either at home or in church. Baptism, however, implies and involves a definite Christian faith and commitment to Christ and the church.

Such conversations can be extremely difficult. But that is true of any conversation raising uncomfortable truths. The alternative of a Thanksgiving is rarely popular with parents concerned that it is 'not the real thing' but this response then provides the opportunity to ask the parents why baptism is being sought. If clergy can hold their nerve at this point, it both can and should lead to a fruitful discussion about the meaning and significance of baptism. Such a meeting is probably the key moment in any process of trying to ensure that baptism possesses integrity. If the parents decide that they do wish for their child to be baptized, it is good for the preparation to continue with regular church attendance accompanied by their attendance on a course. Many churches now run courses such as Emmaus, Alpha and Christianity Explained which provide those coming with a taste of Christian community alongside the opportunity to ask about and discuss the claims that it is based upon. An alternative is a three- to four-week course focused more directly upon baptism and its meaning. It is of the greatest value if lay people play a major role in this preparation. If attendance on such a course is expected of everyone, including regular church attenders having their first child baptized, this will help with its acceptance. The style and content will vary according to the culture and area, but it should involve a major investment of thought and effort. This is front-line evangelism and pastoral care. Its aim is to bring parents to faith, or to clearer faith in Christ, and understanding of Christian life.

One of the frequent complications is *godparents*. It is quite common for parents to have already asked their friends to become godparents for their child before they even approach the church for baptism. The instructions and responsibilities regarding godparents in Canon B 23 should nonetheless be brought to their attention, and it is made clear that the godparents that they choose must be people who can say the promises in baptism with integrity. In most cases, it is not possible to ask godparents to attend a course but effort should nonetheless be made to meet the spirit of the law in this regard. It is rare but not impossible, if the welcome to the church has been powerful enough, for the parents to even choose existing members of the church for this vital role.

Another complication can occur when one parent wants to affirm their Christian faith in the baptism service and the other doesn't. In this case it is good to affirm the honesty and integrity of the parent who cannot say the promises and still include them within the baptism. They should still be invited, if they wish, to stand alongside their partner and child during the baptism and it made clear to the congregation in an honest and confident manner why they will not be saying the promises. An appropriate way of reinforcing their inclusion is to include a promise that the parents say together after the baptism publicly affirming their love and commitment for their child. It has been known for the respect that this displays to make a considerable impact upon the non-Christian parent and perhaps sow the seeds of future faith. If all of this process takes places within the context of a church where the welcome and kindness to the family couldn't be stronger, it will provide the best possible preparation for baptism. If the course is completed, attendance at church has continued and the parents are still clear that they want baptism for their child, then the date should be agreed and the baptism proceeded with. There will be some families that continue as regular attenders at church hopefully growing as the years go past in Christian faith and loving service. Many of them are willing to testify: 'We are so glad the vicar made us stop and think about the meaning of baptism. It has changed our lives!' Sadly and despite the very best efforts of the church, there will be others who then become less regular or even fairly soon disappear. This won't mean that the preparation and the baptism itself has been in vain and the church will know that it has done all it can to both communicate the love of God and be true to the meaning and importance of baptism.

The battle lines between those who advocate general and open baptism and those who advance the case for discriminate household baptism have often been more fraught than those between both groups and Baptists. However, if the church is serious about its call to mission, then all the best instincts of the open position in terms of love and generosity and welcome can be included within a policy of careful and responsible discrimination in regard to the sacrament and covenant sign of baptism.

# 'Rebaptism' – is it ever justified?

The New Testament writers affirm that there is one baptism (Ephesians 4.5) into the one Lord Jesus Christ. There is therefore one biblical theology of baptism, although the various Christian churches may not equally or fully embrace and teach that theology. A second baptism is, in the strict sense of the term, nonsense – it is a self-contradiction. Either the first so-called 'baptism' was really not a baptism and so the second one was a baptism, or the first one was baptism and the second one was not. But there cannot be two baptismal initiations into the Christian life. How has any suggestion or debate about 'rebaptism' come about?

## The request for 'rebaptism'

The issue is increasingly common in recent years although it has been known for centuries. It is more complex than is often realized, and so the issues will be illustrated by some typical cases.[1]

## The adult convert

George is twenty-five and Christianity held no meaning in his life. Now suddenly he has come to know Jesus Christ in a vivid, personal, life-transforming way. He is eager to join the church. As he reads the Acts of the Apostles he sees baptism as the way to express his new relationship with God and his people. However, when he discusses it with his vicar it transpires that he was baptized as a baby, and so the vicar kindly but firmly indicates that another baptism is quite out of the question. George is perplexed because his parents never attended church and did not bring him up in faith in Jesus Christ or in the church. What could that splashing with water on the little baby mean? And what has it got to do with the excitement and reality of his new-found life in Christ?

A similar problem confronted Sarah who is in her thirties. She went to a Youth Group in a church where they practised 'believer's baptism'. At the age of twelve she went to a Christian summer camp and the leaders pressed the young people to follow Jesus. Several of her friends asked to be baptized and Sarah did not want to be out of step with the gang of friends. She said the right things, was baptized, but a year or two later she stopped going to church. Now twenty years later she knows that she has met with Jesus in a real way and wishes to commit her life to him and the church. As she looks back on her childhood she is grateful for Christian youth leaders but doubtful of the wisdom of their pressurizing children into 'a decision' and almost completely sure that her profession of faith and baptism was due to external pressures. How should she, now, proclaim her mature discipleship and desire to join the church?

## Moving to a 'Baptist' church

Mary's parents are deeply committed Christians. Mary was baptized as a baby and grew up from her earliest days to know God and love Jesus Christ. She gladly went to church with the family, and although there were ups and downs in her faith and discipleship, she never regretted being confirmed at the age of fourteen. Mary has married a Christian man who has moved around many parts of the country and attended many churches of different denominations. On moving to a new area they find themselves close to a lively Baptist church where their children have good friends. They want to be full members, but the church requires that Mary be baptized. What is she to do? Does she effectively renounce her infant baptism that has meant so much to her as God's covenant sign and an indication of her parents' godly upbringing? Or does she threaten the family unity and full involvement in their local church?

## 'Charismatic' renewal

Andrew grew up in a Christian home, was baptized and confirmed and has always been glad to be a member of the church. It was important to him, but if truth be told, it was not exciting. In his mid-twenties he went to a charismatic conference and had a deep experience of spiritual renewal. His awareness of the personal intimacy of God as Father brought him to a radically new joy in worship, prayer and reading the Bible. He felt as though he could tell everyone about Jesus, and remarkable signs of God's power resulted from his prayers, witness and gifts. 'If this is "baptism in the Spirit"', he reasoned, 'should it not be testified to or expressed in "baptism in water"?' The vicar is delighted that Andrew has 'come alive' in his faith but cannot even consider a second baptism. But Andrew just wants to demonstrate somehow the overwhelming change that has made such an impact on his life.

In real life, George may find a Baptist Church or Brethren Assembly where he can be baptized and, perhaps, return to his Church of England parish with mixed feelings of perplexity, sadness and embarrassment. Sarah would almost certainly not be offered a 'rebaptism' in a Baptist Church. She might be tempted into a 'house-church' where the theology of baptism is less significant than its experience, but either way is not a happy solution for her. Mary might decide to go through 'believer baptism' in order to join the church with her husband, but is sad to hurt her parents and does not see the ceremony as baptism into Christ, but just a rite of entry to that particular church, Andrew will either get stuck in to his local church in a more committed way or go off to a 'house-church' of similar-minded folk. But will his decision be based on scriptural and theological considerations or on his own subjective feelings and emotional needs?

The charismatic movement has, in some situations, reinforced the sacramental dimension of the outward expression of the reality of God's grace. In other contexts it leads to a downgrading of the significance of sacramental signs compared with the experienced reality of 'baptism in Spirit' (see Chapter 13). The individuals in the stories and the Christian leaders they consult should think not only in terms of 'what is right for them' but also 'what is right'. The emphasis in much pastoral work is 'non-directive' or person-centred rather than truth-centred. This can reinforce a personalized and subjective view of Christian faith, church and sacraments which loses touch with the givenness of God's word in Scripture and the necessity for order and discipline in church life.

## The case against 'rebaptism'

The question 'What is right?' implies theological judgement rather than a reliance on merely subjective feeling. Within postmodern culture, it is increasingly difficult to stop the feelings of the individual being seen as the supreme factor that should govern any decision that affects them. If a proper and responsible approach is to be taken to 'rebaptism', this needs to be recognized and resisted. The depth of emotional need (or even anguish) involved is not the only, or even the most, significant factor. It is significant but other issues are also crucial. There are formidable arguments against 'rebaptism'.

The first of these is *theological* – the very nature and meaning of baptism is at stake. There is one baptism because of the oneness of the people of God into whom it brings entry. There are not separate baptisms for different churches nor to represent different experiences. Baptism must be seen (like Holy Communion) as primarily a sign God gives us rather than a symbol we undergo for him. It is God's covenant sign which must be met by faith. The relationship in time between the baptism and the faith may not always be tidy or certain, but the sign is not made invalid by untidiness or uncertainties about quality of faith. The validity and efficacy of baptism must be distinguished. Validity must depend on objective factors, even though efficacy is a matter known only to God (see Chapter 6). The major argument against 'rebaptism' is the proper understanding of the meaning of baptism in itself (covered in the earlier chapters of this book). If baptism (of infant or adult) does not appear to have been a credible initiation into Christ and his church, then there is a theological anomaly and pastoral problem. However, any repetition of baptism might meet the emotional needs of some individuals, but at the expense of further theological confusion for all and pastoral problems in the future.

Important *pastoral issues* are at stake as well. If the reality or validity of a baptism rests upon any kind of subjective consideration, this means that some people might never be certain about their baptism and repeatedly seek to renew it. New Testament theology encourages Christians to be confident about God's covenant love and the security of their salvation in Christ but every church leader knows Christians who are either occasionally or even regularly subjected to bouts of insecurity and lack of assurance. It would surely be a pastoral (as well as theological and ecclesiological) tragedy if such insecurities and/or the move to different churches was marked by another 'baptism'.

The World Council of Churches report *Baptism, Eucharist and Ministry* declared unambiguously: 'Baptism is an unrepeatable act. Any practice which might be interpreted as "re-baptism" must be avoided.'[2] Responses to the issue of rebaptism by the mainstream churches in Britain show a mixture of similarity and diversity.

The Church of England and Roman Catholic Church baptize believing adults and infant children of parents who confess their faith. This is followed by confirmation when the candidate is old enough to assume personal responsibility. Christian baptism conducted within other churches is recognized and cannot be repeated, although there is a form of 'conditional' baptism where there is genuine uncertainty about whether a person has been baptized or not. *Common Worship* also makes provision for the 'Corporate Renewal of Baptismal Vows'.

The Methodist Church has broadly similar practice. The Methodist Conference has ruled against rebaptism but has stressed the need for more opportunity for public testimony as a means of giving expression to deeper spiritual experience. Some use a rededication service involving immersion in water and making clear it is not baptism, but this is not authorized.

The Baptist Union churches do not agree on the necessity for 'believer's baptism' (or any baptism) as a condition for church membership. Many, probably most, Baptist pastors would baptize George (in the stories that began this chapter) on the grounds that the circumstances of his 'baptism' rendered it meaningless. Many would similarly 'baptize' Mary if she requested it with strong personal conviction but there are some who would say that she need not, and probably should not, undergo this. They would recognize the validity of an infant baptism involving believing parents followed by profession of conscious faith in confirmation. However, it would be very rare (perhaps impossible) to find a pastor to 'rebaptize' Sarah, in spite of their emphasis on baptism following and expressing faith.

The official Baptist Union response to *Baptism, Eucharist and Ministry* objected strongly to indiscriminate baptism rather than to infant baptism itself. It declared that the section on 'rebaptism' (quoted above) was 'wholly unacceptable in its present form'. It added, 'In cases of infant baptism which are neither accompanied nor followed by any of the significant features of the initiatory process to which the Report amply draws attention and where the individual involved is convinced out of an instructed conscience that Christian obedience requires believer baptism, we cannot agree that an a priori universal bar should operate.'[3]

There is a strong element of individual decision and local variation in Baptist churches. When one moves beyond the Baptist Union to independent chapels, Brethren Assemblies and 'house-churches' it becomes almost impossible to generalize on their baptismal practices in these situations.

The United Reformed Church accommodates both infant and believer baptism while formally declaring rebaptism unacceptable. Most of the united churches in the URC follow their traditional pattern of initiation but the Churches of Christ (following Baptist practice) merged with the URC in 1981. Part of the agreement was that both modes of baptism were to continue, that no URC minister was required to perform a mode of baptism to which they had conscientious objection and that 'nothing should be done in conformity with one practice that casts doubt on the integrity of the other'.

This dual system is in operation in several areas of ecumenical experiment – i.e. where churches of different parent denominations are engaged in ministry and mission together. In this context a request for 'rebaptism' can threaten a delicate situation. In the United Church of North India, for instance, the local bishop decides the policy at this most sensitive point.

## The pastoral response to rebaptism

Considerable gentleness, pastoral and teaching skills are needed to cope with requests for 'rebaptism' particularly when the applications are in the context of strong emotional experience and/or peer pressure. There are many parallels with the pastoral problems of discrimination in applications for 'first' baptism. Three dimensions of pastoral care and provision are needed:

## Reduction of the scale of the problem

It is important, where possible, to take certain steps before the issue arises. In fact the problem can be largely pre-empted in this way. An important part of this is regular and careful teaching about the significance of baptism including the nature of God's covenant love, plan and signs, and the place of the sacraments in God's provision for church life. It is only good teaching that will keep out bad teaching. Too often there has been a vacuum on this subject which has inevitably been filled by subjective and erroneous ideas. Preaching and teaching about baptism will be given more attention in Chapter 14.

Careful discrimination over initial candidature for baptism of both adult and infant is another factor that will significantly reduce both the size and the bitterness of the problem. The case for this was covered in the previous chapter. It is the fueling of hurt and loss through the abuse of baptism in the case study of George that is so difficult to deal with. Indiscriminate baptism devalues the sacrament and provides substantial theological, pastoral and emotional grounds for George's dilemma. Speaking of this issue, *Baptism, Eucharist and Ministry* declared: 'This contributes to the reluctance of churches which practise believer's baptism to acknowledge the validity of infant baptism; this fact should lead to more critical reflection on the meaning of baptism, within those majority churches themselves' (i.e. in Europe and North America).[4] It is quite clear from the Baptist Union response and the writings of other Baptist theologians that for many of them the real scandal and stumbling block is at this point of indiscriminate use of baptism rather than the baptism of children of believing parents. The Church of England response to the issue of rebaptism failed to show a clear enough appreciation of this crucial dimension of the problem and greater engagement with it is still needed.[5]

Good relationships and consultation between church leaders in a locality will increasingly mean that baptism is seen as not a matter for individual whim or even the concern of a single church but a joy for the whole Church of God in Christ Jesus. So 'rebaptism' is a concern not just for the individual and a local church but for the whole church. It is hoped that leaders would consult and pray together even where they finally cannot agree. It is at this point that questions of initiation are especially difficult with Christian groups that have no clear leadership, or are recently schismatic or who regard other denominations as heretical or beyond fellowship. In parts of the country 'house-church' or 'Restorationist' leaders are realizing the value of better relationships, co-operation and consultation but time is needed for the healing of some wounds of division.

## Offering a significant alternative to rebaptism

The person most in need of pastoral provision of a public and liturgical character is George, the adult convert whose infant baptism was apparently in the context of parental unbelief and led to no nurture in Christ. He needs assurance that he can still look back to that baptism as God's sign of his covenant love, but he also needs a suitably joyful and impressive ceremony in which he can both testify to his new-found faith and 'be confirmed' by the prayer, the welcome and the joy of the Christian community. The provision may be the service of Confirmation itself. It may be in the context of a regular congregational use of the Renewal of Baptismal Vows. The Methodist annual Covenant Renewal service (often used at the first Sunday of the New Year) is increasingly used in other churches. Services of Marriage renewal are becoming popular, and many dioceses offer an annual opportunity for clergy to renew their ordination vows. Some element of testimony or spoken response is important, and some element of dramatic action which meets the emotional need for expression of renewal.

It is desire for the latter which is often the driving force in requests for rebaptism. Those who have experienced a deeper spiritual renewal will often badly want the sacramental experience of (re)baptism to accompany this. It is ironic that it is those churches that are least sacramental in their understanding of baptism that are often happiest to provide this because it reinforces their stance on believer's baptism. This factor has led to some churches adopting the practice of renewing baptismal vows in or with water.[6] This meets the pressure for a rite symbolizing washing or an immersion symbolizing death and resurrection with Christ. First there is an introductory address emphasizing the significance of the earlier baptism as God's gift and action, and the subsequent acceptance by the candidate of God's grace through the Spirit in repentance and faith. Then after affirmation of faith the minister immerses the candidate saying appropriate words such as:

*'As you were baptised in the name of the Father and of the Son and of the Holy Spirit, so now I confirm to you the cleansing, forgiveness, new life and promised gift of God's Spirit which are in his covenant'* or

*'As into Jesus Christ you were baptised, so I pray God who began a good work in you, to bring it to completion at the day of Christ Jesus.'*

The theological and pastoral problem associated with this has been termed 'sacramental and liturgical brinkmanship'.[7] Brinkmanship is the practice of seeking to pursue a dangerous policy to the limits of safety before stopping. The danger is that what people hear and see in a church event is as significant as what the minister has to say about it. Although the minister will *say* a renewing of baptismal vows with water is not baptism, the congregation (and the candidate) will all too easily hear and see it as such, and the validity of all baptisms will be undermined. On the other hand indiscriminate baptism using the New Testament language of efficacy where there is no credible profession of faith is also 'liturgical and sacramental brinkmanship'. It would be better to do without either but until we get rid of the latter, the pressure for renewing of baptismal vows with water is completely understandable.

## Acceptance of a measure of untidiness

Untidiness is unavoidable in an imperfect world and in imperfect church life. It should never be an aim, particularly within our theology of baptism. In another aspect of baptism, for instance, those who favour two-stage initiation (covered in the next chapter) have sometimes sought to cover their lack of theological argument by saying that the denial that Confirmation is a sacrament that completes baptism is 'perhaps a result of an overly tidy frame of mind'.[8] Such an approach is simply an attempt to disguise the lack of a proper theological argument, usually to preserve tradition and the status quo. However, when it comes to the way in which people's Christian lives work out, it is important for all of us to accept that there are things that will happen that are less than ideal. Students away from home for the first time are particularly vulnerable into being pressurized or themselves feeling the need for rebaptism. This is often done as a *fait accompli* before anyone can question it and too strong a subsequent reaction by, for instance, their vicar at their home church can sometimes win the argument but lose the friend. Anglicans, in particular, have to accept that their long-term practice of indiscriminate infant baptism is the chief factor in causing the phenomena of rebaptism and accept a measure of collective responsibility for the untidiness this has created.

Others take a tougher line. Colin Buchanan has argued that not only should Christians be dissuaded from 'rebaptism' but also, if they have received it, they should be urged to repent and renounce it. This would include signing a certificate renouncing any belief that this 'rebaptism' was their Christian baptism and reverting to their original baptism as their true Christian baptism.[9]

This is quite logical in terms of theology and is probably important for ordination candidates. They must work through this sacramental issue before they have responsibility for theological and pastoral leadership to others. However, there are considerable pastoral problems in pursuing the policy of renunciation further. What sanctions would be appropriate, if any? At what point, and for how long, should pressure be applied? The hurt and misunderstanding that so easily arise means that it is often preferable to go with a level of liturgical and pastoral untidiness even if it is with a heavy heart. The earlier proposals to reduce the scale of the problem are the most significant contributions to the issue of 'rebaptism'.

# Baptism and its completion?

We have seen that all of the blessings of the gospel, without exception, are contained in and conveyed by baptism – union with Christ, divine son/daughtership, the gift of the Holy Spirit and eternal life. We have also seen that the response of faith is crucial to receiving these promises: 'baptism effects what it symbolises in the context of faith'.

This response of faith needs to be lifelong and continuous. In fact the whole of the Christian life can be summarized as the calling to live out our baptism. Churches are encouraged to work out what it means to be communities defined and shaped by baptism, and this is also true of the lives of its members. The hallmarks of this baptized life are holiness, unity and the willingness to suffer for the gospel. By living in this manner, baptized communities shine God's light into a dark world (Philippians 2.14-16) with their lives eventually causing the unbelievers living around them to ask them to give a reason for the hope that they have (1 Peter 3.8-17).

It is baptism that provides the ongoing motivation, guidance and energy for this task. Continuing to respond to the grace of baptism with active faith ensures that, through our ongoing union with Christ, the Holy Spirit continues to flow through our lives constantly energizing and equipping us for fresh challenges and opportunities. Baptism is a past event but with constantly unfolding significance for our lives.

The New Testament is clear that other means are provided to strengthen and sustain the relationship with God begun in baptism. The Scriptures are given to 'make you wise for salvation through faith in Christ Jesus' and inspired or 'God-breathed' to make them 'useful for teaching, rebuking, correcting and training in righteousness, so that the man of God may be thoroughly equipped for every good work' (2 Timothy 3.15-16). Constant prayer to God as Father is another vital means of our union with Christ being strengthened and sustained (Colossians 4.2-4; 1 Thessalonians 5.17). Rather than being individually expressed, the assumption is that both the reading of Scripture and prayer have their greatest effect within the body of Christ (1 Timothy 4.13; Romans 15.30). Joyful worship of various kinds and mutual accountability within a loving and peaceful Christian community are other means provided by God to strengthen and sustain the covenant relationship with him begun in baptism (Colossians 3.15-17).

But another means of sustaining and strengthening Christians is, of course, the other sacrament authorized by Jesus – Holy Communion – also known as the Eucharist, the Lord's Supper, the Mass or the Breaking of Bread. Whereas baptism is, by definition, a once and for all event, Holy Communion is a repeated action or ritual, to be shared regularly by followers of Jesus. However, in many of its essential characteristics, Holy Communion is remarkably similar to baptism.

Like baptism, Holy Communion is firmly grounded in the covenant story of Israel and its greatest moment of the exodus – specifically, in the case of Communion, the Passover meal instituted to celebrate the freedom from slavery that the exodus brought about.

Like baptism, Holy Communion remembers and proclaims that, through the death and resurrection of Jesus Christ, God had brought the covenant story to its climax by bringing about the supreme exodus of freedom from the slavery to sin. Like baptism, Holy Communion declares that God's presence is found within the single, united community formed around the union it expresses with the body of Jesus Christ.

As with baptism, there are some who insist that Holy Communion conveys what it represents *ex opere operato*. Others are equally insistent that Communion is a symbol of God's blessings but does not convey them. However, like baptism, the New Testament combines strongly efficacious language about Holy Communion (John 6.53-58; 1 Corinthians 10.3-4; 15–16; 11.23-26) with an equal emphasis upon the necessity of faithful obedience for the blessings that it signifies to be received (1 Corinthians 10.5-14; 11.17-22; 27–34). In the light of this, the best way of doing justice to this biblical material is to affirm that Holy Communion, like baptism, effects what it symbolizes in the context of faith.

However, whereas baptism brings about this union with Christ, sharing the bread and wine of Holy Communion represents the means which God has provided for the covenant people of God to continue to be nourished, sustained and strengthened in this union with Christ. This is true of the other means that God has provided to help Christians grow in their faith. As we have seen from the many references and allusions to it in the epistles, baptism and what it has established remain the firm basis of the entire Christian life with everything that nourishes that relationship with God through Jesus Christ built upon it.

However, there are some who argue that baptism doesn't complete Christian initiation. For full initiation to take place, baptism needs to be supplemented by a further act of God's grace. This view has come from two major traditions. Some from a more *Catholic* perspective sometimes argue that Christian initiation is a two-stage process, with baptism needing to be supplemented by the apostolic laying on of hands or Confirmation. Others, coming from a more *Pentecostal or charismatic* perspective, have spoken of the importance of Christians receiving 'baptism in the Holy Spirit', understood as a necessary and distinct stage from receiving baptism with water. Despite the different contexts in which they have arisen, the arguments used for both positions share a strong degree of similarity. Both undermine the position that water-baptism completes Christian initiation and so it is important that their arguments are understood and addressed.

## Confirmation

It is within Western churches that practise infant baptism that this is normally accompanied by the distinct rite known as Confirmation. The most obvious use of Confirmation is to provide the opportunity for those who have been baptized as infants to make a personal and public affirmation of their Christian faith and acknowledge their desire to live out their response to their baptism. Whilst the parents and godparents declared their faith at the baptism and promised to bring up the child in the Christian family, Confirmation provides the opportunity for the one so baptized, to affirm their faith and commitment for themselves, usually as a teenager or adult. Confirmation within the Church of England is exclusively conducted by bishops and, until relatively recently, the right to receive Holy Communion was restricted to those who had been confirmed. Increasingly, the link between Confirmation and Communion has become less emphatic within the Church of England, with a growing number of churches gaining permission to offer children Holy Communion, usually from the age of around seven and prior to Confirmation. Within the Roman Catholic Church, Confirmation is understood to be a sacrament alongside Baptism, Penance, Communion, Marriage, Ordination and Extreme Unction/Anointing of the Sick. However, Confirmation is less tied to Communion with a much longer tradition of children being admitted to their first communion prior to Confirmation, again usually around the age of seven.

Confirmation can be a very solemn and joyful occasion as someone brought up in the family of the church declares their determination to live out the Christian life. It is equally moving when someone whose infant baptism was not accompanied by the same Christian nurture nonetheless takes the step of confirming their response to that baptism. Throughout this book, we have emphasized the biblical imperative of God's promise in baptism requiring the response of faith and obedience if those promises are to be received. Confirmation, rightly practised, provides a very helpful means of providing this response with a means of public and liturgical expression. It models the decisive decision to live out the Christian faith that baptism insists upon within the context of the grace of God in baptism that enables this to happen.

However, the question is whether Confirmation is more than this? So far we have stressed its role in giving those baptized as infants the chance to personally affirm their faith and response to their baptism. However, those coming from a more Catholic perspective have often sought to give Confirmation a greater sacramental significance. According to this understanding, Confirmation represents God specially strengthening those who have previously been baptized and, as part of this, freshly imparting the Holy Spirit to them. The sacramental action understood as bringing this about is the laying on of hands, sometimes accompanied by an anointing with oil. Crucial to this sacramental view of Confirmation is the role of bishops with their laying on of hands in the rite seen as acting in succession to the similar practice of the apostles in the early church (e.g. Acts 8.17).

It is this understanding that has led to the view that Confirmation *completes* the process of Christian initiation begun in baptism. Particularly following infant baptism, Confirmation has been seen as God's equipping of the adult Christian with the Holy Spirit and thus as 'the sacrament of spiritual maturity'.[1] This is obviously reinforced in those settings where Confirmation is a necessary precursor to being admitted to Holy Communion. Even in contexts where Confirmation isn't accorded a sacramental understanding, the rite is quite commonly understood and presented as what makes someone into 'a full member' of the church.

Clarity over this issue is thus vital to understanding baptism. As emphasized, baptism needs to be responded to with faithful obedience for the promises that it contains to be effective. However, it is quite another thing to see another sacrament as being needed to complete Christian initiation. Baptism is either complete as sacramental initiation or it isn't. Establishing the true nature of Confirmation is vital to achieving clarity on this matter.

## Does Confirmation complete the initiation begun in baptism?

The Second Vatican Council of the Roman Catholic Church declared in the 'Constitution of the Church' that Christians

> are more perfectly bound to the Church by the sacrament of Confirmation, and the Holy Spirit endows them with special strength so that they are more strictly obliged to spread and defend the faith, both by word and deed, as true witnesses of Christ.[2]

Confirmation is thus presented as completing the sacramental initiation begun by baptism. It represents both a distinct strengthening with the Holy Spirit and a distinct commissioning to serve God in the world. Anglican advocates of this position include, from the past, A.J. Mason (1851–1928) and Gregory Dix (1901–1952), who went as far as to see the Holy Spirit as sacramentally imparted for the first time in Confirmation. More recent proponents of a sacramental understanding of Confirmation, such as Paul Avis, tend to present it instead as completing the bestowal of the Holy Spirit begun in baptism.[3]

Those who argue for the place of Confirmation within a two-stage understanding of Christian initiation normally place great importance upon tradition and, in particular, defending the sacraments of the Roman Catholic Church. The biblical case is built upon those examples in the New Testament where baptism is followed by a subsequent laying on of apostolic hands to impart the Holy Spirit. One of these is Acts 8.4-25. In this chapter, Philip preaches in Samaria with the result that a number of the Samaritans believed and were baptized into the name of the Lord Jesus but without receiving the Holy Spirit. This only occurred once the apostles Peter and John had come to Samaria from Jerusalem: 'Then Peter and John placed their hands on them, and they received the Holy Spirit' (8.17). Another example is said to be found in Acts 19.1-7 where Paul encounters 'some disciples' in Ephesus who had not received the Holy Spirit when they believed and received only the baptism of John the Baptist. After Paul informed them that John's baptism pointed to Jesus, they were baptized in Jesus's name and when Paul placed his hands upon them, they received the Holy Spirit. Another piece of biblical evidence is drawn from Hebrews 6.1-2 where the writer's summary of foundational Christian teaching refers to 'baptisms' followed by 'the laying on of hands'.

It is from these examples that some argue that the pattern for initiation within the early church was that of baptism, followed by an apostolic laying on of hands. This two-stage understanding is seen to gain support from Jesus telling Nicodemus about the necessity of rebirth by 'water and the Spirit' (John 3.5), which is taken as referring to two separate rites. Where the laying on of hands isn't mentioned, it is argued that this probably formed part of the process that would have accompanied the baptisms we hear about. It has further been suggested that the mention of the 'seal of the Spirit' (2 Corinthians 1.22; Ephesians 1.13-14 and 4.30) and 'anointing' (2 Corinthians 1.21; 1 John 2.20, 27) may also suggest a post-baptismal second ceremony.

All of this results in an understanding of Confirmation as a sacrament through which the Holy Spirit specially strengthens or 'makes firm' those who have previously been baptized. Advocates of this perspective sometimes present Confirmation as 'the ordination of the laity', conferring an authority and role within the body of Christ that has not been present before.[4] The frequent occurrence of Confirmation in adolescence adds a layer of sociological factors to this. Both society and psychology create the impulse for a rite of passage between childhood and adulthood, and Confirmation can therefore become easily seen as the point where God makes the child 'member in waiting' into a full adult member of the church.

However, as Colin Buchanan has shown, the biblical evidence cannot bear the weight that this view seeks to place upon it. None of the other seven references to baptism in Acts refer to baptism being followed by laying on of hands and in some cases the context makes this unlikely or impossible. When Peter declared at Pentecost 'Repent and be baptised ... and you will receive the gift of the Holy Spirit' (Acts 2.38), it is stretching credibility to argue that the latter only followed a (unrecorded) laying on of apostolic hands on the 3,000 converts. Likewise after Philip baptized the Ethiopian in the desert, he sent him on his way rejoicing, rather than sending him back to Jerusalem so that an apostle could supplement his baptism (Acts 8.36-38). In the eight explicit references to baptism in Paul's letters (Romans 6.3-4; 1 Corinthians 1.13-17; 10.1-2; 12.12-23; 15.29; Galatians 3.27; Ephesians 4.4; Colossians 2.11; as well as the implicit references in 1 Corinthians 6.11 and Titus 3.5) and also in 1 Peter 3.21, there is not a hint of a second ceremony needed to supplement baptism. In all of these passages we see baptism alone conveying all the blessings of the gospel with, as we have seen, the consistent message that these blessings need to be received with faith.[5] When Paul revisits the churches that he had planted, it is with the specific aim of 'strengthening the disciples and encouraging them to remain true to the faith' (Acts 14.21-22; cf. 15.41; 18.23). However, the emphasis here is upon his message regarding the suffering that these new Christians needed to endure, with no laying on of hands reported (Acts 14.22).

So what about Acts 8.4-25? If the two-stage process that we see there was atypical rather than archetypal, what were the circumstances that brought it about? The crucial contextual factor is the way in which this section of Acts is focused upon the momentous period during the early church when those who had previously been outsiders were admitted into the renewed people of God – Samaritans (8.4-25), Gentile proselytes to Judaism (8.26-40), God-fearing Gentiles (Acts 10–11) and eventually Gentiles coming straight from paganism (Acts 13.46 onwards). There are two emphases that are particularly important to the writer of Acts in the description of this process: firstly, that this development was by a sovereign act of God and, secondly, that it was wholeheartedly endorsed by the apostles in Jerusalem with these converts joining the one, united people of God. It is in order to clarify the importance of both of these factors that we see their separation in the two key episodes reported in Acts 8.4-25 and Acts 10–11. When Philip proclaims the Christ in Samaria, the healings and exorcisms that accompany the Samaritans' response make it clear that this represented a sovereign act of God (8.4-8). However, it was also very possible that, given the history of Jewish-Samaritan enmity (reflected in Luke 9.51-56; 10.25-37; John 4), this development would have then led to the formation of two separate churches. It was in order to prevent this that the atypical process reported in Samaria occurred. Acts 2 had established the archetypal pattern for initiation into the Christian community with baptism and the Holy Spirit received together. However, the conversion of Samaritans to Christianity was so momentous that its process was slowed to two stages in order to show its nature as both a sovereign act of God and one fully endorsed by the apostles and Jerusalem church. The clear evidence of God's grace to the Samaritans was therefore accompanied by the covenant sign of baptism (8.12) but reception of the Spirit (which normally went with the former) was delayed until what had occurred in Samaria had received the affirmation of the apostles, represented by Peter and John (8.14-17). What this process made clear was that the very same Holy Spirit that had filled the apostles and those baptized in Jerusalem on the day of Pentecost had now come upon those who had received the grace of God in Samaria. However, it is to make absolutely clear that this process was *not* seen as archetypal that we see the complete opposite occur a few chapters later when Cornelius and his household receive the Holy Spirit *prior* to baptism. As Peter preaches the good news, the Holy Spirit came on all those who heard the message causing him to declare: 'Can anyone keep these people from being baptised with water? They have received the Holy Spirit just as we have' (10.47). Once again the dual emphasis is upon the sovereignty of God in bringing these former outsiders to faith and the recognition and endorsement of this by the apostolic church. But the process is deliberately reversed precisely in order to make it clear that nothing typical was to be drawn about initiation from the unique context surrounding these crucial episodes in the early church. Both episodes actually presuppose that baptism and reception of the Holy Spirit, under normal circumstances, belong together. It was the special circumstances involved in the startling new development of Samaritan/Gentile inclusion and the importance of acknowledging the apostolic recognition of this act of God that necessitated the atypical process that occurred.

Acts 19.1-7 is different in its circumstances but nonetheless bears some similarities in terms of the ecclesiological factors involved. Paul's assumption was that Christian baptism brought the gift of the Spirit and it was the ignorance of the Ephesian 'disciples' about the Holy Spirit that led to his question about the baptism they had therefore received. The context here is the introduction into the narrative of Acts, just prior to this, of the influential Christian leader Apollos (18.24-28; cf. 1 Corinthians 1.12). Apollos is endorsed as a dynamic and largely orthodox Christian leader who, nonetheless and until instructed more adequately, 'knew only the baptism of John' (18.25). Given the positive report of his proclamation about Jesus, the specific shortcoming in Apollos' understanding that Priscilla and Aquila corrected (18.26) appears to been the same ignorance about the Holy Spirit then shown by the Ephesian disciples, who were similar in only knowing the baptism of John (19.3). After Paul provided instruction presumably similar to that given to Apollos, the Ephesian disciples were then baptized 'into the name of the Lord Jesus' and received the Holy Spirit precisely as a complete package. Rather than providing any support for a process of two-stage Christian initiation, the episode instead witnesses to the single-stage nature of sacramental initiation into the church. The role of Acts 18.24–19.7 thus possesses some similarity to the earlier episodes examined. In those episodes the emphasis was upon the Samaritan and Gentile converts entering the renewed people of God on precisely the same basis as Jewish Christians. Here the emphasis is upon the inclusion into the church of those who were formerly unorthodox in their discipleship, being conducted precisely under the same single rite of initiation that orthodox Christians had entered the church, i.e. baptism in the name of Jesus Christ with all of the fullness of blessings that this contained. The aim is to express the same truth as Paul when he declares that 'there is one body and one Spirit – just as you were called to one hope when you were called – one Lord, one faith, one baptism' (Ephesians 4.4-5).

As mentioned, Hebrews 6.1-2 is the third passage often cited as lending support to a two-stage process of sacramental initiation with its reference to 'baptisms' being followed by 'the laying on of hands' and the inclusion of these within 'the foundation' that also includes 'repentance from acts that lead to death', 'faith in God', 'the resurrection of the dead' and 'eternal judgement'. However, the reason why some would not have included this passage within the definite references to baptism in the New Testament epistles that we listed in Chapter 2 is because it uses a word that is related but distinct from the normal New Testament word for baptism. The normal word used for baptism is *baptisma*, whilst Hebrews 6.2 refers to *baptismōn* with this genitive plural drawn from the different word *baptismos*. The same word is found in Hebrews 9.10 and also Mark 7.4 where it refers to the ceremonial and domestic washings that were part of Judaism under the old covenant. The plural form would also be odd if it refers to the same baptism consistently referred to elsewhere (and for good theological reasons) in the singular form. It is for this reason that many doubt whether Christian baptism is being referred to in Hebrews 6.2. In fact a number of translations prefer to render it as 'ablutions', 'cleansing rites' or 'washings'. However, it would also be odd, particularly in the context of Hebrews, for its writer to include such old covenant style ablutions within their summary of elementary Christian teaching. It therefore seems most likely that the verse does refers to baptisms with the plural possibly used because, like the gospels, the Christian teaching it refers to included instruction about the decisive difference between the baptism of John and that brought about by Jesus. The probable reference to Christian baptism in 10.22 does then refer to it in a more singular fashion. However, even if baptism is referred to in Hebrews 6.2 (and the element of doubt is important), this doesn't prove in any way that its following reference to 'the laying on of hands' supports the theory of a two-stage understanding of Christian initiation. No details of what this laying on of hands involved (particularly any mention of the Holy Spirit being imparted) is given, and it is possible that it refers to the commissioning (or ordination) to specific tasks similar to when the leaders of the church at Antioch placed their hands upon Paul and Barnabas prior to their first missionary journey (Acts 13.3).

It is clear that the biblical evidence cannot support the case for a two-stage initiation with baptism completed by the laying on of hands in Confirmation. The biblical arguments commonly employed for this actually prove too much because if they support the case made for them, they involve the denial that the Holy Spirit is sacramentally imparted in baptism. This is biblically unsustainable with the result that more recent arguments prefer to present the sacramental nature of Confirmation as being derived from baptism, which still leaves the latter as sacramentally incomplete. Recognizing the weakness of their case, advocates of this view fall back on the vague claim that those who deny this status for Confirmation 'seek for a tidy, minimal vision' and their view 'is perhaps a result of an overly tidy frame of mind'.[6] This is bolstered by the slippery use of the term 'Christian initiation' which Andrew Davison describes as 'never complete in this life' because 'baptism inducts us into a life of growth into Christ, into a life of initiation'.[7] Baptism indeed inducts us into a life of growth into Christ and such growth is vital. But to describe this as 'a life of initiation' is to change what the word 'initiation' means. Initiation refers to the start or beginning of something and the New Testament makes it clear that baptism is the sole sacrament that represents and conveys the beginning of the Christian life. Baptism, as we have stressed throughout this book, effects what it symbolizes in the context of faith. But to present the initiation that baptism represents as needing to be completed by other sacramental actions of God is to deny this efficacy and, in consequence, the assurance that baptism should bring.

The major source of this perspective is insecurity over the role of bishops. Maintaining the sacramental nature of Confirmation is seen as essential for maintaining the credibility of their ministry. However, the price for this is the undermining of baptism. Complete clarity is needed on this point. Confirmation is a good and helpful opportunity for people baptized as infants to give public expression to the confession of faith that baptism requires. It can also be a powerful way of confirming to the candidate, the promises that God has made to them in their baptism which they are receiving through their faith. But it is not a sacrament because, unlike baptism and the Lord's Supper, Confirmation lacks 'dominical institution', i.e. command (and promise) by Jesus Christ. Confusion over this results in the understandable accusation that Anglicans say that baptism makes someone a member of the church but then behave as though Confirmation does. Clarity over the sacramental status of baptism necessitates denial of the sacramental status of Confirmation.

A particularly unhelpful aspect of Confirmation is when it is still presented as necessary after an *adult* baptism. The personal confession of faith involved in an adult baptism means that Confirmation is at best unnecessary and at worst an undermining of that baptism. The justification normally given is that such a Confirmation marks out the candidate's admission into a particular denomination. It is usually required, for instance, of ordinands who have previously belonged to a different denomination to demonstrate their commitment to the Church of England. But other ways should be found of doing this and avoiding the confusion that it brings to the nature and status of baptism.

## Indiscriminate/open Confirmation?

Before we leave the subject of Confirmation, it is important to acknowledge an issue concerning it very similar to that addressed in regard to baptism in Chapter 11. In that chapter we examined the case for indiscriminate or open baptism and found it wanting on the basis of its failure to recognize the importance of baptized infants being brought up in the context of a living faith in Jesus Christ. It was acknowledged that the pressures upon clergy to conduct a baptism without evidence of faith within the family bringing the child to baptism are immense. These pressures, it was argued, both can and should be resisted if baptism is to retain its meaning and credibility. In theory, Confirmation shouldn't face the same issues, since its entire rationale is based upon those who reached an age of responsibility taking their own decision regarding it.

Things, however, are sometimes more complex. In a similar manner to the popular pressure to baptize infants outside of the context of faith, a pressure can exist in regard to Confirmation. Admittedly in the post-Christian context of Britain, this is far less common than it used to be. Forty years ago, particularly in the upper classes, Confirmation was still seen as almost as automatic a process for young adults as baptism for babies and often just as lacking in the context of a living faith. Entire year groups within certain public schools were often expected to get confirmed and it was viewed as part of the rite of passage to adult society. Part of this was a hangover from an earlier period when admission to most universities and indeed public office was restricted to confirmed communicants within the Church of England.

These days, somewhat ironically, it is more common for the pressure to conduct Confirmation outside of the context of faith to come from Christian parents anxious for their almost adult children to 'have something nailed down' before they leave home. Even where preparatory classes are required and taken seriously by the church, this can and often does result in Confirmation representing something like a 'passing out' ceremony. Unlike 'open baptism', there are very few who argue for such an approach to be taken to Confirmation. As with infant baptism, however, pastoral practice can sometimes differ quite considerably from official theology.

Part of the reason this issue is covered here is to show that the pressures to sit lightly to the context of faith are not limited to infant baptism. Neither are they limited to Confirmation. Adult baptism too can, on occasion, possess a similar external pressure. In much the same way as infant baptism, Confirmation must be practised in the context of faith, in this case the personal faith of those being confirmed. Once again, expectations, particularly of the ability to articulate this faith, should be age and personality appropriate. A shy teenager should not be expected to vocalize his or her faith in the same manner as someone much older or more extrovert. But for Confirmation to have credibility, evidence of personal faith in the candidate should be present in much the same manner as parents bringing children to baptism. It is perfectly fitting for this to include regular attendance at church services and/or church groups run for young people plus an appropriate measure of Christian service. Often it is encouragement of the latter that can make a major difference to the development of Christian faith and provide a very fitting and exciting context for Confirmation.

## 'Baptism in the Holy Spirit'

It is usually within Pentecostal and charismatic traditions that belief in 'baptism with the Holy Spirit', as distinct from 'baptism by water', has arisen. On the surface, these traditions couldn't be further from more catholic ones with little, if any, reference to the language of sacraments, apostolic succession or initiation. Confirmation is rarely an issue within such traditions since, in many of them, adult or believer's baptism is the norm, only conducted once people are able to make a public declaration of their faith. This, however, is often carefully described as '*water* baptism' in order to distinguish it from the (usually) subsequent and more vital stage of receiving 'baptism in the *Holy Spirit*'. The latter refers to an overwhelming, datable experience of God's Spirit which floods the life of the believer, normally accompanied by receiving supernatural gifts such as prophecy and the ability to speak in tongues.

Whilst very different in its language and style, this understanding is actually very similar to the view of those who believe that Confirmation completes sacramental initiation. Water-baptism is generally seen by Pentecostal or charismatic Christians in a non-sacramental manner rather than actually conveying God's blessings. But it is nonetheless taken seriously as the rite of entry into God's family and a sign that the person baptized has begun their relationship with God. Given their public confession of Jesus as Lord, it is rarely denied that the Holy Spirit is at work in them (1 Corinthians 12.3). However, the event that really completes their entry into the blessings God intends for his people is the further experience of being 'baptized in the Holy Spirit'. Water-baptism and Spirit-baptism can occur together and it is even possible (as with Cornelius and his household in Acts 10) for Spirit-baptism to precede water-baptism. But most commonly, baptism in the Holy Spirit comes as a 'second blessing', received some time after someone has become a Christian and through which God imparts the fullness of his blessings. Baptism in the Holy Spirit brings a much greater depth of experience than when the person first became a Christian: a deeper knowledge of God's love, a deeper desire to express that love to others and a deeper experience of the Spirit's gifts.

The parallels to the more catholic understanding of Confirmation are obvious. The blessings that the Bible associates with baptism are divided, with baptism in the Holy Spirit seen as the decisive act of God bringing these blessings to completion. The biblical argument for this rests quite heavily upon the distinction which John and Jesus made between John's baptism with water and Jesus's baptism with the Holy Spirit and with fire (Matthew 3.11; Mark 1.7-8; Luke 3.16; Acts 1.5), with all water-baptism associated with the former. Like those who see Confirmation as completing Christian initiation, advocates of a separate 'baptism in the Holy Spirit' also make strong use of Acts 8.4-25 and the Holy Spirit coming upon the Samaritan believers subsequent to their baptism through the laying on of hands by Peter and John. Acts 19.1-7 is also used, although less so because the original baptism of John that the Ephesian disciples received was clearly followed by a second water-baptism into Jesus through which they received the Holy Spirit.

There is no doubt at all that the Pentecostal and charismatic movements have brought huge blessings to the church and to many millions of Christians. Numerous Christians whose faith was failing to nourish them or address their deepest needs have been transformed by an increased expectation and experience of the power of the Holy Spirit in their lives. Gifts of the Holy Spirit such as healing, prophecy and speaking in tongues, all present in the Scriptures but sidelined for a very long time, have found their way back into Christians' experience bringing a great deal of blessing with them. It is also true that there has been little church growth in the last thirty years that has not owed a great deal of its success to the charismatic movement and an increased emphasis upon encouraging a greater openness to the power of the Holy Spirit. The spectacular success of the Alpha course, for example, and the many thousands of people transformed by it, is overwhelmingly due to the centrality given to its members experiencing the power of the Holy Spirit in their lives. Throughout this book, we have emphasized that for the blessings contained in baptism to be received, there needs to be a response of faith. An increased expectation and excitement about experiencing the blessings of the Holy Spirit and fervent prayer for these to come is all part of the faith that we are called to show to God's promises conveyed in baptism. This, ideally, will be a constant process throughout the lives of those seeking to live out the truth of their baptism into Christ.

However, it is also true to say that any understanding of a distinct and second act of God, separate from water-baptism and necessary to complete it, is a denial of the Bible's witness in regard to baptism. The teaching of the New Testament, as we have seen, is that all the blessings of the gospel are contained in water-baptism into the name of Jesus Christ. Paul refers to 'the God and Father of our Lord Jesus Christ, who has blessed us in the heavenly realms with every spiritual blessing in Christ' (Ephesians 1.3). This includes the indwelling of the Holy Spirit which is presented as the great uniting factor given to all Christians through their baptism (1 Corinthians 12.13; Ephesians 4.4; cf. Hebrews 6.4-5).

Rather than exhorting them to experience a new, distinct blessing, the emphasis of the New Testament is upon reminding Christians of the grace that they have received and urging them to live by it: to display the continuous response of faith that seeks to appropriate these blessings. So the apostles beg their readers not to 'grieve the Spirit' (Ephesians 4.30), to 'walk with the Spirit' (Galatians 5.16), 'keep in step with the Spirit' (Galatians 5.25) and to go on being 'filled with the Spirit' (Ephesians 5.18 using a continuous present imperative) but *never* to 'be baptised with the Spirit' because this is assumed to have already occurred.[8] In fact of the seven references to baptism in the Holy Spirit (six contrasting the baptism of John with that of Jesus plus 1 Corinthians 12.13), none is an exhortation in the imperative or even hints at a second, distinct blessing. The exhortation instead is for every Christian to go on being constantly refilled with the Spirit given in baptism.

What is often referred to as 'baptism in the Holy Spirit' is often, in reality, a further appropriation of the gift of the Holy Spirit given to that person in their baptism. An illustration at this point may help. When a couple are married, they commonly receive many presents, most of which they open sometime after their wedding day when they return from their honeymoon. Unpacking these gifts and expressing thanks for them are often all part of what gets their married life off to an exciting and uplifting beginning. However, it has been known for a present given on the wedding day to go astray and remain unopened and therefore unenjoyed by those to whom it was given. The present has the couple's name upon it, it has been given to them and belongs to them but, for whatever reason, they are not fully conscious of their possession of it. Then one day, the gift comes to light and is opened. Thanks is belatedly expressed to those who gave it and the gift is finally able to be enjoyed by those to whom it was given way back on their wedding day.

It is probably most helpful to understand the missing wedding gift in this illustration as representing a particular aspect of the Spirit's ministry, rather than the gift of the Holy Spirit in his entirety. Indeed one of the problems with the understanding of baptism of the Holy Spirit as a second and distinct act of God is the way in which the evidence for this is often limited to particular experiences. Speaking in tongues, prophecy and gifts of healing are all, without doubt, examples of people receiving gifts of the Holy Spirit. But so too are followers of Jesus Christ being given and using equally biblical gifts such as encouragement, administration and service to others. Paul's major point in 1 Corinthians 12–14 is that all of these different gifts are given by the one Spirit through whom Christians were baptized into one body. They are given for the common good, none of them should be despised or undervalued and they must always be exercised within the context of the greatest gift of the Holy Spirit which is love. Through their divisions and lack of love, the Corinthian Christians, indeed, are an example of how it is possible to be baptized with the Holy Spirit, gifted by the Spirit and yet not filled with the Spirit (1 Corinthians 2.14). The chief mark of fullness of the Spirit throughout the New Testament is in terms of the character or fruit of the Spirit rather than gifts.[9] Both Stephen and Barnabas are described in this way (Acts 7.55; 11.24) and when Paul urges Christians to go on being filled with the Spirit, the qualities he then commends are all relational ones – thankful worship of God and loving submission to one another (Ephesians 5.18ff).

Understanding all God's blessings as given in baptism but with the constant response of faith being needed to receive (and in some cases discover) these blessings avoids further danger connected with 'baptism in the Holy Spirit'. The most obvious of these is a privileging of the more obviously supernatural gifts over those seen as more mundane and the inevitable elitism then accorded to those who possess the former. The oneness of baptism means that all those who are baptized into Christ are equally blessed with the gift of the Holy Spirit with the ongoing response of faith equally required of all to receive the Spirit's blessings. This will include openness to discovering or receiving fresh and surprising gifts of the Spirit but within the context of existing possession of the Spirit given in their baptism and already evidenced by their confession of Jesus as Lord (1 Corinthians 12.3).

God's blessings are therefore fully contained within baptism. These blessings, including all those associated with the Holy Spirit, are received by responding to this baptism through a life of faith. If it is right to speak of the completion of baptism, this can only be in terms of the constant response of faith to its promises. The alternative understanding of baptism needing to be supplemented by further acts of grace by God fatally undermines its status. Whether through a sacramental understanding of Confirmation or belief in a 'baptism of the Holy Spirit', such approaches declare that the blessings of God given through baptism are incomplete. Complete clarity over this matter is vital. God's blessings are all, without exception, contained within baptism but need to be received by the ongoing response of faith.

## The participation of baptized infants within Holy Communion

If the argument of this chapter is correct and baptism indeed represents full sacramental initiation into the Christian faith, and if household baptism is indeed a valid form of this baptism, then household or infant communion immediately possesses a compelling case. Many are increasingly recognizing that if the sacrament of baptism does bring full membership of the church, there are no grounds for withholding the sacrament of Holy Communion from any who are baptized, including infants and children.

Throughout much of Christian history, this has not been the case. It was during the Middle Ages that admittance to Holy Communion in the Western Church became dependent upon Confirmation and this remained the case after the Reformation. This helped build towards the later idea that Confirmation completed Christian initiation. It was probably following the start of the Parish Communion movement in the 1930s (the Anglo-Catholic movement seeking to make Communion the main act of Sunday worship in a parish) that the custom began of children receiving a blessing as their parents received the bread and wine of Holy Communion. The dominance of the Mason-Dix school of two-stage initiation, plus a hefty dose of natural conservatism, ensured that this non-inclusion of baptized children within Holy Communion was rarely questioned. From the early 1970s, however, this began to change with many increasingly starting to realize its inconsistency.

As with infant baptism, trying to establish clarity about infant communion in the earliest church is a hazardous process. Most studies of primitive Christian practice do suggest that baptism (in whatever form it was administered) always led to participation in the Lord's Supper. However, as with baptism, the most important factor in the rightness or otherwise of infant communion is what *the Bible* points us towards. In the first place, this will concern the establishment of whether a biblical case exists for some being baptized but not admitted to Holy Communion.

No such case exists. The New Testament speaks with one voice on this issue which is to assume that all those who are baptized then receive Holy Communion. In Acts we are told that 'all the believers', referring to the newly baptized, 'broke bread in their homes and ate together' (Acts 2.42-47). In 1 Corinthians 10, as we have seen, Paul uses baptism and the Lord's Supper to interpret Israel's exodus experience. Whilst it refers to 'our fathers', Paul's message is to the Corinthians about the importance of responding to the sacraments that God has given them with faith and obedience. In the process he assumes that all the Corinthian Christians that he is writing to are both baptized and communicant and that both sacraments belong together. This is reinforced by 1

Corinthians 10.17 in conjunction with 12.13. In the former of these verses, Paul says that the Corinthian Christians are sustained as 'one body' by receiving the shared bread of communion whilst in the latter he says that it is baptism that admitted them into 'one body'. As Colin Buchanan has said, 'Far and away the most comfortable holding together of his thought is to conclude that baptism admitted to communion.'[10]

The exceptions to this would be those baptized Christians who had fallen away or who had been removed from the Christian fellowship for disciplinary reasons. Paul advocates such an expulsion in 1 Corinthians 5 where one of the members of the church has been involved in sexual immorality. When he says 'with such a man do not even eat' (5.11), he is referring to any form of table fellowship. But this would obviously include the Lord's Supper. Excommunication on disciplinary grounds is thus the only biblical basis that we find for someone who has been baptized not being allowed to participate in Holy Communion.

Having established that baptism and Holy Communion belong together, we must then consider whether good grounds exist for excluding baptized children from participating in the latter. The major argument used for this surrounds infants and young people not having the understanding seen as necessary for receiving Holy Communion. When the Bible is used to support this perspective, examples are usually drawn from 1 Corinthians 11 where Paul speaks of valid participation in the Lord's Supper depending on its participants recognizing or discerning the body of Christ and examining themselves so that that they do not eat the bread and drink the wine in an unworthy manner (1 Corinthians 11.27f). Since infants are not capable of doing either of these things, they should not be allowed to receive Holy Communion until they are older.

There are several problems with the broader issue of a necessary level of understanding being required before admission is permitted to Holy Communion. In most churches, children are encouraged to grow in their understanding of things such as worship, prayer and reading the Bible, precisely through experiencing these features of the Christian life. In fact, in all of these cases it could be argued that little understanding of them can be reached *until* they are experienced. But, at a more fundamental level, such an attitude betrays an overly cerebral approach to the sacraments which cannot be applied consistently. Adults are not scrutinized in terms of their understanding of the Lord's Supper (and excommunicated if they fall short!) and this is because of the recognition that Holy Communion speaks powerfully and yet mysteriously and inclusively to the whole Christian community of the saving death of Jesus. In fact Holy Communion is particularly inclusive of those with different intellectual aptitudes. This is because of the power and clarity with which its multi-sensory nature proclaims Jesus in a manner that is more accessible than other forms of proclamation, particularly to those with learning difficulties. It is this same multi-sensory nature that makes Holy Communion overwhelmingly suitable for the Christian nurture of children being brought up to respond to their baptism with a life of faith in Jesus Christ.[11]

It is within this perspective that we need to interpret Paul's injunctions about fruitful reception of the Lord's Supper requiring discernment from its participants. Paul's criticism is focused upon the divisions, apparently between rich and poor, which marred the celebration of the Lord's Supper at Corinth. It is as part of this that he speaks of the need to examine oneself before eating the bread and drinking the cup because 'anyone who eats and drinks without recognising the body of the Lord, eats and drinks judgement upon himself' (11.28-29f). The context makes it clear that this failure to recognize or discern the body is referring very specifically to participants at the Lord's Supper not displaying that unity in the body of Christ that they share with their fellow Christians. Ironically, the most obvious application of this, in terms of infant communion, lies in the lack of unity in the body of Christ displayed by the non-inclusion of baptized infants. As with other aspects of Christian nurture, respect for and responsibility towards other members of the body of Christ is something that is most appropriately taught to Christian children from within, rather than outside, the body of Christ. Self-examination is something that children are encouraged to do as soon it becomes possible and it should be no different when it comes to Holy Communion. In fact, a major difference between children and adults within church is that children are the ones who generally receive far more accountability for their behaviour and attitudes. Within many churches, it is the behaviour of the adults that is by far the bigger issue! Of course in the earliest stages of their life, infants are incapable of seeing much beyond their own needs. But just as parents undertake to make their children aware of the rights and importance of others as early as it becomes appropriate to expect this, so the same should be the case within the body of Christ.

The supposedly biblical arguments against infant communion are therefore extremely weak. In reality, the strongest arguments made against it don't attempt a biblical basis and rely upon some variation of 'it's good for children to have to wait'. At a deeper level, more powerful through being less stated and therefore recognized, is the sense many established churchgoers possess that 'it just feels wrong'. Much of the resistance to infant communion has also come from bishops anxious again about what will happen to Confirmation (as their major public role) if the former is established.

But the same principles must apply to both of the sacraments that Jesus instituted and to deny the sacrament of Holy Communion to those who have received the sacrament of baptism is to undermine the validity of that baptism. Although baptism completes sacramental initiation, the withholding of Holy Communion from baptized children forms a practical denial of this. Issues of course exist concerning how Holy Communion is administered to the very young. But, in reality, these issues are often not that different to those involved in administering communion to the very old and infirm. Embracing infant communion, as much as seeking to build child-friendly churches, is often the definitive sign of whether churches really believe in infant baptism.

In 1997 the bishops of the Church of England issued guidelines for parishes wishing to introduce 'communion before Confirmation'.[12] Whilst this represented a major breakthrough for those advancing the case for infant communion, the nature of these guidelines retained much of the thinking that had previously been used to exclude children. This was most obviously shown in their stipulation that the time of children first receiving Holy Communion should be determined 'not so much by the child's chronological age as by his or her appreciation of the significance of the sacrament'. As part of this, the bishops added that 'an appropriate and serious pattern of preparation should be followed'. Recognizing the problems this created, the guidelines then softened this by adding that 'the Church needs to encourage awareness of many different levels of understanding, and support the inclusion of those with learning difficulties in the Christian community. Particular care needs to be taken with the preparation of any who have learning difficulties, including children'. Despite this softening, the guidelines therefore maintained the theological principle, inconsistent with infant baptism, that instruction and the response of faith should *precede* reception of the sacrament of Holy Communion, rather than be expected and encouraged in response to it. Despite the non-stipulation of a particular age, the requirement of an 'appreciation of the significance of the sacrament' meant that the guidelines envisaged child communion rather than its administration to baptized babies. Within many dioceses, in fact, the age of seven was specified to clarify this. The rest of the guidelines generally comprised details of what was required before the 'special permission' needed for 'communion before confirmation' would be granted by the bishop. The overall tone spoke of pastoral concession rather than any change of theological principle. It therefore remained clear that, despite the theology and official position claimed for it, baptism (certainly in its infant form) was not yet seen by the Church of England as representing full sacramental initiation into the family of God.[13]

It is now time for the timidity to end and for the implications of baptism as complete sacramental initiation to be implemented in full. Baptism brings full membership of the people of God and access to all the blessings of salvation, including all those represented by Holy Communion. Participation in the Lord's Supper needs to be seen as the right of all those who have been baptized rather than something requiring 'special permission'. Once this happens, the confusion caused by the sacramental claims made about Confirmation will finally go and it will assume its proper place as a helpful means by which those baptized as infants can publicly affirm their faith. More importantly, baptism will finally become what the New Testament claims for it. The instinctive reaction against infant communion that many display is, in reality, further indication of the indefensible nature of indiscriminate infant baptism. Baptism should be restored to its place as God's sign of covenant membership for Christian households responding to his grace with a life of faithful obedience, and this will be fully signified when that same baptism admits children of the covenant, from their earliest memories, into the covenant family meal that Jesus instituted for the people of God.

# 14

# Living and preaching baptism

## Living baptism

Baptism is a specific moment which then provides a pattern and shape for the whole of Christian life. It is not so much a single service or event, more a way of life. The truth of baptism as an event will only be fully understood when the reality of baptism as a way of life is lived out and experienced.

Within most churches and for very many Christians, however, baptism retains very little importance once it has occurred. The baptism event, whether involving adult or child, is often profound and deeply moving. But, even within the context of the most committed Christian faith, it can then be left in the past as life moves on. Very few Christians and churches are aware that the significance of baptism should be ongoing and enduring.The World Council of Churches Faith and Order Commission Paper directly challenged this when it spoke of the high significance of baptism for the practical life of the church:

> *Since baptism encompasses the whole Christian life, lack of clarity concerning the meaning of baptism leads to uncertainty all along the line. It is beyond dispute that in no church body does baptism have the decisive significance which the witness of the New Testament ascribes to it. Here we all have much to learn. A serious penetration into the meaning of baptism and an appropriation of the treasure given in baptism would give preaching and teaching both a centrally focussed content and a new breadth, together with an insight which clarifies and unifies the whole of Christian life. The more the baptised learn to see their whole life in the light of their baptism, the more does their life take on the pattern of life 'in Christ'.*[1]

Baptism, in this sense, is rather like marriage. Just as the marriage ceremony is a decisive event which must then be worked out through married life, so too baptism is a decisive event but must be worked out through the Christian life. The marriage ceremony marks the beginning of a new way of life and so too with baptism. Baptism is for living.

We observed this back in Chapter 6 when we looked at baptism in the early church. There we saw the way in which the New Testament writers constantly use and appeal to baptism as the decisive factor in defining, shaping and motivating the Christian life.

For Paul, in particular, it can be said that the whole of Christian life for both churches and the Christians within them can be summed up as the calling to work out the significance of their baptism.

## Baptism as the source of reassurance about our status in Christ

Martin Luther (1483–1546) is for many Christians a great hero for his role in sparking the sixteenth-century reformation which changed the Christian world forever. But he was also a complex and rather tormented Christian regularly assailed by feelings of doubt and temptation about his status before God. Luther's reformation theology was built around 'justification by faith', which he understood to mean that human beings had nothing whatsoever to contribute to their salvation and could merely receive it with empty hands. This was then worked out in immense detail and in regard to various different topics in his voluminous writings. But when he suffered the painful assaults of doubt and temptation that continued to afflict him, Luther had one phrase that summed up his entire theology of grace and which he hurled back at the Devil: *baptizatus sum* – 'I am baptised!'. Luther understood that the whole of a Christian's security in God rested upon what he had done for them in their baptism. Baptism was the completely reliable divine pledge of his good standing before God.

The power of this reassurance is something that Christians and churches need to rediscover today. All Christians struggle and find life difficult and in these moments it is all too easy to doubt whether we really belong to God. An aspect of modern society making this worse are the endless messages conveyed by TV, advertising and social media suggesting that our value is dependent on what we have achieved and possess, what we look like and the quality of our relationships and experiences. Increasing isolation and the breakdown of family and community life have caused many to lack a sense of belonging and identity. All of these factors have contributed to soaring problems with mental health and anxiety, often affecting Christians as much as anyone else.

Baptism possesses the power to speak strongly into this. As God's covenant sign, it first and foremost speaks of the love of God by reminding Christians of the priority and initiative of God's grace, the faithfulness of his covenant promise through the ages and the incredible costliness of God's salvation in Christ. But precisely because of this, baptism provides believers with a reassurance that should be truly transforming.

In overall terms, baptism is a communal statement of identity proclaiming that those marked out by it are God's people, rescued from the slavery of sin and on their way to the inheritance that God has promised them. When a baptism takes place, it should thus serve as a powerful reminder to all the congregation present of who they are in Jesus Christ. The emphasis upon God's grace means there is no place within this for pride or any sense of superiority. But it should nevertheless convey a common status before God and a sense of identity and belonging that then leads to that community being a place of humility and joy, leading to acts of love and generosity towards one another as fellow members of God's family. This of course is reinforced by the other sacrament ordained by Christ, the Lord's Supper, through which the church regularly celebrates its identity in Jesus Christ.

Extra depth is added to this affirmation of identity by reflection upon the specific blessings of baptism covered in Chapter 6. Part of this is its promise of permanent forgiveness and cleansing. Regular confession of sin accompanied by the assurance of God's forgiveness is both biblical (1 John 1.9) and common practice within many churches. But baptism reminds the believer that this awareness of sin and its confession occur within the larger context of their existing status as God's permanently forgiven and cleansed people. In fact, rather than bringing this forgiven status into doubt, awareness of sin and its regular confession become a positive sign of the reality of this status. Much as it did for Martin Luther, baptism is intended to act as a powerful pledge of a Christian's good conscience before God (1 Peter 3.21). Many Christians suffer from the crippling effects of guilt about things that they have done or failed to do in their lives, and the power of this guilt can sometimes threaten to destroy those lives. Living out baptism is partly about living with the full consciousness that this sin was completely washed away when we were forgiven and cleansed through our baptism into Jesus Christ.

Closely associated with this is the reassurance brought by baptism that Christians are adopted as precious sons or daughters of God. As mentioned, a great source of insecurity for many people lies within their human relationships and, in particular, the relationship (or sometimes non-relationship) with their parents. Baptism speaks directly into this hurt through its assurance of divine son and daughtership. Rather than being individual, the major way in which this reassurance is experienced is through the believer's welcome into and inclusion within a church that reinforces this status by treating them as a cherished brother or sister in Christ. Emphasis should be laid at this point, without any disrespect, on the contrast with Islam and its express denial that human beings can know Allah as Father. Muslims who have converted to Christianity are clear about the decisive difference that it makes to their identity and security to know God as Father.[2] This should encourage all Christians to invest more significance in the declaration through baptism of their divine son and daughtership and the reassurance this should bring.

A further aspect of the reassurance brought by baptism lies in its nature as a mark of God's indwelling presence within us through the Holy Spirit. Some Christians can feel rather second class if they don't possess the inward glow, certainty or specific gifts sometimes seen as the definitive sign of the Spirit's presence. However, as we saw in Chapter 13, a biblical understanding of baptism involves the decisive rejection of any separate blessing being needed to receive the Holy Spirit. This isn't to deny that all Christians should seek greater renewal through the Holy Spirit or be open to receiving more gifts of the Spirit. What baptism should do, however, is bring the reassurance to all those responding to their baptism with faith that they are already indwelt by God's Spirit. From this basis, they can then be encouraged to see all their acts of service and love towards others, however seemingly unspectacular, as evidence that the Holy Spirit is at work in their life. This will lead Christians to a greater appreciation of the gifts of the Spirit that God has given them through their baptism and the affirmation that comes from the clarification of their baptismal vocation to serve God in the world.

As with the Lord's Supper, there is no greater encouragement and reassurance to the Christian than recalling the status and blessings that we receive through being joined to Jesus Christ. We have seen that these blessings are not automatic or unconditional but are offered through the gospel to those who receive the good news by faith. But baptism, nonetheless, reminds us that our status and our value emphatically rest upon the person whom God alone has declared us to be through our baptism into his Son, Jesus Christ.

## Baptism as the source of clarity about our calling in Christ

This is an equally significant aspect of living out our baptism. Christians are rescued entirely by God's grace rather than by anything that we do but we are then called to 'continue to work out your salvation with trembling and fear' (Philippians 2.12). This means living out our status as 'children of God without fault in a crooked and depraved generation, in which you shine like stars in the universe, as you hold out the word of life' (Philippians 2.15-16). The whole purpose of the covenant with its climax in Jesus Christ was God's intention of restoring the people made in his image so that they could finally fulfil their calling of ruling over his similarly restored creation. This future is anticipated in the present by the manner in which those who are baptized are called to live as a tangible witness to this future hope. Christians today, just like those in the first century, are called through their baptism to express this through lives of holiness, unity and the willingness to suffer for their faithfulness to Jesus Christ.

## The baptismal call to holiness

Holiness is an unfashionable concept today. For many, it is associated with a joyless and timid avoidance of everything that is fun and exciting about life. But, clarified by baptism, holiness should be understood instead as the very opposite. It forms an essential part of the exciting calling that Christians possess to anticipate their future rule over creation and demonstrate what living 'life to the full' is all about.

Much of this holiness involves the decisive rejection of idolatry. Idolatry is taking the good things that God has created to bless us and giving ourselves to these things in the hope of then possessing their fullness. This is most obviously seen in the worship of money, sex and power which manifests itself in the rampant materialism, hedonism and search for achievement and success which dominate Western society. The result of this idolatry is that the good things that God has created to bless us end up cursing both people and the world instead.[3] The pursuit of money, sex and power fails to bring the fullness it appears to promise and instead wreaks devastation and misery – not just in the dehumanization of those who build their lives around this futile search but in the oppression of many others and the world itself which rapidly become its victims. One of the biggest advances in the last twenty years has been the ways in which eyes in the Western world have become opened to the consequences of our way of living upon both the environment and the lives of those, chiefly in other countries, who have paid its cost.

Holiness is the rejection of all of this because of loyalty to God. Right from the start of Israel's establishment as a covenant community, YHWH's presence amongst his people went hand in hand with his call for them to be holy. We saw in Chapter 6 how Paul in 1 Corinthians 10 makes it clear that since baptism and the Lord's Supper now define the new covenant community as the place of God's presence, the result of this is a similar imperative to avoid idolatry. This emphasis was also found in Romans 6 where those baptized are presented as the true exodus people who have been freed from their slavery to sin and must now live in a manner appropriate to this. The challenge there to 'offer the parts of your body to him as instruments of righteousness' (6.13) and 'become slaves to righteousness' (6.18) shows that the holiness of the baptized has a decisive role to play in the ongoing implementation of God's covenant plan. Colossians also follows its reference to baptism with instructions about the practical holiness this then requires with a determined effort to 'put off' idolatrous behaviour and 'put on' that which is good. Paul makes it quite clear that this call to holiness doesn't involve a dualistic rejection of creation itself which fails to address the problem (2.16-23). The answer instead is to focus upon their union with Christ with the approach to living within the world that is consistent with their liberation from evil (3.1ff).

The major way in which the church will display this holiness is through modelling the right and healthy approach to the good things that God has created so that these return to being a blessing rather than a curse. Baptized Christians are called to show what a healthy approach to possessions, relationships and success looks like. This involves both avoiding the dualism that would reject these things as evil and the idolatry that would put them in place of God. In specific terms this will often involve modelling what it means to take a healthy rather than idolatrous approach to good things such as sex, alcohol, entertainment, houses, holidays and education.

This is extraordinarily difficult in the modern age when Christians are surrounded by people living very differently. But often the problems lie with holiness being understood in too individual a manner and the loss of the corporate nature of the baptized life. Churches are intended to be closely knit baptized communities which stand collectively for a different way of living because of their being set apart for God. Its members should work out together what holiness means in an everyday twenty-first-century context and, from that basis, through prayer and fellowship, encourage one another to persevere in living out the baptized life.

## The baptismal call to unity

In both Galatians and Ephesians, Paul emphasizes how baptism brings followers of Jesus into a single community within which is complete equality between Jews and Gentiles, slaves and masters and men and women. The oneness of baptism reflects the oneness of God, and its major practical implication is the firm rejection of any sort of apartheid within the one people of God.

This is something that churches badly need to rediscover today if they are to live out their baptism. Churches, sadly, are often divided by precisely the same factors that divide the surrounding world. Baptism instead calls for segregation of whatever sort within the people of God to be ruthlessly eliminated.

Part of the way in which this is worked out will be in the unity between different churches. Often such unity can be rather nominal and sometimes only expressed in a badly attended 'Churches Together' service held once a year. The call to these churches through baptism is instead to work out really practical and meaningful ways in which they can express their oneness in Christ. One of the best ways that churches can do this is to work together on mission projects to serve the local community. Over the last decade this has particularly occurred within the Night Shelter movement as several churches within a local area have cooperated by each taking a night during the winter months to provide food, shelter and community for people who are homeless. Another approach has been to hold joint services during August, turning a time of lower congregations into something more exciting and vibrant. It is becoming more and more common for churches themselves to be formed out of ecumenical partnerships. Such partnerships are sometimes presented as needing churches to sit more lightly to theology if they are to prosper. A proper theology of baptism declares the very opposite, requiring all who are baptized and confess Jesus as Lord to be acknowledged as fellow brothers and sisters in Christ. As Paul's response to Peter at Antioch shows, any deliberate separation from other Christians is a straightforward denial of the gospel. Another example of the practical implementation of this unity is the collection that Paul organized amongst the Gentile Christians for their starving Jewish Christian brothers and sisters in Jerusalem. Similar care between churches at some distance from one another is another very practical way of living out the radical unity that is proclaimed in baptism.

The implications of this baptismal call to unity exist as much *within* churches as well. The task of any church should be to bring its diverse members together to celebrate the unity that they share through their common baptism into Christ. In Ephesians 3 Paul states that this unity is the way in which 'through the church the manifold wisdom of God should be made known to the rulers and authorities in the heavenly realms' (3.10). The gospel is never more fully displayed than when a church is composed of people united in Jesus Christ who would, under normal circumstances, have nothing to do with one another. This particularly goes for unity across the common divisions of race, age or social class. Many churches organize social events which, however enjoyable, can sometimes be accorded rather marginal significance in church life. Clarity over the baptismal call to unity will lead to such activities assuming a much greater centrality with a determined effort made to bring the very different members of the church together in a meaningful way. The division reported in Galatians 2 manifested itself in Jewish Christians withdrawing from eating with Gentile Christians, and one of the most powerful ways in which the baptismal call to unity is displayed is when churches do the opposite and organize meals at which their most diverse members come together to share fellowship by eating together. The short letter Paul wrote to Philemon nowhere mentions baptism. But the startling degree of fellowship that Paul requires between himself as apostle, Philemon as master and Onesimus as slave is another example of the call to baptismal unity being put into practical action. Churches making a determined effort to cross social boundaries with the gospel and then develop meaningful and loving fellowship across these divisions lies at the heart of the living out of baptism.

Vital to this unity is complete equality. Part of what baptism declares is that everyone who is baptized is an equally valued member of the body of Christ (1 Corinthians 12). Churches then face the challenge of implementing this equality. Where infants are baptized, a specific challenge to churches is to create a culture where these children are accorded the status as full members of the church rather than 'members in waiting'. The overwhelming case for baptized children being admitted to Holy Communion has been covered in the previous chapter. But it is very possible for children to be admitted to Communion within a church that is otherwise fairly neglectful of them. Children should receive an equal level of ministry that is appropriate to their needs, an equal allocation of the resources of the church and an equal opportunity, in an age-appropriate way, to voice their perspective on the church and the direction it should take. One practical way of setting the right tone here is where every child is greeted by name, ideally by the church leader, as they enter the church building for services. Such a greeting is actually beneficial to all of the church's members but it carries a particular weight when the minister of a church takes the time to smile, make eye contact and share some words of greeting with the children that we are hoping and praying will grow up responding to their baptism with a life of faith in Jesus Christ. Obviously this must then proceed to genuine provision for the Christian teaching, nurture and care of that child which must be given the deepest importance and is covered later in this chapter. As mentioned in Chapter 11, children generally know when an effort is being made for them and, from the basis of their status as full members of the church, can be encouraged to show a similar respect and care for the needs of its other members.[4]

This emphasis upon the equality of the baptized has other applications beyond the children. It is often those in couples or those who possess high-status jobs who are accorded greater value within churches. However passages such as Acts 6.1f and 1 Corinthians 11.17f show the importance of churches giving equal standing to all of those within the body of Christ. This has particular reference to those who are often accorded less status by the surrounding world and, as well as crossing social boundaries with God's love, part of what will makes a church distinctive is the way that it accords an equal status to those with learning difficulties or different needs. Thinking through things as practical as accessible entrances and toilets, provision for those hard of hearing and ways of making church more accessible to those with Asperger's or autism all form part of responding to the baptismal call to unity.

This unity is further displayed by these different members using their gifts to serve one another. Earlier in this chapter we saw the reassurance that baptism brings through its assertion that the Holy Spirit is given to all believers in baptism. A vital part of the living out of baptism is where churches develop a culture in which every member is encouraged to discover their gifts and then use them to build up the community. Church leaders possess a particular commission 'to prepare God's people for works of service, so that the body of Christ may be built up until we all reach unity in the faith' (Ephesians 4.12-13).

## Combining the baptismal calls to holiness and unity

Tension can often appear to exist between these callings. It is relatively easy to place an emphasis upon holiness when there is no emphasis on unity but at the price of churches becoming sects and failing to give any practical expression to the oneness that believers in Jesus Christ possess and are called to display. Likewise it is relatively easy to place an emphasis upon unity when there is no emphasis upon holiness but at the price of churches losing any distinctiveness and failing to give any practical expression to the faithfulness to Jesus Christ that they are also called to display. There is no simple formula for how churches should combine these callings. One important aspect of this, however, is being prepared to give authority to what the church has decided, under God, that its norms of behaviour should be. Obviously institutional authority can be abused and the church has had a very mixed history in this regard necessitating deep repentance and change. But it is equally true that both holiness and unity can struggle to retain any importance within the culture of individualism that now pervades many modern forms of Christianity. The critical factor is acceptance that the church, through its elected representatives and its recognition of those whom God has called to leadership, still has an important role in the discipline of its members. This authority must be completely transparent and accountable if is to avoid abuse but its acknowledgement is nonetheless vital if churches are going to live out the baptismal call to holiness and unity with any conviction.

If combining holiness and unity is difficult within local churches, it is more than difficult within church denominations and often appears completely impossible across them. In the latter case this is most obviously due to the lack of any structures of authority comparable to those within local churches and their parent denominations. But the one worldwide covenant community that God has created in Jesus Christ fulfilling its baptismal call to holiness and unity must remain the goal, if the church's call to witness God's salvation to the world is to occur. Progress towards this will be made when all of these churches are prepared to meet together and, under God's authority, humbly and prayerfully reflect upon what he is calling them to through their one baptism.

## The baptismal call to suffering

This is directly linked to the call to holiness and unity because living in this manner issues a major challenge to the status quo which often then brings a strong reaction. Rejecting the kinds of idolatry covered earlier in this chapter, for instance, will very often bring ridicule or marginalization from those who will rightly sense that their own lifestyle choices are being implicitly challenged. For young people, in particular, seeking to live a holy life in the midst of overwhelming pressure from the surrounding culture can frequently bring an immense amount of suffering. But it is not only young people who struggle in this regard. All Christians of whatever age are under pressure to fall back from holiness into idolatry because choosing to live differently from those around us will always bring suffering.

The same is true, though less obviously with unity. Social segregation is as much a reality today as it was back in the first century. This is most obvious in areas where there has been a history of sectarian or racial division. But in reality 'tribes' formed around wealth, social class, race and culture exist in all areas, accompanied by a number of unspoken expectations about how loyalty to these 'tribes' should be expressed. The baptismal call to unity can and should cut right across these tribal loyalties by questioning their very premise and this will often result in very strong opposition to those seeking to form such Christian community. Sadly, some of the opposition in such cases can come from Christians failing to recognize the gospel imperative to unity and preferring to worship only alongside 'people like us'. But a deeper source of opposition will come from secular organizations and philosophies unhappy with any challenge to the alternative 'unity' they are trying to foster around their values. When churches and Christians are divided along much the same lines as the surrounding world, they pose little challenge in this regard. Once Christians start uniting across the traditional boundaries of race, age, wealth, class and culture, it becomes another matter and explains much of the opposition that such churches receive when they seek to express their faith in the public square.

The deeper reason why holiness and Christian unity lead to suffering is because both represent the baptismal proclamation that Jesus is Lord. This, by definition, presents a major challenge to the alternative powers seeking to dominate the world. As Tom Wright has stated, the reason why the Roman Empire persecuted Christians is because their assertion that Jesus is Lord meant that Caesar wasn't.[5] Idolatry and the segregation of 'divide and rule' (under the guise of the pseudo unity of empire) both formed essential elements of Rome's method of control and these were now being directly challenged. Paul and other early Christians, such as the writer of Revelation, were clear that the real enemy behind such structures were the powers of evil (Ephesians 4.12). It was these 'powers and authorities' providing the strongest reaction to baptized Christians proclaiming through their holiness and unity that Jesus is Lord.

Similar structures and the same spiritual realities are in operation today and provide further explanation of why the distinctive living of those baptized will always lead to suffering. It could be seen as rather negative to present suffering as part of the calling of those who are baptized. But, as we have seen, the calling to suffer is completely entwined with the calling to holiness and unity. Being clear about this is actually very helpful to those seeking to live a baptized life firstly because it makes clear that such suffering is not their fault. But it also provides the opportunity for Christians to support one another as they seek to live baptized lives and make a difference to this suffering with their practical love and solidarity.

A further important aspect of the baptismal call to suffering is its role in implementing the victory of God. The New Testament writers are clear that Jesus's death on the cross was unique in winning the victory over sin and evil. But they are equally clear that it is through the ongoing patient suffering of those belonging to Jesus Christ that his sovereign rule continues to advance in the world. Churches need to become communities where those suffering for seeking to live distinctively baptized lives are encouraged to see their suffering as part of God's ongoing work as well as looking ahead to the day when, having persevered through this suffering, they will receive 'the crown of life' (Revelation 2.10). This can be done particularly effectively in smaller groups where Christian believers meet together regularly to have fellowship, study the Bible, be honest about their struggles and pray and support one another.

However, if baptism is going to have this level of impact upon the life of churches and those Christians within them, fresh ways of giving baptism centrality within these churches need to be discovered.

## Ways that Christians can be encouraged to remember their baptism

This should happen every time a baptism takes place, and the congregation confess their faith and witness another member of the family of God being added to their number. Rather than remaining implicit, remembrance of the baptism of those present is something that should be *explicitly* drawn attention to. A fun way in which some clergy remind younger children of their baptism is to flick some of the water from the font or pool over them with the words 'Remember your baptism!' Building a service focused upon the corporate renewal of baptism vows into the church's annual calendar, perhaps on Easter Day, is another way of doing this. Members of the church can be encouraged to bring objects with them that recall their baptism such as the certificate, candle or Bible they were given on its occasion, a picture of the church where their baptism took place or a photo of the key Christians (perhaps their parents) who particularly led them to faith. Such a 'show and tell' is not just for children but forms a powerful way of way of reinforcing for all those present both the personal and corporate significance of their baptism. Young and old can turn to each other and tell part of their different stories united around the status and calling that they have received through being baptized into Jesus Christ.

Another way of doing this is through embracing the importance of making a recording of the actual baptism event. Many clergy are notoriously precious about photography and film during services but there are more grounds for recording an infant baptism than anything else that is done in church. One of the best ways of doing this is for the church itself to organize one of its members to take a really high quality film of the baptism. If well planned, there are hardly any reasons at all why this should be obtrusive or distracting from the solemnity of the occasion. Such a DVD is relatively cheap to produce and makes a lovely gift for the family especially when it is personalized with the name of the one baptized on the cover. Most vitally of all, it provides the opportunity for the member of clergy conducting the baptism to record a direct message to the child who is able to then watch their baptism, and understand God's personal calling to them through it, as they grow older. After the solemn nature of the liturgy and promises, it is a powerful moment when an informal message is spoken directly to the camera by the one conducting the baptism in child-friendly language. This message should be delivered with a smile and convey the two essential elements of baptism by words such as:

*We are making this DVD today so that you can watch it as you grow older. Our prayer is that it will help to remind you of the day that God declared you to be a deeply precious member of his family because of what he did for you in his Son Jesus*

*Christ. We hope that, helped by his Holy Spirit, it will encourage you to carry on following Jesus throughout the whole of your life.*

To clergy not used to speaking to a camera this can initially cause a few nerves. But, if tried, the skill is very swiftly mastered. Visiting with the DVD during the following week is a great way of immediately reinforcing the importance and ongoing significance of the baptism, and it is good to take two copies making it clear that one DVD is for the parents and the other for the child so that there is no future dispute over its ownership when they leave home! The back of the DVD cover can also contain a summary of what baptism is all about and the encouragement to the one baptized to live out its significance in their daily lives. When a later child within the same family is baptized, the family should be encouraged to watch the DVD together as part of their preparation and it is good for the one conducting the baptism to be present as they do so. Questions can be answered and the nature of baptism and its calling and responsibilities can be underlined.

Although personal memory will preserve a measure of its remembrance, filming an adult baptism in a similar manner is just as worthwhile. Many of those baptized as adults give a testimony of their journey of faith to those present and recording this is a powerful way of keeping this story alive. A direct message of encouragement given to the adult watching it in the future to persevere with their Christian faith and stick with Jesus, whatever hardships and difficulties come their way, is also just as helpful as it is for the child unable to remember the actual event.

Baptism is therefore no more mere theoretical theology than it is mere ceremonial rite – it is profoundly practical and relevant to the individual life of the Christian and corporate life of the church. Just as there are no blessings in Christ which are not symbolized in baptism, there are no aspects of discipleship and obedience that are not implied by or consequent upon baptism.

Augustine thought of baptism as like a soldier's badge or uniform. It is, he said, the same sign which both identifies the soldier and convicts the deserter. Baptism then enshrines all the encouragement of God's covenant promises but it also reinforces all the responsibilities of God's covenant requirements. Like a wedding ring, baptism joyfully reminds the Christian of the love and commitment of the One who gives it. It also reminds of the obligation of faithfulness to that One who 'loved me and gave himself for me' (Galatians 2.20).

## Preaching and teaching baptism

'I am convinced', wrote the Scottish theologian Donald M. Baillie (1887–1954), 'that the people of the Church need far more teaching than we have been accustomed to give them on the sacraments... As regards baptism... a great many of our faithful church folk are in a complete fog about its meaning – which is a dreadful condition of affairs'.[6] Pierre Marcel (1910–1992), the French theologian, wrote, 'If no place is found for preaching, and precisely this (covenant of grace) preaching on which the legitimacy of infant baptism is founded, what can baptism be except a rite deprived of its content and meaning?'[7]

The reason for the assertion of the Faith and Order Commission that 'in no church body does baptism have the decisive significance which the witness of the New Testament ascribes to it' is because there is little preaching and teaching about baptism that is fully biblical. So much of the theology is diluted by folk religion on the one hand or a 'witness to faith response' rationale on the other. So much of the practice is indiscriminate or private on the one hand or individual and 'personal conscience' on the other. Where the clergy are weak in theology and embarrassed about the practice, it is little wonder that the lay people are 'in a complete fog'. Baptism needs to be preached because:

## Baptism provides illustration

The New Testament writers never provide a systematic study of baptism. However, as we have seen, they use it again and again to illustrate the deepest significance of life in Christ. The most powerful preaching is often accompanied by the skilful use of illustration and baptism is a wonderful gift in this regard. Baptism illustrates a great range of the aspects of God's blessings through Christ. It speaks of our spiritual washing, anointing and sprinkling by God as well as our burial and rising with Christ all of which can be used to bring home to congregations what God has done for them though Jesus's death and resurrection. Preachers should also reflect the Bible's use of baptism to illustrate the decisiveness of new life in Christ and, therefore, the consequent expectation of holiness, unity and the willingness to suffer in the Christian life.

Baptism is primarily a gift given to us and thus illustrates the initiative of God's grace. It points us outside ourselves to the Christ into whom we are baptized and to the saving events of his life in the power of which, by faith, we now share. The power of the illustration in preaching, however, depends considerably on the power and significance of the experienced event. This is where many a baptism of infants loses out to baptisms of adults. Too often the theology and significance of an infant baptism is attenuated and the dramatic sense of occasion is minimal. There is inevitably a circular chicken-and-egg argument here. Baptism will not be properly administered until there is clearer theology and preaching, and there will not be clear theology and preaching until there is proper administration. The development, then, must go hand in hand but as part of this church leaders should invest time in thinking through how to make the baptism experience as vivid and profound as possible. The church cannot afford to lose this potent source of illustration of what the Christian life is all about.

## Baptism needs explanation

In most churches baptism takes place with little effective explanation of what it is. It is not enough to assume that any liturgy used will provide this explanation because without its words being unpacked and explained, this liturgy will usually be heard with little understanding or appreciation. When baptisms occur, they need to be accompanied by biblical preaching aiming to provide such explanation. In the process this will also work towards making the baptism more fully into a communal event involving the whole congregation.

However, such teaching will make little sense unless it takes place within the context of ongoing preaching and teaching about the wider biblical story in which baptism needs to be understood. There has been profound misunderstanding of the nature of covenant signs and the significance of the sacraments when the climate of thought in Britain has been broadly Christian. The incomprehension is even greater within an increasingly secularist and multi-faith context. The origins, development and fulfilment of God's covenant plan need explanation. This involves a proper understanding of the relation of the two testaments and of promise and fulfilment. The nature of grace and faith and the relation of covenant promise, sign and obligation all need exposition.

The meaning of sacrament also needs explanation, particularly the difference made when a biblical understanding of cosmology and the Christian hope are allowed to replace a sub-biblical one. Furthermore, there is widespread ignorance of the Old Testament among Christians, so many do not appreciate the family principle or the profoundly spiritual character of grace, faith and obedience in the experience of those saints who came before Christ. All of these explanatory issues, covered in the earlier chapters of this book, need to be regularly taught and preached upon to bring about a proper understanding of baptism.

## Baptism involves a teaching obligation for both parents and church leaders

Parenting has always been a tough assignment and families living further apart and the growth of social media have done little to make it easier. However, a key responsibility in teaching about the meaning and responsibilities of baptism rests with Christian parents or guardians who are to bring up their children 'in the training and instruction of the Lord' (Ephesians 6.4). As we have seen, infant baptism only makes sense within the context of the parents being committed to this task of Christian nurture.

God's intention for a growth from childhood in understanding his covenant love and covenant life is nowhere more clearly seen than in Deuteronomy 6.

> Hear, O Israel: the Lord our God, the Lord is one. Love the Lord your God with all your heart, and with all your soul and with all your strength. These commandments that I give you today are to be upon your hearts. *Impress them on your children.* Talk about them when you sit at home, and when you walk along the road, when you lie down and when you get up. (Deuteronomy 6.4-7)

There follows instructions about phylacteries for hand and forehead and the mezuzah for doorposts. These little containers with portions of God's word in them reminded Israel and remind the Jewish family today that every action and thought and every part of daily life are for submission to the word of YHWH (6.8-9). Parents were to be prepared to explain to their children about God's salvation, covenant signs and the obligations required in response to this (6.20-25). The aim was for the children of the covenant to grow up never knowing a time when they weren't in relationship with YHWH.

None of this disappears under the new covenant. Following the coming of Jesus Christ, the ideal is for children born into Christian families to grow up like Timothy who 'from infancy had known the holy scriptures, which are able to make you wise for salvation through faith in Christ Jesus' (2 Timothy 3.15). Christian faith and life need to be caught as well as taught, and the Christian home is the supreme opportunity for that long-term gradual growth in Christian faith, practice and understanding. The responsibility cannot be passed away to others whether in church or school.

Tragically such intentional Christian parenting can be quite rare. Even in homes where both parents are committed Christians, there can be little instruction or teaching. This can be because of a sense of inadequacy on the part of the parents about how equipped they are to provide this. More often than not, embarrassment is a key factor and sometimes other priorities that the parents are reluctant to see relativized by an emphasis on Christian faith. All of these reasons need to be resisted. It's not the *knowledge* of Christian parents that will make an impact upon their child so much as the *earnestness* with which they seek to follow Jesus and the *integrity* that they show in seeking to practice their faith within everyday life. Simple acts such as the parent and child reading a Bible story at bedtime together and each saying a simple, child-like prayer showing honesty before God about their concerns will do an extraordinary amount to nurture faith on the part of both parent and child. Another opportunity is mealtimes. Saying 'grace' before a meal is increasingly seen as a rather dated and unnecessary custom. However, it is firmly biblical (Matthew 14.19-21; 15.34-36; Luke 24.30; Acts 27.35) and provides perhaps the best opportunity a family has to pray together. Mealtimes, more generally, are important times for family members to feedback on their day and learn skills such as listening to others and how to manage conflict. They thus provide an ideal opportunity for low key but regular input and example from Christian parents. When a child expresses worry or concern about something or a cause for celebration arises, it makes a considerable impact when a parent says, 'well let's say a quick prayer about it'. Young children have very little worry about integrating faith with real life and any embarrassment or 'cringe factor' that needs to be overcome is normally on the part of the parents. Obviously this can change as the child grows into a teenager but not as much as sometimes assumed, particularly when the child has grown up seeing this faith match with other aspects of their parent's lives.

Christian parents bringing their children along to church services is also vital. It is not about parents forcing their children to come along to church so much as establishing this into the regular and cheerful routine of 'what we do'. Sunday school teachers and youth workers can be brilliant and wonderfully committed in their teaching and example, but it is almost impossible for these ministries to have the impact that they should if the parents are not in firm support of their efforts. As mentioned, the really crucial factor in the nurture of children within the Christian family is when they are able to see it integrated into the other aspects of their parents' lives. Children seeing their parents apologize to each other when they are wrong, for instance, and admitting, in an appropriate manner, their own doubts and concerns are all part of those parents fulfilling the calling they are given when they bring their child for baptism.

There are no guarantees about how a child will grow up and no magic formula that can ensure they will continue in the Christian faith. It is an issue that can cause a great deal of hurt and anguish, and this section has not sought to add to this. Some of the suggestions made in this chapter may well have been too prescriptive. Where just one parent is a Christian or other difficulties are present, such nurture is much more difficult. But the aim has been to clarify the ideal that infant baptism should be accompanied by real determination on the part of those bringing the child for baptism to do everything possible to see their child growing up responding to their baptism with faith.

But, as mentioned in the chapter on discrimination in baptism, key responsibility for the nurture of baptized children also rests with the church's leaders. It's again deeply tragic when parents are doing their very best to raise their child in the Christian faith when such nurture is well down that church's list of priorities resulting in inadequate provision for that child. Sunday school teachers can sometimes carry out their ministries with minimal interest or support from the rest of the church. It is down to the overall leader of the church to set the tone here. Knowing all the children by name, popping in on the children's groups on a Sunday morning before the service to encourage the leaders and see what they are doing and organizing training sessions for those leaders all make a vast difference to this ministry. Ideally, there should also be frequent occasions when the church leader spends time with the children demonstrating that they are as important as the adults.

Baptism is for living. As mentioned at the start of this chapter, this is a challenge to all Christian traditions and denominations. Churches, families and the baptized themselves all need to take responsibility for implementing what is proclaimed in baptism so that the importance that the New Testament places upon it is worked out in the practical, day-to-day realities of the Christian life. Many of the most formidable challenges currently facing the church in terms of its relevance, distinctiveness, attractiveness and the clarity of its calling will receive their answer in greater reflection upon what baptism means and the way that it should shape and inform the churches' response to the salvation in Jesus Christ that it represents.

# Epilogue
## Changes to baptism in Melton Sudbury

Seventeen months had passed in Melton Sudbury. In the immediate aftermath of the meeting and in response to the obvious consensus that it had gone well, Martin had suggested that a follow-up should happen. 'The proof that we've really listened to one another and sought to learn and develop', he said in an email, 'will probably be whether we can come back in a year or two and talk about how we've all changed in regard to baptism. So why don't we each commit to think, pray and maybe do a bit of a study in the light of what we heard from one another and see where this takes us?' The others responded positively but without a date being set, mainly because the major focus was now upon maintaining the relationships that had been restored within the group. The quarterly 'ministers' meeting' continued with the group sharing lunch in each other's houses, praying together and working on ways of bringing their churches into a more productive unity. A highlight of the shared endeavour of the churches was an outdoor passion play performed over the Easter weekend with sizeable numbers from the five churches participating within it. Both Martin (as Judas) and Bernie (as Peter) took leading roles with the others in strong support and the event was generally seen as a wonderful witness of both Christian unity and love towards the people of the town.

In the months that followed, the relationships were tested in a different way. In the autumn Sally's father suddenly died two days after Alex had left Holy Trinity to become a vicar in Croydon. The support of the group during this time made a big difference to Sally with the care and kindness from Bernie, in particular, touching her greatly and cementing their friendship. Both Sally and Bernie found themselves opening up to one another about insecurities and hurts from their pasts in a way that surprised them both. Something similar happened soon afterwards when Martin was struck down by a serious illness putting him out of action for several months. Lawrence, Sally, Johnny and Bernie all preached at St Mary's during this period and were delighted at the warmth of welcome they received. A visit to his bedside in which a tearful Martin was anointed by Lawrence and then prayed for by the rest of the group was something that the Vicar of St Mary's later described as one of the most moving experiences of his life. Once he was recovered Martin was resolved to improve his fitness, a decision which soon resulted in him and Johnny agreeing to run together once a week. Neither had done any exercise since leaving school but, to their joint amazement (and even more that of their wives), the eventual result was their participation in a half marathon, cheered on by their churches and the rest of the group. It was through the conversations that accompanied their runs that Martin and Johnny discovered how much they had in common, as well as the things that were central to their Christian faith. Both were able to admit how wrong many of their assumptions about each other's traditions had been and started to find one another an invaluable source of advice and support.

It was in January that the subject of the follow-up meeting on baptism was once again mentioned. This time it was Johnny who raised it. 'I think it's important we revisit the baptism debate', he said. 'I know that I've changed in the light of it and perhaps that's true for all of us. It's clear that we've got something very special going on in this group and it would be very easy for us just to park our different perspectives on baptism in the light of this. But I'm sure that God wants us to move on with him together and show that we really believe in the Christian unity through which he wants to shape and change us.' The other ministers agreed with Johnny's suggestion that their next meeting in May would be given over to revisiting baptism and the next few months were a scramble for all of them as they sought, by prayer and as much study and reflection as they could manage, to evaluate where they now were in their understanding and practice of baptism.

On the day of the meeting the group assembled, once again at Martin's spacious vicarage, for their discussion. It was agreed to make the meeting briefer than the one before and to have each minister talk about both the changes and continuity in their approach to baptism since they last met. Questions could be asked for clarification but it was decided to use the time primarily for listening rather than challenge and debate.

The first to go was Johnny Smith. 'Well I called the meeting', Johnny began, 'so I thought it was only fair that I kicked off. And I've got to admit that this isn't easy for me to talk about because for a Baptist to acknowledge that there is anything that we have to learn about baptism from other traditions can seem like I'm being extremely disloyal and letting the side down very badly'. Encouraging smiles from the group acknowledged Johnny's humility plus their own determination to follow a similar approach and the atmosphere immediately relaxed. 'I hasten to add', Johnny continued, 'that I haven't changed in my conviction that baptism should only take place following a profession of faith on the part of the one getting baptized and therefore someone who is old enough for this to be possible. But there are at least two things that stayed with me after our meeting and, if I'm honest, have eventually changed me'. The room and everyone within it felt completely still as they waited for what Johnny was about to share. Johnny himself paused and lightly pursed his lips, conveying the sense that he wanted to get his wording as accurate as possible.

'Well in the first place, it's all the sacramental stuff', Johnny declared. 'Throughout most of my Christian life, including right through my time at college, I've just assumed that because a genuine response of faith to what God has done for us in Jesus is so important, baptism must be a sign of that faith. But I realize now that that's not the case. I think there were two things that influenced me here. The first was hearing Sally put such a major emphasis upon the importance of the response of faith *to* our baptism. I initially found that rather strange before I realized that Sally was attempting to safeguard precisely the same thing that my Baptist tradition has seen as so important'. Sally smiled at Johnny's openness and generosity but it was Martin and Lawrence, who were most obviously fascinated and waiting intently for what

Johnny was about to say next. 'But the second thing was simply reading those passages about baptism in the epistles', Johnny continued, 'and not being able to get away from the truth that they are speaking about baptism as something done by God rather than us. A sacramental understanding has been present in Baptist thinking for a good while but, at a popular level, most of us have rather ignored it and it has certainly not formed part of the understanding of baptism that I have ever presented. But as I heard Martin, Lawrence and Sally and pondered things afterwards, I realized that I need to do a much better job of integrating those passages within my understanding of baptism. I'm still not mad about the term sacrament which, for me, pushes all the wrong buttons and brings ritualistic associations that I'm uncomfortable with. But I now believe that when a believer is baptized, it's the moment when God brings, or perhaps confirms to that person, all those blessings that he promises us in the gospel. I guess this is also being a bit more honest to Baptist experience', Johnny added. The group waited for Johnny's explanation, with Bernie especially looking rather puzzled. 'What I mean', Johnny explained, 'is that when I baptize someone, it's an utterly moving moment for everyone present as they're plunged below the water and then are brought from it. Everyone is deeply moved by this – myself, the person being baptized and all those present. But I've been kidding myself if I've thought this was solely because we were experiencing someone witnessing to their faith. Of course that is immensely important and moving. But what is clearly touching everyone present in the deepest way is that we're witnessing something that God himself is doing in declaring that another precious brother or sister is part of his family because they have died and risen with Jesus Christ and been washed clean by him. Sally may have started me thinking about this but I guess it is as I've listened to Martin during our running together that I've come to realize the immense power and reassurance that God wants us to have through what he has done for us in baptism'.

The room was quiet, acknowledging the way in which Johnny's voice revealed that all of this was extremely difficult to say. 'But that's not actually the biggest change that's happened to me regarding baptism', Johnny continued. 'That has happened in regard to my attitude towards infant baptism.' This time there were puzzled faces from everyone in the room, given what Johnny had said earlier about his continuing commitment to believer's baptism. Johnny smiled as he saw the look on their faces. 'Yes I still believe very strongly in believer's baptism', he said, 'and I still think that is the best and clearest way of giving expression to what baptism and Christianity is all about. But I can now see, and want to acknowledge in a way that I wouldn't have before, the integrity of those Christians who want to baptize their children on the basis of them growing up within the family of God. In the past, if I'm honest, I've not wanted to make a distinction at all between those who take this position and those for whom infant baptism is little other than a baby-naming ceremony. I've not necessarily expressed this but, under the surface, I've believed that only those who take my position on baptism believe that personal faith is important and I'm here today to say sorry for that attitude and admit that it's been wrong'.

Once Johnny had finished, the ministers sat for a few moments in silence, not wanting to spoil the atmosphere of appreciation at the humility and courage that he had shown. Eventually it was Lawrence who spoke. 'Well, I'm praying right now that

God would give me as much grace as you, Johnny, because if more Christian leaders could speak like that, we'd make so much more progress.' The smiles around the group showed that everyone agreed with Lawrence's words. Martin and Sally indicated that they would like to ask questions and it was Martin who went first. 'Yes thanks Johnny, like everyone here, I've really appreciated what you just said. I'll talk shortly about how I've changed on baptism and I hope I can do it as thoughtfully as you have. But, from what you said, it sounds as if it's Sally's position on "household" or discriminate infant baptism that you want to show respect for rather than my position of open baptism. Is that the case? And, because this is where the rubber hits the road, can I also ask how the way in which you have changed will work itself out in regard to rebaptism?'

Johnny smiled in response, acknowledging that the question had been asked in the spirit of the deep friendship that he now shared with Martin. 'We've become great friends Martin', Johnny said, 'and I very definitely wouldn't want to accuse you of lacking integrity. I can see that you honestly want to share God's love with as many people as possible and that's wonderful. But I wouldn't be honest if I didn't admit that I still strongly believe that it does so much damage to Christianity in this country to have so many children christened outside any context of faith. For those present, and perhaps even for the child itself, it seems to act like an inoculation against Christianity rather than anything positive. I'm sorry Martin because I know these words will hurt but I would be the one lacking in integrity if I didn't express them'.

The room fell quiet again, this time more through awareness at the hurt that Martin was clearly trying his best to cover up. 'And I guess the rebaptism question has got an obvious answer?', Martin eventually said, with his smile indicating that he was coping with the discussion. 'Well', said Johnny, 'what happened with Michelle Gough showed that I wouldn't take the decision to baptize or if you prefer to rebaptize someone who was an existing member of another church. I'm not in the business of undermining other churches'. This time anxious faces shot towards Bernie as Johnny realized that he spoke rather hastily and immediately apologized. 'That's fine brother. I accept your rebuke and the Christian love with which it was intended!' was Bernie's humorous response allowing the atmosphere to swiftly recover. 'But', continued Johnny slightly more nervously, 'it would be different if those wanting (re)baptism had joined MSBC. I'm really glad the question has been asked because I've actually changed my position here. If someone joined MSBC who had come to faith as an adult or teenager and happened to have been christened as a child and they wanted to be baptized as a sign of the salvation they had found, I couldn't in all good conscience refuse them. In fact, I've got to say that I would still encourage it because, to my mind, it's not undermining anything about the Christian faith but simply expressing clarity about what has happened to them. But, and this is my big change, I've decided that *I wouldn't do this if someone joined MSBC who had been baptized as a baby or child and then brought up professing the Christian faith.* Whilst I don't think that any form of infant baptism is the best and most helpful way of going about things, I'm no longer in the position where I want to see such baptisms, where there was a clear context of faith, as invalid.' 'So irregular but not invalid', smiled Martin. 'I believe those are the terms', smiled back Johnny. 'Of course that will then bring all sorts of issues to do with church membership and MSBC and whether such people would be able to vote in church member meetings. I also strongly suspect our elders may see things rather differently. But we'll cross that bridge when we come to it!'

'I think you had a further question for Johnny', Lawrence said in the direction of Sally. 'Well it's perhaps been answered', Sally said, 'by implication, at least. I'm grateful for what you've said this morning, Johnny, and its generosity and kindness. Like Lawrence I hope that when it comes to my turn, I'll be able to talk as you have. But I'd like to ask how the discussion and where you've moved to has influenced your approach to bringing up your two boys. Danny and Tom are six and four, I believe, and I think I'm also right that you and Harriet are seeking to bring them up as Christians. You'll remember that my curate Alex, perhaps rather abruptly, brought up the subject of their status within the church and Christian family. How would you answer that question now?'

'Well, I have thought about that since our last meeting', Johnny responded, 'quite a bit in fact. The stuff that was said about God's covenant has had an impact on me and I can also see more clearly the special place of families within his purposes. It's on that basis that I believe Danny and Tom are included within mine and Harriet's relationship with God, until that point where they are old enough to make their own decision to accept Jesus Christ as their Lord and Saviour. When this occurs, and we pray regularly for this, I believe that it will be right for them to receive the sign of what God has done for them by being baptized'. 'And, if I can press you on their status in the meantime?', Sally repeated. 'Well I am a bit uncomfortable with the question, if I'm honest', said Johnny without annoyance, 'and it does make me a bit insecure about my position. But I guess I believe that they are provisional members of God's family covered by his grace ahead of that time when it becomes their responsibility to respond in their own right to God and what he has done for them in Jesus'.

'Well, at the risk of being patronizing', said Lawrence, 'I think Johnny has given us a model of grace, humility and honesty. I'm just hoping the rest of us can keep it up!'. There was a burst of laughter around the group with Martin extending his arm to pat his running partner on the back. 'Well, I wouldn't hold your breath about that', Martin said winking at the group, 'because I'm up next'. There were further smiles as the ministers relaxed and waited for what Martin had to say.

'Right, well I think I have also changed since our meeting last year', Martin began, 'even if it's in quite a different way to Johnny. Despite everything that we discussed two years ago and what we've just heard, I still believe that our primary task as ministers is to show God's grace and make it clear that that grace is for everyone. I believe that Jesus Christ died for everyone and that my job is to make as many people as possible welcome in his name. So I not only continue to believe very strongly in infant baptism but I must confess that I continue to administer the sacrament in as open and inclusive a way as possible'. Martin paused at that point long enough for the others to think that he had maybe said all that he was going to.

'But, as I say, I have nonetheless changed on baptism', Martin eventually continued, 'and its chiefly in terms of where I now am on the importance of faith. Mainly I have to say because of the influence of Sally, and more recently Johnny. Obviously I've always believed that faith in Jesus Christ is crucial. But, particularly when it comes to baptism,

I've been so concerned to present it as a sacrament of God's *grace*, that I'm not sure that faith has had much of a look in!' This time the smiles of appreciation were at Martin's honesty and humility. 'Well, I mustn't exaggerate', Martin continued, 'I guess I've always hoped that families bringing their children for baptism might respond to that baptism with faith. But the truth is that – other than being friendly and welcoming – I've not done nearly enough to encourage this'. The room again went quiet with no one wanting to seem too strongly in agreement with Martin's last sentence.

The silence was just starting to become awkward when Martin again spoke, this time with more of his usual joviality. 'But given "there is more joy in heaven over one sinner that repenteth" etc, I've started to do something about it!' This time the smiles from the group were broader as everyone waited for what Martin had to say. 'It's been a bit of an adjustment but when parents contact me to enquire about baptism for their child, I now ask them if they'd mind coming along to our main service on Sunday where I can explain more of what baptism is about. Normally they sound a little bit thrown at the suggestion but, so far, most of them have come along. After the service, we sit down in the Lady Chapel and have a bit of a chat and I explain that baptism is a sacrament of God's grace and that I'm totally delighted that they have come to St Mary's in search of it. But – and this is the big difference – I also say, much more clearly than I would have done before, that God's dearest wish is for their child to grow up responding to their baptism with a life of faith and trust in their Saviour. And then ... ', Martin paused and said with a satisfied smile, 'I invite them to my new course!'

The other clergy leaned further in, clearly intrigued since it was the first that any of them had heard about this. 'You've kept that quiet', Johnny said with mock indignation, 'we've done all that running together, Martin, and you've never once mentioned that you'd started a baptism course!' 'Well it doesn't mean I haven't been listening carefully to you Johnny and planning', Martin responded. 'I looked at a few courses that already exist, even the Alpha Course that you and Sally both run at MSBC and Holy Trinity. But none of them really floated my boat, so in the end I thought I ought to devise my own. "And what is its format", Lawrence asked, clearly intrigued. "Well it's been a bit trial and error, if I'm honest", Martin replied, but basically I have the parents round here to the vicarage. Normally about three lots of them all together. I have to be clear that if there are two parents, I want them both there, so it often involves them getting a babysitter. I cook them a meal and after we've eaten, I give them a short talk followed by discussion. The first talk is called "God's love and the story of the Bible", the second is called "Where Baptism fits in" and the third is called "How should I respond to God?" And here's the thing – I've absolutely loved doing it! The food has gone down a treat in teeing-up the evening – that's something, Johnny and Sally, which I've definitely learned from Alpha. And from that point I have found that people are happy to have a discussion and bring up all sorts of questions which, if I'm honest, have helped me as much as them! The whole evening is two hours at most. But in that last session, I talk quite a lot about the difference that my Christian faith means to me, the importance of the church and my hope that, after the baptism, they will all see St Mary's as their spiritual home. Its early days and I've only just completed my third go at the course, tinkering with it a bit each time. But I must be honest and say that I'm really quite excited about it all.'

Once again the room fell quiet with the group clearly moved by Martin's sincerity and enthusiasm. Eventually it was Sally who spoke: 'Can I ask a question, Martin?' 'Of course', Martin replied. 'Well what you've said is fantastic and the course sounds brilliant. Doing it in your own home and with your own cooking makes me feel a bit insecure but I guess we can't all be masterchefs!' There were broad smiles again as Sally continued, 'But I guess my question is whether, in the light of the changes that you've have introduced at St Mary's, you would ever say no to a request for baptism? What would you do, or what do you do, if people say that they aren't happy to come on the course and simply want the baptism?' After the energy and excitement of the last few minutes, the atmosphere again became more serious. 'Well, that's a fair question', Martin said a bit more quietly but still with a smile, 'and I suppose that's where I remain a good liberal Catholic. I believe it's my task to welcome everyone with God's love and, even though I now emphasize the importance of a response of faith more than ever before, I still believe that it's my duty to never say no to anyone who asks for baptism. I'm disappointed, of course, but I'm sure I'll be equally disappointed when some, if not all, of those who attend my new course start tailing off. But, at the end of the day, my job is to love people in God's name and their response to his love is really between them and him'. Smiles of appreciation were made to Martin and this time the pat on the back came from Johnny.

Next to go was Lawrence. 'Well after hearing Johnny and Martin, I'm bit worried about whether I've changed enough to keep up with the spirit of this meeting!' 'That's exactly how I'm feeling, brother!' exclaimed Bernie. 'But in truth', continued Lawrence, 'greater reflection on baptism has changed me and I hope St Francis as well over the last year. Mainly, in fact, as result of going back and rereading the Bible passages after our discussion. As you know, within Catholic teaching there are seven sacraments specially given by God to strengthen and equip his people. Like Martin, my major emphasis has been upon baptism as a sacrament of grace, initiating us into a lifetime of receiving God's blessings through the sacramental life. But, as I've studied and prayed, I've come to realize afresh how foundational baptism is to them all and, in particular, how it needs to continue to impact upon the whole of our Christian lives and really shape and direct our response to God. I've always seen baptism as really important, and that's putting it mildly! But it's in the last year that I've grown to see its continuing importance and relevance to the ongoing life of the church'.

'And how has that worked itself out in practice?' asked Sally. Lawrence suddenly looked really animated as he responded. 'Well in the first place, like you Sally, by me preaching a lot more about baptism. Or, perhaps more accurately, by referring to baptism more often within my sermons. I also talk about baptism and its importance a lot more within my preparation of our children for the first Communion and within our Confirmation classes. We're blessed with large numbers coming to St Francis at both our Saturday evening and Sunday masses. But I'm increasingly aware of how most of them are really struggling to live within a culture which is so alien to the teaching of Christ and, in consequence, so full of hardship and difficulty for them. So I now take the members of St Francis back to their baptism quite a bit more to remind them of the identity that God has given us in Christ, the blessings of that union and the way in which our baptism is a picture of the response of faith that God calls us to. It's been especially helpful in dealing with the concept of sin. Most of my congregation, and

I'm sure it's the same in yours, have a rather narrow point of reference when the word sin is mentioned. Normally they think I'm talking exclusively about sex! But baptism has helped me to teach that sin is everything stopping us from being that fully human being that God is making us into through our baptism. Through this positive vision of the resurrection life God has given us in baptism and will one day complete, I've been able to give my congregation a far more positive vision of what the Christian life is all about. What I've particularly tried to emphasize at St Francis over the last year is that every act of love or kindness towards another or honesty or integrity in the face of temptation represents part of that "death to sin" that we're called to in our baptism. And that, if we have the faith, courage and persistence to continue in this baptized life, we will then see a bit more of God's resurrection life coming into the world'. Lawrence paused for moment. 'Don't stop Lawrence', said Martin, 'I'm finding this fascinating!'.

'Well I suppose the other application of baptism that I've tried to make is to our corporate life as a church', Lawrence continued, clearly encouraged by Martin's response. 'Catholics have always placed an emphasis upon the oneness of the church but an emphasis on baptism has helped sharpen up our application of this in church life, particularly in regard to equality. As I've reflected upon God bringing Jews and Gentiles together into his one family through baptism and St Paul's emphasis upon the need to work out the practical applications of this in church life, I've become quite a lot more theological in the way I promote aspects of our common life together. To give just one example, we recently refurbished the whole of the front entrance to St Francis. You've probably seen that it looks far more attractive. But the major reason we did it was to make it more accessible to everyone. Previously we had one entrance for the majority of our congregation but those in wheelchairs or on mobility scooters had to go through another smaller side entrance because it was the only one with a ramp. We had to raise £50,000 from our congregation to pay for the new, accessible entrance and part of the way I promoted this was by saying that everyone being able to come through the same entrance into St Francis was a deeply symbolic and practical application of the truth that we were all baptized by one Spirit into one body. We're now getting quite keen as a church in exploring further ways in which we can become more equal and welcoming to all and of course we've got a very long way to go in all of this. But thinking through the implications of baptism has given vital impetus to a lot of issues that we would previously have seen as 'practical' rather than theological. It's helping us to see that these two things belong completely together.'

There was quiet for a few moments. Eventually it was Bernie who spoke. 'Thank you Lawrence. You and I are perhaps more different than anyone else in this room in the way we express our Christian faith. But I've been so blessed and challenged by what you've just said.' There was a pause as Bernie breathed out before he spoke again. 'But I've got to start my bit with an admission. You see my change in regard to baptism involves something that was said at our meeting twenty one months ago and which I tried pretty hard to dismiss but haven't been able to.' The puzzled looks around the room made it clear that no one knew which part of the discussion Bernie was referring to. Bernie looked down as he spoke again and in a voice more hesitant than usual. 'It was your comment about Marjorie Pullen, Sally, and whether I believed that she was baptized in the Holy Spirit.' 'Well I was far too strong, Bernie', Sally replied. 'I was probably still smarting a bit at what happened with Michelle Gough and it was wrong of me to be so aggressive.' 'But, the thing is', continued Bernie, 'you weren't in the wrong Sally. I was in the wrong and you were right to challenge me. I still believe that most of the Christians I know should be far more open to the gifts of the Spirit because there is loads more that God wants to bless them with. But – and this is a huge change for me – I can now see that I wasn't just wrong but really arrogant to deny that other faithful Christians are baptized with the Holy Spirit just because they don't possess the same gifts as me or have had the same experiences'. Bernie broke into a sudden smile, 'Don't get me wrong. I'll still keep praying for you all to speak in tongues!'. There was a burst of laughter particularly from Johnny and Martin. 'But you'll no longer catch me saying that if you don't speak in tongues or have "words of knowledge", you haven't been baptized with the Holy Spirit. I'll be praying instead that God simply pours out more of his Spirit on all of us!'.

The smiles around the room registered the ministers' gratitude at what Bernie had said as well as the general warmth they felt towards him. 'So does that mean that, like Johnny, you want to acknowledge our baptisms as infants, Bernie', said Lawrence. 'Yes', added Martin with a mischievous wink at Johnny, 'Do you also now see us as "irregular but not invalid"?'. Johnny looked more annoyed than amused at Martin's reference to his earlier statement and for a moment everyone in the room was less comfortable before Bernie responded.

'You see, I can't really take those sort of terms with any seriousness because, for me, they're a big part of the problem. I mean where do you find concepts like "valid but irregular" within the Bible? The reason I said what I did a moment ago about not denying your baptism in the Holy Spirit is because all of you are so obviously living by faith in Jesus. But that doesn't mean that I'm not still hugely unhappy with infant baptism and the way it overwhelmingly undermines rather than promotes the importance of such faith. I can see the care with which Sally's position on infant baptism, in particular, is stated and justified and it can appear quite convincing. Until, that is, we're honest and acknowledge that the number of times that an infant baptism leads to a genuine life of faith in Jesus Christ is totally dwarfed by literally thousands of examples of where it has simply provided people with that inoculation against Christianity Johnny referred to earlier.' This time it was Martin who looked less happy than before. 'Of course I want to acknowledge, Sally, Martin and Lawrence, that you're living out your baptisms with utterly genuine faith', continued Bernie. 'But to me, Sally's case for a practice of discriminate infant baptism is actually the most dangerous of all because it's under the cloak of that sort of justification that the rampantly indiscriminate nature of the majority of infant baptisms in this country are able to happen. That's why I couldn't, in all conscience, take the position that Johnny has moved to where he wouldn't say that someone who joined MSBC who had been christened as a child and brought up in the Christian faith needed to be baptized as an adult. I've acknowledged that I was wrong over Michelle Gough but that's because she's a member of Holy Trinity and I interfered in a situation where I didn't have any pastoral responsibility. But if someone joined Harvest in that position, unlike Johnny, I would definitely urge them to be baptized because otherwise I would be validating the practice of infant baptism and therefore, whatever the context of that person, undermining the call to faith in Jesus that my ministry is all about. I'm sorry, friends, but that's where I'm still coming from on infant baptism and I don't see it changing.' Bernie's smile and use of the word 'friends' took the edge off the tension that had built up as the smiles once again returned.

'Well, last of all it's me', said Sally. 'And in some ways, I'm now going to say the complete opposite of Bernie, so I hope he'll forgive me.' 'How have I changed on baptism in the last two years? Well back then, if I'm honest, I believed that I had thought through baptism thoroughly enough that I had reached my final position on it. Being an Anglican with a number of Baptist members in my family has been quite a factor there!' As she said the last comment, Sally looked at Johnny who returned her smile. 'But I've now recognized that's not true and that my position on baptism wasn't nearly as clear as it needed to be. I've tried for some time to preach about baptism and apply it in church life in a very similar manner to what Lawrence told us about earlier. But there has been at least one area where I now realize that I have been getting baptism and its application to church life badly wrong.'

Once again the ministers looked on with interest, since there was general agreement after the previous meeting that Sally was the one who had invested the most time in studying and reflecting upon the subject. 'Bernie has said that what I said about Marjorie Pullen at our first meeting gave him the greatest challenge. But in my case, it was what my curate, Alex, said. Do you remember right at the end when we were all rather exhausted? And Alex who was really there to observe asked me whether the Church of England really believed in infant baptism? At the time, I thought that Alex was talking about the issue of whether infant baptism completed that child's entry into the church and, in a sense, that was the question. But rather than referring to the issue of whether Confirmation or indeed 'Baptism in the Holy Spirit' was needed to complete that entry, Alex was being more practical. The question being asked was whether baptized children get treated in the Church of England as the full members of the church that their baptism declares them to be? At the time, I thought Alex was being a little bit argumentative. But, as I went away from that meeting and thought about it, I realized that that the treatment of baptized children in church is as big an issue in undermining the credibility of infant baptism as its indiscriminate administration. I must admit that after Alex's comment about budgets, I went away and checked how much Holy Trinity spent on flowers each year compared to what is spent on ministry towards children and young people. Fortunately it wasn't more for the flowers but the amounts were still closer than I was happy with! But I realized that, whilst I've been a firm believer in Christian family baptism for years, I was not really following through on the principles of this position.'

Sally paused for a moment to take breath. 'Particularly on infant communion', she said. 'As you know, at Holy Trinity, we do have child communion for those who are baptized. But for that to happen, I had to get permission from Bishop Helen, provide a list of those baptized children to be admitted to communion, give evidence that I had provided instruction to them by way of preparation and promise that I would still encourage those admitted to be confirmed. Oh yes, and it was essentially made clear that it was only for those over seven. I didn't particularly have a problem with that before, because I was so pleased that child communion had become possible. But I now realize that none of this process is respecting the validity (sorry to use that word again Bernie!) of those children's baptism. Their baptism should be the sole grounds for those children receiving Holy Communion and the fact that it isn't shows that Alex was right in questioning whether the Church of England really believes in infant baptism. I think I'm right in saying that most of its bishops support a policy of more or less indiscriminate infant baptism and the price appears to be their practical denial that it really is baptism. The time I find hardest in this regard is at our Midnight Communion service on Christmas Eve. I'm sure this is also true at Midnight Mass for Martin and Lawrence. Lots of complete strangers flow in to Holy Trinity and happily come up to the rail to receive Communion. And because they are adults, they get it, no questions asked. Most of them probably are baptized but that's just the point. I realized this Christmas Eve that it is totally unfair to our baptized children who come week by week because, even if they are admitted to Holy Communion, they have had to prove their suitability for something that should belong to them by right.'

'So what are you going to do about it, Sally', asked Martin earnestly. 'Well, campaign a lot more for change in this regard', Sally replied. 'Alex has been causing quite a stir about it in Croydon and the two of us plan to get elected to General Synod and take it from there. Both of us are convinced that if we are to be really true to our convictions about Christian family baptism, then baptized infants should be given Holy Communion as soon as it is practicable to do so. I think that's been true in the Eastern Church for some time but it's about time that we in the Church of England caught up. That, as Alex tried to say at our last meeting, isn't the only issue when it comes to baptized children being regarded as full members of the church. There are loads of other ways that we need to make sure that this is practically implemented and I'm trying to work hard on these at Holy Trinity. I don't want to be ticked off in a similar manner by our next curate! I can honesty see where Bernie and Johnny are coming from in all almost every way with their problems about infant baptism. But I guess, I'm saying that given the way that it is often administered and the way that baptized children are treated afterwards, I'm not sure that they are the main ones not really believing in it. There is loads more that I want to go on learning and implementing about baptism. But that, I think, is my major step forward.'

'Well', said Lawrence, 'I think it's been another good and productive meeting with, once again, loads for us all to go away and think about. This fellowship and oneness between us is so special and important and I think the strongest sign of what we all agree about when it comes to baptism. I know I'm not the only one here for whom the Christian support and friendship of this group has made an amazing difference. Let's promise to go on studying, reading, praying and listening to one another as we look to go forward in our understanding and practice of baptism … '.

'Look', cried Martin suddenly rushing over to the French windows and disappearing into his garden. Unsure of what to do, the others looked at one another before proceeding out through the windows themselves. They were met by the smiling Vicar of St Mary's next to one of his rose bushes in spectacular bloom. 'It's a new one, I've been cultivating', Martin said to his friends. 'After a tough old winter, I did wonder whether it had had it. But just look at it now.' Just at that point a cloud moved in the sky filling the garden with sunshine. The ministers smiled at one another and moved back into Martin's lounge for tea.

# Notes

## Preface

1   Stephen Kuhrt, *Tom Wright for Everyone: Putting the Theology of N.T. Wright into Practice in the Local Church.*
2   Examples include Beasley-Murray, *Baptism in the New Testament*; Griffiths, *The Case for Believers Baptism*; Dalby, *Open Baptism*; Taylor, *Paul on Baptism*; Davison, *Why Sacraments?*

## Foreword

1   Martin Luther, *The Holy and Blessed Sacrament of Baptism*, 1519, in *Luther's Works*, Vol. 35.34, Fortress Press, Philadelphia, 1960.

## Introduction

1   Although the story contained in this introduction (and the epilogue) is fictional and deliberately idealized, nearly every situation and perspective that it contains are based upon real examples that the authors have experienced. The writers want to repeat their gratitude to everyone who, from whatever perspective, has helped to shape and form their understanding of baptism.
2   Baptist Christians have variously written and spoken about 'believer's baptism' and 'believers' baptism'. Whilst the latter simply represents its plural form, some Baptists have preferred to speak of 'believer's baptism' to emphasize their understanding of the individual nature of baptism, following a personal acceptance of the gospel. Some omit the apostrophe altogether. Since 'believer's baptism' appears to be the form most commonly used by Baptists and is used on the Baptist Union website, it is used throughout this book.
3   *Common Worship* (2000), p. 361.

## Chapter 1

1   *Common Worship* (2000), p. 353.
2   Ibid., p. 352.
3   Thurian, *Ecumenical Perspectives on BEM*, p. 161.
4   Barrett, *World Christian Encyclopaedia*, p. 9.
5   See Buchanan, *Adult Baptisms*, p. 3 and the Statistical Supplement to the Church of England Yearbook.

6   David Beckham quoted in *The Daily Telegraph*, 23 December 2004, https://www.telegraph.co.uk/news/1479657/Beckhams-sons-christened-in-back-garden-chapel.html (accessed 30 November 2019).

7   *Common Worship* (2000), p. 372.

8   Kuhrt, *Church Growth through the Full Welcome of Children*, pp. 6–7.

9   Particularly important examples of the New Perspective on St Paul include Sanders, *Paul and Palestinian Judaism*; Dunn, *The Theology of Paul the Apostle*; and Wright, *Paul and the Faithfulness of God*.

10  World Council of Churches Faith and Order Paper 111, *Baptism, Eucharist and Ministry* (The Lima Text).

11  Stott, *Baptism and Fullness*; Lucas, *The Message of Colossians*.

# Chapter 2

1   Cullmann, *Baptism in the New Testament*.

2   Lane, *I Want to Be Baptised*, p. 28.

3   Flemington, *The New Testament Doctrine of Baptism*, pp. 105ff.

4   Ibid., p. 109.

5   Beasley-Murray, *Baptism in the New Testament*, pp. 127–262.

6   Sanday and Headlam, *Romans*, p. 107.

7   For a contrary interpretation, see White, *The Biblical Doctrine of Initiation*, pp. 203, 352ff.

8   Beasley-Murray, *Baptism in the New Testament*, p. 247.

9   Lane, *I Want to Be Baptised*, p. 29.

# Chapter 3

1   Much of this chapter rests on the work of others in investigating the covenantal theme throughout the Old Testament. We are particularly indebted to the late William Dumbrell's *Creation and Covenant: A Theology of the Old Testament Covenants* (1984). A more recent resource that has proved just as invaluable is the brilliant online videos produced by *The Bible Project* (*www.thebibleproject.com*) and their sustained covenantal interpretation of each of the Old Testament books.

2   Dumbrell, *Creation and Covenant*, pp. 16–20.

3   Walton, *The Lost World of Genesis 1*.

4   *The Bible Project: Reading Genesis 1–11*.

5   Dumbrell, *Creation and Covenant*, pp. 65–7.

6   Wright, *What St Paul Really Said*, pp. 96–9, *Justification*, pp. 49–51, 65–72.

7   Wright, *Simply Christian*, pp. 66–8.

8   Dumbrell, *Creation and Covenant*, pp. 83–4.

9   Ibid., pp. 102–3.

10  *The Bible Project: Reading Exodus*.

11  Dumbrell, *Creation and Covenant*, pp. 92–3.

12  Ibid., pp. 99–100.

13  Wright, *The New Testament and the People of God*, pp. 224–6.

14  *The Bible Project: Reading Leviticus*.

15  *The Bible Project: Reading Numbers*.

16  Ibid.

17   Dumbrell, *Creation and Covenant*, p. 125.
18   See particularly Wright, *The New Testament and the People of God*, pp. 227–30.
19   Wright, *The Day the Revolution Began*, pp. 73–87.
20   *The Bible Project: Reading Joshua*.
21   *The Bible Project: Reading Judges*.
22   Dumbrell, *Creation and Covenant*, pp. 139–40.
23   Ibid., pp. 143–4.
24   Ibid., pp. 145–50.
25   *The Bible Project: Reading 2 Samuel*.
26   Against Dumbrell, *Creation and Covenant*, p. 162.
27   Ibid., pp. 177–8.
28   The summaries of all of the minor prophets in this section are indebted to their
     respective videos in *The Bible Project*.
29   Wright, *What St Paul Really Said*, pp. 96–9, *Justification*, pp. 49–51; 65–72.
30   Dumbrell, *Creation and Covenant*, pp. 199–200.
31   Wright, *Finding God in the Psalms*.
32   *The Bible Project: Reading Ezra*.
33   *The Bible Project: Reading Nehemiah*.
34   G. H. Jones, *1 and 2 Chronicles*, pp. 54–6.
35   *The Bible Project: Reading Chronicles*.
36   *The Bible Project: Reading Esther*.
37   *The Bible Project: Reading Jonah*.
38   Dumbrell, *Creation and Covenant*, pp. 205–6.
39   *The Bible Project: Reading Proverbs*.
40   *The Bible Project: Reading Ecclesiastes*.
41   *The Bible Project: Reading Job*.
42   *The Bible Project: Reading the Song of Songs*.
43   *The Bible Project: Reading Daniel*.
44   Wright, *The Resurrection of the Son of God*, pp. 109–15.
45   For example, Rowland, *Open Heaven*; Collins, *The Apocalyptic Imagination*; Wright,
     *Paul: Fresh Perspectives*, pp. 40–58.

# Chapter 4

1   Most of this chapter is dependent on the work of N. T. Wright and the covenantal
    reading of the New Testament contained within his many publications. Given the
    considerable overlap across Wright's works, the notes here are, in most cases, limited
    to the section of these works where the most accessible treatment of this aspect of
    the subject can be found. For a broader treatment of Wright's scholarship and its
    relevance to the contemporary church, see Kuhrt, *Tom Wright for Everyone: Putting
    the Theology of N.T. Wright into Practice in the Local Church*.
2   Wright, *The New Testament and the People of God*, Chapters 9–10.
3   Wright, *The Resurrection of the Son of God*, Chapters 3–4.
4   Wright, *The New Testament and the People of God*, Chapter 8.
5   Wright, *Jesus and the Victory of God*, Chapters 5–6.
6   Ibid., pp. 174–82; 229–43.
7   Ibid., pp. 195–6, 201, Chapter 10.4.
8   Ibid., Chapter 7.4–8.
9   Ibid., Chapter 9, also Wright, *John for Everyone*, Part 1.

10    Ibid., Chapter 11.3–5.

11    Ibid., Chapter 13.

12    Ibid., Chapter 8.

13    Ibid., pp. 360–8.

14    Ibid., Chapter 12.5–7.

15    Wright, *The Resurrection of the Son of God*, pp. 585–682.

16    Wright, *Acts for Everyone*, Part 1, pp. 20–5.

17    Ibid., Part 1, pp. 43–7, 73–82.

18    Ibid., Part 1, pp. 61–73, 86–96.

19    Ibid., Part 1, pp. 101–24.

20    Wright, *Acts for Everyone*, Part 2, pp. 7–22.

21    Wright, 'Shipwreck and Kingdom' in *Living Communion*, pp. 106–18.

22    Wright, *The Climax of the Covenant, Paul for Everyone: Romans* (two volumes), *Romans* in *The New Interpreters Bible*, pp. 393–770.

23    Wright, *Paul for Everyone: Romans*, Part 1, pp. 31–51.

24    Ibid., pp. 51–63.

25    Ibid., pp. 64–80.

26    Ibid., Part 1, pp. 80–97.

27    Ibid., pp. 97–139.

28    Ibid., pp. 139–61.

29    Wright, *Paul for Everyone: Romans*, Part 2, pp. 1–33.

30    Ibid., pp. 34–67.

31    Ibid., pp. 67–120.

32    Wright, *Paul for Everyone: 2 Corinthians*, pp. 26–39, *The Climax of the Covenant*, Chapter 9.

33    For example, E. P. Sanders, *Paul and Palestinian Judaism*, Dunn, *The Theology of Paul the Apostle*, Wright, *Paul and the Faithfulness of God*.

34    Wright, *Paul for Everyone: Galatians and Thessalonians*, pp. 27–35.

35    Ibid., pp. 35–43.

36    Ibid., pp. 43–60.

37    Ibid., pp. 60–83.

38    Wright, *Hebrews for Everyone*, pp. 1–114.

39    Ibid., pp. 114–80.

40    Wright, *The Resurrection of the Son of God*, pp. 457–461.

41    Beasley-Murray, *Baptism in the New Testament*, p. 334ff.

42    Ibid., p. 341.

43    Wright, *Revelation for Everyone*, pp. 186–207.

44    Wright, *Galatians and Thessalonians for Everyone*, pp. 122–6.

45    Wright, *Paul for Everyone: 1 Corinthians*, pp. 201–28.

46    Wright, *Paul for Everyone: Romans*, pp. 148–61.

47    Wright, *Virtue Reborn*, pp. 64–87.

48    Wright, *Surprised by Hope*, pp. 201–302.

49    Wright, *Virtue Reborn*, pp. 80ff, 189f, 201ff.

50    Ibid., pp. 156–88.

# Chapter 5

1    Arndt and Gingrich, *A Greek-English Lexicon of the New Testament*.

2    Marshall, *The Meaning of the Verb 'to Baptize'*.

3     Cited in Beasley-Murray, *Baptism in the New Testament*, p. 17.
4     The detailed evidence is conveniently found in Beasley-Murray, *Baptism in the New Testament*, Flemington, *The New Testament Doctrine of Baptism* and Jeremias, *Infant Baptism in the First Four Centuries*.
5     Flemington, *The New Testament Doctrine of Baptism,* p. 4.
6     Buchanan, *A Case for Infant Baptism*, p. 14, n. 1.
7     Wright, *Simply Christian*, p. 182.
8     Wright, *Jesus and the Victory of God*, pp. 268–74.
9     For example, Geldenhuys, *The Gospel of Luke*, p. 140.
10    Against Wright, *Luke for Everyone*, pp. 35–6.
11    Dunn, *Baptism in the Holy Spirit*, p. 10ff; I. H. Marshall, *The Gospel of Luke*, pp. 145ff.

# Chapter 6

1     Dunn, *Baptism in the Holy Spirit*, Chapter 3.
2     Wright, *The Challenge of Jesus*, pp. 52, 79; *Simply Christian*, p. 100; *What St Paul Really Said*, p. 70; *Paul: Fresh Perspectives*, p. 48.
3     Wright, *Climax of the Covenant*, Cpts 2–6; *The New Testament and the People of God*, pp. 448–9; *What St Paul Really Said*, pp. 65–72; *The Meaning of Jesus*, pp. 161–3; *The Resurrection of the Son of God*, pp. 397–8; *Paul: Fresh Perspectives*, pp. 91–6.

# Chapter 7

1     Flavius Josephus, *Antiquities of the Jews*, Book 18, Cpt 3.3; Book 20, Cpt 9.1, on Jesus and on John the Baptist, Book 18, Cpt 5.2.
2     Wright, *The New Testament and the People of God*, p. 447; *Paul and the Faithfulness of God*, pp. 417–27, 1014.
3     Wright, *The Climax of the Covenant*; *Paul: Fresh Perspectives*, pp. 42–50; *Paul and the Faithfulness of God*, pp. 734f, 816–25, 1040, 1413.
4     For example, Dunn, *Unity and Diversity in the New Testament*, p. 155.
5     Wright, *Paul and the Faithfulness of God*, pp. 417–27, Cpt 10.
6     For a further discussion of this, see Taylor, *Paul on Baptism*, pp. 132–8.
7     Wright, *Paul and the Faithfulness of God*, Cpt 10.
8     Wright, *Paul for Everyone: Romans*; 'Romans' in *New Interpreters Bible*.
9     Cited in Davison, *Why Sacraments?*
10    Wright, *Simply Christian*, pp. 31–3.
11    Denney, *The Death of Christ*, p. 185.
12    Cited in Beasley-Murray, *Baptism in the New Testament*, p. 272, n. 3.
13    Ibid., p. 273.
14    Wright, *Paul and the Faithfulness of God*, pp. 962–4.

# Chapter 8

1     E.g. David Horrell, *Solidarity and Difference*, pp. 90f, 101.
2     Wright, *Paul and the Faithfulness of God*, p. 418.

3   Kuhrt, *Believing in Baptism* (First Edition), p. 81.

4   Wright, *Simply Christian*, pp. 53–9; *Surprised by Hope*; *The Resurrection of the Son of God*.

5   Wright, *The Meal Jesus Gave Us*; *The Crown and the Fire*, Chapter 11; 'Time, Space and Matter and the New Creation'; *Simply Christian*, pp. 131–5, 182–4.

6   Wright, *New Tasks for a Renewed Church*, pp. 27–39.

7   Richard Hooker, *Ecclesiastical Polity Book 5*, p. 37, cited in Griffith Thomas, *The Principles of Theology*, p. 362.

8   Stibbs, *Baptism into Christ*, p. 11f.

9   Packer, *I Want to Be a Christian*, p. 94f.

10  Davison, *Why Sacraments*, p. 60.

11  Letters of C. S. Lewis, ed. W. H. Lewis, p. 239.

12  Council of Trent 1547, Session VII, Canon 8.

13  Cf. Augustine on 2 Timothy 2.20ff.

14  J. C. S. Nias, *Gorham and the Bishop of Exeter*, p. 98.

15  Jack, *Believe and Be Baptised*.

16  Thurian, *Ecumenical Perspectives*, p. 161.

17  Beasley-Murray, *Baptism in the New Testament*, p. 273.

## Chapter 9

1   *The Book of Common Prayer* (1662), p. 277.

2   *Common Worship* (2000), p. 355.

3   Ibid., p. 361.

4   *The Book of Common Prayer* (1662), p. 277.

5   *Common Worship* (2000), p. 355.

6   Ibid., p. 359.

## Chapter 10

1   E.g. Watson, *Baptism Not for Infants* and Beasley-Murray, *Baptism in the New Testament*.

2   Jack, *Believe and Be Baptised*.

3   Beasley-Murray, *Baptism in the New Testament*, p. 361.

4   Ibid., p. 376.

5   Davies, *Babies, Believers and Baptism*, pp. 7, 19; Watson, *Baptism Not for Infants*, p. 86.

## Chapter 11

1   *Baptism, Eucharist and Ministry*, IV Cpt 16 and V Cpt 21.

2   Osborne, *Forbid Them Not*.

3   Dalby, *Open Baptism*.

4   *The Canons of the Church of England* (Seventh Edition).

5   *Common Worship* (2000), p. 352.

6    Ibid., p. 353.
7    Ibid., p. 372.
8    Ibid., p. 356.
9    Ibid., p. 373.
10   Ibid., pp. 337–43.
11   Kuhrt, *Church Growth through the Full Welcome of Children*, pp. 6–7.
12   *Common Worship* (2000), p. 361.
13   Kuhrt, *Church Growth through the Full Welcome of Children*, pp. 8–10.
14   See also Stephen Kuhrt, 'Messy Church and the Challenge of Making Disciples' in Ian Paul (ed) *Being Messy, Being Church.*

# Chapter 12

1    Throughout this chapter, the authors are indebted to an unpublished paper produced by a Working Party with Anglican, Methodist, United Reformed and Baptist members under the Chairmanship of Mr Gordon Landreth of the Church of England Evangelical Council.
2    *Baptism, Eucharist and Ministry*, IV A 13.
3    Baptist Union, *Response of the Council to Baptism, Eucharist and Ministry.*
4    BEM 'Baptism Commentary' 21 (b).
5    FOAG (Faith and Order Advisory Group), *Towards a Church of England Response to BEM and ARCIC.*
6    Buchanan, *Adult Baptisms*, pp. 23f; *The Renewal of Baptism Vows.*
7    Buchanan, *Adult Baptisms,* p. 24.
8    Davison, *Why Sacraments?* p. 80.
9    Buchanan, *One Baptism Once*, p. 22.

# Chapter 13

1    Davison, *Why Sacraments?* pp. 77–8.
2    Second Vatican Council, *Lumen Gentium*, p. 11.
3    Paul Avis (ed), *The Journey of Christian Initiation: Theological and Pastoral Perspectives.*
4    Davison, *Why Sacraments?* p. 76.
5    Buchanan, *Baptism as Complete Sacramental Initiation*, pp. 5–9.
6    Davison, *Why Sacraments?* pp. 75, 80.
7    Ibid., p 80.
8    Stott, *Baptism and Fullness*, pp. 47–75; Green, *Baptism*, pp. 127–41.
9    Stott, *Baptism and Fullness*, pp. 76–85.
10   Buchanan, *Children in Communion*, pp. 5–6.
11   See Young, *Welcoming Children to Communion*; Buchanan, *Children in Communion*; Buchanan (ed), *Nurturing Children in Communion*; Holeton, *Infant Communion – Then and Now*; Reiss, *Children and Communion*; Lake, *Let the Children Come to Communion.*

12  'The Admission of Baptised Person to Holy Communion before Confirmation', Guidelines Agreed by the House of Bishops, 1997 in Riess, *Children and Communion*, pp. 14–15.

13  See particularly Riess, *Children and Communion*, pp. 15–17.

# Chapter 14

1  *One Lord, One Baptism*, SCM, 1961, p. 71.

2  Sheikh with Schneider, *I Dared to Call Him Father*; Sutcliffe (ed), *Good News for Asians in Britain*, pp. 15–19.

3  Wright, *New Tasks for a Renewed Church*, pp. 27–39.

4  Kuhrt, *Church Growth through the Full Welcome of Children*.

5  Wright, *What St Paul Really Said*, pp. 56–7, 88, *The Meaning of Jesus*, pp. 219–21, *Paul: Fresh Perspectives*, Cpt 4.

6  Baillie, *The Theology of the Sacraments and Other Papers*, p. 146.

7  Marcel, *The Biblical Doctrine of Infant Baptism*, p. 236.

# Bibliography

Aland, Kurt, *Did the Early Church Baptise Infants?* SCM, London, 1963.

Arndt, W. F. and Gingrich, F. W., *A Greek-English Lexicon of the New Testament*, Cambridge University Press, Cambridge, 1957.

Avis, P. (ed), *The Journey of Christian Initiation*, Church House Publishing, London, 2011.

Baillie, D. M., *The Theology of the Sacraments and Other Papers*, Faber and Faber, London, 1957.

Baillie, J., *Baptism & Conversion*, OUP, London, 1964.

Ball, P., *Journey into Faith*, SPCK, London, 1984.

Baptist Union, *Response of the Council to Baptism, Eucharist and Ministry*, Baptist Union, London, 1985.

Barrett, D. B. (ed), *World Christian Encyclopaedia: Comparative Survey of Churches and Religions in the Modern World*, Oxford University Press, Oxford, 1982.

Barrett, C. K., *Church, Ministry and Sacraments*, Paternoster, Exeter, 1985.

Barth, K., *The Teaching of the Church regarding Baptism* (translated E. A. Payne), SCM, London, 1948.

Beasley-Murray, G. R., *Baptism in the New Testament*, Eerdmans, Grand Rapids, Michigan, 1962/1984.

Beasley-Murray, G. R., *Baptism Today and Tomorrow*, Macmillan, London, 1966.

Beckwith, R. T., 'Infant Baptism' in *New International Dictionary of New Testament Theology*, edited C. Brown, Paternoster, Exeter, 1975.

Beckwith, R. T., Buchanan, C. O. and Prior, K. (ed), *Services of Baptism and Confirmation*, Marcham, Abingdon, 1967.

Booth, Robert R., *Children of the Promise: The Biblical Case for Infant Baptism*, PRP, New Jersey, 1995.

Bridge, D. and Phypers, D., *The Water That Divides*, IVP, Leicester, 1977.

British Council of Churches, *One Lord, One Faith, One Baptism: Guidelines and Materials for Inter-church Worship*, BCC, London, n.d.

British Council of Churches, *Report of the Inter-church Enquiry into Baptismal Practice*, BCC, London, n.d.

Bromiley, G., *Children of Promise*, Eerdmans, Grand Rapids, 1979.

Buchanan, C. O. (ed), *Evangelical Essays on Church and Sacraments*, SPCK, London, 1972.

Buchanan, C. O., *Baptismal Discipline*, Grove, Nottingham, 1972/1974.

Buchanan, C. O., *A Case for Infant Baptism*, Grove, Nottingham, 1973, 2009.

Buchanan, C. O., *ARCIC and LIMA on Baptism and Eucharist*, Grove, Nottingham, 1983.

Buchanan, C. O., *Adult Baptisms*, Grove, Nottingham, 1985.

Buchanan, C. O. (ed), *Nurturing Children in Communion*, Grove, Nottingham, 1985.

Buchanan, C. O., *Anglican Confirmation*, Grove, Nottingham, 1986.

Buchanan, C. O., *Policies for Infant Baptism*, Grove, Nottingham, 1987.

Buchanan, C. O., *One Baptism Once*, Grove, Nottingham, 1978, 1983, 1989.

Buchanan, C. O., *Children in Communion*, Grove, Nottingham, 1990.

Buchanan, C. O., *Infant Baptism and the Gospel*, DLT, London, 1993.

Buchanan, C. O., *The Renewal of Baptism Vows*, Grove, Nottingham, 1993.
Buchanan, C. O., *Infant Baptism in Common Worship*, Grove, Cambridge, 2001.
Buchanan, C. O., *Baptism as Complete Sacramental Initiation*, Grove, Cambridge, 2014.
Burnish, R., *The Meaning of Baptism*, SPCK, London, 1985.
Carey, G., 'Christian Beginning' in Chapter 5 of *Obeying Christ in a Changing World*, edited J. R. W. Stott, Vol. 1. *The Lord Christ*, 123–41, Collins, Glasgow, 1977.
Carr, W., *Brief Encounters: Pastoral Ministry through Baptisms, Weddings and Funerals*, SPCK, London, 1985, 1994.
Collins, John J., *The Apocalyptic Imagination*, Crossroad, New York, 1987.
Craston, R. C., *Baptism*, BCMS, London, n.d.
Crowe, P., *Christian Baptism*, Mowbray, Oxford, 1980.
Cullmann, Oscar, *Baptism in the New Testament* (translated by J. K. S. Reid), SCM, London, 1950.
Dalby, Mark, *Open Baptism*, SPCK, London, 1989.
Dalby, Mark, *Infant Communion: The New Testament to the Reformation*, Grove, Cambridge, 2003.
Davies, J. K., *Babies, Believers and Baptism*, Grace, London, 1983.
Davison, Andrew, *Why Sacraments?* SPCK, London, 2013.
Denney, J., *The Death of Christ*, Hodder and Stoughton, London, 1902.
Dumbrell, W. J., *Covenant and Creation: A Theology of the Old Testament Covenants*, Paternoster, London, 1984.
Dunn, J. D. G., *Baptism in the Holy Spirit: A Re-examination of the New Testament Teaching on the Gift of the Spirit in Relation to Pentecostalism Today*, SCM, London, 1970.
Dunn, J. D. G., 'Baptism' in *The Illustrated Bible Dictionary*, 172–4, IVP, Leicester, 1980.
Dunn, J. D. G., *Unity and Diversity in the New Testament: An Inquiry into the Character of Earliest Christianity* (Second Edition), SCM Press, London, 1990.
Dunn, J. D. G., *The Theology of Paul the Apostle*, T&T Clark, Edinburgh, 1998.
Earey, M., T. Lloyd and I. Tarrant, *Connecting with Baptism: A Practical Guide to Christian Initiation Today*, Church House Publishing, London, 2007.
Eastman, A. T., *The Baptizing Community*, Seabury, Minnesota, 1982.
Ely Report, *Christian Initiation: Birth and Growth in the Christian Society*, CIO, London, 1971.
Faith and Order Advisory Group (Board for Mission and Unity), *Toward a Church of England Response to BEM and ARCIC*, CIO, London, 1985.
Flemington, W. F., *The New Testament Doctrine of Baptism*, SPCK, London, 1948, 1957.
Forsyth, P. T., *The Church and the Sacraments*, Independent, London, 1917, 1947.
Geldenhuys, N., *The Gospel of Luke*, Marshall, Morgan and Scott, London, 1952.
Gilmore, A. (ed), *Christian Baptism*, Lutterworth, London, 1959.
Gilmore, A., *Baptism and Christian Unity*, Lutterworth, London, 1966.
Green, E. M. B., *I Believe in the Holy Spirit*, Hodder, London, 1975.
Green, E. M. B., *Baptism: Its Purpose and Power*, Hodder, London, 1987.
Griffith, Terry, *The Case for Believers Baptism*, Kingsway, Eastbourne, 1990.
Griffith Thomas, W. H., *The Principles of Theology*, Church Book Room Press, London, 1930/1963.
Hart, G., *Right to Baptize*, Hodder, London, 1966.
Hoad, J., *The Baptist*, Grace, London, 1986.
Holeton, David, *Infant Communion – Then and Now*, Grove, Nottingham, 1981.
Holeton, David, *Christian Initiation in the Anglican Communion*, Grove, Nottingham, 1991.

Holeton, David (ed), *Growing in Newness of Life: Christian Initiation in Anglicanism Today*, Anglican Book Centre, Toronto, 1993.

Hooker, Richard, *Ecclesiastical Polity Book 5*, 1597.

Horrell, D. G., *Solidarity and Difference: A Contemporary Reading of Paul's Ethics*, T&T Clark, London, 2005.

Hulse, E., *The Testimony of Baptism*, Carey, Haywards Heath, 1982.

Jack, V., *Believe and Be Baptised*, 10 Publishing, London, 1970.

Jeremias, J., *Infant Baptism in the First Four Centuries*, SCM, London, 1960.

Jeremias, J., *The Origins of Infant Baptism*, SCM, London, 1963.

Jewett, P. K., *Infant Baptism and the Covenant of Grace*, Eerdmans, Grand Rapids, 1978.

Jones, G. H., *1 and 2 Chronicles*, Sheffield Academic Press, Sheffield, 1999.

Kingdon, D., *Children of Abraham*, Walter, Worthing, 1973.

Knaresborough Report, *Communion before Confirmation?* CIO, London, 1985.

Kuhrt, S. J., *Church Growth through the Full Welcome of Children*, Grove, Cambridge, 2009.

Kuhrt, S. J., *Tom Wright for Everyone: Putting the Theology of N.T. Wright into Practice in the Local Church*, SPCK, London, 2011.

Kuhrt, S. J., 'Messy Church and the Challenge of Making Disciples' in *Being Messy, Being Church: Exploring the Direction of Travel in Today's Church*, edited Ian Paul, 155–67, BRF, Abingdon, 2017.

Lake, S., *Let the Children Come to Communion*, SPCK, London, 2006.

Lampe, G. W. H., *The Seal of the Spirit*, SPCK, London, 1951/1956.

Lane, E., *I Want to Be Baptised*, Grace, London, 1986.

Langton, A. A., *Communion for Children? The Current Debate*, Latimer House, Oxford, 1988.

Lewis, W. H., *Letters of C.S. Lewis*, Bles, London, 1966.

Lucas, R. C., *The Message of Colossians and Philemon*, IVP, Leicester, 1980.

Mackie, Timothy and Collins, Jonathan, 'The Bible Project: Visual Storytelling Meets the Bible', *thebibleproject.com*.

Marcel, P., *The Biblical Doctrine of Infant Baptism* (translated P. E. Hughes), James Clark, London, 1951/1953.

Marshall, I. H., *Luke: Historian and Theologian*, Paternoster, Exeter, 1970.

Marshall, I. H., *The Meaning of the Verb 'to Baptize'*, Evangelical Quarterly, Vol. 45, No. 3, 1973.

Marshall, I. H., *The Gospel of Luke*, Paternoster Press, London, 1978.

Martin, R. P., *Worship in the Early Church*, Marshalls, London, 1964.

Moody, D., *Baptism: Foundation for Christian Unity*, Westminster Press, Philadelphia, 1967.

Moore, G. and Briden, T., *Moore's Introduction to English Canon Law*, Mowbray, Oxford, 1985.

Moss, B. S. (ed), *Crisis for Baptism*, SCM, London, 1965.

Motyer, J. A., *Baptism in the Book of Common Prayer*, FEC, Leicester, 1962.

Motyer, J. A., 'Baptism' in *The New Bible Dictionary*, edited J. D. Douglas, IVP, London, 1962.

Moule, C. F. D., *Worship in the New Testament*, Lutterworth, London, 1961.

Moynagh, M., 'Home to Home: Towards a Biblical Model of the Family', *Anvil*, Vol. 3, No. 3, 1986.

Murray, J., *Christian Baptism*, Presbyterian and Reformed Publishing, Philadelphia, 1952.

Nias, J. C. S., *Gorham and the Bishop of Exeter*, SPCK, London, 1951.

Ogilvie, G., *Preaching at Baptisms*, Grove, Nottingham, 1979.

Osborn, R. R., *Forbid Them Not: The Importance and History of General Baptism*, SPCK, London, 1972.

Owen, Clifford (ed), *Reforming Infant Baptism*, Hodder, London, 1990.

Owen, Clifford, *Baptise Every Baby? The Story of One Minister's Struggle to Treat Baptism as if It Really Mattered*, Eastbourne, Monarch, 1991.

Packer, J. I., *I Want to Be a Christian*, Kingsway, Eastbourne, 1977.

Pawson, J. D., *The Normal Christian Birth*, Hodder, London, 1989.

Pawson, J. D. and Buchanan, C. O., *Infant Baptism under Cross-Examination*, Grove, Nottingham, 1974.

Price, Tony, *Evangelical Anglicans and the Lima Text*, Grove, Nottingham, 1985.

Quick, O. C., *The Christian Sacraments*, Nisbet, London, 1927/1932.

Reiss, Peter, *Children and Communion: A Practical Guide for Interested Churches*, Cambridge, Grove, 1998.

Richardson, A., 'Initiation, Christian' in *A Dictionary of Christian Theology*, edited A. Richardson, 170–3, SCM, London, 1969.

Robinson, D. W. B., *The Meaning of Baptism*, Falcon, London, 1956.

Rowland, Christopher C., *The Open Heaven: A Study of Apocalyptic in Judaism and Early Christianity*, Crossroad, New York, 1982.

Sanday, W. and Headlam, A. C., *A Critical and Exegetical Commentary on the Epistle to the Romans* (Fifth Edition), T&T Clark, Edinburgh, 1902.

Sanders, E. P., *Paul and Palestinian Judaism*, SCM, London, 1977.

Sanders, E. P., *Paul, The Law and the Jewish People*, SCM, London, 1983.

Scotland, Church of, *The Biblical Doctrine of Baptism*, St Andrew, Edinburgh, 1958.

Sheikh, Bilquis with Schneider, Richard H., *I Dared to Call Him Father*, Chosen Books, Grand Rapids, 1978, 2003.

Silversides, M., *Folk Religion: Friend or Foe?* Grove, Nottingham, 1986.

Southwell Diocesan Working Party, *Report on Policies Concerning Infant Baptism*, Grove, Nottingham, 1977.

Stibbs, A. M., *Baptism into Christ*, Falcon, London, 1960.

Stibbs, A. M., *Understanding the Sacraments*, Falcon, London, 1960.

Stott, J. R. W., *Baptism and Fullness: The Work of the Holy Spirit Today*, IVP, Leicester, 1964, 1975.

Stott, J. R. W., 'The Evangelical Doctrine of Baptism' in Ch. 6 of *The Anglican Synthesis*, edited W. R. F. Browning, Peter Smith, Derby, 1964.

Sutcliffe, Sally J. (ed), *Good News for Asians in Britain*, Grove, Cambridge, 1998.

Taylor, Nicholas, *Paul on Baptism: Theology, Mission and Ministry in Context*, SCM, London, 2016.

Thurian, M., *Ecumenical Perspectives on Baptism, Eucharist and Ministry*, WCC, Geneva, 1983.

Tovey, Philip, *Of Water and the Spirit: Mission and the Baptismal Liturgy*, Norwich, Canterbury Press, 2015.

Wainwright, G., *Christian Initiation*, Lutterworth, London, 1969.

Walton, J. H., *The Lost World of Genesis One: Ancient Cosmology and the Origins Debate*, IVP, Downers Grove, 2009.

Watson, T. E., *Baptism Not for Infants*, H.E. Walters, London, 1962.

Whitaker, E. C., *Sacramental Initiation Complete in Baptism*, Grove, Nottingham, 1975.

White, R. E. O., *The Biblical Doctrine of Initiation*, Hodder, London, 1960.

William, R. R., 'Baptism' in *A Theological Wordbook of the Bible*, edited A. Richardson, 27–30, SCM, London, 1960.

World Council of Churches Commission on Faith and Order, *One Lord, One Baptism*, SCM, London, 1960.

World Council of Churches, Faith and Order Paper 111, *Baptism, Eucharist and Ministry* (The Lima text), WCC, Geneva, 1982.

Wright, D. F., *Baptism, Eucharist and Ministry: An Evangelical Assessment*, Rutherford Forum Paper, Edinburgh, 1984.

Wright, D. F., *What Has Infant Baptism Done to Baptism? An Enquiry at the End of Christendom*, Paternoster, Milton Keynes, 2005.

Wright, D. F., *Infant Baptism in Historical Perspective*, Paternoster, Milton Keynes, 2007.

Wright, N. T., *The Climax of the Covenant*, SPCK, London, 1991.

Wright, N. T., *The Crown and the Fire*, SPCK, London, 1992.

Wright, N. T., *New Tasks for a Renewed Church*, Hodder, London, 1992.

Wright, N. T., *The New Testament and the People of God*, SPCK, London, 1992.

Wright, N. T., *Jesus and the Victory of God*, SPCK, London, 1996.

Wright, N. T., *What St Paul Really Said*, SPCK, London, 1997.

Wright, N. T. with Borg, Marcus, *The Meaning of Jesus*, SPCK, London, 1999.

Wright, N. T., *The Challenge of Jesus*, SPCK, London, 1999.

Wright, N. T., *John for Everyone*, SPCK, London, 2002.

Wright, N. T., *The Meal Jesus Gave Us* (reissue of *Holy Communion for Amateurs*, 1999), SPCK, London, 2002.

Wright, N. T., *Paul for Everyone: Galatians and Thessalonians*, SPCK, London, 2002.

Wright, N. T., *Paul for Everyone: The Prison Letters: Ephesians, Philippians, Colossians and Philemon*, SPCK, London, 2002.

Wright, N. T., 'Romans' in *The New Interpreters Bible*, Vol. X, edited by Leander E. Keck, 393–770, Nashville, Abingdon, 2002.

Wright, N. T., *Hebrews for Everyone*, SPCK, London, 2003.

Wright, N. T., *Paul for Everyone: 1 Corinthians*, SPCK, London, 2003.

Wright, N. T., *Paul for Everyone: 2 Corinthians*, SPCK, London, 2003.

Wright, N. T., *The Resurrection of the Son of God*, SPCK, London, 2003.

Wright, N. T., *Paul for Everyone: Romans* (two volumes), SPCK, London, 2004.

Wright, N.T., *Paul: Fresh Perspectives*, SPCK, London, 2005.

Wright, N. T., *Evil and the Justice of God*, SPCK, London, 2006.

Wright, N. T., *Simply Christian*, SPCK, London, 2006.

Wright, N. T., 'Shipwreck and Communion: Acts and the Anglican Communion' in *Living Communion: The Official Report of the 13th Meeting of the Anglican Consultative Council*, Nottingham, 2005, edited J. M. Rosenthal and S. T. Erdey, 106–18, Church Publishing Incorporated, New York, 2006.

Wright, N. T., *Surprised by Hope*, SPCK, London, 2007.

Wright, N. T., *Acts for Everyone*, SPCK, London, 2008.

Wright, N. T., *Justification: God's Plan and Paul's Vision*, SPCK, London, 2009.

Wright, N. T., *Virtue Reborn*, SPCK, London, 2010.

Wright, N. T., *Revelation for Everyone*, SPCK, London, 2011.

Wright, N. T., *Paul and the Faithfulness of God* (two volumes), SPCK, London, 2013.

Wright, N. T., *Finding God in the Psalms*, SPCK, London, 2014.

Wright, N. T., *The Day the Revolution Began*, SPCK, London, 2016.

Wright, N. T., *Paul: A Biography*, SPCK, London, 2018.

Young, Daniel, *Welcoming Children to Communion*, Grove, Nottingham, 1983.

Zetterholm, Magnus, *The Formation of Christianity in Antioch*, Routledge, London, 2003.

# Index of biblical references

*Index of Biblical References*

Micah

| | |
|---|---|
| 1.3-4 | 80, 82 |
| 2.6-11 | 80 |
| 2.12-13 | 81 |
| 3.1-11 | 80 |
| 3.12 | 80 |
| 4.1-7 | 81 |
| 5.1-6 | 81 |
| 6-7 | 80 |
| 6.6-8 | 68 |
| 7.14 | 103 |
| 7.15 | 81 |
| 7.20 | 63, 81 |

Nahum

| | |
|---|---|
| 1.1-8 | 82 |
| 1.1-16 | 82 |
| 1.17-21 | 82 |
| 1.8-14 | 82 |
| 2.1-13 | 82 |
| 3.1-19 | 82 |

Habakkuk

| | |
|---|---|
| 1.2-4 | 82 |
| 1.5 | 111 |
| 1.5-2.1 | 82 |
| 2.4 | 82 |
| 2.14 | 19, 66, 126, 180 |
| 2.16 | 152 |
| 3.3-7 | 82 |
| 3.8-15 | 82 |
| 3.16-19 | 82 |

Zephaniah

| | |
|---|---|
| 1.2-3 | 82 |
| 2.4-3.8 | 82 |
| 3.9-10 | 82 |
| 3.11-20 | 82 |

Haggai

| | |
|---|---|
| 1.13-15 | 86 |
| 2.20-23 | 86 |

Zechariah

| | |
|---|---|
| 3.1-2 | 95 |
| 3.8-9 | 86 |
| 4.6 | 86 |
| 4.16-17 | 126 |
| 9.9-10 | 86 |
| 9.11-17 | 86 |
| 9.11 | 106 |
| 12.10b-14 | 86 |
| 13.1 | 138 |
| 13.7 | 86 |
| 14.6-7 | 86 |
| 14.8 | 86 |
| 14.9 | 86 |
| 14.12-15 | 86 |
| 14.16-17 | 126 |
| 14.16-19 | 86 |
| 14.20-21 | 86 |

Malachi

| | |
|---|---|
| 1.2-5 | 96 |
| 1.6-14 | 96 |
| 2.1-9 | 96 |
| 2.4 | 96 |
| 2.10-16 | 96 |
| 2.17 | 96 |
| 3.1-4 | 144 |
| 3.1 | 96 |
| 3.2-5 | 96 |
| 3.10 | 96 |
| 4.1 | 96 |
| 4.4-6 | 96 |
| 4.5f | 99, 139 |

Matthew

| | |
|---|---|
| 1.1-17 | 98, 143 |
| 1.3 | 98 |
| 1.4 | 139 |
| 1.5 | 98 |
| 1.6 | 98 |
| 1.22-23 | 98 |
| 1.23 | 108 |
| 2.14-15 | 98 |
| 2.17-18 | 98 |
| 2.23 | 98 |
| 3.1-2 | 140 |
| 3.3 | 143 |
| 3.3-4 | 99 |
| 3.5-6 | 141 |
| 3.7-10 | 99 |
| 3.8 | 141 |
| 3.9-10 | 142, 198 |
| 3.11-12 | 40, 99, 140, 143 |
| 3.11 | 13, 137, 160, 168, 248 |
| 3.12 | 143, 153 |
| 3.13-17 | 147 |
| 3.14 | 148 |
| 3.15 | 51, 148 |
| 3.16 | 151 |
| 4.1-11 | 99, 105 |
| 4.17 | 99 |
| 5.5 | 105 |
| 5.8 | 138 |
| 5.13-16 | 101 |
| 5.17 | 101, 211 |
| 5.38-42 | 105 |
| 5.43-48 | 105 |
| 7.1-2 | 224 |
| 7.6 | 221 |
| 7.15 | 221 |
| 7.24-27 | 103 |
| 7.28 | 102 |
| 8.1-11 | 102 |
| 8.10 | 102 |
| 8.11 | 102 |
| 8.14-15 | 101 |
| 8.21-23 | 106 |
| 8.23-27 | 100 |
| 8.28-34 | 105 |
| 9.1-8 | 102 |
| 9.9-13 | 100 |
| 9.14-15 | 103 |
| 9.22 | 102 |
| 9.29 | 102 |
| 10.1-4 | 100 |
| 10.28 | 100 |
| 11 | 157 |
| 11.7-19 | 140, 154 |
| 11.9-14 | 143 |
| 11.9-11 | 144 |
| 11.11 | 154 |
| 11.14 | 139 |
| 11.25-27 | 103 |

# General index